Complete
Poetical Works
of
Robert W. Service

BOOKS OF POETRY
BY
ROBERT W. SERVICE

Contained in This Volume

The Spell of the Yukon

Ballads of a Cheechako

Rhymes of a Rolling Stone

Rhymes of a Red Cross Man

Ballads of a Bohemian

Robert W Service

COMPLETE
POETICAL WORKS
OF
ROBERT W. SERVICE

BARSE & HOPKINS
PUBLISHERS
NEW YORK, N. Y.   NEWARK, N. J.

The Spell of the Yukon
and Other Verses

I have no doubt at all the Devil grins,
  As seas of ink I spatter.
Ye gods, forgive my "literary" sins—
  The other kind don't matter.

TO
C. M.

THE LAND GOD FORGOT

The lonely sunsets flare forlorn
  Down valleys dreadly desolate;
The lordly mountains soar in scorn
  As still as death, as stern as fate.

  The lonely sunsets flame and die;
    The giant valleys gulp the night;
  The monster mountains scrape the sky,
    Where eager stars are diamond-bright.

So gaunt against the gibbous moon,
  Piercing the silence velvet-piled,
A lone wolf howls his ancient rune —
  The fell arch-spirit of the Wild.

  O outcast land! O leper land!
    Let the lone wolf-cry all express
  The hate insensate of thy hand,
    Thy heart's abysmal loneliness.

CONTENTS

CONTENTS

CONTENTS

CONTENTS

THE SPELL OF THE YUKON

I wanted the gold, and I sought it;
  I scrabbled and mucked like a slave.
Was it famine or scurvy — I fought it;
  I hurled my youth into a grave.
I wanted the gold, and I got it —
  Came out with a fortune last fall,—
Yet somehow life's not what I thought it,
  And somehow the gold isn't all.

No! There's the land.   (Have you seen it?)
  It's the cussedest land that I know,
From the big, dizzy mountains that screen it
  To the deep, deathlike valleys below.
Some say God was tired when He made it;
  Some say it's a fine land to shun;
Maybe; but there's some as would trade it
  For no land on earth — and I'm one.

THE SPELL OF THE YUKON

You come to get rich (damned good reason);
　　You feel like an exile at first;
You hate it like hell for a season,
　　And then you are worse than the worst.
It grips you like some kinds of sinning;
　　It twists you from foe to a friend;
It seems it's been since the beginning;
　　It seems it will be to the end.

I've stood in some mighty-mouthed hollow
　　That's plumb-full of hush to the brim;
I've watched the big, husky sun wallow
　　In crimson and gold, and grow dim,
Till the moon set the pearly peaks gleaming,
　　And the stars tumbled out, neck and crop;
And I've thought that I surely was dreaming,
　　With the peace o' the world piled on top.

The summer — no sweeter was ever;
　　The sunshiny woods all athrill;
The grayling aleap in the river,
　　The bighorn asleep on the hill.

THE SPELL OF THE YUKON

The strong life that never knows harness;
   The wilds where the caribou call;
The freshness, the freedom, the farness —
   O God! how I'm stuck on it all.

The winter! the brightness that blinds you,
   The white land locked tight as a drum,
The cold fear that follows and finds you,
   The silence that bludgeons you dumb.
The snows that are older than history,
   The woods where the weird shadows slant;
The stillness, the moonlight, the mystery,
   I've bade 'em good-by — but I can't.

There's a land where the mountains are name-
     less,
   And the rivers all run God knows where;
There are lives that are erring and aimless,
   And deaths that just hang by a hair;
There are hardships that nobody reckons;
   There are valleys unpeopled and still;
There's a land — oh, it beckons and beckons,
   And I want to go back — and I will.

THE SPELL OF THE YUKON

They're making my money diminish;
　　I'm sick of the taste of champagne.
Thank God! when I'm skinned to a finish
　　I'll pike to the Yukon again.
I'll fight — and you bet it's no sham-fight;
　　It's hell! — but I've been there before;
And it's better than this by a damsite —
　　So me for the Yukon once more.

There's gold, and it's haunting and haunting;
　　It's luring me on as of old;
Yet it isn't the gold that I'm wanting
　　So much as just finding the gold.
It's the great, big, broad land 'way up yonder,
　　It's the forests where silence has lease;
It's the beauty that thrills me with wonder,
　　It's the stillness that fills me with peace.

THE
HEART OF THE SOURDOUGH

There where the mighty mountains bare their
    fangs unto the moon,
There where the sullen sun-dogs glare in the
    snow-bright, bitter noon,
And the glacier-glutted streams sweep down at
    the clarion call of June.

There where the livid tundras keep their tryst
    with the tranquil snows;
There where the silences are spawned, and the
    light of hell-fire flows
Into the bowl of the midnight sky, violet, amber
    and rose.

THE HEART OF THE SOURDOUGH

There where the rapids churn and roar, and the
    ice-floes bellowing run;
Where the tortured, twisted rivers of blood
    rush to the setting sun —
I've packed my kit and I'm going, boys, ere
    another day is done.

       *   *   *   *   *   *

I knew it would call, or soon or late, as it calls
    the whirring wings;
It's the olden lure, it's the golden lure, it's the
    lure of the timeless things,
And to-night, oh, God of the trails untrod, how
    it whines in my heart-strings!

I'm sick to death of your well-groomed gods,
    your make-believe and your show;
I long for a whiff of bacon and beans, a snug
    shakedown in the snow;
A trail to break, and a life at stake, and an-
    other bout with the foe.

THE HEART OF THE SOURDOUGH

With the raw-ribbed Wild that abhors all life,
    the Wild that would crush and rend,
I have clinched and closed with the naked
    North, I have learned to defy and defend;
Shoulder to shoulder we have fought it out —
    yet the Wild must win in the end.

I have flouted the Wild.   I have followed its
    lure, fearless, familiar, alone;
By all that the battle means and makes I claim
    that land for mine own;
Yet the Wild must win, and a day will come
    when I shall be overthrown.

Then when as wolf-dogs fight we've fought, the
    lean wolf-land and I;
Fought and bled till the snows are red under
    the reeling sky;
Even as lean wolf-dog goes down will I go
    down and die.

21

THE THREE VOICES

The waves have a story to tell me,
　As I lie on the lonely beach;
Chanting aloft in the pine-tops,
　The wind has a lesson to teach;
But the stars sing an anthem of glory
　I cannot put into speech.

The waves tell of ocean spaces,
　Of hearts that are wild and brave,
Of populous city places,
　Of desolate shores they lave,
Of men who sally in quest of gold
　To sink in an ocean grave.

The wind is a mighty roamer;
　He bids me keep me free,

THE THREE VOICES

Clean from the taint of the gold-lust,
  Hardy and pure as he;
Cling with my love to nature,
  As a child to the mother-knee.

But the stars throng out in their glory,
  And they sing of the God in man;
They sing of the Mighty Master,
  Of the loom his fingers span,
Where a star or a soul is a part of the whole
  And weft in the wondrous plan.

Here by the camp-fire's flicker,
  Deep in my blanket curled,
I long for the peace of the pine-gloom,
  When the scroll of the Lord is unfurled,
And the wind and the wave are silent,
  And world is singing to world.

THE LAW OF THE YUKON

This is the law of the Yukon, and ever she
    makes it plain:
"Send not your foolish and feeble; send me
    your strong and your sane —
Strong for the red rage of battle; sane, for I
    harry them sore;
Send me men girt for the combat, men who are
    grit to the core;
Swift as the panther in triumph, fierce as the
    bear in defeat,
Sired of a bulldog parent, steeled in the furnace
    heat.
Send me the best of your breeding, lend me your
    chosen ones;
Them will I take to my bosom, them will I call
    my sons;
Them will I gild with my treasure, them will I
    glut with my meat;

THE LAW OF THE YUKON

But the others — the misfits, the failures — I
    trample under my feet.
Dissolute, damned and despairful, crippled and
    palsied and slain,
Ye would send me the spawn of your gutters —
    Go! take back your spawn again.

" Wild and wide are my borders, stern as death
    is my sway;
From my ruthless throne I have ruled alone for
    a million years and a day;
Hugging my mighty treasure, waiting for man
    to come,
Till he swept like a turbid torrent, and after
    him swept — the scum.
The pallid pimp of the dead-line, the enervate
    of the pen,
One by one I weeded them out, for all that I
    sought was — Men.
One by one I dismayed them, frighting them
    sore with my glooms;
One by one I betrayed them unto my manifold
    dooms.

THE LAW OF THE YUKON

Drowned them like rats in my rivers, starved
them like curs on my plains,
Rotted the flesh that was left them, poisoned
the blood in their veins;
Burst with my winter upon them, searing forever their sight,
Lashed them with fungus-white faces, whimper-
ing wild in the night;

Staggering blind through the storm-whirl,
stumbling mad through the snow,
Frozen stiff in the ice-pack, brittle and bent like
a bow;
Featureless, formless, forsaken, scented by
wolves in their flight,
Left for the wind to make music through ribs
that are glittering white;
Gnawing the black crust of failure, searching
the pit of despair,
Crooking the toe in the trigger, trying to patter
a prayer;
Going outside with an escort, raving with lips
all afoam,

THE LAW OF THE YUKON

Writing a cheque for a million, driveling feebly
    of home;
Lost like a louse in the burning . . . or else
    in the tented town
Seeking a drunkard's solace, sinking and sink-
    ing down;
Steeped in the slime at the bottom, dead to a
    decent world,
Lost 'mid the human flotsam, far on the fron-
    tier hurled;
In the camp at the bend of the river, with its
    dozen saloons aglare,
Its gambling dens ariot, its gramophones all
    ablare;
Crimped with the crimes of a city, sin-ridden
    and bridled with lies,
In the hush of my mountained vastness, in the
    flush of my midnight skies.
Plague-spots, yet tools of my purpose, so nathe-
    less I suffer them thrive,
Crushing my Weak in their clutches, that only
    my Strong may survive.

" But the others, the men of my mettle, the men
    who would 'stablish my fame

THE LAW OF THE YUKON

Unto its ultimate issue, winning me honor, not
    shame;
Searching my uttermost valleys, fighting each
    step as they go,
Shooting the wrath of my rapids, scaling my
    ramparts of snow;
Ripping the guts of my mountains, looting the
    beds of my creeks,
Them will I take to my bosom, and speak as a
    mother speaks.
I am the land that listens, I am the land that
    broods;
Steeped in eternal beauty, crystalline waters and
    woods.
Long have I waited lonely, shunned as a thing
    accurst,
Monstrous, moody, pathetic, the last of the
    lands and the first;
Visioning camp-fires at twilight, sad with a long-
    ing forlorn,
Feeling my womb o'er-pregnant with the seed
    of cities unborn.
Wild and wide are my borders, stern as death
    is my sway,

THE LAW OF THE YUKON

And I wait for the men who will win me — and
    I will not be won in a day;
And I will not be won by weaklings, subtle,
    suave and mild,
But by men with the hearts of vikings, and the
    simple faith of a child;
Desperate, strong and resistless, unthrottled by
    fear or defeat,
Them will I gild with my treasure, them will I
    glut with my meat.

" Lofty I stand from each sister land, patient
    and wearily wise,
With the weight of a world of sadness in my
    quiet, passionless eyes;
Dreaming alone of a people, dreaming alone
    of a day,
When men shall not rape my riches, and curse
    me and go away;
Making a bawd of my bounty, fouling the hand
    that gave —
Till I rise in my wrath and I sweep on their
    path and I stamp them into a grave.
Dreaming of men who will bless me, of women
    esteeming me good,

THE LAW OF THE YUKON

Of children born in my borders of radiant
  motherhood,
Of cities leaping to stature, of fame like a flag
  unfurled,
As I pour the tide of my riches in the eager lap
  of the world."

This is the Law of the Yukon, that only the
  Strong shall thrive;
That surely the Weak shall perish, and only the
  Fit survive.
Dissolute, damned and despairful, crippled and
  palsied and slain,
This is the Will of the Yukon,— Lo, how she
  makes it plain!

THE PARSON'S SON

*This is the song of the parson's son, as he squats
    in his shack alone,
On the wild, weird nights, when the Northern
    Lights shoot up from the frozen zone,
And it's sixty below, and couched in the snow
    the hungry huskies moan:*

"I'm one of the Arctic brotherhood, I'm an
    old-time pioneer.
I came with the first — O God! how I've
    cursed this Yukon — but still I'm here.
I've sweated athirst in its summer heat, I've
    frozen and starved in its cold;
I've followed my dreams by its thousand
    streams, I've toiled and moiled for its gold.

"Look at my eyes — been snow-blind twice;
    look where my foot's half gone;

THE PARSON'S SON

And that gruesome scar on my left cheek, where
 the frost-fiend bit to the bone.
Each one a brand of this devil's land, where
 I've played and I've lost the game,
A broken wreck with a craze for ' hooch,' and
 never a cent to my name.

" This mining is only a gamble; the worst is as
 good as the best;
I was in with the bunch and I might have come
 out right on top with the rest;
With Cormack, Ladue and Macdonald — O
 God! but it's hell to think
Of the thousands and thousands I've squan-
 dered on cards and women and drink.

" In the early days we were just a few, and we
 hunted and fished around,
Nor dreamt by our lonely camp-fires of the
 wealth that lay under the ground.
We traded in skins and whiskey, and I've often
 slept under the shade
Of that lone birch tree on Bonanza, where the
 first big find was made.

THE PARSON'S SON

"We were just like a great big family, and
    every man had his squaw,
And we lived such a wild, free, fearless life
    beyond the pale of the law;
Till sudden there came a whisper, and it mad-
    dened us every man,
And I got in on Bonanza before the big rush
    began.

"Oh, those Dawson days, and the sin and the
    blaze, and the town all open wide!
(If God made me in His likeness, sure He let
    the devil inside.)
But we all were mad, both the good and the
    bad, and as for the women, well —
No spot on the map in so short a space has
    hustled more souls to hell.

"Money was just like dirt there, easy to get
    and to spend.
I was all caked in on a dance-hall jade, but she
    shook me in the end.

THE PARSON'S SON

It put me queer, and for near a year I never
    drew sober breath,
Till I found myself in the bughouse ward with
    a claim staked out on death.

"Twenty years in the Yukon, struggling along
    its creeks;
Roaming its giant valleys, scaling its god-like
    peaks;
Bathed in its fiery sunsets, fighting its fiendish
    cold —
Twenty years in the Yukon . . . twenty years
    — and I'm old.

"Old and weak, but no matter, there's ' hooch '
    in the bottle still.
I'll hitch up the dogs to-morrow, and mush
    down the trail to Bill.
It's so long dark, and I'm lonesome — I'll just
    lay down on the bed;
To-morrow I'll go . . . to-morrow . . . I
    guess I'll play on the red.

THE PARSON'S SON

" . . . Come, Kit, your pony is saddled.   I'm
    waiting, dear, in the court . . .
. . . Minnie, you devil, I'll kill you if you skip
    with that flossy sport . . .
. . . How much does it go to the pan, Bill? . . .
    play up, School, and play the game . . .
. . . Our Father, which art in heaven, hal-
    lowed be Thy name . . ."

*This was the song of the parson's son, as he
    lay in his bunk alone,*
*Ere the fire went out and the cold crept in, and
    his blue lips ceased to moan,*
*And the hunger-maddened malamutes had torn
    him flesh from bone.*

THE CALL OF THE WILD

Have you gazed on naked grandeur where
there's nothing else to gaze on,
  Set pieces and drop-curtain scenes galore,
Big mountains heaved to heaven, which the
blinding sunsets blazon,
  Black canyons where the rapids rip and roar?
Have you swept the visioned valley with the
green stream streaking through it,
  Searched the Vastness for a something you
  have lost?
• Have you strung your soul to silence? Then
for God's sake go and do it;
  Hear the challenge, learn the lesson, pay the
  cost.

Have you wandered in the wilderness, the sage-
brush desolation,
  The bunch-grass levels where the cattle
  graze?

36

THE CALL OF THE WILD

Have you whistled bits of rag-time at the end
    of all creation,
  And learned to know the desert's little
    ways?
Have you camped upon the foothills, have you
    galloped o'er the ranges,
  Have you roamed the arid sun-lands through
    and through?
Have you chummed up with the mesa? Do
    you know its moods and changes?
  Then listen to the Wild — it's calling you.

Have you known the Great White Silence, not
    a snow-gemmed twig aquiver?
  (Eternal truths that shame our soothing
    lies.)
Have you broken trail on snowshoes? mushed
    your huskies up the river,
  Dared the unknown, led the way, and
    clutched the prize?
Have you marked the map's void spaces,
    mingled with the mongrel races,
  Felt the savage strength of brute in every
    thew?

THE CALL OF THE WILD

And though grim as hell the worst is, can you
　　round it off with curses?
　Then hearken to the Wild — it's wanting
　　you.

Have you suffered, starved and triumphed,
　　groveled down, yet grasped at glory,
　Grown bigger in the bigness of the whole?
" Done things " just for the doing, letting bab-
　　blers tell the story,
　Seeing through the nice veneer the naked
　　soul?
Have you seen God in His splendors, heard the
　　text that nature renders?
　(You'll never hear it in the family pew.)
The simple things, the true things, the silent
　　men who do things —
　Then listen to the Wild — it's calling you.

They have cradled you in custom, they have
　　primed you with their preaching,
　They have soaked you in convention through
　　and through;
They have put you in a showcase; you're a
　　credit to their teaching —

THE CALL OF THE WILD

But can't you hear the Wild? — it's calling
you.
Let us probe the silent places, let us seek what
luck betide us;
Let us journey to a lonely land I know.
There's a whisper on the night-wind, there's
a star agleam to guide us,
And the Wild is calling, calling . . . let us
go.

THE LONE TRAIL

*Ye who know the Lone Trail fain would follow
it,*
*Though it lead to glory or the darkness of the
pit.*
*Ye who take the Lone Trail, bid your love
good-by;*
*The Lone Trail, the Lone Trail follow till you
die.*

The trails of the world be countless, and most
of the trails be tried;
You tread on the heels of the many, till you
come where the ways divide;
And one lies safe in the sunlight, and the other
is dreary and wan,
Yet you look aslant at the Lone Trail, and the
Lone Trail lures you on.
And somehow you're sick of the highway, with
its noise and its easy needs,
And you seek the risk of the by-way, and you
reck not where it leads.

THE LONE TRAIL

And sometimes it leads to the desert, and the
    tongue swells out of the mouth,
And you stagger blind to the mirage, to die in
    the mocking drouth.
And sometimes it leads to the mountain, to the
    light of the lone camp-fire,
And you gnaw your belt in the anguish of
    hunger-goaded desire.
And sometimes it leads to the Southland, to the
    swamp where the orchid glows,
And you rave to your grave with the fever, and
    they rob the corpse for its clothes.
And sometimes it leads to the Northland, and
    the scurvy softens your bones,
And your flesh dints in like putty, and you spit
    out your teeth like stones.
And sometimes it leads to a coral reef in the
    wash of a weedy sea,
And you sit and stare at the empty glare where
    the gulls wait greedily.
And sometimes it leads to an Arctic trail,
    and the snows where your torn feet
    freeze,
And you whittle away the useless clay, and
    crawl on your hands and knees.

THE LONE TRAIL

Often it leads to the dead-pit; always it leads
    to pain;
By the bones of your brothers ye know it, but
    oh, to follow you're fain.
By your bones they will follow behind you, till
    the ways of the world are made plain.

*Bid good-by to sweetheart, bid good-by to
    friend;*
*The Lone Trail, the Lone Trail follow to the
    end.*
Tarry not, and fear not, chosen of the true;
*Lover of the Lone Trail, the Lone Trail waits
    for you.*

THE PINES

We sleep in the sleep of ages, the bleak, bar-
    barian pines;
The gray moss drapes us like sages, and closer
    we lock our lines,
And deeper we clutch through the gelid gloom
    where never a sunbeam shines.

On the flanks of the storm-gored ridges are our
    black battalions massed;
We surge in a host to the sullen coast, and we
    sing in the ocean blast;
From empire of sea to empire of snow we grip
    our empire fast.

To the niggard lands were we driven, 'twixt
    desert and floes are we penned;
To us was the Northland given, ours to strong-
    hold and defend;

43

THE PINES

Ours till the world be riven in the crash of the
    ʋtter end;

Ours from the bleak beginning, through the
    æons of death-like sleep;
Ours from the shock when the naked rock was
    hurled from the hissing deep;
Ours through the twilight ages of weary glacier
    creep.

Wind of the East, Wind of the West, wander-
    ing to and fro,
Chant your songs in our topmost boughs, that
    the sons of men may know
The peerless pine was the first to come, and the
    pine will be last to go!

We pillar the halls of perfumed gloom; we
    plume where the eagles soar;
The North-wind swoops from the brooding
    Pole, and our ancients crash and roar;
But where one falls from the crumbling walls
    shoots up a hardy score.

THE PINES

We spring from the gloom of the canyon's
    womb; in the valley's lap we lie;
From the white foam-fringe, where the break-
    ers cringe to the peaks that tusk the sky,
We climb, and we peer in the crag-locked mere
    that gleams like a golden eye.

Gain to the verge of the hog-back ridge where
    the vision ranges free:
Pines and pines and the shadow of pines as far
    as the eye can see;
A steadfast legion of stalwart knights in domi-
    nant empery.

Sun, moon and stars give answer; shall we not
    staunchly stand,
Even as now, forever, wards of the wilder
    strand,
Sentinels of the stillness, lords of the last, lone
    land?

THE LURE OF LITTLE VOICES

There's a cry from out the loneliness — oh,
    listen, Honey, listen!
  Do you hear it, do you fear it, you're a-hold-
    ing of me so?
You're a-sobbing in your sleep, dear, and your
    lashes, how they glisten —
  Do you hear the Little Voices all a-begging
    me to go?

All a-begging me to leave you.   Day and night
    they're pleading, praying,
  On the North-wind, on the West-wind, from
    the peak and from the plain;
Night and day they never leave me — do you
    know what they are saying?
  "He was ours before you got him, and we
    want him once again."

THE LURE OF LITTLE VOICES

Yes, they're wanting me, they're haunting me,
        the awful lonely places;
    They're whining and they're whimpering as
        if each had a soul;
They're calling from the wilderness, the vast
        and God-like spaces,
    The stark and sullen solitudes that sentinel
        the Pole.

They miss my little camp-fires, ever brightly,
        bravely gleaming
    In the womb of desolation, where was never
        man before;
As comradeless I sought them, lion-hearted,
        loving, dreaming,
    And they hailed me as a comrade, and they
        loved me evermore.

And now they're all a-crying, and it's no use me
        denying;
    The spell of them is on me and I'm helpless
        as a child;

THE LURE OF LITTLE VOICES

My heart is aching, aching, but I hear them,
      sleeping, waking;
   It's the Lure of Little Voices, it's the man-
      date of the Wild.

I'm afraid to tell you, Honey, I can take no
      bitter leaving;
   But softly in the sleep-time from your love
      I'll steal away.
Oh, it's cruel, dearie, cruel, and it's God knows
      how I'm grieving;
   But His loneliness is calling, and He knows
      I must obey.

THE SONG OF THE WAGE-SLAVE

When the long, long day is over, and the Big
    Boss gives me my pay,
I hope that it won't be hell-fire, as some of the
    parsons say.
And I hope that it won't be heaven, with some
    of the parsons I've met —
All I want is just quiet, just to rest and forget.
Look at my face, toil-furrowed; look at my
    calloused hands;
Master, I've done Thy bidding, wrought in Thy
    many lands —
Wrought for the little masters, big-bellied they
    be, and rich;
I've done their desire for a daily hire, and I die
    like a dog in a ditch.
I have used the strength Thou hast given, Thou
    knowest I did not shirk;
Threescore years of labor — Thine be the long
    day's work.

THE SONG OF THE WAGE-SLAVE

And now, Big Master, I'm broken and bent and
    twisted and scarred,
But I've held my job, and Thou knowest, and
    Thou will not judge me hard.
Thou knowest my sins are many, and often I've
    played the fool —
Whiskey and cards and women, they made me
    the devil's tool.
I was just like a child with money; I flung it
    away with a curse,
Feasting a fawning parasite, or glutting a har-
    lot's purse;
Then back to the woods repentant, back to the
    mill or the mine,
I, the worker of workers, everything in my line.
Everything hard but headwork (I'd no more
    brains than a kid),
A brute with brute strength to labor, doing as
    I was bid;
Living in camps with men-folk, a lonely and
    loveless life;
Never knew kiss of sweetheart, never caress of
    wife.
A brute with brute strength to labor, and they
    were so far above —

THE SONG OF THE WAGE-SLAVE

Yet I'd gladly have gone to the gallows for one
    little look of Love.
I, with the strength of two men, savage and shy
    and wild —
Yet how I'd ha' treasured a woman, and the
    sweet, warm kiss of a child!
Well, 'tis Thy world, and Thou knowest. I
    blaspheme and my ways be rude;
But I've lived my life as I found it, and I've
    done my best to be good;
I, the primitive toiler, half naked and grimed
    to the eyes,
Sweating it deep in their ditches, swining it
    stark in their styes;
Hurling down forests before me, spanning tu-
    multuous streams;
Down in the ditch building o'er me palaces
    fairer than dreams;
Boring the rock to the ore-bed, driving the road
    through the fen,
Resolute, dumb, uncomplaining, a man in a
    world of men.
Master, I've filled my contract, wrought in Thy
    many lands;

THE SONG OF THE WAGE-SLAVE

Not by my sins wilt Thou judge me, but by the
    work of my hands.
Master, I've done Thy bidding, and the light is
    low in the west,
And the long, long shift is over . . . Master,
    I've earned it — Rest.

GRIN

If you're up against a bruiser and you're getting knocked about —
                                Grin.
If you're feeling pretty groggy, and you're
licked beyond a doubt —
                                Grin.
Don't let him see you're funking, let him know
with every clout,
Though your face is battered to a pulp, your
blooming heart is stout;
Just stand upon your pins until the beggar
knocks you out —
                                And grin.
This life's a bally battle, and the same advice
holds true
                                Of grin.
If you're up against it badly, then it's only one
on you,
                                So grin.

GRIN

If the future's black as thunder, don't let people
    see you're blue;
Just cultivate a cast-iron smile of joy the whole
    day through;
If they call you " Little Sunshine," wish that
    they'd no troubles, too —
                         You may — grin.
Rise up in the morning with the will that,
    smooth or rough,
                         You'll grin.
Sink to sleep at midnight, and although you're
    feeling tough,
                         Yet grin.
There's nothing gained by whining, and you're
    not that kind of stuff;
You're a fighter from away back, and you *won't*
    take a rebuff;
Your trouble is that you don't know when you
    have had enough —
                         Don't give in.
If Fate should down you, just get up and take
    another cuff;
You may bank on it that there is no philosophy
    like bluff,
                         And grin.

THE SHOOTING OF DAN McGREW

A bunch of the boys were whooping it up in the
    Malamute saloon;
The kid that handles the music-box was hitting
    a jag-time tune;
Back of the bar, in a solo game, sat Dangerous
    Dan McGrew,
And watching his luck was his light-o'-love, the
    lady that's known as Lou.

When out of the night, which was fifty below,
    and into the din and the glare,
There stumbled a miner fresh from the creeks,
    dog-dirty, and loaded for bear.
He looked like a man with a foot in the grave
    and scarcely the strength of a louse,
Yet he tilted a poke of dust on the bar, and he
    called for drinks for the house.

THE SHOOTING OF DAN McGREW

There was none could place the stranger's face,
    though we searched ourselves for a clue;
But we drank his health, and the last to drink
    was Dangerous Dan McGrew.

There's men that somehow just grip your eyes,
    and hold them hard like a spell;
And such was he, and he looked to me like a
    man who had lived in hell;
With a face most hair, and the dreary stare of
    a dog whose day is done,
As he watered the green stuff in his glass, and
    the drops fell one by one.
Then I got to figgering who he was, and won-
    dering what he'd do,
And I turned my head — and there watching
    him was the lady that's known as Lou.

His eyes went rubbering round the room, and
    he seemed in a kind of daze,
Till at last that old piano fell in the way of his
    wandering gaze.

THE SHOOTING OF DAN McGREW

The rag-time kid was having a drink; there
    was no one else on the stool,
So the stranger stumbles across the room, and
    flops down there like a fool.
In a buckskin shirt that was glazed with dirt
    he sat, and I saw him sway;
Then he clutched the keys with his talon hands
    — my God! but that man could play.

Were you ever out in the Great Alone, when the
    moon was awful clear,
And the icy mountains hemmed you in with a
    silence you most could *hear;*
With only the howl of a timber wolf, and you
    camped there in the cold,
A half-dead thing in a stark, dead world, clean
    mad for the muck called gold;
While high overhead, green, yellow and red,
    the North Lights swept in bars? —
Then you've a haunch what the music meant
    . . . hunger and night and the stars.

And hunger not of the belly kind, that's ban-
    ished with bacon and beans,

THE SHOOTING OF DAN McGREW

But the gnawing hunger of lonely men for a
    home and all that it means;
For a fireside far from the cares that are, four
    walls and a roof above;
But oh! so cramful of cosy joy, and crowned
    with a woman's love —
A woman dearer than all the world, and true
    as Heaven is true —
(God! how ghastly she looks through her
    rouge,— the lady that's known as Lou.)

Then on a sudden the music changed, so soft
    that you scarce could hear;
But you felt that your life had been looted clean
    of all that it once held dear;
That someone had stolen the woman you loved;
    that her love was a devil's lie;
That your guts were gone, and the best for you
    was to crawl away and die.
'Twas the crowning cry of a heart's despair,
    and it thrilled you through and through —
" I guess I'll make it a spread misere," said
    Dangerous Dan McGrew.

THE SHOOTING OF DAN McGREW

The music almost died away . . . then it burst
    like a pent-up flood;
And it seemed to say, " Repay, repay," and my
    eyes were blind with blood.
The thought came back of an ancient wrong,
    and it stung like a frozen lash,
And the lust awoke to kill, to kill . . . then
    the music stopped with a crash,
And the stranger turned, and his eyes they
    burned in a most peculiar way;
In a buckskin shirt that was glazed with dirt
    he sat, and I saw him sway;
Then his lips went in in a kind of grin, and he
    spoke, and his voice was calm,
And " Boys," says he, " you don't know me,
    and none of you care a damn;
But I want to state, and my words are straight,
    and I'll bet my poke they're true,
That one of you is a hound of hell . . . and
    that one is Dan McGrew."

Then I ducked my head, and the lights went
    out, and two guns blazed in the dark,

THE SHOOTING OF DAN McGREW

And a woman screamed, and the lights went up,
    and two men lay stiff and stark.
Pitched on his head, and pumped full of lead,
    was Dangerous Dan MGrew,
While the man from the creeks lay clutched to
    the breast of the lady that's known as Lou.

These are the simple facts of the case, and I
    guess I ought to know.
They say that the stranger was crazed with
    " hooch," and I'm not denying it's so.
I'm not so wise as the lawyer guys, but strictly
    between us two —
The woman that kissed him and — pinched his
    poke — was the lady that's known as Lou.

THE CREMATION OF SAM McGEE

There are strange things done in the midnight
    sun
  By the men who moil for gold;
The Arctic trails have their secret tales
  That would make your blood run cold;
The Northern Lights have seen queer sights,
  But the queerest they ever did see
Was that night on the marge of Lake Lebarge
  I cremated Sam McGee.

Now Sam McGee was from Tennessee, where
    the cotton blooms and blows.
Why he left his home in the South to roam
    'round the Pole, God only knows.
He was always cold, but the land of gold seemed
    to hold him like a spell;
Though he'd often say in his homely way that
    " he'd sooner live in hell."

THE CREMATION OF SAM McGEE

On a Christmas Day we were mushing our way
over the Dawson trail.
Talk of your cold! through the parka's fold it
stabbed like a driven nail.
If our eyes we'd close, then the lashes froze till
sometimes we couldn't see;
It wasn't much fun, but the only one to whimper
was Sam McGee.

And that very night, as we lay packed tight in
our robes beneath the snow,
And the dogs were fed, and the stars o'erhead
were dancing heel and toe,
He turned to me, and " Cap," says he, " I'll cash
in this trip, I guess;
And if I do, I'm asking that you won't refuse my
last request."

Well, he seemed so low that I couldn't say no;
then he says with a sort of moan:
" It's the cursèd cold, and it's got right hold till
I'm chilled clean through to the bone.

THE CREMATION OF SAM McGEE

Yet 'tain't being dead — it's my awful dread of
  the icy grave that pains;
So I want you to swear that, foul or fair, you'll
  cremate my last remains."

Well,

A pal's last need is a thing to heed, so I swore
  I would not fail;
And we started on at the streak of dawn; but
  God! he looked ghastly pale.
He crouched on the sleigh, ~~and~~ he raved all day
  of his home in Tennessee;
And before nightfall a corpse was all that was
  left of Sam McGee.

There wasn't a breath in that land of death, and
  I hurried, horror-driven,
With a corpse half hid that I couldn't get rid,
  because of a promise given;
It was lashed to the sleigh, and it seemed to say:
  " You may tax your brawn and brains,
But you promised true, and it's up to you to
  cremate those last remains."

THE CREMATION OF SAM McGEE

Now a promise made is a debt unpaid, and the
    trail has its own stern code.
In the days to come, though my lips were dumb,
    in my heart how I cursed that load.
In the long, long night, by the lone firelight,
    while the huskies, round in a ring,
Howled out their woes to the homeless snows
    — O God! how I loathed the thing.

And every day that quiet clay seemed to heavy
    and heavier grow;
And on I went, though the dogs were spent and
    the grub was getting low;
The trail was bad, and I felt half mad, but I
    swore I would not give in;
And I'd often sing to the hateful thing, and it
    hearkened with a grin.

Till I came to the marge of Lake Lebarge, and
    a derelict there lay;
It was jammed in the ice, but I saw in a trice it
    was called the " Alice May."

THE CREMATION OF SAM McGEE

And I looked at it, and I thought a bit, and I
    looked at my frozen chum;
Then " Here," said I, with a sudden cry, " is
    my cre-ma-tor-eum."

Some planks I tore from the cabin floor, and I
    lit the boiler fire;
Some coal I found that was lying around, and I
    heaped the fuel higher;
The flames just soared, and the furnace roared
    — such a blaze you seldom see;
And I burrowed a hole in the glowing coal, and
    I stuffed in Sam McGee.

Then I made a hike, for I didn't like to hear him
    sizzle so;
And the heavens scowled, and the huskies
    howled, and the wind began to blow.
It was icy cold, but the hot sweat rolled down my
    cheeks, and I don't know why;
And the greasy smoke in an inky cloak went
    streaking down the sky.

THE CREMATION OF SAM McGEE

I do not know how long in the snow I wrestled
    with grisly fear;
But the stars came out and they danced about
    ere again I ventured near;
I was sick with dread, but I bravely said: " I'll
    just take a peep inside.
I guess he's cooked, and it's time I looked "; . . .
    then the door I opened wide.

And there sat Sam, looking cool and calm, in the
    heart of the furnace roar;
And he wore a smile you could see a mile, and
    he said: " Please close that door.
It's fine in here, but I greatly fear you'll let in
    the cold and storm —
Since I left Plumtree, down in Tennessee, it's
    the first time I've been warm."

There are strange things done in the midnight sun
    By the men who moil for gold;
The Arctic trails have their secret tales
    That would make your blood run cold;

THE CREMATION OF SAM McGEE

The Northern Lights have seen queer sights,
  But the queerest they ever did see
Was that night on the marge of Lake Lebarge
  I cremated Sam McGee.

fantastic!

MY MADONNA

I haled me a woman from the street,
 Shameless, but, oh, so fair!
I bade her sit in the model's seat
 And I painted her sitting there.

I hid all trace of her heart unclean;
 I painted a babe at her breast;
I painted her as she might have been
 If the Worst had been the Best.

She laughed at my picture and went away.
 Then came, with a knowing nod,
A connoisseur, and I heard him say;
 " 'Tis Mary, the Mother of God."

So I painted a halo round her hair,
 And I sold her and took my fee,
And she hangs in the church of Saint Hillaire,
 Where you and all may see.

UNFORGOTTEN

I know a garden where the lilies gleam,
   And one who lingers in the sunshine there;
   She is than white-stoled lily far more fair,
And oh, her eyes are heaven-lit with dream!

I know a garret, cold and dark and drear,
   And one who toils and toils with tireless pen,
   Until his brave, sad eyes grow weary — then
He seeks the stars, pale, silent as a seer.

And ah, it's strange; for, desolate and dim,
   Between these two there rolls an ocean wide;
   Yet he is in the garden by her side
And she is in the garret there with him.

THE RECKONING

It's fine to have a blow-out in a fancy restau‑
    rant,
With terrapin and canvas-back and all the wine
    you want;
To enjoy the flowers and music, watch the
    pretty women pass,
Smoke a choice cigar, and sip the wealthy
    water in your glass.
It's bully in a high-toned joint to eat and drink
    your fill,
But it's quite another matter when you
                   Pay the bill.

It's great to go out every night on fun or
    pleasure bent;
To wear your glad rags always and to never
    save a cent;

70

THE RECKONING

To drift along regardless, have a good time
    every trip;
To hit the high spots sometimes, and to let your
    chances slip;
To know you're acting foolish, yet to go on
    fooling still,
Till Nature calls a show-down, and you
                      Pay the bill.

Time has got a little bill — get wise while yet
    you may,
For the debit side's increasing in a most alarm-
    ing way;
The things you had no right to do, the things
    you should have done,
They're all put down; it's up to you to pay for
    every one.
So eat, drink and be merry, have a good time
    if you will,
But God help you when the time comes, and you
                   Foot the bill.

QUATRAINS

One said: Thy life is thine to make or mar,
To flicker feebly, or to soar, a star;
    It lies with thee — the choice is thine, is thine,
To hit the ties or drive thy auto-car.

I answered Her: The choice is mine — ah, no!
We all were made or marred long, long ago.
    The parts are written; hear the super wail:
" Who is stage-managing this cosmic show? "

Blind fools of fate and slaves of circumstance,
Life is a fiddler, and we all must dance.
    From gloom where mocks that will-o'-wisp,
        Free-will
I heard a voice cry: " Say, give us a chance."

QUATRAINS

Chance! Oh, there is no chance! The scene
    is set.
Up with the curtain! Man, the marionette,
    Resumes his part. The gods will work the
        wires.
They've got it all down fine, you bet, you bet!

It's all decreed — the mighty earthquake crash,
The countless constellations' wheel and flash;
    The rise and fall of empires, war's red tide;
The composition of your dinner hash.

There's no haphazard in this world of ours.
Cause and effect are grim, relentless powers.
    They rule the world. (A king was shot last
        night;
Last night I held the joker and both bowers.)

From out the mesh of fate our heads we thrust.
We can't do what we would, but what we must.
    Heredity has got us in a cinch —
(Consoling thought when you've been on a
        " bust.")

QUATRAINS

Hark to the song where spheral voices blend:
" There's no beginning, never will be end."
   It makes us nutty; hang the astral chimes!
The tables spread; come, let us dine, my friend.

THE MEN THAT DON'T FIT IN

There's a race of men that don't fit in,
  A race that can't stay still;
So they break the hearts of kith and kin,
  And they roam the world at will.
They range the field and they rove the flood,
  And they climb the mountain's crest;
Theirs is the curse of the gypsy blood,
  And they don't know how to rest.

If they just went straight they might go far;
  They are strong and brave and true;
But they're always tired of the things that are,
  And they want the strange and new.
They say: " Could I find my proper groove,
  What a deep mark I would make! "
So they chop and change, and each fresh move
  Is only a fresh mistake.

THE MEN THAT DON'T FIT IN

And each forgets, as he strips and runs
  With a brilliant, fitful pace,
It's the steady, quiet, plodding ones
  Who win in the lifelong race.
And each forgets that his youth has fled,
  Forgets that his prime is past,
Till he stands one day, with a hope that's dead,
  In the glare of the truth at last.

He has failed, he has failed; he has missed his
      chance;
  He has just done things by half.
Life's been a jolly good joke on him,
  And now is the time to laugh.
Ha, ha! He is one of the Legion Lost;
  He was never meant to win;
He's a rolling stone, and it's bred in the bone;
  He's a man who won't fit in.

MUSIC IN THE BUSH

O'er the dark pines she sees the silver moon,
    And in the west, all tremulous, a star;
And soothing sweet she hears the mellow tune
    Of cow-bells jangled in the fields afar.

Quite listless, for her daily stent is done,
    She stands, sad exile, at her rose-wreathed
        door,
And sends her love eternal with the sun
    That goes to gild the land she'll see no more.

The grave, gaunt pines imprison her sad gaze,
    All still the sky and darkling drearily;
She feels the chilly breath of dear, dead days.
    Come sifting through the alders eerily.

MUSIC IN THE BUSH

Oh, how the roses riot in their bloom!
    The curtains stir as with an ancient pain;
Her old piano gleams from out the gloom
    And waits and waits her tender touch in vain.

But now her hands like moonlight brush the keys
    With velvet grace — melodious delight;
And now a sad refrain from over seas
    Goes sobbing on the bosom of the night;

And now she sings.   (O! singer in the gloom,
    Voicing a sorrow we can ne'er express,
Here in the Farness where we few have room
    Unshamed to show our love and tenderness,

Our hearts will echo, till they beat no more,
    That song of sadness and of motherland;
And, stretched in deathless love to England's
        shore,
    Some day she'll hearken and she'll under-
        stand.)

MUSIC IN THE BUSH

A prima-donna in the shining past,
  But now a mother growing old and gray,
She thinks of how she held a people fast
  In thrall, and gleaned the triumphs of a day.

She sees a sea of faces like a dream;
  She sees herself a queen of song once more;
She sees lips part in rapture, eyes agleam;
  She sings as never once she sang before.

She sings a wild, sweet song that throbs with
      pain,
  The added pain of life that transcends art —
A song of home, a deep, celestial strain,
  The glorious swan-song of a dying heart.

A lame tramp comes along the railway track,
  A grizzled dog whose day is nearly done;
He passes, pauses, then comes slowly back
  And listens there — an audience of one.

MUSIC IN THE BUSH

She sings — her golden voice is passion-fraught,
 As when she charmed a thousand eager ears;
He listens trembling, and she knows it not,
 And down his hollow cheeks roll bitter tears.

She ceases and is still, as if to pray;
 There is no sound, the stars are all alight —
Only a wretch who stumbles on his way,
 Only a vagrant sobbing in the night.

THE RHYME OF THE REMIT-
TANCE MAN

There's a four-pronged buck a-swinging in the
    shadow of my cabin,
And it roamed the velvet valley till to-day;
But I tracked it by the river, and I trailed it in
    the cover,
And I killed it on the mountain miles away.
Now I've had my lazy supper, and the level
    sun is gleaming
On the water where the silver salmon play;
And I light my little corn-cob, and I linger,
    softly dreaming,
In the twilight, of a land that's far away.

Far away, so faint and far, is flaming London,
    fevered Paris,
That I fancy I have gained another star;

RHYME OF THE REMITTANCE MAN

Far away the din and hurry, far away the sin
    and worry,
  Far away — God knows they cannot be too
    far.
Gilded galley-slaves of Mammon — how my
    purse-proud brothers taunt me!
  I might have been as well-to-do as they
Had I clutched like them my chances,
    learned their wisdom, crushed my
    fancies,
  Starved my soul and gone to business every
    day.

Well, the cherry bends with blossom and the
    vivid grass is springing,
  And the star-like lily nestles in the
    green;
And the frogs their joys are singing, and my
    heart in tune is ringing,
  And it doesn't matter what I might have
    been.
While above the scented pine-gloom, piling
    heights of golden glory,
  The sun-god paints his canvas in the west,

RHYME OF THE REMITTANCE MAN

I can couch me deep in clover, I can listen to
    the story
  Of the lazy, lapping water — it is best.

While the trout leaps in the river, and the blue
    grouse thrills the cover,
  And the frozen snow betrays the panther's
    track,
And the robin greets the dayspring with the
    rapture of a lover,
  I am happy, and I'll nevermore go back.
For I know I'd just be longing for the little old
    log cabin,
  With the morning-glory clinging to the door,
Till I loathed the city places, cursed the care
    on all the faces,
  Turned my back on lazar London evermore.

So send me far from Lombard Street, and write
    me down a failure;
  Put a little in my purse and leave me free.
Say: " He turned from Fortune's offering to
    follow up a pale lure,
  He is one of us no longer — let him be."

RHYME OF THE REMITTANCE MAN

I am one of you no longer; by the trails my feet
    have broken,
    The dizzy peaks I've scaled, the camp-fire's
        glow;
By the lonely seas I've sailed in — yea, the final
    word is spoken,
    I am signed and sealed to nature.   Be it so.

THE LOW-DOWN WHITE

This is the pay-day up at the mines, when the
    bearded brutes come down;
There's money to burn in the streets to-night,
    so I've sent my klooch to town,
With a haggard face and a ribband of red en-
    twined in her hair of brown.

And I know at the dawn she'll come reeling
    home with the bottles, one, two, three —
One for herself, to drown her shame, and two
    big bottles for me,
To make me forget the thing I am and the man
    I used to be.

THE LOW-DOWN WHITE

To make me forget the brand of the dog, as I
    crouch in this hideous place;
To make me forget once I kindled the light of
    love in a lady's face,
Where even the squalid Siwash now holds me
    a black disgrace.

Oh, I have guarded my secret well! And who
    would dream as I speak
In a tribal tongue like a rogue unhung, 'mid the
    ranch-house filth and reek,
I could roll to bed with a Latin phrase and rise
    with a verse of Greek?

Yet I was a senior prizeman once, and the pride
    of a college eight;
Called to the bar — my friends were true! but
    they could not keep me straight;
Then came the divorce, and I went abroad and
    " died " on the River Plate.

THE LOW-DOWN WHITE

But I'm not dead yet; though with half a lung
    there isn't time to spare,
And I hope that the year will see me out, and,
    thank God, no one will care —
Save maybe the little slim Siwash girl with the
    rose of shame in her hair.

She will come with the dawn, and the dawn is
    near; I can see its evil glow,
Like a corpse-light seen through a frosty pane
    in a night of want and woe;
And yonder she comes by the bleak bull-pines,
    swift staggering through the snow.

THE LITTLE OLD LOG CABIN

When a man gits on his uppers in a hard-pan
    sort of town,
  An' he ain't got nothin' comin' an' he can't
    afford ter eat,
An' he's in a fix for lodgin' an' he wanders up
    an' down,
  An' you'd fancy he'd been boozin', he's so
    locoed 'bout the feet;
When he's feelin' sneakin' sorry an' his belt is
    hangin' slack,
  An' his face is peaked an' gray-like an' his
    heart gits down an' whines,
Then he's apt ter git a-thinkin' an' a-wishin' he
    was back
  In the little ol' log cabin in the shadder of
    the pines.

THE LITTLE OLD LOG CABIN

When he's on the blazin' desert an' his canteen's
    sprung a leak,
  An' he's all alone an' crazy an' he's crawlin'
    like a snail,
An' his tongue's so black an' swollen that it
    hurts him fer to speak,
  An' he gouges down fer water an' the raven's
    on his trail;
When he's done with care and cursin' an' he
    feels more like to cry,
  An' he sees ol' Death a-grinnin' an' he thinks
    upon his crimes,
Then he's like ter hev' a vision, as he settles
    down ter die,
  Of the little ol' log cabin an' the roses an'
    the vines.

Oh, the little ol' log cabin, it's a solemn shinin'
    mark,
  When a feller gits ter sinnin' an' a-goin' ter
    the wall,
An' folks don't understand him an' he's gropin'
    in the dark,

THE LITTLE OLD LOG CABIN

An' he's sick of bein' cursed at an' he's
    longin' fer his call!
When the sun of life's a-sinkin' you can see it
    'way above,
    On the hill from out the shadder in a glory
        'gin the sky,
An' your mother's voice is callin', an' her arms
    are stretched in love,
    An' somehow you're glad you're goin', an'
        you ain't a-scared to die;
When you'll be like a kid again an' nestle to
    her breast,
An' never leave its shelter, an' forget, an' love,
    an' rest.

THE YOUNGER SON

If you leave the gloom of London and you seek
    a glowing land,
  Where all except the flag is strange and new,
There's a bronzed and stalwart fellow who will
    grip you by the hand,
  And greet you with a welcome warm and
    true;
For he's your younger brother, the one you
    sent away
  Because there wasn't room for him at home;
And now he's quite contented, and he's glad he
    didn't stay,
  And he's building Britain's greatness o'er the
    foam.

When the giant herd is moving at the rising of
    the sun,
  And the prairie is lit with rose and gold,

THE YOUNGER SON

And the camp is all abustle, and the busy day's
    begun,
  He leaps into the saddle sure and bold.
Through the round of heat and hurry, through
    the racket and the rout,
  He rattles at a pace that nothing mars;
And when the night-winds whisper and camp-
    fires flicker out,
  He is sleeping like a child beneath the stars.

When the wattle-blooms are drooping in the
    sombre shed-oak glade,
  And the breathless land is lying in a swoon,
He leaves his work a moment, leaning lightly
    on his spade,
  And he hears the bell-bird chime the Austral
    noon.
The parrakeets are silent in the gum-tree by the
    creek;
  The ferny grove is sunshine-steeped and
    still;
But the dew will gem the myrtle in the twilight
    ere he seek
  His little lonely cabin on the hill.

THE YOUNGER SON

Around the purple, vine-clad slope the argent
river dreams;
The roses almost hide the house from view;
A snow-peak of the Winterberg in crimson
splendor gleams;
The shadow deepens down on the karroo.
He seeks the lily-scented dusk beneath the
orange tree;
His pipe in silence glows and fades and
glows;
And then two little maids come out and climb
upon his knee,
And one is like the lily, one the rose.

He sees his white sheep dapple o'er the green
New Zealand plain,
And where Vancouver's shaggy ramparts
frown,
When the sunlight threads the pine-gloom he is
fighting might and main
To clinch the rivets of an Empire down.
You will find him toiling, toiling, in the south
or in the west,
A child of nature, fearless, frank and free;

THE YOUNGER SON

And the warmest heart that beats for you is
    beating in his breast,
  And he sends you loyal greeting o'er the sea.

You've a brother in the army, you've another in
    the Church;
  One of you is a diplomatic swell;
You've had the pick of everything and left him
    in the lurch,
  And yet I think he's doing very well.
I'm sure his life is happy, and he doesn't envy
    yours;
  I know he loves the land his pluck has won;
And I fancy in the years unborn, while Eng-
    land's fame endures,
  She will come to bless with pride — The
    Younger Son.

THE MARCH OF THE DEAD

The cruel war was over — oh, the triumph was
        so sweet!
  We watched the troops returning, through
        our tears;
There was triumph, triumph, triumph down the
        scarlet glittering street,
  And you scarce could hear the music for the
        cheers.
And you scarce could see the house-tops for the
        flags that flew between;
  The bells were pealing madly to the sky;
And everyone was shouting for the Soldiers of
        the Queen,
  And the glory of an age was passing by.

And then there came a shadow, swift and sud-
        den, dark and drear;
  The bells were silent, not an echo stirred.

THE MARCH OF THE DEAD

The flags were drooping sullenly, the men for-
      got to cheer;
  We waited, and we never spoke a word.
The sky grew darker, darker, till from out the
      gloomy rack
  There came a voice that checked the heart
      with dread:
"Tear down, tear down your bunting now, and
      hang up sable black;
  They are coming — it's the Army of the
      Dead."

They were coming, they were coming, gaunt and
      ghastly, sad and slow;
  They were coming, all the crimson wrecks of
      pride;
With faces seared, and cheeks red smeared, and
      haunting eyes of woe,
  And clotted holes the khaki couldn't hide.
Oh, the clammy brow of anguish! the livid,
      foam-flecked lips!
  The reeling ranks of ruin swept along!
The limb that trailed, the hand that failed, the
      bloody finger tips!
  And oh, the dreary rhythm of their song!

THE MARCH OF THE DEAD

" They left us on the veldt-side, but we felt we
    couldn't stop
  On this, our England's crowning festal day;
We're the men of Magersfontein, we're the men
    of Spion Kop,
  Colenso — we're the men who had to pay.
We're the men who paid the blood-price. Shall
    the grave be all our gain?
  You owe us. Long and heavy is the score.
Then cheer us for our glory now, and cheer us
    for our pain,
  And cheer us as ye never cheered before."

The folks were white and stricken, and each
    tongue seemed weighted with lead;
  Each heart was clutched in hollow hand of ice;
And every eye was staring at the horror of the
    dead,
  The pity of the men who paid the price.
They were come, were come to mock us, in the
    first flush of our peace;
  Through writhing lips their teeth were all
    agleam;

THE MARCH OF THE DEAD

They were coming in their thousands — oh,
    would they never cease!
  I closed my eyes, and then — it was a dream.

There was triumph, triumph, triumph down the
    scarlet gleaming street;
  The town was mad; a man was like a boy.
A thousand flags were flaming where the sky and
    city meet;
  A thousand bells were thundering the joy.
There was music, mirth and sunshine; but some
    eyes shone with regret;
  And while we stun with cheers our homing
    braves,
O God, in Thy great mercy, let us nevermore
    forget
  The graves they left behind, the bitter graves.

"FIGHTING MAC"

A LIFE TRAGEDY

A pistol shot rings round and round the world;
    In pitiful defeat a warrior lies.
A last defiance to dark Death is hurled,
    A last wild challenge shocks the sunlit skies.
    Alone he falls, with wide, wan, woeful eyes:
Eyes that could smile at death — could not face
        shame.

Alone, alone he paced his narrow room,
    In the bright sunshine of that Paris day;
Saw in his thought the awful hand of doom;
    Saw in his dream his glory pass away;
    Tried in his heart, his weary heart, to pray:
" O God! who made me, give me strength to
        face
The spectre of this bitter, black disgrace."

    *   *   *   *   *   *

99

"FIGHTING MAC"

The burn brawls darkly down the shaggy
     glen;
   The bee-kissed heather blooms around the
     door;
He sees himself a barefoot boy again,
   Bending o'er page of legendary lore.
   He hears the pibroch, grips the red clay-
     more,
Runs with the Fiery Cross, a clansman true,
Sworn kinsman of Rob Roy and Roderick
     Dhu.

Eating his heart out with a wild desire,
   One day, behind his counter trim and
     neat,
He hears a sound that sets his brain afire —
   The Highlanders are marching down the
     street.
   Oh, how the pipes shrill out, the mad drums
     beat!
" On to the gates of Hell, my Gordons gay! "
He flings his hated yardstick away.

" FIGHTING MAC "

He sees the sullen pass, high-crowned with
    snow,
    Where Afghans cower with eyes of gleaming
       hate.
He hurls himself against the hidden foe.
    They try to rally — ah, too late, too late!
    Again, defenseless, with fierce eyes that wait
For death, he stands, like baited bull at bay,
And flouts the Boers, that mad Majuba day.

He sees again the murderous Soudan,
    Blood-slaked and rapine-swept. He seems
      to stand
Upon the gory plain of Omdurman.
    Then Magersfontein, and supreme command
    Over his Highlanders. To shake his hand
A King is proud, and princes call him friend.
And glory crowns his life — and now the end,

The awful end. His eyes are dark with doom;
    He hears the shrapnel shrieking overhead;
He sees the ravaged ranks, the flame-stabbed
    gloom.

" FIGHTING MAC "

Oh, to have fallen! — the battle-field his bed,
  With Wauchope and his glorious brother-
    dead.
Why was he saved for this, for this? And now
He raises the revolver to his brow.

      *   *   *   *   *   *

In many a Highland home, framed with rude
    art,
  You'll find his portrait, rough-hewn, stern and
    square ;
It's graven in the Fuyam fellah's heart ;
  The Ghurka reads it at his evening prayer ;
  The raw lands know it, where the fierce suns
    glare ;
The Dervish fears it. Honor to his name
Who holds aloft the shield of England's fame.

Mourn for our hero, men of Northern race !
  We do not know his sin ; we only know
His sword was keen. He laughed death in the
    face,
  And struck, for Empire's sake, a giant blow.

" FIGHTING MAC "

His arm was strong.   Ah! well they learnt,
    the foe
The echo of his deeds is ringing yet —
Will ring for aye.   All else . . . let us forget.

THE WOMAN AND THE ANGEL

An angel was tired of heaven, as he lounged in
    the golden street;
His halo was tilted sideways, and his harp lay
    mute at his feet;
So the Master stooped in His pity, and gave him
    a pass to go,
For the space of a moon, to the earth-world, to
    mix with the men below.

He doffed his celestial garments, scarce waiting
    to lay them straight;
He bade good by to Peter, who stood by the
    golden gate;
The sexless singers of heaven chanted a fond
    farewell,
And the imps looked up as they pattered on the
    red-hot flags of hell.

THE WOMAN AND THE ANGEL

Never was seen such an angel — eyes of
     heavenly blue,
Features that shamed Apollo, hair of a golden
     hue;
The women simply adored him; his lips were
     like Cupid's bow;
But he never ventured to use them — and so
     they voted him slow.

Till at last there came One Woman, a marvel
     of loveliness,
And she whispered to him: " Do you love me? "
     And he answered that woman, " Yes."
And she said: " Put your arms around me, and
     kiss me, and hold me — so —"
But fiercely he drew back, saying: " This thing
     is wrong, and I know."

Then sweetly she mocked his scruples, and softly
     she him beguiled:
" You, who are verily man among men, speak
     with the tongue of a child.

THE WOMAN AND THE ANGEL

We have outlived the old standards; we have
    burst, like an over-tight thong,
The ancient, outworn, Puritanic traditions of
    Right and Wrong."

Then the Master feared for His angel, and
    called him again to His side,
For oh, the woman was wondrous, and oh, the
    angel was tried!
And deep in his hell sang the Devil, and this
    was the strain of his song:
" The ancient, outworn, Puritanic traditions of
    Right and Wrong."

THE RHYME OF THE RESTLESS ONES

We couldn't sit and study for the law;
  The stagnation of a bank we couldn't stand;
For our riot blood was surging, and we didn't
      need much urging
  To excitements and excesses that are banned.
So we took to wine and drink and other things,
  And the devil in us struggled to be free;
Till our friends rose up in wrath, and they
      pointed out the path,
  And they paid our debts and packed us o'er
      the sea.

Oh, they shook us off and shipped us o'er the
      foam,
To the larger lands that lure a man to roam;
      And we took the chance they gave
      Of a far and foreign grave,
And we bade good-by for evermore to home.

RHYME OF THE RESTLESS ONES

And some of us are climbing on the peak,
    And some of us are camping on the plain;
By pine and palm you'll find us, with never claim
        to bind us,
    By track and trail you'll meet us once again.

We are fated serfs to freedom — sky and sea;
    We have failed where slummy cities overflow;
But the stranger ways of earth know our pride
        and know our worth,
    And we go into the dark as fighters go.

Yes, we go into the night as brave men go,
Though our faces they be often streaked with
        woe;
    Yet we're hard as cats to kill,
    And our hearts are reckless still,
And we've danced with death a dozen times or
    so.

And you'll find us in Alaska after gold,
    And you'll find us herding cattle in the South.

RHYME OF THE RESTLESS ONES

We like strong drink and fun, and, when the
    race is run,
  We often die with curses in our mouth.
We are wild as colts unbroke, but never mean.
  Of our sins we've shoulders broad to bear the
    blame;
But we'll never stay in town and we'll never
    settle down,
  And we'll never have an object or an aim.

No, there's that in us that time can never tame;
And life will always seem a careless game;
    And they'd better far forget —
    Those who say they love us yet —
Forget, blot out with bitterness our name.

NEW YEAR'S EVE

It's cruel cold on the water-front, silent and
    dark and drear;
  Only the black tide weltering, only the hissing
    snow;
And I, alone, like a storm-tossed wreck, on this
    night of the glad New Year,
  Shuffling along in the icy wind, ghastly and
    gaunt and slow.

They're playing a tune in McGuffy's saloon, and
    it's cheery and bright in there
  (God! but I'm weak — since the bitter dawn,
    and never a bite of food);
I'll just go over and slip inside — I mustn't give
    way to despair —
  Perhaps I can bum a little booze if the boys
    are feeling good.

NEW YEAR'S EVE

They'll jeer at me, and they'll sneer at me, and
 they'll call me a whiskey soak;
 (" Have a drink?   Well, thankee kindly, sir,
  I don't mind if I do.")
A drivelling, dirty, gin-joint fiend, the butt of the
 bar-room joke;
 Sunk and sodden and hopeless —" Another?
  Well, here's to you! "

McGuffy is showing a bunch of the boys how
 Bob Fitzsimmons hit;
 The barman is talking of Tammany Hall,
  and why the ward boss got fired.
I'll just sneak into a corner and they'll let me
 alone a bit;
 The room is reeling round and round . . .
  O God! but I'm tired, I'm tired. . . .

  * * * * * *

Roses she wore on her breast that night.   Oh,
 but their scent was sweet!
 Alone we sat on the balcony, and the fan-
  palms arched above;

NEW YEAR'S EVE

The witching strain of a waltz by Strauss came
    up to our cool retreat,
And I prisoned her little hand in mine, and
    I whispered my plea of love.

Then sudden the laughter died on her lips, and
    lowly she bent her head;
And oh, there came in the deep, dark eyes a
    look that was heaven to see;
And the moments went, and I waited there, and
    never a word was said,
And she plucked from her bosom a rose of
    red and shyly gave it to me.

Then the music swelled to a crash of joy, and
    the lights blazed up like day,
And I held her fast to my throbbing heart,
    and I kissed her bonny brow.
" She is mine, she is mine for evermore ! " the
    violins seemed to say,
And the bells were ringing the New Year in
    — O God! I can hear them now.

NEW YEAR'S EVE

Don't you remember that long, last waltz, with
    its sobbing, sad refrain?
  Don't you remember that last good-by, and
    the dear eyes dim with tears?
Don't you remember that golden dream, with
    never a hint of pain,
  Of lives that would blend like an angel-song
    in the bliss of the coming years?

Oh, what have I lost! What have I lost!
    Ethel, forgive, forgive!
  The red, red rose is faded now, and it's fifty
    years ago.
'Twere better to die a thousand deaths than live
    each day as I live!
  I have sinned, I have sunk to the lowest
    depths — but oh, I have suffered so!

Hark! Oh, hark! I can hear the bells! . . .
    Look! I can see her there,
  Fair as a dream . . . but it fades . . . And
    now — I can hear the dreadful hum

Of the crowded court . . . See! the Judge
    looks down . . . NOT GUILTY, my
    Lord, I swear . . .
The bells — I can hear the bells again! . . .
    Ethel, I come, I come! . . .

      *   *   *   *   *   *

" Rouse up, old man, it's twelve o'clock.   You
    can't sleep here, you know.
Say! ain't you got no sentiment?   Lift up
    your muddled head;
Have a drink to the glad New Year, a drop
    before you go —
You darned old dirty hobo . . . My God!
    Here, boys!   He's DEAD! "

COMFORT

Say! You've struck a heap of trouble —
  Bust in business, lost your wife;
No one cares a cent about you,
  You don't care a cent for life;
Hard luck has of hope bereft you,
  Health is failing, wish you'd die —
Why, you've still the sunshine left you
  And the big, blue sky.

Sky so blue it makes you wonder
  If it's heaven shining through;
Earth so smiling 'way out yonder,
  Sun so bright it dazzles you;
Birds a-singing, flowers a-flinging
  All their fragrance on the breeze;
Dancing shadows, green, still meadows —
  Don't you mope, you've still got these.

COMFORT

These, and none can take them from you;
 These, and none can weigh their worth.
What! you're tired and broke and beaten? —
 Why, you're rich — you've got the earth!
Yes, if you're a tramp in tatters,
 While the blue sky bends above
You've got nearly all that matters —
 You've got God, and God is love.

THE HARPY

There was a woman, and she was wise; woefully
wise was she;
She was old, so old, yet her years all told were
but a score and three;
And she knew by heart, from finish to start, the
Book of Iniquity.

There is no hope for such as I on earth, nor yet
in Heaven;
Unloved I live, unloved I die, unpitied, unfor-
given;
A loathèd jade, I ply my trade, unhallowed and
unshriven.

THE HARPY

I paint my cheeks, for they are white, and cheeks
    of chalk men hate;
Mine eyes with wine I make them shine, that
    man may seek and sate;
With overhead a lamp of red I sit me down and
    wait

Until they come, the nightly scum, with drunken
    eyes aflame;
Your sweethearts, sons, ye scornful ones —'tis
    I who know their shame.
The gods, ye see, are brutes to me — and so I
    play my game.

For life is not the thing we thought, and not the
    thing we plan;
And Woman in a bitter world must do the best
    she can —
Must yield the stroke, and bear the yoke, and
    serve the will of man;

THE HARPY

Must serve his need and ever feed the flame of
    his desire,
Though be she loved for love alone, or be she
    loved for hire;
For every man since life began is tainted with
    the mire.

And though you know he love you so and set
    you on love's throne;
Yet let your eyes but mock his sighs, and let
    your heart be stone,
Lest you be left (as I was left) attainted and
    alone.

From love's close kiss to hell's abyss is one sheer
    flight, I trow,
And wedding ring and bridal bell are will-o'-
    wisps of woe,
And 'tis not wise to love too well, and this all
    women know.

THE HARPY

Wherefore, the wolf-pack having gorged upon
  the lamb, their prey,
With siren smile and serpent guile I make the
  wolf-pack pay —
With velvet paws and flensing claws, a tigress
  roused to slay.

One who in youth sought truest truth and found
  a devil's lies;
A symbol of the sin of man, a human sacrifice.
Yet shall I blame on man the shame? Could it
  be otherwise?

Was I not born to walk in scorn where others
  walk in pride?
The Maker marred, and, evil-starred, I drift
  upon His tide;
And He alone shall judge His own, so I His
  judgment bide.

THE HARPY

Fate has written a tragedy; its name is " The
    Human Heart."
The Theatre is the House of Life, Woman the
    mummer's part;
The Devil enters the prompter's box and the
    play is ready to start.

PREMONITION

'Twas a year ago and the moon was bright
   (Oh, I remember so well, so well) ;
I walked with my love in a sea of light,
   And the voice of my sweet was a silver bell.
      And sudden the moon grew strangely dull,
        And sudden my love had taken wing;
     I looked on the face of a grinning skull,
      I strained to my heart a ghastly thing.

'Twas but fantasy, for my love lay still
   In my arms, with her tender eyes aglow,
And she wondered why my lips were chill,
   Why I was silent and kissed her so.
      A year has gone and the moon is bright,
        A gibbous moon, like a ghost of woe;
     I sit by a new-made grave to-night,
      And my heart is broken — it's strange,
       you know.

THE TRAMPS

Can you recall, dear comrade, when we tramped
    God's land together,
  And we sang the old, old Earth-song, for our
    youth was very sweet;
When we drank and fought and lusted, as we
    mocked at tie and tether,
  Along the road to Anywhere, the wide world
    at our feet —

Along the road to Anywhere, when each day
    had its story;
  When time was yet our vassal, and life's jest
    was still unstale;
When peace unfathomed filled our hearts as,
    bathed in amber glory,
  Along the road to Anywhere we watched the
    sunsets pale?

THE TRAMPS

Alas! the road to Anywhere is pitfalled with
    disaster;
  There's hunger, want, and weariness, yet O
    we loved it so!
As on we tramped exultantly, and no man was
    our master,
  And no man guessed what dreams were ours,
    as, swinging heel and toe,
We tramped the road to Anywhere, the magic
    road to Anywhere,
  The tragic road to Anywhere, such dear, dim
    years ago.

L'ENVOI

You who have lived in the land,
*   You who have trusted the trail,*
You who are strong to withstand,
*   You who are swift to assail:*
*   Songs have I sung to beguile,*
*   Vintage of desperate years,*
*   Hard as a harlot's smile,*
*   Bitter as unshed tears.*

Little of joy or mirth,
*   Little of ease I sing;*
Sagas of men of earth
*   Humanly suffering,*
*   Such as you all have done;*
*   Savagely faring forth,*
*   Sons of the midnight sun,*
*   Argonauts of the North.*

125

L'ENVOI

Far in the land God forgot
   Glimmers the lure of your trail;
Still in your lust are you taught
   Even to win is to fail.
      Still you must follow and fight
       Under the vampire wing;
      There in the long, long night
       Hoping and vanquishing.

Husbandman of the Wild,
   Reaping a barren gain;
Scourged by desire, reconciled
   Unto disaster and pain;
      These, my songs, are for you,
       You who are seared with the brand.
      God knows I have tried to be true;
       Please God you will understand.

Ballads of a Cheechako

CONTENTS

7

CONTENTS

CONTENTS

Contents

TO THE MAN OF THE HIGH NORTH

My rhymes are rough, and often in my rhyming
  I've drifted, silver-sailed, on seas of dream,
Hearing afar the bells of Elfland chiming,
  Seeing the groves of Arcadie agleam.

I was the thrall of Beauty that rejoices
  From peak snow-diademed to regal star;
Yet to mine aerie ever pierced the voices,
  The pregnant voices of the Things That Are.

The Here, the Now, the vast Forlorn around us;
  The gold-delirium, the ferine strife;
The lusts that lure us on, the hates that hound us;
  Our red rags in the patch-work quilt of Life.

The nameless men who nameless rivers travel,
  And in strange valleys greet strange deaths alone;
The grim, intrepid ones who would unravel
  The mysteries that shroud the Polar Zone.

These will I sing, and if one of you linger
  Over my pages in the Long, Long Night,
And on some lone line lay a calloused finger,
  Saying: " It's human-true—it hits me right;"
Then will I count this loving toil well spent;
Then will I dream awhile—content, content.

11

MEN OF THE HIGH NORTH

Men of the High North, the wild sky is blazing;
  Islands of opal float on silver seas;
Swift splendors kindle, barbaric, amazing;
  Pale ports of amber, golden argosies.
Ringed all around us the proud peaks are glowing;
  Fierce chiefs in council, their wigwam the sky;
Far, far below us the big Yukon flowing,
  Like threaded quicksilver, gleams to the eye.

Men of the High North, you who have known it;
  You in whose hearts its splendors have abode;
Can you renounce it, can you disown it?
  Can you forget it, its glory and its goad?
Where is the hardship, where is the pain of it?
  Lost in the limbo of things you've forgot;
Only remain the guerdon and gain of it;
  Zest of the foray, and God, how you fought!

12

MEN OF THE HIGH NORTH

You who have made good, you foreign faring;
   You money magic to far lands has whirled;
Can you forget those days of vast daring,
   There with your soul on the Top o' the World?
Nights when no peril could keep you awake on
   Spruce boughs you spread for your couch in
      the snow;
Taste all your feasts like the beans and the bacon
   Fried at the camp-fire at forty below?

Can you remember your huskies all going,
   Barking with joy and their brushes in air;
You in your parka, glad-eyed and glowing,
   Monarch, your subjects the wolf and the bear?
Monarch, your kingdom unravisht and gleaming;
   Mountains your throne, and a river your car:
Crash of a bull moose to rouse you from dreaming;
   Forest your couch, and your candle a star.

You who this faint day the High North is luring
   Unto her vastness, taintlessly sweet;
You who are steel-braced, straight-lipped, enduring,
   Dreadless in danger and dire in defeat:
Honor the High North ever and ever,
   Whether she crown you, or whether she slay;
Suffer her fury, cherish and love her—
   He who would rule he must learn to obey.

MEN OF THE HIGH NORTH

Men of the High North, fierce mountains love you;
  Proud rivers leap when you ride on their breast.
See, the austere sky, pensive above you,
  Dons all her jewels to smile on your rest.
Children of Freedom, scornful of frontiers,
  We who are weaklings honor your worth.
Lords of the wilderness, Princes of Pioneers,
  Let's have a rouse that will ring round the
    earth.

THE BALLAD OF THE NORTHERN LIGHTS

One of the Down and Out—that's me. Stare at
   me well, ay, stare!
Stare and shrink—say! you wouldn't think that
   I was a millionaire.
Look at my face, it's crimped and gouged—one of
   them death-mask things;
Don't seem the sort of man, do I, as might be the
   pal of kings?
Slouching along in smelly rags, a bleary-eyed, no-
   good bum;
A knight of the hollow needle, pard, spewed from
   the sodden slum.
Look me all over from head to foot; how much
   would you think I was worth?
A dollar? a dime? a nickel? Why, *I'm the wealth-
iest man on earth.*

No, don't you think that I'm off my base. You'll
   sing a different tune
If only you'll let me spin my yarn. Come over to
   this saloon;

BALLAD OF THE NORTHERN LIGHTS

Wet my throat—it's as dry as chalk, and seeing as
    how it's you,
I'll tell the tale of a Northern trail, and so help me
    God, it's true.
I'll tell of the howling wilderness and the haggard
    Arctic heights,
Of a reckless vow that I made, and how *I staked
    the Northern Lights.*

Remember the year of the Big Stampede and the
    trail of Ninety-eight,
When the eyes of the world were turned to the
    North, and the hearts of men elate;
Hearts of the old dare-devil breed thrilled at the
    wondrous strike,
And to every man who could hold a pan came the
    message, "Up and hike."
Well, I was there with the best of them, and I knew
    I would not fail.
You wouldn't believe it to see me now; but wait
    till you've heard my tale.

You've read of the trail of Ninety-eight, but its
    woe no man may tell;
It was all of a piece and a whole yard wide, and the
    name of the brand was "Hell."
We heard the call and we staked our all; we were
    plungers playing blind,

16

BALLAD OF THE NORTHERN LIGHTS

And no man cared how his neighbor fared, and no
    man looked behind;
For a ruthless greed was born of need, and the
    weakling went to the wall,
And a curse might avail where a prayer would fail,
    and the gold lust crazed us all.

Bold were we, and they called us three the "Unholy
    Trinity;"
There was Ole Olson, the sailor Swede, and the
    Dago Kid and me.
We were the discards of the pack, the foreloopers
    of Unrest,
Reckless spirits of fierce revolt in the ferment of
    the West.
We were bound to win and we revelled in the hard-
    ships of the way.
We staked our ground and our hopes were crowned,
    and we hoisted out the pay.
We were rich in a day beyond our dreams, it was
    gold from the grass-roots down;
But we weren't used to such sudden wealth, and
    there was the siren town.
We were crude and careless frontiersmen, with
    much in us of the beast;
We could bear the famine worthily, but we lost our
    heads at the feast.

BALLAD OF THE NORTHERN LIGHTS

The town looked mighty bright to us, with a bunch
    of dust to spend,
And nothing was half too good them days, and
    everyone was our friend.
Wining meant more than mining then, and life was
    a dizzy whirl,
Gambling and dropping chunks of gold down the
    neck of a dance-hall girl;
Till we went clean mad, it seems to me, and we
    squandered our last poke,
And we sold our claim, and we found ourselves one
    bitter morning—broke.

The Dago Kid he dreamed a dream of his mother's
    aunt who died—
In the dawn-light dim she came to him, and she
    stood by his bedside,
And she said: "Go forth to the highest North till
    a lonely trail ye find;
Follow it far and trust your star, and fortune will
    be kind."
But I jeered at him, and then there came the Sailor
    Swede to me,
And he said: "I dreamed of my sister's son, who
    croaked at the age of three.
From the herded dead he sneaked and said: 'Seek
    you an Arctic trail;

BALLAD OF THE NORTHERN LIGHTS

'Tis pale and grim by the Polar rim, but seek and
     ye shall not fail.' ''
And lo! that night I too did dream of my mother's
     sister's son,
And he said to me: "By the Arctic Sea there's a
     treasure to be won.
Follow and follow a lone moose trail, till you come
     to a valley grim,
On the slope of the lonely watershed that borders
     the Polar brim."
Then I woke my pals, and soft we swore by the
     mystic Silver Flail,
'Twas the hand of Fate, and to-morrow straight
     we would seek the lone moose trail.

We watched the groaning ice wrench free, crash on
     with a hollow din;
Men of the wilderness were we, freed from the
     taint of sin.
The mighty river snatched us up and it bore us
     swift along;
The days were bright, and the morning light was
     sweet with jewelled song.
We poled and lined up nameless streams, portaged
     o'er hill and plain;
We burnt our boat to save the nails, and built our
     boat again;

BALLAD OF THE NORTHERN LIGHTS

We guessed and groped, North, ever North, with
    many a twist and turn;
We saw ablaze in the deathless days the splendid
    sunsets burn.
O'er soundless lakes where the grayling makes a
    rush at the clumsy fly;
By bluffs so steep that the hard-hit sheep falls
    sheer from out the sky;
By lilied pools where the bull moose cools and wal-
    lows in huge content;
By rocky lairs where the pig-eyed bears peered at
    our tiny tent.
Th ough the black canyon's angry foam we
    hurled to dreamy bars,
And round in a ring the dog-nosed peaks bayed to
    the mocking stars.
Spring and summer and autumn went; the sky
    had a tallow gleam,
Yet North and ever North we pressed to the land
    of our Golden Dream.

So we came at last to a tundra vast and dark and
    grim and lone;
And there was the little lone moose trail, and we
    knew it for our own.
By muskeg hollow and nigger-head it wandered
    endlessly;

BALLAD OF THE NORTHERN LIGHTS

Sorry of heart and sore of foot, weary men were
we.
The short-lived sun had a leaden glare and the
darkness came too soon,
And stationed there with a solemn stare was the
pinched, anaemic moon.
Silence and silvern solitude till it made you dumbly
shrink,
And you thought to hear with an outward ear the
things you thought to think.

Oh, it was wild and weird and wan, and ever in
camp o' nights
We would watch and watch the silver dance of the
mystic Northern Lights.
And soft they danced from the Polar sky and swept
in primrose haze;
And swift they pranced with their silver feet, and
pierced with a blinding blaze.
They danced a cotillion in the sky; they were rose
and silver shod;
It was not good for the eyes of man—'twas a sight
for the eyes of God.
It made us mad and strange and sad, and the gold
whereof we dreamed
Was all forgot, and our only thought was of the
lights that gleamed.

BALLAD OF THE NORTHERN LIGHTS

Oh, the tundra sponge it was golden brown, and
    some was a bright blood-red;
And the reindeer moss gleamed here and there like
    the tombstones of the dead.
And in and out and around about the little trail
    ran clear,
And we hated it with a deadly hate and we feared
    with a deadly fear.
And the skies of night were alive with light, with a
    throbbing, thrilling flame;
Amber and rose and violet, opal and gold it came.
It swept the sky like a giant scythe, it quivered
    back to a wedge;
Argently bright, it cleft the night with a wavy
    golden edge.
Pennants of silver waved and streamed, lazy ban-
    ners unfurled;
Sudden splendors of sabres gleamed, lightning
    javelins were hurled.
There in our awe we crouched and saw with our
    wild, uplifted eyes
Charge and retire the hosts of fire in the battle-
    field of the skies.

But all things come to an end at last, and the
    muskeg melted away,
And frowning down to bar our path a muddle of
    mountains lay.

BALLAD OF THE NORTHERN LIGHTS

And a gorge sheered up in granite walls, and the
    moose trail crept betwixt;
'Twas as if the earth had gaped too far and her
    stony jaws were fixt.
Then the winter fell with a sudden swoop, and the
    heavy clouds sagged low,
And earth and sky were blotted out in a whirl of
    driving snow.

We were climbing up a glacier in the neck of a
    mountain pass,
When the Dago Kid slipped down and fell into a
    deep crevasse.
When we got him out one leg hung limp, and his
    brow was wreathed with pain,
And he says: "'Tis badly broken, boys, and I'll
    never walk again.
It's death for all if ye linger here, and that's no
    curséd lie;
Go on, go on while the trail is good, and leave me
    down to die."
He raved and swore, but we tended him with our
    uncouth, clumsy care.
The camp-fire gleamed and he gazed and dreamed
    with a fixed and curious stare.
Then all at once he grabbed my gun and he put
    it to his head,
And he says: "I'll fix it for you, boys"—them are
    the words he said.

BALLAD OF THE NORTHERN LIGHTS

So we sewed him up in a canvas sack and we slung
      him to a tree;
And the stars like needles stabbed our eyes, and
      woeful men were we.
And on we went on our woeful way, wrapped in a
      daze of dream,
And the Northern Lights in the crystal nights
      came forth with a mystic gleam.
They danced and they danced the devil-dance over
      the naked snow;
And soft they rolled like a tide upshoaled with a
      ceaseless ebb and flow.
They rippled green with a wondrous sheen, they
      fluttered out like a fan;
They spread with a blaze of rose-pink rays never
      yet seen of man.
They writhed like a brood of angry snakes, hissing
      and sulphur pale;
Then swift they changed to a dragon vast, lashing
      a cloven tail.
It seemed to us, as we gazed aloft with an ever-
      lasting stare,
The sky was a pit of bale and dread, and a monster
      revelled there.

We climbed the rise of a hog-back range that was
      desolate and drear,
When the Sailor Swede had a crazy fit, and he got
      to talking queer.

BALLAD OF THE NORTHERN LIGHTS

He talked of his home in Oregon and the peach
     trees all in bloom,
And the fern head-high, and the topaz sky, and the
     forest's scented gloom.
He talked of the sins of his misspent life, and then
     he seemed to brood,
And I watched him there like a fox a hare, for I
     knew it was not good.
And sure enough in the dim dawn-light I missed
     him from the tent,
And a fresh trail broke through the crusted snow,
     and I knew not where it went.
But I followed it o'er the seamless waste, and I
     found him at shut of day,
Naked there as a new-born babe—so I left him
     where he lay.

Day after day was sinister, and I fought fierce-eyed
     despair,
And I clung to life, and I struggled on, I knew not
     why nor where.
I packed my grub in short relays, and I cowered
     down in my tent,
And the world around was purged of sound like a
     frozen continent.
Day after day was dark as death, but ever and
     ever at nights,
With a brilliancy that grew and grew, blazed up
     the Northern Lights.

BALLAD OF THE NORTHERN LIGHTS

They rolled around with a soundless sound like
    softly bruiséd silk;
They poured into the bowl of the sky with the
    gentle flow of milk.
In eager, pulsing violet their wheeling chariots
    came,
Or they poised above the Polar rim like a coronal
    of flame.
From depths of darkness fathomless their lancing
    rays were hurled,
Like the all-combining search-lights of the navies
    of the world.
There on the roof-pole of the world as one be-
    witched I gazed,
And howled and grovelled like a beast as the awful
    splendors blazed.
My eyes were seared, yet thralled I peered through
    the parka hood nigh blind;
But I staggered on to the lights that shone, and
    never I looked behind.

There is a mountain round and low that lies by
    the Polar rim,
And I climbed its height in a whirl of light, and I
    peered o'er its jaggéd brim;
And there in a crater deep and vast, ungained,
    unguessed of men,
The mystery of the Arctic world was flashed into
    my ken.

BALLAD OF THE NORTHERN LIGHTS

For there these poor dim eyes of mine beheld the
    sight of sights—
That hollow ring was the source and spring of the
    mystic Northern Lights.

Then I staked that place from crown to base, and
    I hit the homeward trail.
Ah, God! it was good, though my eyes were blurred,
    and I crawled like a sickly snail.
In that vast white world where the silent sky
    communes with the silent snow,
In hunger and cold and misery I wandered to and
    fro.
But the Lord took pity on my pain, and He led me
    to the sea,
And some ice-bound whalers heard my moan, and
    they fed and sheltered me.
They fed the feeble scarecrow thing that stumbled
    out of the wild
With the ravaged face of a mask of death and the
    wandering wits of a child—
A craven, cowering bag of bones that once had been
    a man.
They tended me and they brought me back to the
    world, and here I am.

Some say that the Northern Lights are the glare
    of the Arctic ice and snow;

BALLAD OF THE NORTHERN LIGHTS

And some that it's electricity, and nobody seems
to know.
But I'll tell you now—and if I lie, may my lips be
stricken dumb—
It's a *mine*, a mine of the precious stuff that men
call radium.
It's a million dollars a pound, they say, and there's
tons and tons in sight.
You can see it gleam in a golden stream in the
solitudes of night.
And it's mine, all mine—and say! if you have a
hundred plunks to spare,
I'll let you have the chance of your life, I'll sell
you a quarter share.
You turn it down? Well, I'll make it ten, seeing
as you are my friend.
Nothing doing? Say! don't be hard—have you
got a dollar to lend?
Just a dollar to help me out, I know you'll treat me
white;
I'll do as much for you some day . . . God
bless you, sir; good-night.

THE BALLAD OF THE BLACK FOX SKIN

There was Claw-fingered Kitty and Windy Ike
    living the life of shame,
When unto them in the Long, Long Night came
    the man-who-had-no-name;
Bearing his prize of a black fox pelt, out of the Wild
    he came.

His cheeks were blanched as the flume-head foam
    when the brown spring freshets flow;
Deep in their dark, sin-calcined pits were his sombre
    eyes aglow;
They knew him far for the fitful man who spat
    forth blood on the snow.

"Did ever you see such a skin?" quoth he; "there's
    nought in the world so fine—
Such fullness of fur as black as the night, such
    lustre, such size, such shine;
It's life to a one-lunged man like me; it's London,
    it's women, it's wine.

29

BALLAD OF THE BLACK FOX SKIN

"The Moose-hides called it the devil-fox, and
    swore that no man could kill;
That he who hunted it, soon or late, must surely
    suffer some ill;
But I laughed at them and their old squaw-tales.
    Ha! Ha! I'm laughing still.

"For look ye, the skin—it's as smooth as sin, and
    black as the core of the Pit.
By gun or by trap, whatever the hap, I swore I
    would capture it;
By star and by star afield and afar, I hunted and
    would not quit.

"For the devil-fox, it was swift and sly, and it
    seemed to fleer at me;
I would wake in fright by the camp-fire light,
    hearing its evil glee;
Into my dream its eyes would gleam, and its
    shadow would I see.

"It sniffed and ran from the ptarmigan I had
    poisoned to excess;
Unharmed it sped from my wrathful lead ('twas
    as if I shot by guess);
Yet it came by night in the stark moonlight to
    mock at my weariness.

BALLAD OF THE BLACK FOX SKIN

"I tracked it up where the mountains hunch like
    the vertebrae of the world;
I tracked it down to the death-still pits where the
    avalanche is hurled;
From the glooms to the sacerdotal snows, where the
    carded clouds are curled.

"From the vastitudes where the world protrudes
    through clouds like seas up-shoaled,
I held its track till it led me back to the land I had
    left of old—
The land I had looted many moons. I was weary
    and sick and cold.

"I was sick, soul-sick, of the futile chase, and there
    and then I swore
The foul fiend fox might scathless go, for I would
    hunt no more;
Then I rubbed mine eyes in a vast surprise—it
    stood by my cabin door.

"A rifle raised in the wraith-like gloom, and a
    vengeful shot that sped;
A howl that would thrill a cream-faced corpse—
    and the demon fox lay dead. . . .
Yet there was never a sign of wound, and never a
    drop he bled.

31

BALLAD OF THE BLACK FOX SKIN

"So that was the end of the great black fox, and
    here is the prize I've won;
And now for a drink to cheer me up—I've mushed
    since the early sun;
We'll drink a toast to the sorry ghost of the fox
    whose race is run."

II.

Now Claw-fingered Kitty and Windy Ike, bad as
    the worst were they;
In their road-house down by the river-trail they
    waited and watched for prey;
With wine and song they joyed night long, and
    they slept like swine by day.

For things were done in the Midnight Sun that no
    tongue will ever tell;
And men there be who walk earth-free, but whose
    names are writ in hell—
Are writ in flames with the guilty names of Fournier
    and Labelle.

Put not your trust in a poke of dust would ye sleep
    the sleep of sin;
For there be those who would rob your clothes ere
    yet the dawn comes in;
And a prize likewise in a woman's eyes is a peerless
    black fox skin.

BALLAD OF THE BLACK FOX SKIN

Put your faith in the mountain cat if you lie within
    his lair;
Trust the fangs of the mother-wolf, and the claws
    of the lead-ripped bear;
But oh, of the wiles and the gold-tooth smiles of a
    dance-hall wench beware!

Wherefore it was beyond all laws that lusts of man
    restrain,
A man drank deep and sank to sleep never to wake
    again;
And the Yukon swallowed through a hole the cold
    corpse of the slain.

III.

The black fox skin a shadow cast from the roof nigh
    to the floor;
And sleek it seemed and soft it gleamed, and the
    woman stroked it o'er;
And the man stood by with a brooding eye, and
    gnashed his teeth and swore.

When thieves and thugs fall out and fight there's
    fell arrears to pay;
And soon or late sin meets its fate, and so it fell
    one day
That Claw-fingered Kitty and Windy Ike fanged
    up like dogs at bay.

33

BALLAD OF THE BLACK FOX SKIN

"The skin is mine, all mine," she cried; "I did the
    deed alone."
"It's share and share with a guilt-yoked pair," he
    hissed in a pregnant tone;
And so they snarled like malamutes over a mil-
    dewed bone.

And so they fought, by fear untaught, till haply it
    befell
One dawn of day she slipped away to Dawson town
    to sell
The fruit of sin, this black fox skin that had made
    their lives a hell.

She slipped away as still he lay, she clutched the
    wondrous fur;
Her pulses beat, her foot was fleet, her fear was as
    a spur;
She laughed with glee, she did not see him rise
    and follow her.

The bluffs uprear and grimly peer far over Dawson
    town;
They see its lights a blaze o' nights and harshly
    they look down;
They mock the plan and plot of man with grim,
    ironic frown.

BALLAD OF THE BLACK FOX SKIN

The trail was steep; 'twas at the time when swiftly
    sinks the snow;
All honey-combed, the river ice was rotting down
    below;
The river chafed beneath its rind with many a
    mighty throe.

And up the swift and oozy drift a woman climbed
    in fear,
Clutching to her a black fox fur as if she held it
    dear;
And hard she pressed it to her breast—then Windy
    Ike drew near.

She made no moan—her heart was stone—she read
    his smiling face,
And like a dream flashed all her life's dark horror
    and disgrace;
A moment only—with a snarl he hurled her into
    space.

She rolled for nigh an hundred feet; she bounded
    like a ball;
From crag to crag she carromed down through snow
    and timber fall; . . .
A hole gaped in the river ice; the spray flashed—
    that was all.

35

BALLAD OF THE BLACK FOX SKIN

A bird sang for the joy of spring, so piercing sweet
    and frail;
And blinding bright the land was dight in gay and
    glittering mail;
And with a wondrous black fox skin a man slid
    down the trail.

IV.

A wedge-faced man there was who ran along the
    river bank,
Who stumbled through each drift and slough, and
    ever slipped and sank,
And ever cursed his Maker's name, and ever
    "hooch" he drank.

He travelled like a hunted thing, hard harried, sore
    distrest;
The old grandmother moon crept out from her
    cloud-quilted nest;
The aged mountains mocked at him in their prim-
    eval rest.

Grim shadows diapered the snow; the air was
    strangely mild;
The valley's girth was dumb with mirth, the
    laughter of the wild;
The still, sardonic laughter of an ogre o'er a child.

BALLAD OF THE BLACK FOX SKIN

The river writhed beneath the ice; it groaned like
    one in pain,
And yawning chasms opened wide, and closed and
    yawned again;
And sheets of silver heaved on high until they split
    in twain

From out the road-house by the trail they saw a
    man afar
Make for the narrow river-reach where the swift
    cross-currents are;
Where, frail and worn, the ice is torn and the angry
    waters jar.

But they did not see him crash and sink into the
    icy flow;
They did not see him clinging there, gripped by
    the undertow,
Clawing with bleeding finger-nails at the jagged
    ice and snow.

They found a note beside the hole where he had
    stumbled in:
"Here met his fate by evil luck a man who lived
    in sin,
And to the one who loves me least I leave this
    black fox skin."

BALLAD OF THE BLACK FOX SKIN

And strange it is; for, though they searched the
    river all around,
No trace or sign of black fox skin was ever after
    found;
Though one man said he saw the tread of *hoofs*
    deep in the ground.

THE BALLAD OF PIOUS PETE

"The North has got him."—Yukonism.

I tried to refine that neighbor of mine, honest to
  God, I did.
I grieved for his fate, and early and late I watched
  over him like a kid.
I gave him excuse, I bore his abuse in every way
  that I could;
I swore to prevail; I camped on his trail; I plotted
  and planned for his good.
By day and by night I strove in men's sight to
  gather him into the fold,
With precept and prayer, with hope and despair, in
  hunger and hardship and cold.
I followed him into Gehennas of sin, I sat where
  the sirens sit;
In the shade of the Pole, for the sake of his soul, I
  . strove with the powers of the Pit.
I shadowed him down to the scrofulous town; I
  dragged him from dissolute brawls;
But I killed the galoot when he started to shoot
  electricity into my walls.

THE BALLAD OF PIOUS PETE

God knows what I did he should seek to be rid of
      one who would save him from shame.
God knows what I bore that night when he swore
      and bade me make tracks from his claim.
I started to tell of the horrors of hell, when sudden
      his eyes lit like coals;
And "Chuck it," says he, "don't persecute me with
      your cant and your saving of souls."
I'll swear I was mild as I'd be with a child, but he
      called me the son of a slut;
And, grabbing his gun with a leap and a run, he
      threatened my face with the butt.
So what could I do (I leave it to you)? With curses
      he harried me forth;
Then he was alone, and I was alone, and over us
      menaced the North.

Our cabins were near; I could see, I could hear;
      but between us there rippled the creek;
And all summer through, with a rancor that grew,
      he would pass me and never would speak.
Then a shuddery breath like the coming of Death
      crept down from the peaks far away;
The water was still; the twilight was chill; the sky
      was a tatter of gray.
Swift came the Big Cold, and opal and gold the
      lights of the witches arose;

THE BALLAD OF PIOUS PETE

The frost-tyrant clinched, and the valley was
    cinched by the stark and cadaverous snows.
The trees were like lace where the star-beams
    could chase, each leaf was a jewel agleam.
The soft white hush lapped the Northland and
    wrapped us round in a crystalline dream;
So still I could hear quite loud in my ear the swish
    of the pinions of time;
So bright I could see, as plain as could be, the wings
    of God's angels ashine.

As I read in the Book I would oftentimes look to
    that cabin just over the creek.
Ah me, it was sad and evil and bad, two neighbors
    who never would speak!
I knew that full well like a devil in hell he was
    hatching out, early and late,
A system to bear through the frost-spangled air
    the warm, crimson waves of his hate.
I only could peer and shudder and fear—'twas
    ever so ghastly and still;
But I knew over there in his lonely despair he was
    plotting me terrible ill.
I knew that he nursed a malice accurst, like the
    blast of a winnowing flame;
I pleaded aloud for a shield, for a shroud—Oh,
    God! then calamity came.

41

THE BALLAD OF PIOUS PETE

Mad! If I'm mad then you too are mad; but it's
    all in the point of view.
If you'd looked at them things gallivantin' on
    wings, all purple and green and blue;
If you'd noticed them twist, as they mounted and
    hissed like scorpions dim in the dark;
If you'd seen them rebound with a horrible sound,
    and spitefully spitting a spark;
If you'd watched *It* with dread, as it hissed by your
    bed, that thing with the feelers that crawls—
You'd have settled the brute that attempted to
    shoot electricity into your walls.

Oh, some they were blue, and they slithered right
    through; they were silent and squashy and
    round;
And some they were green; they were wriggly and
    lean; they writhed with so hateful a sound.
My blood seemed to freeze; I fell on my knees;
    my face was a white splash of dread.
Oh, the Green and the Blue, they were gruesome to
    view; but the worst of them all were the Red.
They came through the door, they came through
    the floor, they came through the moss-
    creviced logs.
They were savage and dire; they were whiskered
    with fire; they bickered like malamute dogs.

THE BALLAD OF PIOUS PETE

They ravined in rings like iniquitous things; they
  gulped down the Green and the Blue.
I crinkled with fear whene'er they drew near, and
  nearer and nearer they drew.

And then came the crown of Horror's grim crown,
  the monster so loathsomely red.
Each eye was a pin that shot out and in, as, squid-
  like, it oozed to my bed;
So softly it crept with feelers that swept and quivered like fine copper wire;
Its belly was white with a sulphurous light, its
  jaws were a-drooling with fire.
It came and it came; I could breathe of its flame,
  but never a wink could I look.
I thrust in its maw the Fount of the Law; I fended
  it off with the Book.
I was weak—oh, so weak—but I thrilled at its
  shriek, as wildly it fled in the night;
And deathlike I lay till the dawn of the day. (Was
  ever so welcome the light?)

I loaded my gun at the rise of the sun; to his cabin
  so softly I slunk.
My neighbor was there in the frost-freighted air,
  all wrapped in a robe in his bunk.

43

THE BALLAD OF PIOUS PETE

It muffled his moans; it outlined his bones, as
      feebly he twisted about;
His gums were so black, and his lips seemed to
      crack, and his teeth all were loosening out.
'Twas a death's head that peered through the
      tangle of beard; 'twas a face I will never
      forget;
Sunk eyes full of woe, and they troubled me so
      with their pleadings and anguish, and yet
As I rested my gaze in a misty amaze on the
      scurvy-degenerate wreck,
I thought of the Things with the dragon-fly wings,
      then laid I my gun on his neck.
He gave out a cry that was faint as a sigh, like a
      perishing malamute,
And he says unto me, "I'm converted," says he;
      "for Christ's sake, Peter, don't shoot!"

     *   *   *   *   *   *

They're taking me out with an escort about, and
      under a sergeant's care;
I am humbled indeed, for I'm 'cuffed to a Swede
      that thinks he's a millionaire.
But it's all Gospel true what I'm telling to you—
      up there where the Shadow falls—
That I settled Sam Noot when he started to shoot
      electricity into my walls.

THE BALLAD OF BLASPHEMOUS
BILL

I took a contract to bury the body of blasphemous
    Bill MacKie,
Whenever, wherever or whatsoever the manner of
    death he die—
Whether he die in the light o' day or under the
    peak-faced moon;
In cabin or dance-hall, camp or dive, mucklucks
    or patent shoon;
On velvet tundra or virgin peak, by glacier, drift
    or draw;
In muskeg hollow or canyon gloom, by avalanche,
    fang or claw;
By battle, murder or sudden wealth, by pestilence,
    hooch or lead—
I swore on the Book I would follow and look till I
    found my tombless dead.

For Bill was a dainty kind of cuss, and his mind
    was mighty sot
On a dinky patch with flowers and grass in a civil-
    ized bone-yard lot.

BALLAD OF BLASPHEMOUS BILL

And where he died or how he died, it didn't matter
    a damn
So long as he had a grave with frills and a tomb-
    stone "epigram."
So I promised him, and he paid the price in good
    cheechako coin
(Which the same I blowed in that very night down
    in the Tenderloin).
Then I painted a three-foot slab of pine: "Here
    lies poor Bill MacKie,"
And I hung it up on my cabin wall and I waited
    for Bill to die.

Years passed away, and at last one day came a
    squaw with a story strange,
Of a long-deserted line of traps 'way back of the
    Bighorn range;
Of a little hut by the great divide, and a white man
    stiff and still,
Lying there by his lonesome self, and I figured it
    must be Bill.
So I thought of the contract I'd made with him,
    and I took down from the shelf
The swell black box with the silver plate he'd picked
    out for hisself;
And I packed it full of grub and "hooch," and I
    slung it on the sleigh;
Then I harnessed up my team of dogs and was off
    at dawn of day.

BALLAD OF BLASPHEMOUS BILL

You know what it's like in the Yukon wild when
    it's sixty-nine below;
When the ice-worms wriggle their purple heads
    through the crust of the pale blue snow;
When the pine-trees crack like little guns in the
    silence of the wood,
And the icicles hang down like tusks under the
    parka hood;
When the stove-pipe smoke breaks sudden off, and
    the sky is weirdly lit,
And the careless feel of a bit of steel burns like a
    red-hot spit;
When the mercury is a frozen ball, and the frost-
    fiend stalks to kill—
Well, it was just like that that day when I set out
    to look for Bill.

Oh, the awful hush that seemed to crush me down
    on every hand,
As I blundered blind with a trail to find through
    that blank and bitter land;
Half dazed, half crazed in the winter wild, with its
    grim heart-breaking woes,
And the ruthless strife for a grip on life that only
    the sourdough knows!
North by the compass, North I pressed; river and
    peak and plain
Passed like a dream I slept to lose and I waked to
    dream again

BALLAD OF BLASPHEMOUS BILL

River and plain and mighty peak—and who could
    stand unawed ?
As their summits blazed, he could stand undazed
    at the foot of the throne of God.
North, aye, North, through a land accurst, shunned
    by the scouring brutes,
And all I heard was my own harsh word and the
    whine of the malamutes,
Till at last I came to a cabin squat, built in the side
    of a hill,
And I burst in the door, and there on the floor,
    frozen to death, lay Bill.

Ice, white ice, like a winding-sheet, sheathing each
    smoke-grimed wall;
Ice on the stove-pipe, ice on the bed, ice gleaming
    over all;
Sparkling ice on the dead man's chest, glittering
    ice in his hair,
Ice on his fingers, ice in his heart, ice in his glassy
    stare;
Hard as a log and trussed like a frog, with his arms
    and legs outspread.
I gazed at the coffin I'd brought for him, and I
    gazed at the gruesome dead,
And at last I spoke: "Bill liked his joke; but still,
    goldarn his eyes,
A man had ought to consider his mates in the way
    he goes and dies."

BALLAD OF BLASPHEMOUS BILL

Have you ever stood in an Arctic hut in the shadow
  of the Pole,
With a little coffin six by three and a grief you
  can't control?
Have you ever sat by a frozen corpse that looks
  at you with a grin,
And that seems to say: "You may try all day, but
  you'll never jam me in?"
I'm not a man of the quitting kind, but I never
  felt so blue
As I sat there gazing at that stiff and studying
  what I'd do.
Then I rose and I kicked off the husky dogs that
  were nosing round about,
And I lit a roaring fire in the stove, and I started
  to thaw Bill out.

Well, I thawed and thawed for thirteen days, but
  it didn't seem no good;
His arms and legs stuck out like pegs, as if they
  was made of wood.
Till at last I said: "It ain't no use—he's froze too
  hard to thaw;
He's obstinate, and he won't lie straight, so I guess
  I got to—*saw*."
So I sawed off poor Bill's arms and legs, and I laid
  him snug and straight
In the little coffin he picked hisself, with the dinky
  silver plate;

49

BALLAD OF BLASPHEMOUS BILL

And I came nigh near to shedding a tear as I nailed
    him safely down;
Then I stowed him away in my Yukon sleigh, and
    I started back to town.

So I buried him as the contract was in a narrow
    grave and deep,
And there he's waiting the Great Clean-up, when
    the Judgment sluice-heads sweep;
And I smoke my pipe and I meditate in the light of
    the Midnight Sun,
And sometimes I wonder if they *was*, the awful
    things I done.
And as I sit and the parson talks, expounding of
    the Law,
I often think of poor old Bill—*and how hard he was
    to saw.*

THE BALLAD OF ONE-EYED MIKE

THE BALLAD OF ONE-EYED MIKE

*This is the tale that was told to me by the man with
the crystal eye,
As I smoked my pipe in the camp-fire light, and the
Glories swept the sky;
As the Northlights gleamed and curved and streamed,
and the bottle of "hooch" was dry.*

A man once aimed that my life be shamed, and
wrought me a deathly wrong;
I vowed one day I would well repay, but the heft
of his hate was strong.
He thonged me East and he thonged me West; he
harried me back and forth,
Till I fled in fright from his peerless spite to the
bleak, bald-headed North.

And there I lay, and for many a day I hatched plan
after plan,
For a golden haul of the wherewithal to crush and
to kill my man;

THE BALLAD OF ONE-EYED MIKE

And there I strove, and there I clove through the
    drift of icy streams;
And there I fought, and there I sought for the pay-
    streak of my dreams.

So twenty years, with their hopes and fears and
    smiles and tears and such,
Went by and left me long bereft of hope of the
    Midas touch;
About as fat as a chancel rat, and lo! despite my
    will,
In the weary fight I nad clean lost sight of the man
    I sought to kill.

'Twas so far away, that evil day when I prayed
    the Prince of Gloom
For the savage strength and the sullen length of
    life to work his doom.
Nor sign nor word had I seen or heard, and it
    happed so long ago;
My youth was gone and my memory wan, and I
    willed it even so.

It fell one night in the waning light by the Yukon's
    oily flow,
I smoked and sat as I marvelled at the sky's port-
    winey glow;

THE BALLAD OF ONE-EYED MIKE

Till it paled away to an absinthe gray, and the
   river seemed to shrink,
All wobbly flakes and wriggling snakes and goblin
   eyes a-wink.

'Twas weird to see and it 'wildered me in a queer,
   hypnotic dream,
Till I saw a spot like an inky blot come floating
   down the stream;
It bobbed and swung; it sheered and hung; it
   romped round in a ring;
It seemed to play in a tricksome way; it sure was
   a merry thing.

In freakish flights strange oily lights came fluttering
   round its head,
Like butterflies of a monster size—then I knew it
   for the Dead.
Its face was rubbed and slicked and scrubbed as
   smooth as a shaven pate;
In the silver snakes that the water makes it gleamed
   like a dinner-plate.

It gurgled near, and clear and clear and large and
   large it grew;
It stood upright in a ring of light and it looked me
   through and through.

THE BALLAD OF ONE-EYED MIKE

It weltered round with a woozy sound, and ere I
      could retreat,
With the witless roll of a sodden soul it wantoned
      to my feet.

And here I swear by this Cross I wear, I heard that
      "floater" say:
"I am the man from whom you ran, the man you
      sought to slay.
That you may note and gaze and gloat, and say
      'Revenge is sweet,'
In the grit and grime of the river's slime I am
      rotting at your feet.

"The ill we rue we must e'en undo, though it rive
      us bone from bone;
So it came about that I sought you out, for I prayed
      I might atone.
I did you wrong, and for long and long I sought
      where you might live;
And now you're found, though I'm dead and
      drowned, I beg you to forgive."

So sad it seemed, and its cheek-bones gleamed,
      and its fingers flicked the shore;
And it lapped and lay in a weary way, and its hands
      met to implore;

THE BALLAD OF ONE-EYED MIKE

That I gently said: "Poor, restless dead, I would
    never work you woe;
Though the wrong you rue you can ne'er undo,
    I forgave you long ago."

Then, wonder-wise, I rubbed my eyes and I woke
    from a horrid dream.
The moon rode high in the naked sky, and some-
    thing bobbed in the stream.
It held my sight in a patch of light, and then it
    sheered from the shore;
It dipped and sank by a hollow bank, and I never
    saw it more.

This was the tale he told to me, that man so warped
    and gray,
Ere he slept and dreamed, and the camp-fire gleamed
    in his eye in a wolfish way—
That crystal eye that raked the sky in the weird
    Auroral ray.

THE BALLAD OF THE BRAND

'Twas up in a land long famed for gold, where
women were far and rare,
Tellus, the smith, had taken to wife a maiden
amazingly fair;
Tellus, the brawny worker in iron, hairy and heavy
of hand,
Saw her and loved her and bore her away from the
tribe of a Southern land;
Deeming her worthy to queen his home and mother
him little ones,
That the name of Tellus, the master smith, might
live in his stalwart sons.

Now there was little of law in the land, and evil
doings were rife,
And every man who joyed in his home guarded the
fame of his wife;
For there were those of the silver tongue and the
honeyed art to beguile,
Who would cozen the heart from a woman's breast
and damn her soul with a smile.

56

THE BALLAD OF THE BRAND

And there were women too quick to heed a look
or a whispered word,
And once in a while a man was slain, and the ire
of the King was stirred;
So far and wide he proclaimed his wrath, and this
was the law he willed:
"That whosoever killeth a man, even shall he be
killed."

Now Tellus, the smith, he trusted his wife; his
heart was empty of fear.
High on the hill was the gleam of their hearth, a
beacon of love and cheer.
High on the hill they builded their bower, where
the broom and the bracken meet;
Under a grave of oaks it was, hushed and drowsily
sweet.
Here he enshrined her, his dearest saint, his idol,
the light of his eye;
Her kisses rested upon his lips as brushes a butterfly.
The weight of her arms around his neck was light
as the thistle down;
And sweetly she studied to win his smile, and gently
she mocked his frown.
And when at the close of the dusty day his clang-
orous toil was done,
She hastened to meet him down the way all lit by
the amber sun.

THE BALLAD OF THE BRAND

Their dove-cot gleamed in the golden light, a
    temple of stainless love;
Like the hanging cup of a big blue flower was the
    topaz sky above.
The roses and lilies yearned to her, as swift through
    their throng she pressed;
A little white, fragile, fluttering thing that lay like
    a child on his breast.
Then the heart of Tellus, the smith, was proud, and
    sang for the joy of life,
And there in the bronzing summertide he thanked
    the gods for his wife.

Now there was one called Philo, a scribe, a man of
    exquisite grace,
Carved like the god Apollo in limb, fair as Adonis
    in face;
Eager and winning of manner, full of such radiant
    charm,
Womenkind fought for his favor and loved to their
    uttermost harm.
Such was his craft and his knowledge, such was his
    skill at the game,
Never was woman could flout him, so be he plotted
    her shame.
And so he drank deep of pleasure, and then it fell
    on a day
He gazed on the wife of Tellus and marked her
    out for his prey.

58

THE BALLAD OF THE BRAND

Tellus, the smith, was merry, and the time of the
    year it was June,
So he said to his stalwart helpers: "Shut down
    the forge at noon.
Go ye and joy in the sunshine, rest in the coolth of
    the grove,
Drift on the dreamy river, every man with his love."
Then to himself: "Oh, Beloved, sweet will be your
    surprise;
To-day will we sport like children, laugh in each
    other's eyes;
Weave gay garlands of poppies, crown each other
    with flowers,
Pull plump carp from the lilies, rifle the ferny
    bowers.
To-day with feasting and gladness the wine of
    Cyprus will flow;
To-day is the day we were wedded only a twelve-
    month ago."

The larks trilled high in the heavens; his heart was
    lyric with joy;
He plucked a posy of lilies; he sped like a love-sick
    boy.
He stole up the velvety pathway—his cottage was
    sunsteeped and still;
Vines honeysuckled the window; softly he peeped
    o'er the sill.

THE BALLAD OF THE BRAND

The lilies dropped from his fingers; devils were
    choking his breath;
Rigid with horror, he stiffened; ghastly his face
    was as death.
Like a nun whose faith in the Virgin is met with
    a prurient jibe,
He shrank—'twas the wife of his bosom in the
    arms of Philo, the scribe.

Tellus went back to his smithy; he reeled like a
    drunken man;
His heart was riven with anguish; his brain was
    brooding a plan.
Straight to his anvil he hurried; started his furnace
    aglow;
Heated his iron and shaped it with savage and
    masterful blow.
Sparks showered over and round him; swiftly under
    his hand
There at last it was finished—a hideous and in-
    famous Brand.

That night the wife of his bosom, the light of joy
    in her eyes,
Kissed him with words of rapture; but he knew
    that her words were lies.
Never was she so beguiling, never so merry of
    speech

THE BALLAD OF THE BRAND

(For passion ripens a woman as the sunshine
    ripens a peach).
He clenched his teeth into silence; he yielded up
    to her lure,
Though he knew that her breasts were heaving
    from the fire of her paramour.
"To-morrow," he said, "to-morrow"—he wove
    her hair in a strand,
Twisted it round his fingers and smiled as he
    thought of the Brand.

The morrow was come, and Tellus swiftly stole up
    the hill.
Butterflies drowsed in the noon-heat; coverts were
    sunsteeped and still.
Softly he padded the pathway unto the porch, and
    within
Heard he the low laugh of dalliance, heard he the
    rapture of sin.
Knew he her eyes were mystic with light that no
    man should see,
No man kindle and joy in, no man on earth save
    he.
And never for him would it kindle. The blood-
    lust surged in his brain;
Through the senseless stone could he see them,
    wanton and warily fain.

THE BALLAD OF THE BRAND

Horrible! Heaven he sought for, gained it and
    gloried and fell—
Oh, it was sudden—headlong into the nether-
    most hell. . . .

Was this he, Tellus, this marble? Tellus . . .
    not dreaming a dream?
Ah! sharp-edged as a javelin, was that a woman's
    scream?
Was it a door that shattered, shell-like, under his
    blow?
Was it his saint, that strumpet, dishevelled and
    cowering low?
Was it her lover, that wild thing, that twisted and
    gouged and tore?
Was it a man he was crushing, whose head he beat
    on the floor?
Laughing the while at its weakness, till sudden
    he stayed his hand—
Through the red ring of his madness flamed the
    thought of the Brand.

Then bound he the naked Philo with thongs that
    cut in the flesh,
And the wife of his bosom, fear-frantic, he gagged
    with a silken mesh,

THE BALLAD OF THE BRAND

Choking her screams into silence; bound her down
     by the hair;
Dragged her lover unto her under her frenzied
     stare.
In the heat of the hearth-fire embers he heated the
•   hideous Brand;
Twisting her fingers open, he forced its haft in her
     hand.
He pressed it downward and downward; she felt
     the living flesh sear;
She saw the throe of her lover; she heard the scream
     of his fear.
Once, twice and thrice he forced her, heedless of
     prayer and shriek—
Once on the forehead of Philo, twice in the soft of
     his cheek.
Then (for the thing was finished) he said to the
     woman: "See
How you have branded your lover! Now will I
     let him go free."
He severed the thongs that bound him, laughing:
     "Revenge is sweet,"
And Philo, sobbing in anguish, feebly rose to his
     feet.
The man who was fair as Apollo, god-like in
     woman's sight,
Hideous now as a satyr, fled to the pity of night.

THE BALLAD OF THE BRAND

*Then came they before the Judgment Seat, and thus
  spoke the Lord of the Land:*
*"He who seeketh his neighbor's wife shall suffer the
  doom of the Brand.*
*Brutish and bold on his brow be it stamped, deep in
  his cheek let it sear,*
*That every man may look on his shame, and shudder
  and sicken and fear.*
*He shall hear their mock in the market-place, their
  fleering jibe at the feast;*
*He shall seek the caves and the shroud of night, and
  the fellowship of the beast.*
*Outcast forever from homes of men, far and far shall
  he roam.*
*Such be the doom, sadder than death, of him who
  shameth a home."*

THE BALLAD OF HARD-LUCK HENRY

Now wouldn't you expect to find a man an awful
    crank
That's staked out nigh three hundred claims, and
    every one a blank;
That's followed every fool stampede, and seen the
    rise and fall
Of camps where men got gold in chunks and he got
    none at all;
That's prospected a bit of ground and sold it for
    a song
To see it yield a fortune to some fool that came
    along;
That's sunk a dozen bed-rock holes, and not a speck
    in sight,
Yet sees them take a million from the claims to
    left and right?
Now aren't things like that enough to drive a man
    to booze?
But Hard-Luck Smith was hoodoo-proof—he knew
    the way to lose.

BALLAD OF HARD-LUCK HENRY

'Twas in the fall of nineteen four—leap-year I've
    heard them say—
When Hard-Luck came to Hunker Creek and took
    a hillside lay.
And lo! as if to make amends for all the futile
    past,
Late in the year he struck it rich, the real pay-
    streak at last.
The riffles of his sluicing-box were choked with
    speckled earth,
And night and day he worked that lay for all that
    he was worth.
And when in chill December's gloom his lucky
    lease expired,
He found that he had made a stake as big as he
    desired.

One day while meditating on the waywardness of
    fate,
He felt the ache of lonely man to find a fitting mate;
A petticoated pard to cheer his solitary life,
A woman with soft, soothing ways, a confidant, a
    wife.
And while he cooked his supper on his little Yukon
    stove,
He wished that he had staked a claim in Love's
    rich treasure-trove;

BALLAD OF HARD-LUCK HENRY

When suddenly he paused and held aloft a Yukon
    egg,
For there in pencilled letters was the magic name
    of Peg.

You know these Yukon eggs of ours—some pink,
    some green, some blue—
A dollar per, assorted tints, assorted flavors too.
The supercilious cheechako might designate them
    high,
But one acquires a taste for them and likes them
    by-and-by.
Well, Hard-Luck Henry took this egg and held it
    to the light,
And there was more faint pencilling that sorely
    taxed his sight.
At last he made it out, and then the legend ran like
    this—
"Will Klondike miner write to Peg, Plumhollow,
    Squashville, Wis.?"

That night he got to thinking of this far-off, un-
    known fair;
It seemed so sort of opportune, an answer to his
    prayer.

BALLAD OF HARD-LUCK HENRY

She flitted sweetly through his dreams, she haunted
him by day,
She smiled through clouds of nicotine, she cheered
his weary way.
At last he yielded to the spell; his course of love
he set—
Wisconsin his objective point; his object, Margaret.

With every mile of sea and land his longing grew
and grew.
He practised all his pretty words, and these, I fear,
were few.
At last, one frosty evening, with a cold chill down
his spine,
He found himself before her house, the threshold
of the shrine.
His courage flickered to a spark, then glowed with
sudden flame—
He knocked; he heard a welcome word; she came
—his goddess came.
Oh, she was fair as any flower, and huskily he spoke:
"I'm all the way from Klondike, with a mighty
heavy poke.
I'm looking for a lassie, one whose Christian name
is Peg,
Who sought a Klondike miner, and who wrote it
on an egg."

68

BALLAD OF HARD-LUCK HENRY

The lassie gazed at him a space, her cheeks grew
    rosy red;
She gazed at him with tear-bright eyes, then ten-
    derly she said:
"Yes, lonely Klondike miner, it is true my name is
    Peg.
It's also true I longed for you and wrote it on an
    egg.
My heart went out to someone in that land of night
    and cold;
But oh, I fear that Yukon egg must have been
    mighty old.
I waited long, I hoped and feared; you should have
    come before;
I've been a wedded woman now for eighteen months
    or more.
I'm sorry, since you've come so far, you ain't the
    one that wins;
But won't you take a step inside—*I'll let you see
the twins.*"

THE MAN FROM ELDORADO

He's the man from Eldorado, and he's just arrived
    in town,
    In moccasins and oily buckskin shirt.
He's gaunt as any Indian, and pretty nigh as brown;
    He's greasy, and he smells of sweat and dirt.
He sports a crop of whiskers that would shame a
    healthy hog;
    Hard work has racked his joints and stooped
    his back;
He slops along the sidewalk followed by his yellow
    dog,
    But he's got a bunch of gold-dust in his sack.

He seems a little wistful as he blinks at all the
    lights,
    And maybe he is thinking of his claim
And the dark and dwarfish cabin where he lay and
    dreamed at nights,
    (Thank God, he'll never see the place again!)

THE MAN FROM ELDORADO

Where he lived on tinned tomatoes, beef embalmed
    and sourdough bread,
  On rusty beans and bacon furred with mould;
His stomach's out of kilter and his system full of
    lead,
  But it's over, and his poke is full of gold.

He has panted at the windlass, he has loaded in the
    drift,
  He has pounded at the face of oozy clay;
He has taxed himself to sickness, dark and damp
    and double shift,
  He has labored like a demon night and day.
And now, praise God, it's over, and he seems to
    breathe again
  Of new-mown hay, the warm, wet, friendly loam;
He sees a snowy orchard in a green and dimpling
    plain,
  And a little vine-clad cottage, and it's—Home.

II.

He's the man from Eldorado, and he's had a bite
    and sup,
  And he's met in with a drouthy friend or two;
He's cached away his gold-dust, but he's sort of
    bucking up,
  So he's kept enough to-night to see him through.

THE MAN FROM ELDORADO

His eye is bright and genial, his tongue no longer
 lags;
 His heart is brimming o'er with joy and mirth;
He may be far from savory, he may be clad in rags,
 But to-night he feels as if he owns the earth.

Says he: "Boys, here is where the shaggy North
 and I will shake;
 I thought I'd never manage to get free.
I kept on making misses; but at last I've got my
 stake;
 There's no more thawing frozen muck for me.
I am going to God's Country, where I'll live the
 simple life;
 I'll buy a bit of land and make a start;
I'll carve a little homestead, and I'll win a little
 wife,
 And raise ten little kids to cheer my heart."

They signified their sympathy by crowding to the
 bar;
 They bellied up three deep and drank his health.
He shed a radiant smile around and smoked a rank
 cigar;
 They wished him honor, happiness and wealth.
They drank unto his wife to be—that unsuspecting
 maid;
 They drank unto his children half a score;

THE MAN FROM ELDORADO

And when they got through drinking very ten-
        derly they laid
    The man from Eldorado on the floor.

III.

He's the man from Eldorado, and he's only start-
        ing in
    To cultivate a thousand-dollar jag.
His poke is full of gold-dust and his heart is full of
        sin,
    And he's dancing with a girl called Muckluck Mag.
She's as light as any fairy; she's as pretty as a peach;
    She's mistress of the witchcraft to beguile;
There's sunshine in her manner, there is music in
        her speech,
    And there's concentrated honey in her smile.

Oh, the fever of the dance-hall and the glitter and
        the shine,
    The beauty, and the jewels, and the whirl,
The madness of the music, the rapture of the wine,
    The languorous allurement of a girl!
She is like a lost madonna; he is gaunt, unkempt
        and grim;
    But she fondles him and gazes in his eyes;
Her kisses seek his heavy lips, and soon it seems
        to him
    He has staked a little claim in Paradise.

THE MAN FROM ELDORADO

'Who's for a juicy two-step?" cries the master of
    the floor;
The music throbs with soft, seductive beat.
There's glitter, gilt and gladness; there are pretty
    girls galore;
There's a woolly man with moccasins on feet.
They know they've got him going; he is buying
    wine for all;
They crowd around as buzzards at a feast,
Then when his poke is empty they boost him from
    the hall,
And spurn him in the gutter like a beast.

He's the man from Eldorado, and he's painting
    red the town;
Behind he leaves a trail of yellow dust;
In a whirl of senseless riot he is ramping up and
    down;
There's nothing checks his madness and his
    lust.
And soon the word is passed around—it travels
    like a flame;
They fight to clutch his hand and call him friend,
The chevaliers of lost repute, the dames of sorry
    fame;
Then comes the grim awakening—the end.

THE MAN FROM ELDORADO

IV.

He's the man from Eldorado, and he gives a grand
    affair;
  There's feasting, dancing, wine without re-
    straint.
The smooth Beau Brummels of the bar, the faro
    men, are there;
  The tinhorns and purveyors of red paint;
The sleek and painted women, their predacious
    eyes aglow—
  Sure Klondike City never saw the like;
Then Muckluck Mag proposed the toast, "The giver
    of the show,
  The livest sport that ever hit the pike."

The "live one" rises to his feet; he stammers to
    reply—
And then there comes before his muddled brain
A vision of green vastitudes beneath an April
    sky,
  And clover pastures drenched with silver rain.
He knows that it can never be, that he is down and
    out;
  Life leers at him with foul and fetid breath;
And then amid the revelry, the song and cheer and
    shout,
  He suddenly grows grim and cold as death.

THE MAN FROM ELDORADO

He grips the table tensely, and he says: "Dear
      friends of mine,
  I've let you dip your fingers in my purse;
I've crammed you at my table, and I've drowned
      you in my wine,
  And I've little left to give you but—my curse.
I've failed supremely in my plans; it's rather late
      to whine;
  My poke is mighty weasened up and small.
I thank you each for coming here; the happiness
      is mine—
  And now, you thieves and harlots, take it all."

He twists the thong from off his poke; he swings
      it o'er his head;
  The nuggets fall around their feet like grain.
They rattle over roof and wall; they scatter, roll
      and spread;
  The dust is like a shower of golden rain.
The guests a moment stand aghast, then grovel on
      the floor;
  They fight, and snarl, and claw, like beasts of
      prey;
And then, as everybody grabbed and everybody
      swore,
  The man from Eldorado slipped away.

THE MAN FROM ELDORADO

v.

He's the man from Eldorado, and they found him
 stiff and dead,
  Half covered by the freezing ooze and dirt.
A clotted Colt was in his hand, a hole was in his
 head,
  And he wore an old and oily buckskin shirt.
His eyes were fixed and horrible, as one who hails
 the end;
  The frost had set him rigid as a log;
And there, half lying on his breast, his last and only
 friend,
  There crouched and whined a mangy yellow dog.

MY FRIENDS

The man above was a murderer, the man below
was a thief;
And I lay there in the bunk between, ailing beyond
belief;
A weary armful of skin and bone, wasted with pain
and grief.

My feet were froze, and the lifeless toes were purple
and green and gray;
The little flesh that clung to my bones, you could
punch it in holes like clay;
The skin on my gums was a sullen black, and slowly
peeling away.

I was sure enough in a direful fix, and often I wondered why
They did not take the chance that was left and
leave me alone to die,
Or finish me off with a dose of dope—so utterly
lost was I.

MY FRIENDS

But no; they brewed me the green-spruce tea, and
    nursed me there like a child;
And the homicide he was good to me, and bathed
    my sores and smiled;
And the thief he starved that I might be fed, and
    his eyes were kind and mild.

Yet they were woefully wicked men, and often at
    night in pain
I heard the murderer speak of his deed and dream
    it over again;
I heard the poor thief sorrowing for the dead self
    he had slain.

I'll never forget that bitter dawn, so evil, askew
    and gray,
When they wrapped me round in the skins of
    beasts and they bore me to a sleigh,
And we started out with the nearest post an hun-
    dred miles away.

I'll never forget the trail they broke, with its tense,
    unuttered woe;
And the crunch, crunch, crunch as their snow-
    shoes sank through the crust of the hollow
    snow;
And my breath would fail, and every beat of my
    heart was like a blow.

79

MY FRIENDS

And oftentimes I would die the death, yet wake
    up to life anew;
The sun would be all ablaze on the waste, and the
    sky a blighting blue,
And the tears would rise in my snow-blind eyes
    and furrow my cheeks like dew.

And the camps we made when their strength out-
    played and the day was pinched and wan;
And oh, the joy of that blessed halt, and how I
    did dread the dawn;
And how I hated the weary men who rose and
    dragged me on.

And oh, how I begged to rest, to rest—the snow
    was so sweet a shroud;
And oh, how I cried when they urged me on, cried
    and cursed them aloud;
Yet on they strained, all racked and pained, and
    sorely their backs were bowed.

And then it was all like a lurid dream, and I prayed
    for a swift release
From the ruthless ones who would not leave me to
    die alone in peace;
Till I wakened up and I found myself at the post
    of the Mounted Police.

MY FRIENDS

And there was my friend the murderer, and there
    was my friend the thief,
With bracelets of steel around their wrists, and
    wicked beyond belief:
But when they come to God's judgment seat—
    may I be allowed the brief.

THE PROSPECTOR

I strolled up old Bonanza, where I staked in ninety-
    eight,
  A-purpose to revisit the old claim.
I kept thinking mighty sadly of the funny ways of
    Fate,
  And the lads who once were with me in the
    game.
Poor boys, they're down-and-outers, and there's
    scarcely one to-day
  Can show a dozen colors in his poke;
And me, I'm still prospecting, old and battered,
    gaunt and gray,
  And I'm looking for a grub-stake, and I'm
    broke.

I strolled up old Bonanza. The same old moon
    looked down;
  The same old landmarks seemed to yearn to me;
But the cabins all were silent, and the flat, once like
    a town,
  Was mighty still and lonesome-like to see.

THE PROSPECTOR

There were piles and piles of tailings where we
    toiled with pick and pan,
  And turning round a bend I heard a roar,
And there a giant gold-ship of the very newest plan
  Was tearing chunks of pay-dirt from the shore.

It wallowed in its water-bed; it burrowed, heaved
    and swung;
  It gnawed its way ahead with grunts and sighs;
Its bill of fare was rock and sand; the tailings
    were its dung;
  It glared around with fierce electric eyes.
Full fifty buckets crammed its maw; it bellowed
    out for more;
  It looked like some great monster in the gloom.
With two to feed its sateless greed, it worked for
    seven score,
  And I sighed: "Ah, old-time miner, here's your
    doom!"

The idle windlass turns to rust; the sagging sluice-
    box falls;
  The holes you digged are water to the brim;
Your little sod-roofed cabins with the snugly moss-
    chinked walls
  Are deathly now and mouldering and dim.
The battle-field is silent where of old you fought
    it out;
  The claims you fiercely won are lost and sold;

THE PROSPECTOR

But there's a little army that they'll never put to
      rout—
  The men who simply live to seek the gold.

The men who can't remember when they learned
      to swing a pack,
  Or in what lawless land the quest began;
The solitary seeker with his grub-stake on his back,
  The restless buccaneer of pick and pan.
On the mesas of the Southland, on the tundras of
      the North,
  You will find us, changed in face but still the
      same;
And it isn't need, it isn't greed that sends us faring
      forth—
  It's the fever, it's the glory of the game.

For once you've panned the speckled sand and seen
      the bonny dust,
  Its peerless brightness blinds you like a spell;
It's little else you care about; you go because you
      must,
  And you feel that you could follow it to hell.
You'd follow it in hunger, and you'd follow it in
      cold;
  You'd follow it in solitude and pain;

THE PROSPECTOR

And when you're stiff and battened down let some-
      one whisper "Gold,"
  You're lief to rise and follow it again.

Yet look you, if I find the stuff it's just like so much
      dirt;
  I fling it to the four winds like a child.
It's wine and painted women and the things that
      do me hurt,
  Till I crawl back, beggared, broken, to the Wild.
Till I crawl back, sapped and sodden, to my grub-
      stake and my tent—
  There's a city, there's an army (hear them
      shout).
There's the gold in millions, millions, but I haven't
      got a cent;
  And oh, it's me, it's me that found it out.

It was my dream that made it good, my dream
      that made me go
  To lands of dread and death disprized of man;
But oh, I've known a glory that their hearts will
      never know,
  When I picked the first big nugget from my pan.
It's still my dream, my dauntless dream, that drives
      me forth once more
  To seek and starve and suffer in the Vast;

THE PROSPECTOR

That heaps my heart with eager hope, that glim-
      mers on before—
  My dream that will uplift me to the last.

Perhaps I am stark crazy, but there's none of you
      too sane;
  It's just a little matter of degree.
My hobby is to hunt out gold; it's fortressed in
      my brain;
  It's life and love and wife and home to me.
And I'll strike it, yes, I'll strike it; I've a hunch
      I cannot fail;
  I've a vision, I've a prompting, I've a call;
I hear the hoarse stampeding of an army on my
      trail,
  To the last, the greatest gold camp of them all.

Beyond the shark-tooth ranges sawing savage at
      the sky
  There's a lowering land no white man ever struck;
There's gold, there's gold in millions, and I'll find
      it if I die,
  And I'm going there once more to try my luck.
Maybe I'll fail—what matter? It's a mandate, it's
      a vow;
  And when in lands of dreariness and dread
You seek the last lone frontier, far beyond your
      frontiers now,
  You will find the old prospector, silent, dead.

THE PROSPECTOR

You will find a tattered tent-pole with a ragged robe
      below it;
  You will find a rusted gold-pan on the sod;
You will find the claim I'm seeking, with my bones
      as stakes to show it;
  But I've sought the last Recorder, and He's—God.

THE BLACK SHEEP

"The aristocratic ne'er-do-well in Canada frequently finds his way into the ranks of the Royal North-West Mounted Police."—*Extract.*

Hark to the ewe that bore him:
"What has muddied the strain?
Never his brothers before him
Showed the h nt of a stain."
Hark 'o the tups and wethers;
Hark to the old gray ram:
"We're all of us white, but he's black as night,
And he'll never be worth a damn."

I'm up on the bally wood-pile at the back of the
　　barracks yard;
"A damned disgrace to the force, sir." with a
　　comrade standing guard;
Making the bluff I'm busy, doing my six months
　　hard.

THE BLACK SHEEP

"Six months hard and dismissed, sir." Isn't that
     rather hell?
And all because of the liquor laws and the wiles
     of a native belle—
Some "hooch" I gave to a siwash brave who swore
     that he wouldn't tell.

At least they *say* that I did it. It's so in the town
     report.
All that I can recall is a night of revel and sport,
When I woke with a "head" in the guard-room,
     and they dragged me sick into court.

And the O. C. said: "You are guilty," and I said
     never a word;
For, hang it, you see I couldn't—I didn't know *what*
     had occurred,
And, under the circumstances, denial would be
     absurd.

But the one that cooked my bacon was Grubbe, of
     the City Patrol.
He fagged for my room at Eton, and didn't I devil
     his soul!
And now he is getting even, landing me down in
     the hole.

THE BLACK SHEEP

Plugging away on the wood-pile; doing chores
round the square.
There goes an officer's lady—gives me a haughty
stare—
Me that's an earl's own nephew—that is the
hardest to bear.

To think of the poor old mater awaiting her prodi-
gal son.
Tho' I broke her heart with my folly, I was always
the white-haired one.
(That fatted calf that they're cooking will surely
be overdone.)

I'll go back and yarn to the Bishop; I'll dance
with the village belle;
I'll hand round tea to the ladies, and everything
will be well.
Where I have been won't matter; what I have
seen I won't tell.

I'll soar to their ken like a comet. They'll see me
with never a stain;
But will they reform me?—far from it. We pay
for our pleasure with pain;
But the dog will return to his vomit, the hog to
his wallow again.

THE BLACK SHEEP

I've chewed on the rind of creation, and bitter I've
    tasted the same ;
Stacked up against hell and damnation, I've man-
    aged to stay in the game;
I've had my moments of sorrow; I've had my
    seasons of shame.

That's past; when one's nature's a cracked one,
    it's too jolly hard to mend.
So long as the road is level, so long as I've cash to
    spend,
I'm bound to go to the devil, and it's all the same
    in the end

The bugle is sounding for stables; the men troop
    off through the gloom;
An orderly laying the tables sings in the bright
    mess-room.
(I'll wash in the prison bucket, and brush with the
    prison broom.)

I'll lie in my cell and listen; I'll wish that I couldn't
    hear
The laugh and the chaff of the fellows swigging the
    canteen beer;
The nasal tone of the gramophone playing "The
    Bandolier."

THE BLACK SHEEP

And it seems to me, though it's misty, that night
    of the flowing bowl,
That the man who potlatched the whiskey and
    landed me into the hole
Was Grubbe, that unmerciful bounder, Grubbe, of the
    City Patrol.

THE TELEGRAPH OPERATOR

I will not wash my face;
    I will not brush my hair;
I "pig" around the place—
    There's nobody to care.
Nothing but rock and tree;
    Nothing but wood and stone,
Oh, God, it's hell to be
    Alone, alone, alone!

Snow-peaks and deep-gashed draws
    Corral me in a ring.
I feel as if I was
    The only living thing
On all this blighted earth;
    And so I frowst and shrink,
And crouching by my hearth
    I hear the thoughts I think.

I think of all I miss—
    The boys I used to know;
The girls I used to kiss;
    The coin I used to blow:

93

THE TELEGRAPH OPERATOR

The bars I used to haunt;
  The racket and the row;
The beers I didn't want
  (I wish I had 'em now).

Day after day the same,
  Only a little worse;
No one to grouch or blame—
  Oh, for a loving curse!
Oh, in the night I fear,
  Haunted by nameless things,
Just for a voice to cheer,
  Just for a hand that clings!

Faintly as from a star
  Voices come o'er the line;
Voices of ghosts afar,
  Not in this world of mine;
Lives in whose loom I grope;
  Words in whose weft I hear
Eager the thrill of hope,
  Awful the chill of fear.

I'm thinking out aloud;
  I reckon that is bad:
(The snow is like a shroud)—
  Maybe I'm going mad.

THE TELEGRAPH OPERATOR

Say! wouldn't that be tough?
  This awful hush that hugs
And chokes one is enough
  To make a man go "bugs."

There's not a thing to do;
  I cannot sleep at night;
No wonder I'm so blue;
  Oh, for a friendly fight!
The din and rush of strife;
  A music-hall aglow;
A crowd, a city, life—
  Dear God, I miss it so!

Here, you have moped enough!
  Brace up and play the game!
But say, it's awful tough—
  Day after day the same
(I've said that twice, I bet).
  Well, there's not much to say.
I wish I had a pet,
  Or something I could play.

Cheer up! don't get so glum
  And sick of everything;
The worst is yet to come;
  God help you till the Spring.

THE TELEGRAPH OPERATOR

God shield you from the Fear;
   Teach you to laugh, not moan.
Ha! ha! it sounds so queer—
   Alone, alone, alone!

THE WOOD-CUTTER

The sky is like an envelope,
  One of those blue official things;
And, sealing it, to mock our hope,
  The moon, a silver wafer, clings.
What shall we find when death gives leave
To read—our sentence or reprieve?

I'm holding it down on God's scrap-pile, up on the
    fag-end of earth;
  O'er me a menace of mountains, a river that
    grits at my feet;
Face to face with my soul-self, weighing my life
    at its worth;
  Wondering what I was made for, here in my
    last retreat.

Last! Ah, yes, it's the finish. Have ever you heard
    a man cry?
  (Sobs that rake him and rend him, right from
    the base of the chest.)

THE WOOD-CUTTER

That's how I've cried, oh, so often; and now
      that my tears are dry,
   I sit in the desolate quiet and wait for the
      infinite Rest.

Rest! Well, it's restful around me; it's quiet clean
      to the core.
   The mountains pose in their ermine, in golden
      the hills are clad;
The big, blue, silt-freighted Yukon seethes by my
      cabin door,
   And I think it's only the river that keeps me
      from going mad.

By day it's a ruthless monster, a callous, insatiate
      thing,
   With oily bubble and eddy, with sudden swirling
      of breast;
By night it's a writhing Titan, sullenly murmuring,
   Ever and ever goaded, and ever crying for rest.

It cries for its human tribute, but me it will never
      drown.
   I've learned the lore of my river; my river
      obeys me well.
I hew and I launch my cordwood, and raft it to
      Dawson town,
   Where wood means wine and women, and,
      incidentally, hell.

THE WOOD-CUTTER

Hell and the anguish thereafter. Here as I sit
    alone
I'd give the life I have left me to lighten some
    load of care:
(The bitterest part of the bitter is being denied to
    atone;
Lips that have mocked at Heaven lend them-
    selves ill to prayer.)

Impotent as a beetle pierced on the needle of Fate;
    A wretch in a cosmic death-cell, peaks for my prison
      bars;
'Whelmed by a world stupendous, lonely and listless
    I wait,
    Drowned in a sea of silence, strewn with confetti
      of stars.

See! from far up the valley a rapier pierces the
    night,
    The white search-ray of a steamer. Swiftly,
      serenely it nears;
A proud, white, alien presence, a glittering galley
    of light,
    Confident-poised, triumphant, freighted with
      hopes and fears.

I look as one looks on a vision; I see it pulsating by;
    I glimpse joy-radiant faces; I hear the thresh
    of the wheel.

THE WOOD-CUTTER

Hoof-like my heart beats a moment; then silence
    swoops from the sky.
  Darkness is piled upon darkness. God only
    knows how I feel.

Maybe you've seen me sometimes; maybe you've
    pitied me then—
  The lonely waif of the wood-camp, here by my
    cabin door.
Some day you'll look and see not; futile and out-
    cast of men,
  I shall be far from your pity, resting forevermore.

My life was a problem in ciphers, a weary and
    profitless sum.
  Slipshod and stupid I worked it, dazed by negation
    and doubt.
Ciphers the total confronts me. Oh, Death, with thy
    moistened thumb,
  Stoop like a petulant schoolboy, wipe me forever out!

THE SONG OF THE MOUTH-ORGAN

(With apologies to the singer of the "Song of the Banjo.")

I'm a homely little bit of tin and bone;
  I'm beloved by the Legion of the Lost;
I haven't got a "vox humana" tone,
  And a dime or two will satisfy my cost.
I don't attempt your high-falutin' flights;
  I am more or less uncertain on the key;
But I tell you, boys, there's lots and lots of nights
  When you've taken mighty comfort out of me.

I weigh an ounce or two, and I'm so small
  You can pack me in the pocket of your vest;
And when at night so wearily you crawl
  Into your bunk and stretch your limbs to rest,
You take me out and play me soft and low,
  The simple songs that trouble your heartstrings:
The tunes you used to fancy long ago,
  Before you made a rotten mess of things.

101

THE SONG OF THE MOUTH-ORGAN

Then a dreamy look will come into your eyes,
   And you break off in the middle of a note;
And then, with just the dreariest of sighs,
   You drop me in the pocket of your coat.
But somehow I have bucked you up a bit;
   And, as you turn around and face the wall,
You don't feel quite so spineless and unfit—
   You're not so bad a fellow after all.

Do you recollect the bitter Arctic night;
   Your camp beside the canyon on the trail;
Your tent a tiny square of orange light;
   The moon above consumptive-like and pale;
Your supper cooked, your little stove aglow;
   You tired, but snug and happy as a child?
Then 'twas "Turkey in the Straw" till your lips
      were nearly raw,
   And you hurled your bold defiance at the Wild

Do you recollect the flashing, lashing pain;
   The gulf of humid blackness overhead;
The lightning making rapiers of the rain;
   The cattle-horns like candles of the dead
You sitting on your bronco there alone,
   In your slicker, saddle-sore and sick with cold?
Do you think the silent herd did not hear "The
      Mocking Bird,"
   Or relish "Silver Threads among the Gold?"

THE SONG OF THE MOUTH-ORGAN

Do you recollect the wild Magellan coast;
  The head-winds and the icy, roaring seas;
The nights you thought that everything was lost;
  The days you toiled in water to your knees;
The frozen ratlines shrieking in the gale;
  The hissing steeps and gulfs of livid foam:
When you cheered your messmates nine with "Ben
        Bolt" and "Clementine,"
  And "Dixie Land" and "Seeing Nellie Home?"

Let the jammy banjo voice the Younger Son,
  Who waits for his remittance to arrive;
I represent the grimy, gritty one,
  Who sweats his bones to keep himself alive;
Who's up against the real thing from his birth;
  Whose heritage is hard and bitter toil;
I voice the weary, smeary ones of earth,
  The helots of the sea and of the soil.

I'm the Steinway of strange mischief and mischance;
  I'm the Stradivarius of blank defeat;
In the down-world, when the devil leads the dance,
  I am simply and symbolically meet;
I'm the irrepressive spirit of mankind;
  I'm the small boy playing knuckle down with
        Death;
At the end of all things known, where God's rubbish-
        heap is thrown,
  I shrill impudent triumph at a breath.

103

THE SONG OF THE MOUTH-ORGAN

I'm a humble little bit of tin and horn;
   I'm a byword, I'm a plaything, I'm a jest;
The virtuoso looks on me with scorn;
    But there's times when I am better than the
      best.
Ask the stoker and the sailor of the sea;
   Ask the mucker and the hewer of the pine;
Ask the herder of the plain, ask the gleaner of the
    grain—
    There's a lowly, loving kingdom—and it's mine.

THE TRAIL OF NINETY-EIGHT

I

Gold! We leapt from our benches. Gold! We
sprang from our stools.
Gold! We wheeled in the furrow, fired with the
faith of fools.
Fearless, unfound, unfitted, far from the night and
the cold,
Heard we the clarion summons, followed the master-
lure—Gold!

Men from the sands of the Sunland; men from the
woods of the West;
Men from the farms and the cities, into the Northland we pressed.
Graybeards and striplings and women, good men
and bad men and bold,
Leaving our homes and our loved ones, crying
exultantly—"Gold!"

Never was seen such an army, pitiful, futile, unfit;
Never was seen such a spirit, manifold courage and
grit

THE TRAIL OF NINETY-EIGHT

Never has been such a cohort under one banner
    unrolled
As surged to the ragged-edged Arctic, urged by
    the arch-tempter—Gold.

"Farewell!" we cried to our dearests; little we
    cared for their tears.
"Farewell!" we cried to the humdrum and the yoke
    of the hireling years;
Just like a pack of school-boys, and the big crowd
    cheered us good-bye.
Never were hearts so uplifted, never were hopes so
    high.

The spectral shores flitted past us, and every whirl
    of the screw
Hurled us nearer to fortune, and ever we planned
    what we'd do—
Do with the gold when we got it—big, shiny
    nuggets like plums,
There in the sand of the river, gouging it out with
    our thumbs.

And one man wanted a castle, another a racing
    stud;
A third would cruise in a palace yacht like a red-
    necked prince of blood.

THE TRAIL OF NINETY-EIGHT

And so we dreamed and we vaunted, millionaires
    to a man,
Leaping to wealth in our visions long ere the trail
    began.

II.

We landed in wind-swept Skagway. We joined
    the weltering mass,
Clamoring over their outfits, waiting to climb the
    Pass.
We tightened our girths and our pack-straps; we
    linked on the Human Chain,
Struggling up to the summit, where every step was
    a pain.

Gone was the joy of our faces, grim and haggard
    and pale;
The heedless mirth of the shipboard was changed
    to the care of the trail.
We flung ourselves in the struggle, packing our
    grub in relays,
Step by step to the summit in the bale of the winter
    days.

Floundering deep in the sump-holes, stumbling out
    again;
Crying with cold and weakness, crazy with fear and
    pain.

THE TRAIL OF NINETY-EIGHT

Then from the depths of our travail, ere our spirits
    were broke,
Grim, tenacious and savage, the lust of the trail
    awoke.

"Klondike or bust!" rang the slogan; every man
    for his own.
Oh, how we flogged the horses, staggering skin and
    bone!
Oh, how we cursed their weakness, anguish they
    could not tell,
Breaking their hearts in our passion, lashing them
    on till they fell!

For grub meant gold to our thinking, and all that
    could walk must pack;
The sheep for the shambles stumbled, each with a
    load on its back;
And even the swine were burdened, and grunted
    and squealed and rolled,
And men went mad in the moment, huskily clam-
    oring "Gold!"

Oh, we were brutes and devils, goaded by lust and
    fear!
Our eyes were strained to the summit; the weak-
    lings dropped to the rear,

THE TRAIL OF NINETY-EIGHT

Falling in heaps by the trail-side, heart-broken
    limp and wan;
But the gaps closed up in an instant, and heedless
    the chain went on.

Never will I forget it, there on the mountain face,
Antlike, men with their burdens, clinging in icy
    space;
Dogged, determined and dauntless, cruel and cal-
    lous and cold,
Cursing, blaspheming, reviling, and ever that battle-
    cry—"Gold!"

Thus toiled we, the army of fortune, in hunger and
    hope and despair,
Till glacier, mountain and forest vanished, and,
    radiantly fair,
There at our feet lay Lake Bennett, and down to
    its welcome we ran:
The trail of the land was over, the trail of the water
    began.

III.

We built our boats and we launched them.   Never
    has been such a fleet;
A packing-case for a bottom, a mackinaw for a sheet.
Shapeless, grotesque, lopsided, flimsy, makeshift
    and crude,
Each man after his fashion builded as best he could

THE TRAIL OF NINETY-EIGHT

Each man worked like a demon, as prow to rudder
    we raced;
The winds of the Wild cried "Hurry!" the voice of
    the waters, "Haste!"
We hated those driving before us; we dreaded
    those pressing behind;
We cursed the slow current that bore us; we prayed
    to the God of the wind.

Spring! and the hillsides flourished, vivid in jew-
    elled green;
Spring! and our hearts' blood nourished envy and
    hatred and spleen.
Little cared we for the Spring-birth; much cared
    we to get on—
Stake in the Great White Channel, stake ere the
    best be gone.

The greed of the gold possessed us; pity and love
    were forgot;
Covetous visions obsessed us; brother with brother
    fought.
Partner with partner wrangled, each one claiming
    his due;
Wrangled and halved their outfits, sawing their
    boats in two.

THE TRAIL OF NINETY-EIGHT

Thuswise we voyaged Lake Bennett, Tagish,
  then Windy Arm,
Sinister, savage and baleful, boding us hate and
  harm.
Many a scow was shattered there on that iron
  shore;
Many a heart was broken straining at sweep and
  oar.

We roused Lake Marsh with a chorus, we drifted
  many a mile;
There was the canyon before us—cave-like its
  dark defile;
The shores swept faster and faster; the river nar-
  rowed to wrath;
Waters that hissed disaster reared upright in our
  path.

Beneath us the green tumult churning, above us
  the cavernous gloom;
Around us, swift twisting and turning, the black,
  sullen walls of a tomb.
We spun like a chip in a mill-race; our hearts ham-
  mered under the test;
Then—oh, the relief on each chill face!—we soared
  into sunlight and rest.

THE TRAIL OF NINETY-EIGHT

Hand sought for hand on the instant. Cried we,
    "Our troubles are o'er!"
Then, like a rumble of thunder, heard we a canorous
    roar.
Leaping and boiling and seething, saw we a cauldron
    afume;
There was the rage of the rapids, there was the
    menace of doom.

The river springs like a racer, sweeps through a
    gash in the rock;
Buts at the boulder-ribbed bottom, staggers and
    rears at the shock;
Leaps like a terrified monster, writhes in its fury
    and pain;
Then with the crash of a demon springs to the
    onset again.

Dared we that ravening terror; heard we its din
    in our ears;
Called on the Gods of our fathers, juggled forlorn
    with our fears;
Sank to our waists in its fury, tossed to the sky
    like a fleece;
Then, when our dread was the greatest, crashed
    into safety and peace.

THE TRAIL OF NINETY-EIGHT

But what of the others that followed, losing their
    boats by the score?
Well could we see them and hear them, strung
    down that desolate shore.
What of the poor souls that perished? Little of
    them shall be said—
On to the Golden Valley, pause not to bury the
    dead.

Then there were days of drifting, breezes soft as a
    sigh;
Night trailed her robe of jewels over the floor of
    the sky.
The moonlit stream was a python, silver, sinuous,
    vast,
That writhed on a shroud of velvet—well, it was
    done at last.

There were the tents of Dawson, there the scar of
    the slide;
Swiftly we poled o'er the shallows, swiftly leapt
    o'er the side.
Fires fringed the mouth of Bonanza; sunset gilded
    the dome;
The test of the trail was over—thank God, thank
    God, we were Home!

THE BALLAD OF GUM-BOOT BEN

He was an old prospector with a vision bleared and dim.

He asked me for a grubstake, and the same I gave to him.

He hinted of a hidden trove, and when I made so bold

To question his veracity, this is the tale he told.

"I do not seek the copper streak, nor yet the yellow dust;

I am not fain for sake of gain to irk the frozen crust;

Let fellows gross find gilded dross, far other is my mark;

Oh, gentle youth, this is the truth—I go to seek the Ark.

"I prospected the Pelly bed, I prospected the White;

The Nordenscold for love of gold I piked from morn till night;

THE BALLAD OF GUM-BOOT BEN

Afar and near for many a year I led the wild
     stampede,
Until I guessed that all my quest was vanity and
     greed.

"Then came I to a land I knew no man had ever
     seen,
A haggard land, forlornly spanned by mountains
     lank and lean;
The nitchies said 'twas full of dread, of smoke and
     fiery breath,
And no man dare put foot in there for fear of pain
     and death.

"But I was made all unafraid, so, careless and alone,
Day after day I made my way into that land
     unknown;
Night after night by camp-fire light I crouched in
     lonely thought;
Oh, gentle youth, this is the truth—I knew not
     what I sought.

"I rose at dawn; I wandered on. 'Tis somewhat
     fine and grand
To be alone and hold your own in God's vast
     awesome land;

THE BALLAD OF GUM-BOOT BEN

Come woe or weal, 'tis fine to feel a hundred
    miles between
The trails you dare and pathways where the feet
    of men have been.

"And so it fell on me a spell of wander-lust was
    cast.
The land was still and strange and chill, and
    cavernous and vast;
And sad and dead, and dull as lead, the valleys
    sought the snows;
And far and wide on every side the ashen peaks
    arose.

"The moon was like a silent spike that pierced
    the sky right through;
The small stars popped and winked and hopped
    in vastitudes of blue;
And unto me for company came creatures of the
    shade,
And formed in rings and whispered things that
    made me half afraid.

"And strange though be, 'twas borne on me that
    land had lived of old,
And men had crept and slain and slept where now
    they toiled for gold;

THE BALLAD OF GUM-BOOT BEN

Through jungles dim the mammoth grim had
  sought the oozy fen,
And on his track, all bent of back, had crawled the
  hairy men.

"And furthermore, strange deeds of yore in this
  dead place were done.
They haunted me, as wild and free I roamed from
  sun to sun;
Until I came where sudden flame uplit a terraced
  height,
A regnant peak that seemed to seek the coronal
  of night.

"I scaled the peak; my heart was weak, yet on
  and on I pressed.
Skyward I strained until I gained its dazzling
  silver crest;
And there I found, with all around a world supine
  and stark,
Swept clean of snow, a flat plateau, and on it
  lay—the Ark.

"Yes, there, I knew, by two and two the beasts did
  disembark,
And so in haste I ran and traced in letters on the
  Ark

THE BALLAD OF GUM-BOOT BEN

My human name—Ben Smith's the same.   And
    now I want to float
A syndicate to haul and freight to town that noble
    boat."

I met him later in a bar and made a gay remark
Anent an ancient miner and an option on the Ark.
He gazed at me reproachfully, as only topers can;
But what he said I can't repeat—he was a bad old
    man.

CLANCY OF THE MOUNTED POLICE

CLANCY OF THE MOUNTED POLICE

In the little Crimson Manual it's written plain
    and clear
That who would wear the scarlet coat shall say
    good-bye to fear;
Shall be a guardian of the right, a sleuth-hound of
    the trail—
In the little Crimson Manual there's no such word
    as "fail"—
Shall follow on though heavens fall, or hell's top-
    turrets freeze,
Half round the world, if need there be, on bleeding
    hands and knees.
It's duty, duty, first and last, the Crimson Manual
    saith;
The Scarlet Rider makes reply: "It's duty—to
    the death."
And so they sweep the solitudes, free men from all
    the earth;
And so they sentinel the woods, the wilds that
    know their worth;
And so they scour the startled plains and mock
    at hurt and pain,

119

And read their Crimson Manual, and find their
    duty plain.
Knights of the lists of unrenown, born of the
    frontier's need,
Disdainful of the spoken word, exultant in the
    deed;
Unconscious heroes of the waste, proud players
    of the game,
Props of the power behind the throne, upholders
    of the name:
For thus the Great White Chief hath said, "In
    all my lands be peace,"
And to maintain his word he gave his West the
    Scarlet Police.

Livid-lipped was the valley, still as the grave of
    God;
  Misty shadows of mountain thinned into mists
    of cloud;
Corpselike and stark was the land, with a quiet
    that crushed and awed,
  And the stars of the weird sub-arctic glimmered
    over its shroud.

Deep in the trench of the valley two men stationed
    the Post,
  Seymour and Clancy the reckless, fresh from
    the long patrol;

CLANCY OF THE MOUNTED POLICE

Seymour, the sergeant, and Clancy—Clancy who
    made his boast
  He could cinch like a bronco the Northland,
    and cling to the prongs of the Pole.

Two lone men on detachment, standing for law
    on the trail;
  Undismayed in the vastness, wise with the
    wisdom of old—
Out of the night hailed a half-breed telling a pitiful
    tale,
  "White man starving and crazy on the banks
    of the Nordenscold."

Up sprang the red-haired Clancy, lean and eager
    of eye;
  Loaded the long toboggan, strapped each dog
    at its post;
Whirled his lash at the leader; then, with a whoop
    and a cry,
  Into the Great White Silence faded away like
    a ghost.

The clouds were a misty shadow, the hills were
    a shadowy mist;
  Sunless, voiceless and pulseless, the day was a
    dream of woe;

CLANCY OF THE MOUNTED POLICE

Through the ice-rifts the river smoked and bubbled
and hissed;
  Behind was a trail fresh broken, in front the un-
trodden snow.

Ahead of the dogs ploughed Clancy, haloed by
steaming breath;
  Through peril of open water, through ache of
insensate cold;
Up rivers wantonly winding in a land affianced
to death,
  Till he came to a cowering cabin on the banks
of the Nordenscold.

Then Clancy loosed his revolver, and he strode
through the open door;
  And there was the man he sought for, crouching
beside the fire;
The hair of his beard was singeing, the frost on his
back was hoar,
  And ever he crooned and chanted as if he never
would tire:—

*"I panned and I panned in the shiny sand, and I
sniped on the river bar;*
*But I know, I know, that it's down below that
the golden treasures are;*

CLANCY OF THE MOUNTED POLICE

So I'll wait and wait till the floods abate, and I'll
sink a shaft once more,
And I'd like to bet that I'll go home yet with a
brass band playing before."

He was nigh as thin as a sliver, and he whined like
a Moose-hide cur;
So Clancy clothed him and nursed him as a
mother nurses a child;
Lifted him on the toboggan, wrapped him in robes
of fur,
Then with the dogs sore straining started to
face the Wild.

Said the Wild, "I will crush this Clancy, so fearless
and insolent;
For him will I loose my fury, and blind and
buffet and beat;
Pile up my snows to stay him; then when his
strength is spent,
Leap on him from my ambush and crush him
under my feet.

"Him will I ring with my silence, compass him
with my cold;
Closer and closer clutch him unto mine icy
breast;

123

CLANCY OF THE MOUNTED POLICE

Buffet him with my blizzards, deep in my snows
    enfold,
  Claiming his life as my tribute, giving my
    wolves the rest."

Clancy crawled through the vastness; o'er him
    the hate of the Wild;
  Full on his face fell the blizzard; cheering his
    huskies he ran;
Fighting, fierce-hearted and tireless, snows that
    drifted and piled,
  With ever and ever behind him singing the
    crazy man.

   "Sing hey, sing ho, for the ice and snow,
     And a heart that's ever merry;
     Let us trim and square with a lover's care
     (For why should a man be sorry?)
     A grave deep, deep, with the moon a-peep,
     A grave in the frozen mould.
     Sing hey, sing ho, for the winds that blow,
     And a grave deep down in the ice and snow,
     A grave in the land of gold."

Day after day of darkness, the whirl of the seeth·
    ing snows;
  Day after day of blindness, the swoop of the
    stinging blast;

CLANCY OF THE MOUNTED POLICE

On through a blur of fury the swing of staggering
 blows;
 On through a world of turmoil, empty, inane
 and vast.

Night with its writhing storm-whirl, night des-
 pairingly black;
 Night with its hours of terror, numb and end-
 lessly long;
Night with its weary waiting, fighting the shadows
 back,
 And ever the crouching madman singing his
 crazy song.

Cold with its creeping terror, cold with its sudden
 clinch;
 Cold so utter you wonder if 'twill ever again be
 warm;
Clancy grinned as he shuddered, "Surely it isn't
 a cinch
 Being wet-nurse to a looney in the teeth of an
 arctic storm."

The blizzard passed and the dawn broke, knife-
 edged and crystal clear;
 The sky was a blue-domed iceberg, sunshine
 outlawed away;

CLANCY OF THE MOUNTED POLICE

Ever by snowslide and ice-rip haunted and hovered
the Fear;
  Ever the Wild malignant poised and panted to
  slay.

The lead-dog freezes in harness—cut him out of
the team!
  The lung of the wheel-dog's bleeding—shoot
  him and let him lie!
On and on with the others—lash them until they
scream!
  "Pull for your lives, you devils! On! To halt
  is to die."

There in the frozen vastness Clancy fought with
his foes;
  The ache of the stiffened fingers, the cut of the
  snowshoe thong;
Cheeks black-raw through the hood-flap, eyes that
tingled and closed,
  And ever to urge and cheer him quavered the
  madman's song.

Colder it grew and colder, till the last heat left the
earth,
  And there in the great stark stillness the bale
  fires glinted and gleamed,

CLANCY OF THE MOUNTED POLICE

And the Wild all around exulted and shook with
    a devilish mirth,
  And life was far and forgotten, the ghost of a
    joy once dreamed.

Death! And one who defied it, a man of the
    Mounted Police;
  Fought it there to a standstill long after hope
    was gone;
Grinned through his bitter anguish, fought with-
    out let or cease,
  Suffering, straining, striving, stumbling, strug-
    gling on.

Till the dogs lay down in their traces, and rose and
    staggered and fell;
  Till the eyes of him dimmed with shadows, and
    the trail was so hard to see;
Till the Wild howled out triumphant, and the
    world was a frozen hell—
  Then said Constable Clancy: "I guess that it's
    up to me."

Far down the trail they saw him, and his hands
    they were blanched like bone;
  His face was a blackened horror, from his eye-
    lids the salt rheum ran;

CLANCY OF THE MOUNTED POLICE

His feet he was lifting strangely, as if they were
    made of stone,
    But safe in his arms and sleeping he carried
    the crazy man.

So Clancy got into Barracks, and the boys made
    rather a scene;
    And the O. C. called him a hero, and was nice
    as a man could be;
But Clancy gazed down his trousers at the place
    where his toes had been,
    And then he howled like a husky, and sang in
    a shaky key:

"When I go back to the old love that's true to the
    finger-tips,
I'll say: 'Here's bushels of gold, love,' and I'll kiss
    my girl on the lips;
'It's yours to have and to hold, love.' It's the proud,
    proud boy I'll be,
When I go back to the old love that's waited so long
    for me."

LOST

"Black is the sky, but the land is white—
  (O the wind, the snow and the storm!)—
Father, where is our boy to-night?
  Pray to God he is safe and warm."

"Mother, mother, why should you fear?
  Safe is he, and the Arctic moon
Over his cabin shines so clear—
  Rest and sleep, 'twill be morning soon."

"It's getting dark awful sudden. Say, this is
    mighty queer!
  Where in the world have I got to? It's still
    and black as a tomb.
I reckoned the camp was yonder, I figured the
    trail was here—
  Nothing! Just draw and valley packed with
    quiet and gloom;

LOST

Snow that comes down like feathers, thick and
gobby and gray;
Night that looks spiteful ugly—seems that I've
lost my way.

"The cold's got an edge like a jackknife—it must
be forty below;
Leastways that's what it seems like—it cuts so
fierce to the bone.
The wind's getting real ferocious; it's heaving and
whirling the snow;
It shrieks with a howl of fury, it dies away to
a moan;
Its arms sweep round like a banshee's, swift and
icily white,
And buffet and blind and beat me.   Lord! it's
a hell of a night.

"I'm all tangled up in a blizzard.   There's only
one thing to do—
Keep on moving and moving; it's death, it's
death if I rest.
Oh, God! if I see the morning, if only I struggle
through,
I'll say the prayers I've forgotten since I lay on
my mother's breast.
I seem going round in a circle; maybe the camp is
near.

130

LOST

Say! did somebody holler? Was it a light I
    saw?
Or was it only a notion? I'll shout, and maybe
    they'll hear—
No! the wind only drowns me—shout till my
    throat is raw.

"The boys are all round the camp-fire wondering
    when I'll be back.
They'll soon be starting to seek me; they'll
    scarcely wait for the light.
What will they find, I wonder, when they come to
    the end of my track—
A hand stuck out of a snowdrift, frozen and
    stiff and white.
That's what they'll strike, I reckon; that's how
    they'll find their pard,
A pie-faced corpse in a snowbank—curse you,
    don't be a fool!
Play the game to the finish; bet on your very last
    card;
Nerve yourself for the struggle. Oh, you coward,
    keep cool!

"I'm going to lick this blizzard; I'm going to live
    the night.
It can't down me with its bluster—I'm not the
    kind to be beat.

LOST

On hands and knees will I buck it; with every
    breath will I fight;
  It's life, it's life that I fight for—never it seemed
    so sweet.
I know that my face is frozen; my hands are
    numblike and dead;
  But oh, my feet keep a-moving, heavy and hard
    and slow;
They're trying to kill me, kill me, the night that's
    black overhead,
  The wind that cuts like a razor, the whipcord
    lash of the snow.
Keep a-moving, a-moving; don't, don't stumble,
    you fool!
  Curse this snow that's a-piling a-purpose to
    block my way.
It's heavy as gold in the rocker, it's white and
    fleecy as wool;
  It's soft as a bed of feathers, it's warm as a
    stack of hay.
Curse on my feet that slip so, my poor tired,
    stumbling feet—
  I guess they're a job for the surgeon, they feel
    so queerlike to lift—
I'll rest them just for a moment—oh, but to rest
    is sweet!
  The awful wind cannot get me, deep, deep down
    in the drift."

LOST

"Father, a bitter cry I heard,
  Out of the night so dark and wild.
Why is my heart so strangely stirred?
  'Twas like the voice of our erring child."

"Mother, mother, you only heard
  A waterfowl in the locked lagoon—
Out of the night a wounded bird—
  Rest and sleep, 'twill be morning soon."

Who is it talks of sleeping?   I'll swear that some-
    body shook
  Me hard by the arm for a moment, but how on
    earth could it be?
See how my feet are moving—awfully funny they
    look—
  Moving as if they belonged to a someone that
    wasn't me.
The wind down the night's long alley bowls me
    down like a pin;
  I stagger and fall and stagger, crawl arm-deep
    in the snow.
Beaten back to my corner, how can I hope to win?
  And there is the blizzard waiting to give me the
    knockout blow.

Oh, I'm so warm and sleepy! No more hunger and
    pain.
  Just to rest for a moment; was ever rest such
    a joy?

LOST

Ha! what was that? I'll swear it, somebody
    shook me again;
  Somebody seemed to whisper: "Fight to the
    last, my boy."
Fight! That's right, I must struggle. I know
    that to rest means death;
  Death, but then what does death mean?—ease
    from a world of strife.
Life has been none too pleasant; yet with my
    failing breath
  Still and still must I struggle, fight for the gift
    of life.

   *   *   *   *   *   *

Seems that I must be dreaming! Here is the old
    home trail;
  Yonder a light is gleaming; oh, I know it so well!
The air is scented with clover; the cattle wait by
    the rail;
  Father is through with the milking; there goes
    the supper-bell.

   *   *   *   *   *   *

Mother, your boy is crying, out in the night and
    cold;
  Let me in and forgive me, I'll never be bad
    any more:

134

LOST

I'm, oh, so sick and so sorry: please, dear mother,
    don't scold—
It's just your boy, and he wants you. . . .
    Mother, open the door. . . .

"Father, father, I saw a face
    Pressed just now to the window-pane!
Oh, it gazed for a moment's space,
    Wild and wan, and was gone again!"

"Mother, mother, you saw the snow
    Drifted down from the maple tree
(Oh, the wind that is sobbing so!
    Weary and worn and old are we)—
Only the snow and a wounded loon—
Rest and sleep, 'twill be morning soon."

L'ENVOI

We talked of yesteryears, of trails and treasure,
  Of men who played the game and lost or won;
Of mad stampedes, of toil beyond all measure,
  Of camp-fire comfort when the day was done.
We talked of sullen nights by moon-dogs haunted,
  Of bird and beast and tree, of rod and gun;
Of boat and tent, of hunting-trip enchanted
  Beneath the wonder of the midnight sun;
Of bloody-footed dogs that gnawed the traces,
  Of prisoned seas, wind-lashed and winter-locked
The ice-gray dawn was pale upon our faces,
  Yet still we filled the cup and still we talked.

The city street was dimmed.   We saw the glitter
  Of moon-picked brilliants on the virgin snow,
And down the drifted canyon heard the bitter,
  Relentless slogan of the winds of woe.
The city was forgot, and, parka-skirted,
  We trod that leagueless land that once we knew;

L'ENVOI

We saw stream past, down valleys glacier-girted,
  The wolf-worn legions of the caribou.
We smoked our pipes, o'er scenes of triumph dwelling,
  Of deeds of daring, dire defeats, we talked;
And other tales that lost not in the telling,
  Ere to our beds uncertainly we walked.

And so, dear friends, in gentler valleys roaming,
  Perhaps, when on my printed page you look,
Your fancies by the firelight may go homing
  To that lone land that haply you forsook.
And if perchance you hear the silence calling,
  The frozen music of star-yearning heights,
Or, dreaming, see the seines of silver trawling
  Across the sky's abyss on vasty nights,
You may recall that sweep of savage splendor,
  That land that measures each man at his worth,
And feel in memory, half fierce, half tender,
  The brotherhood of men that know the North.

Rhymes of a Rolling Stone

Contents

CONTENTS

PRELUDE

I SING no idle songs of dalliance days,
  No dreams Elysian inspire my rhyming;
I have no Celia to enchant my lays,
No pipes of Pan have set my heart to chiming.
I am no wordsmith dripping gems divine
Into the golden chalice of a sonnet;
If love songs witch you, close this book of mine,
      Waste no time on it.

Yet bring I to my work an eager joy,
A lusty love of life and all things human;
Still in me leaps the wonder of the boy,
A pride in man, a deathless faith in woman.
Still red blood calls, still rings the valiant fray;
Adventure beacons through the summer gloaming:
Oh long and long and long will be the day
      Ere I come homing!

PRELUDE

This earth is ours to love: lute, brush and pen,
They are but tongues to tell of life sincerely;
The thaumaturgic Day, the might of men,
O God of Scribes, grant us to grave them clearly!
Grant heart that homes in heart, then all is well.
Honey is honey-sweet, howe'er the hiving.
Each to his work, his wage at evening bell
      The strength of striving.

A ROLLING STONE

THERE'S sunshine in the heart of me,
    My blood sings in the breeze;
The mountains are a part of me,
I'm fellow to the trees.
My golden youth I'm squandering,
Sun-libertine am I;
A-wandering, a-wandering,
Until the day I die.

I was once, I declare, a Stone-Age man,
    And I roomed in the cool of a cave;
I have known, I will swear, in a new life-span,
    The fret and the sweat of a slave:
For far over all that folks hold worth,
    There lives and there leaps in me
A love of the lowly things of earth,
    And a passion to be free.

To pitch my tent with no prosy plan,
    To range and to change at will;
To mock at the mastership of man,
    To seek Adventure's thrill.

3

A ROLLING STONE

Carefree to be, as a bird that sings;
 To go my own sweet way;
To reck not at all what may befall,
 But to live and to love each day.

To make my body a temple pure
 Wherein I dwell serene;
To care for the things that shall endure,
 The simple, sweet and clean.
To oust out envy and hate and rage,
 To breathe with no alarm;
For Nature shall be my anchorage,
 And none shall do me harm.

To shun all lures that debauch the soul,
 The orgied rites of the rich;
To eat my crust as a rover must
 With the rough-neck down in the ditch.
To trudge by his side whate'er betide;
 To share his fire at night;
To call him friend to the long trail-end,
 And to read his heart aright.

To scorn all strife, and to view all life
 With the curious eyes of a child;
From the plangent sea to the prairie,
 From the slum to the heart of the Wild.

A ROLLING STONE

From the red-rimmed star to the speck of sand,
    From the vast to the greatly small;
For I know that the whole for good is planned,
    And I want to see it all.

To see it all, the wide world-way,
    From the fig-leaf belt to the Pole;
With never a one to say me nay,
    And none to cramp my soul.
In belly-pinch I will pay the price,
    But God! let me be free;
For once I know in the long ago,
    They made a slave of me.

In a flannel shirt from earth's clean dirt,
    Here, pal, is my calloused hand!
Oh, I love each day as a rover may,
    Nor seek to understand.
To *enjoy* is good enough for me;
    The gipsy of God am I;
Then here's a hail to each flaring dawn!
And here's a cheer to the night that's gone!
And may I go a-roaming on
    Until the day I die!

A ROLLING STONE

Then every star shall sing to me
Its song of liberty;
And every morn shall bring to me
Its mandate to be free.
In every throbbing vein of me
I'll feel the vast Earth-call;
O body, heart and brain of me
Praise Him who made it all!

THE SOLDIER OF FORTUNE

"DENY your God!" they ringed me with their
spears;
Blood-crazed were they, and reeking from the strife;
Hell-hot their hate, and venom-fanged their sneers,
And one man spat on me and nursed a knife.
And there was I, sore wounded and alone,
I, the last living of my slaughtered band.
Oh sinister the sky, and cold as stone!
In one red laugh of horror reeled the land.
And dazed and desperate I faced their spears,
And like a flame out-leaped that naked knife,
And like a serpent stung their bitter jeers:
"Deny your God, and we will give you life."

Deny my God! Oh life was very sweet!
And it is hard in youth and hope to die;
And there my comrades dear lay at my feet,
And in that blear of blood soon must I lie.
And yet . . . I almost laughed — it seemed so odd,
For long and long had I not vainly tried
To reason out and body forth my God,
And prayed for light, and doubted — and *denied:*
Denied the Being I could not conceive,

Denied a life-to-be beyond the grave. . . .
And now they ask me, who do not believe,
Just to deny, to voice my doubt, to save
This life of mine that sings so in the sun,
The bloom of youth yet red upon my cheek,
My only life!—O fools! 'tis easy done,
I will deny . . . and yet I do not speak.

"Deny your God!" their spears are all agleam,
And I can see their eyes with blood-lust shine;
Their snarling voices shrill into a scream,
And, mad to slay, they quiver for the sign.
Deny my God. yes, I could do it well;
Yet if I did, what of my race, my name?
How they would spit on me, these dogs of hell!
Spurn me, and put on me the brand of shame.
A white man's honour! what of that, I say?
Shall these black curs cry "Coward" in my face?
They who would perish for their gods of clay —
Shall I defile my country and my race?
My country! what's my country to me now?
Soldier of Fortune, free and far I roam;
All men are brothers in my heart, I vow;
The wide and wondrous world is all my home.
My country! reverent of her splendid Dead,
Her heroes proud, her martyrs pierced with pain:

For me her puissant blood was vainly shed;
For me her drums of battle beat in vain,
And free I fare, half-heedless of her fate:
No faith, no flag I owe — then why not seek
This last loop-hole of life? Why hesitate?
I will deny . . . and yet I do not speak.

"Deny your God!" their spears are poised on high,
And tense and terrible they wait the word;
And dark and darker glooms the dreary sky,
And in that hush of horror no thing stirred.
Then, through the ringing terror and sheer hate
Leaped there a vision to me — Oh, how far!
A face, Her face . . . through all my stormy fate
A joy, a strength, a glory and a star.
Beneath the pines, where lonely camp-fires gleam,
In seas forlorn, amid the deserts drear,
How I had gladdened to that face of dream!
And never, never had it seemed so dear.
O silken hair that veils the sunny brow!
O eyes of grey, so tender and so true!
O lips of smiling sweetness! must I now
For ever and for ever go from you?
Ah, yes, I must . . . for if I do this thing,
How can I look into your face again?
Knowing you think me more than half a king,
I with my craven heart, my honour slain.

A SOLDIER OF FORTUNE

No! no! my mind's made up. I gaze above,
Into that sky insensate as a stone;
Not for my creed, my country, but my Love
Will I stand up and meet my death alone.
Then though it be to utter dark I sink,
The God that dwells in me is not denied;
" Best " triumphs over " Beast,"— and so I think
Humanity itself is glorified. . . .

" And now, my butchers, I embrace my fate.
" Come! let my heart's blood slake the thirsty sod.
" Curst be the life you offer! Glut your hate!
" Strike! Strike, you dogs! I'll *not* deny my God."

I saw the spears that seemed a-leap to slay,
All quiver earthward at the headman's nod;
And in a daze of dream I heard him say:
" Go, set him free who serves so well his God!"

THE GRAMAPHONE AT FOND-DU-LAC

NOW Eddie Malone got a swell grammyfone to
    draw all the trade to his store;
An' sez he: "Come along for a season of song, which
    the like ye had niver before."
Then Dogrib, an' Slave, an' Yellow-knife brave, an' Cree
    in his dinky canoe,
Confluated near, to see an' to hear Ed's grammyfone
    make its dayboo.

Then Ed turned the crank, an' there on the bank they
    squatted like bumps on a log.
For acres around there wasn't a sound, not even the
    howl of a dog.
When out of the horn there sudden was born such a
    marvellous elegant tone;
An' then like a spell on that auddyence fell the voice
    of its first grammyfone.

"Bad medicine!" cried Old Tom, the One-eyed, an'
    made for to jump in the lake;
But no one gave heed to his little stampede, so he
    guessed he had made a mistake.

Then Roll-in-the-Mud, a chief of the blood, observed in
   choice Chippewayan:
" You've brought us canned beef, an' it's now my belief
   that this here's a case of ' *canned man.*' "

Well, though I'm not strong on the Dago in song, that
   sure got me goin' for fair.
There was Crusoe an' Scotty, an' Ma'am Shoeman Hank,
   an' Melber an' Bonchy was there.
'Twas silver an' gold, an' sweetness untold to hear all
   them big guinneys sing;
An' thick all around an' inhalin' the sound, them Indians
   formed in a ring.

So solemn they sat, an' they smoked an' they spat, but
   their eyes sort o' glistened an' shone;
Yet niver a word of approvin' occurred till that guy
   Harry Lauder came on.
Then hunter of moose, an' squaw an' papoose jest
   laughed till their stummicks was sore;
Six times Eddie set back that record an' yet they hol-
   lered an' hollered for more.

THE GRAMAPHONE AT FOND-DU-LAC

I'll never forget that frame-up, you bet; them caverns
    of sunset agleam;
Them still peaks aglow, them shadders below, an' the
    lake like a petrified dream;
The teepees that stood by the edge of the wood; the
    evenin' star blinkin' alone;
The peace an' the rest, an' final an' best, the music of
    Ed's grammyfone.

Then sudden an' clear there rang on my ear a song
    mighty simple an' old;
Heart-hungry an' high it thrilled to the sky, all about
    " silver threads in the gold."
'Twas tender to tears, an' it brung back the years, the
    mem'ries that hallow an' yearn;
'Twas home-love an' joy, 'twas the thought of my boy
    . . . an' right there I vowed I'd return.

Big Four-finger Jack was right at my back, an' I saw
    with a kind o' surprise,
He gazed at the lake with a heartful of ache, an' the
    tears irrigated his eyes.
An' sez he: " Cuss me, pard! but that there hits me
    hard; I've a mother does nuthin' but wait.
" She's turned eighty-three, an' she's only got me, an'
    I'm scared it'll soon be too late."

*　　*　　*　　*　　*　　*　　*　　*

THE GRAMAPHONE AT FOND-DU-LAC

On Fond-du-lac's shore I'm hearin' once more that blessed
  old grammyfone play.
The summer's all gone, an' I'm still livin' on in the same
  old haphazardous way.
Oh, I cut out the booze, an' with muscles an' thews I
  corralled all the coin to go back;
But it wasn't to be: he'd a mother, you see, so I —
  slipped it to Four-finger Jack.

THE LAND OF BEYOND

HAVE ever you heard of the Land of Beyond,
    That dreams at the gates of the day?
Alluring it lies at the skirts of the skies,
    And ever so far away;
Alluring it calls: O ye the yoke galls,
    And ye of the trail overfond,
With saddle and pack, by paddle and track,
    Let's go to the Land of Beyond!

Have ever you stood where the silences brood,
    And vast the horizons begin,
At the dawn of the day to behold far away
    The goal you would strive for and win?
Yet ah! in the night when you gain to the height,
    With the vast pool of heaven star-spawned,
Afar and agleam, like a valley of dream,
    Still mocks you a Land of Beyond.

THE LAND OF BEYOND

Thank God! there is always a Land of Beyond
    For us who are true to the trail;
A vision to seek, a beckoning peak,
    A farness that never will fail;
A pride in our soul that mocks at a goal,
    A manhood that irks at a bond,
And try how we will, unattainable still,
    Behold it, our Land of Beyond!

SUNSHINE

I

FLAT as a drum-head stretch the haggard snows;
   The mighty skies are palisades of light;
The stars are blurred; the silence grows and grows;
Vaster and vaster vaults the icy night.
Here in my sleeping-bag I cower and pray:
"Silence and night, have pity! stoop and slay."

I have not slept for many, many days.
I close my eyes with weariness — that's all.
I still have strength to feed the drift-wood blaze,
That flickers weirdly on the icy wall.
I still have strength to pray: "God rest her soul,
Here in the awful shadow of the Pole."

There in the cabin's alcove low she lies,
Still candles gleaming at her head and feet;
All snow-drop white, ash-cold, with closéd eyes,
Lips smiling, hands at rest — O God, how sweet!
How all unutterably sweet she seems. . . .
Not dead, not dead indeed — she dreams, she dreams.

SUNSHINE

II

"Sunshine," I called her, and she brought, I vow,
  God's blessed sunshine to this life of mine.
I was a rover, of the breed who plough
  Life's furrow in a far-flung, lonely line;
The wilderness my home, my fortune cast
In a wild land of dearth, barbaric, vast.

When did I see her first? Long had I lain
  Groping my way to life through fevered gloom.
Sudden the cloud of darkness left my brain;
  A velvet bar of sunshine pierced the room,
And in that mellow glory aureoled
She stood, she stood, all golden in its gold.

Sunshine! O miracle! the earth grew glad;
  Radiant each blade of grass, each living thing.
What a huge strength, high hope, proud will I had!
  All the wide world with rapture seemed to ring.
Would she but wed me? *Yes:* then fared we forth
Into the vast, unvintageable North.

SUNSHINE

III

In Muskrat Land the conies leap,
The wavies linger in their flight;
The jewelled, snakelike rivers creep;
The sun, sad rogue, is out all night;
The great wood bison paws the sand,
In Muskrat Land, in Muskrat Land.

In Muskrat Land dim streams divide
The tundras belted by the sky.
How sweet in slim canoe to glide,
And dream, and let the world go by!
Build gay camp-fires on greening strand!
In Muskrat Land, in Muskrat Land.

SUNSHINE

IV

And so we dreamed and drifted, she and I;
And how she loved that free, unfathomed life!
There in the peach-bloom of the midnight sky,
The silence welded us, true man and wife.
Then North and North invincibly we pressed
Beyond the Circle, to the world's white crest.

And on the wind-flailed Arctic waste we stayed,
Dwelt with the Huskies by the Polar sea.
Fur had they, white fox, marten, mink to trade,
And we had food-stuff, bacon, flour and tea.
So we made snug, chummed up with all the band:
Sudden the Winter swooped on Husky Land.

SUNSHINE

V

What was that ill so sinister and dread,
Smiting the tribe with sickness to the bone?
So that we waked one morn to find them fled;
So that we stood and stared, alone, alone.
Bravely she smiled and looked into my eyes;
Laughed at their troubled, stern, foreboding pain;
Gaily she mocked the menace of the skies,
Turned to our cheery cabin once again,
Saying: " 'Twill soon be over, dearest one,
The long, long night: then O the sun, the sun!"

SUNSHINE

VI

God made a heart of gold, of gold,
Shining and sweet and true;
Gave it a home of fairest mould,
Blest it, and called it — You.

God gave the rose its grace of glow,
And the lark its radiant glee;
But, better than all, I know, I know
God gave you, Heart, to me.

SUNSHINE

VII

She was all sunshine in those dubious days;
Our cabin beaconed with defiant light;
We chattered by the friendly drift-wood blaze;
Closer and closer cowered the hag-like night.
A wolf-howl would have been a welcome sound,
And there was none in all that stricken land;
Yet with such silence, darkness, death around,
Learned we to love as few can understand.
Spirit with spirit fused, and soul with soul,
There in the sullen shadow of the Pole.

SUNSHINE

VIII

What was that haunting horror of the night?
Brave was she; buoyant, full of sunny cheer.
Why was her face so small, so strangely white?
Then did I turn from her, heart-sick with fear;
Sought in my agony the outcast snows;
Prayed in my pain to that insensate sky;
Grovelled and sobbed and cursed, and then arose:
"Sunshine! O heart of gold! to die! to die!"

SUNSHINE

IX

She died on Christmas day — it seems so sad
That one you love should die on Christmas day.
Head-bowed I knelt by her; O God! I had
No tears to shed, no moan, no prayer to pray.
I heard her whisper: "Call me, will you, dear?
They say Death parts, but I won't go away.
I will be with you in the cabin here;
Oh I will plead with God to let me stay!
Stay till the Night is gone, till Spring is nigh,
Till sunshine comes . . . be brave . . . I'm
    tired . . . good-bye. . . ."

X

For weeks, for months I have not seen the sun;
The minatory dawns are leprous pale;
The felon days malinger one by one;
How like a dream Life is! how vain! how stale!
I, too, am faint; that vampire-like disease
Has fallen on me; weak and cold am I,
Hugging a tiny fire in fear I freeze:
The cabin must be cold, and so I try
To bear the frost, the frost that fights decay,
The frost that keeps her beautiful alway.

SUNSHINE

XI

She lies within an icy vault;
It glitters like a cave of salt.
All marble-pure and angel-sweet
With candles at her head and feet,
Under an ermine robe she lies.
I kiss her hands, I kiss her eyes:
" Come back, come back, O Love, I pray,
Into this house, this house of clay!
Answer my kisses soft and warm;
Nestle again within my arm.
Come! for I know that you are near:
Open your eyes and look, my dear.
Just for a moment break the mesh;
Back from the spirit leap to flesh.
Weary I wait; the night is black;
Love of my life, come back, come back!"

XII

Last night maybe I was a little mad,
For as I prayed despairful by her side,
Such a strange, antic visioning I had:
Lo! it did seem *her eyes were open wide.*
Surely I must have dreamed! I stared once more. . . .
No, 'twas a candle's trick, a shadow cast.
There were her lashes locking as before.
(Oh, but it filled me with a joy so vast!)
No, 'twas a freak, a fancy of the brain,
(Oh, but to-night I'll try again, again!)

SUNSHINE

XIII

It was no dream; now do I know that Love
Leapt from the starry battlements of Death;
For in my vigil as I bent above,
Calling her name with eager, burning breath,
Sudden there came a change: again I saw
The radiance of the rose-leaf stain her cheek;
Rivers of rapture thrilled in sunny thaw;
Cleft were her coral lips as if to speak;
Curved were her tender arms as if to cling;
Open the flower-like eyes of lucent blue,
Looking at me with love so pitying
That I could fancy Heaven shining through.
 "Sunshine," I faltered, "stay with me, oh, stay!"
Yet ere I finished, in a moment's flight,
There in her angel purity she lay —
Ah! but I know she'll come again to-night.
Even as radiant sword leaps from the sheath,
Soul from the body leaps — we call it Death.

XIV

Even as this line I write,
Do I know that she is near;
Happy am I, every night
Comes she back to bid me cheer;
Kissing her, I hold her fast;
Win her into life at last.

Did I dream that yesterday
On yon mountain ridge a glow
Soft as moonstone paled away,
Leaving less forlorn the snow?
Could it be the sun? Oh, fain
Would I see the sun again!

Oh, to see a coral dawn
Gladden to a crocus glow!
Day's a spectre dim and wan,
Dancing on the furtive snow;
Night's a cloud upon my brain:
Oh, to see the sun again!

You who find us in this place,
Have you pity in your breast;
Let us in our last embrace,
Under earth sun-hallowed rest.
Night's a claw upon my brain:
Oh, to see the sun again!

SUNSHINE

XV

The Sun! at last the Sun! I write these lines.
Here on my knees, with feeble, fumbling hand.
Look! in yon mountain cleft a radiance shines,
Gleam of a primrose — see it thrill, expand,
Grow glorious. Dear God be praised! it streams
Into the cabin in a gush of gold.
Look! there she stands, the angel of my dreams,
All in the radiant shimmer aureoled;
First as I saw her from my bed of pain;
First as I loved her when the darkness passed.
Now do I know that Life is not in vain;
Now do I know God cares, at last, at last!
Light outlives dark, joy grief, and Love's the sum:
Heart of my heart! Sunshine! I come . . . I
come. . . ,

THE IDEALIST

OH you who have daring deeds to tell!
　　And you who have felt Ambition's spell!
Have you heard of the louse who longed to dwell
　In the golden hair of a queen?
He sighed all day and he sighed all night,
　And no one could understand it quite,
For the head of a slut is a louse's delight,
　But he pined for the head of a queen.

So he left his kinsfolk in merry play,
　And off by his lonesome he stole away,
From the home of his youth so bright and gay,
　And gloriously unclean.
And at last he came to the palace gate,
　And he made his way in a manner straight
(For a louse may go where a man must wait)
　To the tiring-room of the queen.

THE IDEALIST

The queen she spake to her tiring-maid:
" There's something the matter, I'm afraid.
To-night ere for sleep my hair ye braid,
    Just see what may be seen."
And lo, when they combed that shining hair
    They found him alone in his glory there,
And he cried: " I die, but I do not care,
    For I've lived in the head of a queen! "

ATHABASKA DICK

WHEN the boys come out from Lac Labiche in the
lure of the early Spring,
To take the pay of the " Hudson's Bay," as their fathers
did before,
They are all a-glee for the jamboree, and they make the
Landing ring
With a whoop and a whirl, and a " Grab your girl," and
a rip and a skip and a roar.
For the spree of Spring is a sacred thing, and the boys
must have their fun;
Packer and tracker and half-breed Cree, from the boat
to the bar they leap;
And then when the long flotilla goes, and the last of
their pay is done,
The boys from the banks of Lac Labiche swing to the
heavy sweep.
And oh, how they sigh! and their throats are dry, and
sorry are they and sick:
Yet there's none so cursed with a lime-kiln thirst as that
Athabaska Dick.

ATHABASKA DICK

He was long and slim and lean of limb, but strong as a
    stripling bear;
And by the right of his skill and might he guided the
    Long Brigade.
All water-wise were his laughing eyes, and he steered
    with a careless care,
And he shunned the shock of foam and rock, till they
    came to the Big Cascade.
And here they must make the long *portãge,* and the
    boys sweat in the sun;
And they heft and pack, and they haul and track, and
    each must do his trick;
But their thoughts are far in the Landing bar, where
    the founts of nectar run:
And no man thinks of such gorgeous drinks as that
    Athabaska Dick.

'Twas the close of day and his long boat lay just over
    the Big Cascade,
When there came to him one Jack-pot Jim, with a wild
    light in his eye;
And he softly laughed, and he led Dick aft, all eager,
    yet half afraid,
And snugly stowed in his coat he showed a pilfered
    flask of " rye."

35

And in haste he slipped, or in fear he tripped, but —
Dick in warning roared —
And there rang a yell, and it befell that Jim was over-
board.

Oh, I heard a splash, and quick as a flash I knew he
could not swim.
I saw him whirl in the river swirl, and thresh his arms
about.
In a queer, strained way I heard Dick say: " I'm going
after him,"
Throw off his coat, leap down the boat — and then I
gave a shout:
" Boys, grab him, quick! You're crazy, Dick! Far better one than two!
" Hell, man! You know you've got no show! It's sure
and certain death. . . ."
And there we hung, and there we clung, with beef and
brawn and thew,
And sinews cracked and joints were racked, and panting
came our breath;
And there we swayed and there we prayed, till strength
and hope were spent —
Then Dick, he threw us off like rats, and after Jim he
went.

36

With mighty urge amid the surge of river-rage he leapt,
And gripped his mate and desperate he fought to gain
  the shore;
With teeth a-gleam he bucked the stream, yet swift and
  sure he swept
To meet the mighty cataract that waited all a-roar.
And there we stood like carven wood, our faces sickly
  white,
And watched him as he beat the foam, and inch by inch
  he lost;
And nearer, nearer drew the fall, and fiercer grew the
  fight,
Till on the very cáscade crest a last farewell he tossed.
Then down and down and down they plunged into that
  pit of dread;
And mad we tore along the shore to claim our bitter
  dead.

And from that hell of frenzied foam, that crashed and
  fumed and boiled,
Two little bodies bubbled up, and they were heedless
  then;
And oh, they lay like senseless clay! and bitter hard we
  toiled,

Yet never, never gleam of hope, and we were weary men.
And moments mounted into hours, and black was our
    despair;
And faint were we, and we were fain to give them up
    as dead,
When suddenly I thrilled with hope: " Back, boys! and
    give him air;
" I feel the flutter of his heart. . . ." And, as the
    word I said,
Dick gave a sigh, and gazed around, and saw our breath-
    less band;
And saw the sky's blue floor above, all strewn with
    golden fleece;
And saw his comrade Jack-pot Jim, and touched him
    with his hand:
And then there came into his eyes a look of perfect
    peace.
And as there, at his very feet, the thwarted river raved,
I heard him murmur low and deep:

        " Thank God! the *whiskey's* saved."

CHEER

IT'S a mighty good world, so it is, dear lass,
  When even the worst is said.
There's a smile and a tear, a sigh and a cheer,
  But better be living than dead;
A joy and a pain, a loss and a gain;
  There's honey and may be some gall:
Yet still I declare, foul weather or fair,
  It's a mighty good world after all.

For look, lass! at night when I break from the fight,
  My Kingdom's awaiting for me;
There's comfort and rest, and the warmth of your breast,
  And little ones climbing my knee.
There's fire-light and song — Oh, the world may be
      wrong!
  Its empires may topple and fall:
My home is my care — if gladness be there,
  It's a mighty good world after all.

CHEER

O heart of pure gold! I have made you a fold,
    It's sheltered, sun-fondled and warm.
O little ones, rest! I have fashioned a nest;
    Sleep on! you are safe from the storm.
For there's no foe like fear, and there's no friend like
      cheer,
    And sunshine will flash at our call;
So crown Love as King, and let us all sing —
    " It's a mighty good world after all."

THE RETURN

THEY turned him loose; he bowed his head.
    A felon, bent and grey.
His face was even as the Dead,
    He had no word to say.

He sought the home of his old love,
    To look on her once more;
And where her roses breathed above,
    He cowered beside the door.

She sat there in the shining room;
    Her hair was silver grey.
He stared and stared from out the gloom;
    He turned to go away.

Her roses rustled overhead.
    She saw, with sudden start.
"I knew that you would come," she said,
    And held him to her heart.

THE RETURN

Her face was rapt and angel-sweet;
    She touched his hair of grey;

, ...   °

But he, sob-shaken, at her feet,
    Could only pray and pray.

THE JUNIOR GOD

THE Junior God looked from his place
    In the conning towers of heaven,
And he saw the world through the span of space
    Like a giant golf-ball driven.
And because he was bored, as some gods are,
    With high celestial mirth,
He clutched the reins of a shooting star,
    And he steered it down to earth.

The Junior God, 'mid leaf and bud,
    Passed on with a weary air,
Till lo! he came to a pool of mud,
    And some hogs were rolling there.
Then in he plunged with gleeful cries,
    And down he lay supine;
For they had no mud in paradise,
    And they likewise had no swine.

The Junior God forgot himself;
    He squelched mud through his toes;
With the careless joy of a wanton boy
    His reckless laughter rose.

THE JUNIOR GOD

Till, tired at last, in a brook close by,
    He washed off every stain;
Then softly up to the radiant sky
    He rose, a god again.

The Junior God now heads the roll
    In the list of heaven's peers;
He sits in the House of High Control,
    And he regulates the spheres.
Yet does he wonder, do you suppose,
    If, even in gods divine,
The best and wisest may not be those
    Who have wallowed awhile with the swine?

THE NOSTOMANIAC

*O*N the ragged edge of the world I'll roam,
   And the home of the wolf shall be my home,
And a bunch of bones on the boundless snows
The end of my trail . . . who knows, who knows!

I'm dreaming to-night in the fire-glow, alone in my study
   tower,
My books battalioned around me, my Kipling flat on my
   knee;
But I'm not in the mood for reading, I haven't moved
   for an hour;
Body and brain I'm weary, weary the heart of me;
Weary of crushing a longing it's little I understand,
For I thought that my trail was ended, I thought I had
   earned my rest;
But oh, it's stronger than life is, the call of the heartless
   land!
And I turn to the North in my trouble, as a child to the
   mother-breast.

THE NOSTOMANIAC

Here in my den it's quiet; the sea-wind taps on the pane;
There's comfort and ease and plenty, the smile of the
South is sweet.
All that a man might long for, fight for and seek in vain,
Pictures and books and music, pleasure my last retreat.
Peace! I thought I had gained it, I swore that my tale
was told;
By my hair that is grey I swore it, by my eyes that are
slow to see;
Yet what does it all avail me? to-night, to-night as of old,
Out of the dark I hear it — the Northland calling to me.

And I'm daring a rampageous river that runs the devil
knows where;
My hand is athrill on the paddle, the birch-bark bounds
like a bird.
Hark to the rumble of rapids! Here in my morris chair
Eager and tense I'm straining — isn't it most absurd?
Now in the churn and the lather, foam that hisses and
stings,
Leap I, keyed for the struggle, fury and fume and roar;
Rocks are spitting like hell-cats — Oh, it's a sport for
kings,
Life on a twist of the paddle . . . there's my
"Kim" on the floor.

46

THE NOSTOMANIAC

How I thrill and I vision! Then my camp of a night;
Red and gold of the fire-glow, net afloat in the stream;
Scent of the pines and silence, little " pal " pipe alight,
Body a-purr with pleasure, sleep untroubled of dream:
Banquet of paystreak bacon! moment of joy divine,
When the bannock is hot and gluey, and the teapot's
    nearing the boil!
Never was wolf so hungry, stomach cleaving to
    spine. . . .
Ha! there's my servant calling, says that dinner will
    spoil.

What do I want with dinner? Can I eat any more?
Can I sleep as I used to? . . . Oh, I abhor this
    life!
Give me the Great Uncertain, the Barren Land for a
    floor,
The Milky Way for a roof-beam, splendour and space
    and strife:
Something to fight and die for — the limpid Lake of
    the Bear,
The Empire of Empty Bellies, the dunes where the Dog-
    ribs dwell;
Big things, real things, live things . . . here or
    my morris chair
How I ache for the Northland! " Dinner and serv-
    ants "— Hell!!

47

Am I too old, I wonder? Can I take one trip more?
Go to the granite-ribbed valleys, flooded with sunset
　　wine,
Peaks that pierce the aurora, rivers I must explore,
Lakes of a thousand islands, millioning hordes of the
　　Pine?
Do they not miss me, I wonder, valley and peak and
　　plain?
Whispering each to the other: "Many a moon has
　　passed . . .
"Where has he gone, our lover? Will he come back
　　again?
"Star with his fires our tundra, leave us his bones at
　　last?"

Yes, I'll go back to the Northland, back to the way of
　　the bear,
Back to the muskeg and mountain, back to the ice-
　　leaguered sea.
Old am I! what does it matter? Nothing I would
　　not dare;
Give me a trail to conquer — Oh, it is "meat" to me!
I will go back to the Northland, feeble and blind and
　　lame;

THE NOSTOMANIAC

Sup with the sunny-eyed Husky, eat moose-nose with the
  Cree;
Play with the Yellow-knife bastards, boasting my blood
  and my name:
I will go back to the Northland, for the Northland is
  calling to me.

Then give to me paddle and whiplash, and give to me
  tumpline and gun;
Give to me salt and tobacco, flour and a gunny of tea;
Take me up over the Circle, under the flamboyant sun;
Turn me foot-loose like a savage — that is the finish
  of me.
I know the trail I am seeking, it's up by the Lake of the
  Bear;
It's down by the Arctic Barrens, it's over to Hudson's
  Bay;
Maybe I'll get there,— maybe: death is set by a
  hair. . . .
Hark! it's the Northland calling! now must I go
  away. . . .

  Go to the Wild that waits for me;
  Go where the moose and the musk-ox be;
  Go to the wolf and the secret snows;
  Go to my fate . . . who knows, who knows!

AMBITION

THEY brought the mighty chief to town;
　　They showed him strange, unwonted sights;
Yet as he wandered up and down,
He seemed to scorn their vain delights.
His face was grim, his eye lacked fire,
As one who mourns a glory dead;
And when they sought his heart's desire:
"Me like'um tooth same gold," he said.

A dental place they quickly found.
He neither moaned nor moved his head.
They pulled his teeth so white and sound;
They put in teeth of gold instead.
Oh, never saw I man so gay!
His very being seemed to swell:
"Ha! ha!" he cried, "Now Injun say
Me heap big chief, *me look like hell.*"

TO SUNNYDALE

THERE lies the trail to Sunnydale,
　　Amid the lure of laughter.
Oh, how can we unhappy be
Beneath its leafy rafter!
Each perfect hour is like a flower,
Each day is like a posy.
How can you say the skies are grey?
You're wrong, my friend, they're rosy.

With right good will let's climb the hill
And leave behind all sorrow.
Oh, we'll be gay! a bright to-day
Will make a bright to-morrow.
Oh, we'll be strong! the way is long
That never has a turning;
The hill is high, but there's the sky,
And how the West is burning!

51

TO SUNNYDALE

And if through chance of circumstance
We have to go bare-foot, sir,
We'll not repine — a friend of mine
Has got no feet to boot, sir.
This Happiness a habit is,
And Life is what we make it:
See! there's the trail to Sunnydale!
Up, friend! and let us take it.

THE BLIND AND THE DEAD

SHE lay like a saint on her copper couch;
　　Like an angel asleep she lay,
In the stare of the ghoulish folks that slouch
　　Past the Dead and sneak away.

Then came old Jules of the sightless gaze,
　　Who begged in the streets for bread.
Each day he had come for a year of days,
　　And groped his way to the Dead.

"What's the Devil's Harvest to-day?" he cried;
　　"A wanton with eyes of blue!
I've known too many a such," he sighed;
　　"Maybe I know this . . . mon Dieu!"

He raised the head of the heedless Dead;
　　He fingered the frozen face. . . .
Then a deathly spell on the watchers fell —
　　God! it was still, that place!

THE BLIND AND THE DEAD

He raised the head of the careless Dead;
  He fumbled a vagrant curl;
And then with his sightless smile he said:
  "It's only my little girl."

"Dear, my dear, did they hurt you so!
  Come to your daddy's heart. . . .
Aye, and he held so tight, you know,
  They were hard to force apart.

No! Paris isn't always gay;
  And the morgue has its stories too:
You are a writer of tales, you say —
  Then there is a tale for you.

THE ATAVIST

WHAT are you doing here, Tom Thorne, on the
  white top-knot o' the world,
Where the wind has the cut of a naked knife and the
  stars are rapier keen?
Hugging a smudgy willow fire, deep in a lynx robe curled,
You that's a lord's own son, Tom Thorne — what does
  your madness mean?

Go home, go home to your clubs, Tom Thorne! home to
  your evening dress!
Home to your place of power and pride, and the feast
  that waits for you!
Why do you linger all alone in the splendid emptiness,
Scouring the Land of the Little Sticks on the trail of
  the caribou?

Why did you fall off the Earth, Tom Thorne, out of
  our social ken?
What did your deep damnation prove? What was your
  dark despair?

THE ATAVIST

Oh with the width of a world between, and years to the
    count of ten,
If they cut out your heart to-night, Tom Thorne, *Her*
    name would be graven there!

And you fled afar for the thing called Peace, and you
    thought you would find it here,
In the purple tundras vastly spread, and the mountains
    whitely piled;
It's a weary quest and a dreary quest, but I think that
    the end is near;
For they say that the Lord has hidden it in the secret
    heart of the Wild.

And you know that heart as few men know, and your
    eyes are fey and deep,
With a " something lost " come welling back from the
    raw, red dawn of life:
With woe and pain have you greatly lain, till out of
    abysmal sleep
The soul of the Stone Age leaps in you, alert for the
    ancient strife.

THE ATAVIST

And if you came to our feast again, with its pomp and
    glee and glow,
I think you would sit stone-still, Tom Thorne, and see
    in a daze of dream,
A mad sun goading to frenzied flame the glittering gems
    of the snow,
And a monster musk-ox bulking black against the blood-
    red gleam.

I think you would see berg-battling shores, and stammer
    and halt and stare,
With a sudden sense of the frozen void, serene and
    vast and still;
And the aching gleam and the hush of dream, and the
    track of a great white bear,
And the primal lust that surged in you as you sprang
    to make your kill.

I think you would hear the bull-moose call, and the
    glutted river roar;
And spy the hosts of the caribou shadow the shining
    plain;
And feel the pulse of the Silences, and stand elate once
    more
On the verge of the yawning vastitudes that call to you
    in vain.

THE ATAVIST

For I think you are one with the stars and the sun, and
  the wind and the wave and the dew;
And the peaks untrod that yearn to God, and the valleys
  undefiled;
Men soar with wings, and they bridle kings, but what
  is it all to you,
Wise in the ways of the wilderness, and strong with the
  strength of the Wild?

You have spent your life, you have waged your strife
  where never we play a part;
You have held the throne of the Great Unknown, you
  have ruled a kingdom vast:

   .   .   .   .

*But to-night there's a strange, new trail for you, and you
  go, O weary heart!*
To the peace and rest of the Great Unguessed . . .
  at last, Tom Thorne, at last.

THE SCEPTIC

MY Father Christmas passed away
When I was barely seven.
At twenty-one, alack-a-day,
I lost my hope of heaven.

Yet not in either lies the curse:
The hell of it's because
I don't know which loss hurt the worse —
My God or Santa Claus.

THE ROVER

I

OH, how good it is to be
    Foot-loose and heart-free!
Just my dog and pipe and I, underneath the vast sky;
Trail to try and goal to win, white road and cool inn;
Fields to lure a lad afar, clear spring and still star;
Lilting feet that never tire, green dingle, fagot fire;
None to hurry, none to hold, heather hill and hushed fold;
Nature like a picture book, laughing leaf and bright
    brook;
Every day a jewel bright, set serenely in the night;
Every night a holy shrine, radiant for a day divine.

Weathered cheek and kindly eye, let the wanderer go by.
Woman-love and wistful heart, let the gipsy one depart.
For the farness and the road are his glory and his goad.
Oh, the lilt of youth and Spring! Eyes laugh and lips
    sing.
                    Yea, but it is good to be
                    Foot-loose and heart-free!

THE ROVER

II

Yet how good it is to come
Home at last, home, home!
On the clover swings the bee, overhead's the hale tree
Sky of turquoise gleams through, yonder glints the lake's
    blue.
In a hammock let's swing, weary of wandering;
Tired of wild, uncertain lands, strange faces, faint hands

Has the wondrous world gone cold? Am I growing
    old, old?
Grey and weary . . . let me dream, glide on the
    tranquil stream.
Oh, what joyous days I've had, full, fervid, gay, glad!
Yet there comes a subtile change, let the stripling rove,
    range.
From sweet roving comes sweet rest, after all, home's
    best.
And if there's a little bit of woman-love with it,
I will count my life content, God-blest and well
    spent. . . .

        Oh but it is good to be
        Foot-loose and heart-free!
        Yet how good it is to come
        Home at last, home, home!

BARB-WIRE BILL

A T dawn of day the white land lay all gruesome-
like and grim,
When Bill Mc'Gee he says to me: "We've *got* to do it,
Jim.
"We've got to make Fort Liard quick. I know the
river's bad,
"But, oh! the little woman's sick . . . why! don't
you savvy, lad?"
And me! Well, yes, I must confess it wasn't hard to
see
Their little family group of two would soon be one of
three.
And so I answered, careless-like: "Why, Bill! you don't
suppose
"I'm scared of that there 'babbling brook'? Whatever
you say — goes."

A real live man was Barb-wire Bill, with insides copper-
lined;
For "barb-wire" was the brand of "hooch" to which
he most inclined.
They knew him far; his igloos are on Kittiegazuit strand.

62

BARB-WIRE BILL

They knew him well, the tribes who dwell within the
    Barren Land.
From Koyokuk to Kuskoquim his fame was everywhere;
And he did love, all life above, that little Julie Claire,
The lithe, white slave-girl he had bought for seven hun-
    dred skins,
And taken to his wickiup to make his moccasins.

We crawled down to the river bank and feeble folk
    were we,
That Julie Claire from God-knows-where, and Barb-wire
    Bill and me.
From shore to shore we heard the roar the heaving ice-
    floes make,
And loud we laughed, and launched our raft, and fol-
    lowed in their wake.
The river swept and seethed and leapt, and caught us
    in its stride;
And on we hurled amid a world that crashed on every
    side.
With sullen din the banks caved in; the shore-ice lanced
    the stream;
The naked floes like spooks arose, all jiggling and agleam.
Black anchor-ice of strange device shot upward from its
    bed,
As night and day we cleft our way, and arrow-like we
    sped.

But " Faster still! " cried Barb-wire Bill, and looked the
    live-long day

In dull despair at Julie Claire, as white like death she
    lay.

And sometimes he would seem to pray and sometimes
    seem to curse,

And bent above, with eyes of love, yet ever she grew
    worse.

And as we plunged and leapt and lunged, her face was
    plucked with pain,

And I could feel his nerves of steel a-quiver at the strain.

And in the night he gripped me tight as I lay fast asleep:

" The river's kicking like a steer . . . run out the
    forward sweep!

" That's Hell-gate Canyon right ahead; I know of old
    its roar,

" And . . . I'll be damned! *the ice is jammed!*
    We've *got* to make the shore."

With one wild leap I gripped the sweep. The night was
    black as sin.

The float-ice crashed and ripped and smashed, and stunned
    us with its din.

And near and near, and clear and clear I heard the can-
    yon boom;

And swift and strong we swept along to meet our awful
    doom.
And as with dread I glimpsed ahead the death that waited
    there,
My only thought was of the girl, the little Julie Claire;
And so, like demon mad with fear, I panted at the oar,
And foot by foot, and inch by inch, we worked the raft
    ashore.

The bank was staked with grinding ice, and as we scraped
    and crashed,
I only knew one thing to do, and through my mind it
    flashed:
Yet while I groped to find the rope, I heard Bill's savage
    cry:
"That's my job, lad! It's me that jumps. I'll snub
    this raft or die!"
I saw him leap, I saw him creep, I saw him gain the
    land;
I saw him crawl, I saw him fall, then run with rope in
    hand.
And then the darkness gulped him up, and down we
    dashed once more,
And nearer, nearer drew the jam, and thunder-like its
    roar.

Oh God! all's lost . . . from Julie Claire there
    came a wail of pain,
And then — the rope grew sudden taut, and quivered at
    the strain;
It slacked and slipped, it whined and gripped, and oh, I
    held my breath!
And there we hung and there we swung right in the
    jaws of death.

A little strand of hempen rope, and how I watched it
    there,
With all around a hell of sound, and darkness and despair;
A little strand of hempen rope, I watched it all alone,
And somewhere in the dark behind I heard a woman
    moan;
And somewhere in the dark ahead I heard a man cry out,
Then silence, silence, silence fell, and mocked my hollow
    shout.
And yet once more from out the shore I heard that cry
    of pain,
A moan of mortal agony, then all was still again.

That night was hell with all the frills, and when the
    dawn broke dim,
I saw a lean and level land, but never sign of him.
I saw a flat and frozen shore of hideous device,

I saw a long-drawn strand of rope that vanished through
    the ice.
And on that treeless, rockless shore I found my partner
    — dead.
No place was there to snub the raft, so — *he had served
    instead;*
And with the rope lashed round his waist, in last de-
    fiant fight,
He'd thrown himself beneath the ice, that closed and
    gripped him tight;
And there he'd held us back from death, as fast in death
    he lay. . . .
Say, boys! I'm not the pious brand, but — I just tried
    to pray.
And then I looked to Julie Claire, and sore abashed was I,
For from the robes that covered her, *I — heard — a —
    baby — cry.* . . .

Thus was Love conqueror of death, and life for life was
    given;
And though no saint on earth, d'ye think — Bill's squared
    hisself with Heaven?

IF you had the choice of two women to wed,
 (Though of course the idea is quite absurd)
And the first from her heels to her dainty head
Was charming in every sense of the word:
And yet in the past (I grieve to state),
She never had been exactly " straight."

And the second — she was beyond all cavil,
A model of virtue, I must confess;
And yet, alas! she was dull as the devil,
And rather a dowd in the way of dress;
Though what she was lacking in wit and beauty,
She more than made up for in " sense of duty."

Now, suppose you must wed, and make no blunder,
And either would love you, and let you win her —
Which of the two would you choose, I wonder,
The stolid saint or the sparkling sinner?

JUST THINK!

JUST think! some night the stars will gleam
 Upon a cold, grey stone,
And trace a name with silver beam,
 And lo! 'twill be your own.

That night is speeding on to greet
 Your epitaphic rhyme.
Your life is but a little beat
 Within the heart of Time.

A little gain, a little pain,
 A laugh, lest you may moan;
A little blame, a little fame,
 A star-gleam on a stone.

THE LUNGER

JACK would laugh an' joke all day;
   Never saw a lad so gay;
Singin' like a medder lark,
Loaded to the Plimsoll mark
With God's sunshine was that boy;
Had a strangle-holt on Joy.
Held his head 'way up in air,
Left no callin' cards on Care;
Breezy, buoyant, brave and true;
Sent his sunshine out to you;
Cheerfulest when clouds was black —
     Happy Jack! Oh, Happy Jack!

Sittin' in my shack alone
I could hear him in his own,
Singin' far into the night,
Till it didn't seem just right
One man should corral the fun,
Live his life so in the sun;
Didn't seem quite natural
Not to have a grouch at all;
Not a trouble, not a lack —
     Happy Jack! Oh, Happy Jack!

THE LUNGER

He was plumbful of good cheer
Till he struck that low-down year;
Got so thin, so little to him,
You could most see day-light through him.
Never was his eye so bright,
Never was his cheek so white.
Seemed as if somethin' was wrong,
Sort o' quaver in his song.
Same old smile, same hearty voice:
" Bless you, boys! let's all rejoice! "
But old Doctor shook his head:
" Half a lung," was all he said.
Yet that half was surely right,
For I heard him every night,
Singin', singin' in his shack —
      Happy Jack! Oh, Happy Jack!

Then one day a letter came
Endin' with a female name;
Seemed to get him in the neck,
Sort o' pile-driver effect;
Paled his lip and plucked his breath,
Left him starin' still as death.
Somethin' had gone awful wrong,
Yet that night he sang his song.
Oh, but it was good to hear!

THE LUNGER

For there clutched my heart a fear,
So that I quaked listenin'
Every night to hear him sing.
But each day he laughed with me,
An' his smile was full of glee.
Nothin' seemed to set him back —
    Happy Jack! Oh, Happy Jack!

Then one night the singin' stopped . . .
Seemed as if my heart just flopped;
For I'd learned to love the boy
With his gilt-edged line of joy,
With his glorious gift of bluff,
With his splendid fightin' stuff.
Sing on, lad, and play the game!
O dear God! . . . no singin' came,
But there surged to me instead —
Silence, silence, deep and dread;
Till I shuddered, tried to pray,
Said: " He's maybe gone away."

Oh, yes, he had gone away,
Gone forever and a day.
But he'd left behind him there,
In his cabin, pinched and bare,
His poor body, skin and bone,

THE LUNGER

His sharp face, cold as a stone.
An' his stiffened fingers pressed
Somethin' bright upon his breast:
Locket with a silken curl,
Poor, sweet portrait of a girl.
Yet I reckon at the last
How defiant-like he passed;
For there sat upon his lips
Smile that death could not eclipse;
An' within his eyes lived still
Joy that dyin' could not kill.

An' now when the nights are long,
How I miss his cheery song!
How I sigh an' wish him back!
    Happy Jack! Oh, Happy Jack!

THE MOUNTAIN AND THE LAKE

I KNOW a mountain thrilling to the stars,
  Peerless and pure, and pinnacled with snow;
Glimpsing the golden dawn o'er coral bars,
Flaunting the vanisht sunset's garnet glow;
Proudly patrician, passionless, serene;
Soaring in silvered steeps where cloud-surfs break;
Virgin and vestal — Oh, a very Queen!
And at her feet there dreams a quiet lake.

My lake adores my mountain — well I know,
For I have watched it from its dawn-dream start,
Stilling its mirror to her splendid snow,
Framing her image in its trembling heart;
Glassing her graciousness of greening wood,
Kissing her throne, melodiously mad,
Thrilling responsive to her every mood,
Gloomed with her sadness, gay when she is glad.

THE MOUNTAIN AND THE LAKE

My lake has dreamed and loved since time was born;
Will love and dream till time shall cease to be;
Gazing to Her in worship half forlorn,
Who looks towards the stars and will not see —
My peerless mountain, splendid in her scorn. . . .
Alas! poor little lake! Alas! poor me!

THE HEADLINER AND THE BREADLINER

MOKO, the Educated Ape is here,
  The pet of vaudeville, so the posters say,
And every night the gaping people pay
To see him in his panoply appear;
To see him pad his paunch with dainty cheer,
  Puff his perfecto, swill champagne, and sway
  Just like a gentleman, yet all in play,
Then bow himself off stage with brutish leer.

And as to-night, with noble knowledge crammed,
  I 'mid this human compost take my place,
I, once a poet, now so dead and damned,
  The woeful tears half freezing on my face:
"O God!" I cry, "let me but take his shape,
  Moko's, the Blest, the Educated Ape."

DEATH IN THE ARCTIC

I

I TOOK the clock down from the shelf;
  "At eight," said I, " I shoot myself."
It lacked a *minute* of the hour,
And as I waited all a-cower,
A skinful of black, boding pain,
Bits of my life came back again. . . .

" Mother, there's nothing more to eat —
Why don't you go out on the street?
Always you sit and cry and cry;
Here at my play I wonder why.
Mother, when you dress up at night,
Red are your cheeks, your eyes are bright;
Twining a ribband in your hair,
Kissing good-bye you go down-stair.
Then I'm as lonely as can be.
Oh, how I wish you were with me!
Yet when you go out on the street,
Mother, there's always lots to eat. . .

II

For days the igloo has been dark;
But now the rag wick sends a spark
That glitters in the icy air,
And wakes frost sapphires everywhere;
Bright, bitter flames, that adder-like
Dart here and there, yet fear to strike
The gruesome gloom wherein *they* lie,
My comrades, oh, so keen to die!
And I, the last — well, here I wait
The clock to strike the hour of eight. . . .

" *Boy, it is bitter to be hurled*
Nameless and naked on the world;
Frozen by night and starved by day,
Curses and kicks and clouts your pay.
But you must fight! Boy, look on me!
Anarch of all earth-misery;
Beggar and tramp and shameless sot;
Emblem of ill, in rags that rot.
Would you be foul and base as I?
Oh, it is better far to die!
Swear to me now you'll fight and fight,
Boy, or I'll kill you here to-night. . . ."

DEATH IN THE ARCTIC

III

Curse this silence soft and black!
Sting, little light, the shadows back!
Dance, little flame, with freakish glee!
Twinkle with brilliant mockery!
Glitter on ice-robed roof and floor!
Jewel the bear-skin of the door!
Gleam in my beard, illume my breath,
Blanch the clock face that times my death!
But do not pierce that murk so deep,
Where in their sleeping-bags they sleep!
But do not linger where they lie,
They whc had all the luck to die! . . .

" *There is nothing more to say;*
Let us part and go our way.
Since it seems we can't agree,
I will go across the sea.
Proud of heart and strong am I;
Not for woman will I sigh;
Hold my head up gay and glad:
You can find another lad. . . .*

IV

Above the igloo piteous flies
Our frayed flag to the frozen skies.
Oh, would you know how earth can be
A hell — go north of Eighty-three!
Go, scan the snows day after day,
And hope for help, and pray and pray;
Have seal-hide and sea-lice to eat;
Melt water with your body's heat;
Sleep all the fell, black winter through
Beside the dear, dead men you knew.
(The walrus blubber flares and gleams —
O God! how long a minute seems!) . .

Mary, many a day has passed,
Since that morn of hot-head youth.
Come I back at last, at last,
Crushed with knowing of the truth;
How through bitter, barren years
You loved me, and me alone;
Waited, wearied, wept your tears —
Oh, could I atone, atone,
I would pay a million-fold!
Pay you for the love you gave.
Mary, look down as of old —
I am kneeling by your grave." . .

DEATH IN THE ARCTIC

V

Olaf, the Blonde, was first to go;
Bitten his eyes were by the snow;
Sightless and sealed his eyes of blue,
So that he died before I knew.
Here in those poor weak arms he died:
"Wolves will not get you, lad," I lied;
"For I will watch till Spring come round;
Slumber you shall beneath the ground."
Oh, how I lied! I scarce can wait:
Strike, little clock, the hour of eight! . . .

"Comrade, can you blame me quite?
The horror of the long, long night
Is on me, and I've borne with pain
So long, and hoped for help in vain.
So frail am I, and blind and dazed;
With scurvy sick, with silence crazed.
Beneath the Arctic's heel of hate,
Avid for Death I wait, I wait.
Oh if I falter, fail to fight,
Can you, dear comrade, blame me quite?" . . .

VI

Big Eric gave up months ago.
But seldom do men suffer so.
His feet sloughed off, his fingers died,
His hands shrunk up and mummified.
I had to feed him like a child;
Yet he was valiant, joked and smiled,
Talked of his wife and little one
(Thanks be to God that I have none),
Passed in the night without a moan,
Passed, and I'm here, alone, alone. . .

"I've got to kill you, Dick.
Your life for mine, you know.
Better to do it quick,
A swift and sudden blow.
See! here's my hand to lick;
A hug before you go —
God! but it makes me sick:
Old dog, I love you so.
Forgive, forgive me, Dick —
A swift and sudden blow. . . .

DEATH IN THE ARCTIC

VII

Often I start up in the dark,
Thinking the sound of bells to hear.
Often I wake from sleep: " Oh, hark!
Help . . . it is coming . . . near and
    near."
Blindly I reel toward the door;
There the snow billows bleak and bare;
Blindly I seek my den once more,
Silence and darkness and despair.
Oh, it is all a dreadful dream!
Scurvy and cold and death and dearth;
I will awake to warmth and gleam,
Silvery seas and greening earth.
Life is a dream, its wakening,
Death, gentle shadow of God's wing.   .   .   .

" *Tick, little clock, my life away!*
Even a second seems a day.
Even a minute seems a year,
Peopled with ghosts, that press and peer
Into my face so charnel white,
Lit by the devilish, dancing light.
Tick, little clock! mete out my fate:
Tortured and tense I wait, I wait.   .   .   ."

VIII

Oh, I have sworn! the hour is nigh:
When it strikes eight, I die, I die.
Raise up the gun — it stings my brow —
When it strikes eight . . . all ready . . .
    now —

         *   *   *   *

Down from my hand the weapon dropped;
Wildly I stared. . . .
        THE CLOCK HAD STOPPED.

DEATH IN THE ARCTIC

IX

Phantoms and fears and ghosts have gone.
Peace seems to nestle in my brain.
Lo! the clock stopped, I'm living on;
Heart-sick I was, and less than sane.
Yet do I scorn the thing I planned,
Hearing a voice: " O coward, fight! "
Then the clock stopped . . . whose was the
    hand?
Maybe 'twas God's — ah well, all's right.
Heap on me darkness, fold on fold!
Pain! wrench and rack me! What care I?
Leap on me, hunger, thirst and cold!
I will await my time to die;
Looking to Heaven that shines above;
Looking to God, and love . . . and love.

X

Hark! what is that? Bells, dogs again!
Is it a dream? I sob and cry.
See! the door opens, fur-clad men
Rush to my rescue; frail am I;
Feeble and dying, dazed and glad.
There is the pistol where it dropped.
" Boys, it was hard — but I'm not mad. . . .
Look at the clock — it stopped, it stopped.
Carry me out. The heavens smile.
See! there's an arch of gold above.
Now, let me rest a little while —
Looking to God and love . . . and love. . . .

DREAMS ARE BEST

I JUST think that dreams are best,
     Just to sit and fancy things;
   Give your gold no acid test,
Try not how your silver rings;
Fancy women pure and good,
     Fancy men upright and true:
     Fortressed in your solitude,
Let Life be a dream to you.

For I think that Thought is all;
     Truth's a minion of the mind;
     Love's ideal comes at call;
As ye seek so shall ye find.
But ye must not seek too far;
     Things are never what they seem:
     Let a star be just a star,
And a woman — just a dream.

O you Dreamers, proud and pure,
     You have gleaned the sweet of life!
     Golden truths that shall endure
Over pain and doubt and strife.

DREAMS ARE BEST

I would rather be a fool
    Living in my Paradise,
    Than the leader of a school,
Sadly sane and weary wise.

O you Cynics with your sneers,
    Fallen brains and hearts of brass,
    Tweak me by my foolish ears,
Write me down a simple ass!
I'll believe the real " you "
    Is the " you " without a taint;
    I'll believe each woman too,
But a slightly damaged saint.

Yes, I'll smoke my cigarette,
    Vestured in my garb of dreams,
    And I'll borrow no regret;
All is gold that golden gleams.
So I'll charm my solitude
    With the faith that Life is blest,
    Brave and noble, bright and good,
Oh, I think that dreams are best!

THE QUITTER

WHEN you're lost in the Wild, and you're scared
 as a child,
And Death looks you bang in the eye,
And you're sore as a boil, it's according to Hoyle
 To cock your revolver and . . . die.
But the Code of a Man says: "Fight all you can,"
 And self-dissolution is barred.
In hunger and woe, oh, it's easy to blow . . .
 It's the hell-served-for-breakfast that's hard.

"You're sick of the game!" Well, now, that's a shame.
 You're young and you're brave and you're bright.
"You've had a raw deal!" I know — but don't squeal,
 Buck up, do your damnedest, and fight.
It's the plugging away that will win you the day,
 So don't be a piker, old pard!
Just draw on your grit; it's so easy to quit:
 It's the keeping-your-chin-up that's hard.

It's easy to cry that you're beaten — and die;
 It's easy to crawfish and crawl;
But to fight and to fight when hope's out of sight —
 Why, that's the best game of them all!

THE QUITTER

And though you come out of each gruelling bout,
    All broken and beaten and scarred,
Just have one more try — it's dead easy to die,
    It's the keeping-on-living that's hard.

THE COW JUICE CURE

THE clover was in blossom, an' the year was at the
    June,
When Flap-jack Billy hit the town, likewise O'Flynn's
    saloon.
The frost was on the fodder an' the wind was growin'
    keen,
When Billy got to seein' snakes in Sullivan's shebeen.

Then in meandered Deep-hole Dan, once comrade of the
    cup:
" Oh Billy, for the love of Mike, why don't ye sober up?
I've got the gorgus recipay, 'tis smooth an' slick as silk —
Jest quit yer strangle-holt on hooch, an' irrigate with
    milk.
Lackteeal flooid is the lubrication you require;
Yer nervus frame-up's like a bunch of snarled pianc wire.
You want to get it coated up with addypose tishoo,
So's it will work elastic-like, an' milk's the dope for you."

Well, Billy was complyable, an' in a month it's strange,
That cow-juice seemed to oppyrate a most amazin' change.

"Call up the water-wagon, Dan, an' book my seat,"
    sez he.
" 'Tis mighty queer," sez Deep-hole Dan, " 'twas just the
    same with me."
They shanghaied little Tim O'Shane, they cached him
    safe away,
An' though he objurgated some, they " cured " him night
    an' day;
An' pretty soon there came the change amazin' to explain:
" I'll never take another drink," sez Timothy O'Shane.
They tried it out on Spike Muldoon, that toper of renown;
They put it over Grouch McGraw, the terror of the
    town.
They roped in " tanks " from far and near, an' every test
    was sure,
An' like a flame there ran the fame of Deep-hole's Cow-
    juice Cure.

" It's mighty queer," sez Deep-hole Dan, " I'm puzzled
    through and through;
It's only milk from Riley's ranch, no other milk will do."
An' it jest happened on that night with no predictive plan,
He left some milk from Riley's ranch a-settin' in a pan;
An' picture his amazement when he poured that milk
    next day —
There in the bottom of the pan a dozen " colours " lay.

" Well, what d'ye know 'bout that," sez Dan; " Gosh ding
    my dasted eyes,
We've been an' had the Gold Cure, Bill, an' none of us
    was wise.
The milk's free-millin' that's a cinch; there's colours
    everywhere.
Now, let us figger this thing out — how does the dust
    git there?
' Gold from the grass-roots down,' they say — why, Bill!
    we've got it cold —
Them cows what nibbles up the grass, jest nibbles up the
    gold.
We're blasted, bloomin' millionaires; dissemble an' lie
    low:
We'll follow them gold-bearin' cows, an' prospect where
    they go."

An' so it came to pass, fer weeks them miners might be
    found
A-sneakin' round on Riley's ranch, an' snipin' at the
    ground;
Till even Riley stops an' stares, an' presently allows:
" Them boys appear to take a mighty interest in cows."
An' night an' day they shadowed each auriferous bovine,
An' panned the grass-roots on their trail, yet nivver gold
    they seen.

THE COW JUICE CURE

An' all that season, secret-like, they worked an' nothin'
    found;

An' there was colours in the milk, but none was in the
    ground.

An' mighty desperate was they, an' down upon their luck,

When sudden, inspirationlike, the source of it they struck.

An' where d'ye think they traced it too? it grieves my
    heart to tell —

In the black sand at the bottom of that wicked milkman's
    well.

WHILE THE BANNOCK BAKES

LIGHT up your pipe again, old chum, and sit awhile
    with me;
I've got to watch the bannock bake — how restful is the
    air!
You'd little think that we were somewhere north of
    Sixty-three,
Though where I don't exactly know, and don't precisely
    care.
The man-size mountains palisade us round on every side;
The river is a-flop with fish, and ripples silver-clear;
The midnight sunshine brims yon cleft — we think it's
    the Divide;
We'll get there in a month, maybe, or maybe in a year.

It doesn't matter, does it, pal? We're of that breed of
    men
With whom the world of wine and cards and women dis-
    agree;
Your trouble was a roofless game of poker now and then,
And "raising up my elbow." that's what got away
    with me.

WHILE THE BANNOCK BAKES

We're merely " Undesirables," artistic more or less;
My horny hands are Chopin-wise; you quote your Browning well;
And yet we're fooling round for gold in this damned wilderness:
The joke is, if we found it, we would both go straight to hell.

Well, maybe we won't find it — and at least we've got the " life."
We're both as brown as berries, and could wrestle with a bear:
(That bannock's raising nicely, pal; just jab it with your knife.)
Fine specimens of manhood they would reckon us out there.
It's the tracking and the packing and the poling in the sun;
It's the sleeping in the open, it's the rugged, unfaked food;
It's the snow-shoe and the paddle, and the campfire and the gun,
And when I think of what I was, I know that it is good.

WHILE THE BANNOCK BAKES

Just think of how we've poled all day up this strange
    little stream;
Since life began no eye of man has seen this place before;
How fearless all the wild things are! the banks with
    goose-grass gleam,
And there's a bronzy musk-rat sitting sniffing at his door.
A mother duck with brood of ten comes squattering along;
The tawny, white-winged ptarmigan are flying all about;
And in that swirly, golden pool, a restless, gleaming
    throng,
The trout are waiting till we condescend to take them out.

Ah, yes, it's good! I'll bet that there's no doctor like
    the Wild:
(Just turn that bannock over there; it's getting nicely
    brown.)
I might be in my grave by now, forgotten and reviled,
Or rotting like a sickly cur in some far, foreign town.
I might be that vile thing I was,— it all seems like a
    dream;
I owed a man a grudge one time that only life could pay;
And yet it's half-forgotten now — how petty these things
    seem!
(But that's "another story," pal; I'll tell it you some
    day.)

How strange two "irresponsibles" should chum away
    up here!
But round the Arctic Circle friends are few and far
    between.
We've shared the same camp-fire and tent for nigh on
    seven year,
And never had a word that wasn't cheering and serene.
We've halved the toil and split the spoil, and borne each
    other's packs;
By all the Wild's freemasonry we're brothers, tried and
    true;
We've swept on danger side by side, and fought it back
    to back,
And you would die for me, old pal, and I would die
    for you.

Now there was that time I got lost in Rory Bory Land,
(How quick the blizzards sweep on one across that
    Polar sea!)
You formed a rescue crew of One, and saw a frozen hand
That stuck out of a drift of snow — and, partner, it
    was Me.
But I got even, did I not, that day the paddle broke?
White water on the Coppermine — a rock — a split
    canoe —
Two fellows struggling in the foam (one couldn't swim
    a stroke):

98

WHILE THE BANNOCK BAKES

A half-drowned man I dragged ashore . . . and
partner, it was You.

*   *   *   *   *

In Rory Borealis Land the winter's long and black.
The silence seems a solid thing, shot through with wolfish
woe;
And rowelled by the eager stars the skies vault vastly
back,
And man seems but a little mite on that weird-lit plateau.
No thing to do but smoke and yarn of wild and mis-
spent lives,
Beside the camp-fire there we sat — what tales you told
to me
Of love and hate, and chance and fate, and temporary
wives!
In Rory Borealis Land, beside the Arctic Sea.

One yarn you told me in those days I can remember still;
It seemed as if I visioned it, so sharp you sketched it in;
Bellona was the name, I think; a coast town in Brazil,
Where nobody did anything but serenade and sin.
I saw it all — the jewelled sea, the golden scythe of sand,
The stately pillars of the palms, the feathery bamboo,
The red-roofed houses and the swart, sun-dominated land,
The people ever children, and the heavens ever blue.

WHILE THE BANNOCK BAKES

You told me of that girl of yours, that blossom of old
    Spain,
All glamour, grace and witchery, all passion, verve and
    glow.
How maddening she must have been! You made me see
    her plain,
There by our little camp-fire, in the silence and the snow.
You loved her and she loved you. She'd a husband, too,
    I think,
A doctor chap, you told me, whom she treated like a dog,
A white man living on the beach, a hopeless slave to
    drink —
(Just turn that bannock over there, that's propped
    against the log.)

That story seemed to strike me, pal — it happens every
    day:
You had to go away awhile, then somehow it befell
The doctor chap discovered, gave her up, and disappeared;
You came back, tired of her in time . . . there's
    nothing more to tell.
Hist! see those willows silvering where swamp and river
    meet!
Just reach me up my rifle quick; that's Mister Moose, I
    know —

WHILE THE BANNOCK BAKES

There now, *I've got him dead to rights* . . . but
    hell! we've lots to eat
I don't believe in taking life — we'll let the beggar go.

Heigh ho! I'm tired; the bannock's cooked; it's time we
    both turned in.
The morning mist is coral-kissed, the morning sky is gold.
The camp-fire's a confessional — what funny yarns we
    spin!
It sort of made me think a bit, that story that you told.
The fig-leaf belt and Rory Bory are such odd extremes,
Yet after all how very small this old world seems to
    be . . .
Yes, that was quite a yarn, old pal, and yet to me it
    seems
You missed the point: the point is that the " doctor chap "
    . . . was ME. . . .

THE LOST MASTER

"AND when I come to die," he said,
 "Ye shall not lay me out in state,
Nor leave your laurels at my head,
Nor cause your men of speech orate;
No monument your gift shall be,
No column in the Hall of Fame;
But just this line ye grave for me:
 "He played the game."

So when his glorious task was done,
It was not of his fame we thought;
It was not of his battles won,
But of the pride with which he fought;
But of his zest, his ringing laugh,
His trenchant scorn of praise or blame:
And so we graved his epitaph,
 "He played the game."

And so we, too, in humbler ways
Went forth to fight the fight anew,
And heeding neither blame nor praise,
We held the course he set us true.
And we, too, find the fighting sweet;

THE LOST MASTER

And we, too, fight for fighting's sake;
And though we go down in defeat,
And though our stormy hearts may break,
We will not do our Master shame:
We'll play the game, please God,
     We'll play the game.

LITTLE MOCCASINS

COME out, O Little Moccasins, and frolic on the
    snow!
Come out, O tiny beaded feet, and twinkle in the light!
I'll play the old Red River reel, you used to love it so:
Awake, O Little Moccasins, and dance for me to-night!

Your hair was all a gleamy gold, your eyes a corn-flower
    blue;
Your cheeks were pink as tinted shells, you stepped light
    as a fawn;
Your mouth was like a coral bud, with seed pearls peep-
    ing through;
As gladdening as Spring you were, as radiant as dawn.

Come out, O Little Moccasins! I'll play so soft and
    low,
The songs you loved, the old heart-songs that in my
    mem'ry ring;

LITTLE MOCCASINS

O child, I want to hear you now beside the campfire
glow!
With all your heart a-throbbing in the simple words
you sing.

For there was only you and I, and you were all to me;
And round us were the barren lands, but little did we
fear;
Of all God's happy, happy folks the happiest were
we. . . .
(Oh, call her, poor old fiddle mine, and maybe she will
hear!)

Your mother was a half-breed Cree, but you were white
all through;
And I, your father was — but well, that's neither here
nor there;
I only know, my little Queen, that all my world was you,
And now that world can end to-night, and I will never
care.

For there's a tiny wooden cross that pricks up through
the snow:
(Poor little Moccasins! you're tired, and so you lie at
rest.)

And there's a grey-haired, weary man beside the camp-
  fire glow:
(O fiddle mine! the tears to-night are drumming on
  your breast.)

THE WANDERLUST

THE Wanderlust has lured me to the seven lonely
    seas,
Has dumped me on the tailing-piles of dearth;
The Wanderlust has haled me from the morris chairs
    of ease,
Has hurled me to the ends of all the earth.
How bitterly I've cursed it, oh, the Painted Desert
    knows,
The wraithlike heights that hug the pallid plain,
The all-but-fluid silence,— yet the longing grows and
    grows,
And I've got to glut the Wanderlust again.

    Soldier, sailor, in what a plight I've been!
    Tinker, tailor, oh what a sight I've seen!
    And I'm hitting the trail in the morning, boys,
    And you won't see my heels for dust;
    For it's " all day " with you
    When you answer the cue
        Of the Wan-der-lust.

The Wanderlust has got me . . . by the belly-ach-
    ing fire,
By the fever and the freezing and the pain;
By the darkness that just drowns you, by the wail of
    home desire,
I've tried to break the spell of it — in vain.
Life might have been a feast for me, now there are only
    crumbs;
In rags and tatters, beggar-wise I sit;
Yet there's no rest or peace for me, imperious it drums,
The Wanderlust, and I must follow it.

    Highway, by-way, many a mile I've done;
    Rare way, fair way, many a height I've won;
    But I'm pulling my freight in the morning, boys,
    And it's over the hills or bust;
    For there's never a cure
    When you list to the lure
        Of the Wan-der-lust.

The Wanderlust has taught me . . . it has whis-
    pered to my heart
Things all you stay-at-homes will never know.
The white man and the savage are but three short days
    apart,

THE WANDERLUST

Three days of cursing, crawling, doubt and woe.
Then it's down to chewing muclucs, to the water you
    can *eat,*
To fish you bolt with nose held in your hand.
When you get right down to cases, it's King's Grub that
    rules the races,
And the Wanderlust will help you understand.

    Haunting, taunting, that is the spell of it;
    Mocking, baulking, that is the hell of it;
    But I'll shoulder my pack in the morning, boys,
    And I'm going because I must;
    For it's so-long to all
    When you answer the call
          Of the Wan-der-lust.

The Wanderlust has blest me . . . in a ragged
    blanket curled,
I've watched the gulf of Heaven foam with stars;
I've walked with eyes wide open to the wonder of the
    world,
I've seen God's flood of glory burst its bars.
I've seen the gold a-blinding in the riffles of the sky,
Till I fancied me a bloated plutocrat;

But I'm freedom's happy bond-slave, and I will be till
    I die,
And I've got to thank the Wanderlust for that.

    Wild heart, child heart, all of the world your home.
    Glad heart, mad heart, what can you do but roam?
    Oh, I'll beat it once more in the morning, boys,
    With a pinch of tea and a crust;
    For you cannot deny
    When you hark to the cry
        Of the Wan-der-lust.

The Wanderlust will claim me at the finish for its own.
I'll turn my back on men and face the Pole.
Beyond the Arctic outposts I will venture all alone;
Some Never-never Land will be my goal.
Thank God! there's none will miss me, for I've been a
    bird of flight;
And in my moccasins I'll take my call;
For the Wanderlust has ruled me,
And the Wanderlust has schooled me,
And I'm ready for the darkest trail of all.

THE WANDERLUST

Grim land, dim land, oh, how the vastness calls!
Far land, star land, oh, how the stillness falls!
For you never can tell if it's heaven or hell,
And I'm taking the trail on trust;
But I haven't a doubt
That my soul will leap out
　　　On its Wan-der-lust.

THE TRAPPER'S CHRISTMAS EVE

IT'S mighty lonesome-like and drear.
    Above the Wild the moon rides high,
And shows up sharp and needle-clear
The emptiness of earth and sky;
No happy homes with love a-glow;
No Santa Claus to make believe:
Just snow and snow, and then more snow;
It's Christmas Eve, it's Christmas Eve.

And here am I where all things end,
And Undesirables are hurled;
A poor old man without a friend,
Forgot and dead to all the world;
Clean out of sight and out of mind . . .
Well, maybe it is better so;
We all in life our level find,
And mine, I guess, is pretty low.

Yet as I sit with pipe alight
Beside the cabin-fire, it's queer
This mind of mine must take to-night
The backward trail of fifty year.

THE TRAPPER'S CHRISTMAS EVE

The school-house and the Christmas tree;
The children with their cheeks a-glow;
Two bright blue eyes that smile on me 。 。 ﹡
Just half a century ago.

Again (it's maybe forty years),
With faith and trust almost divine,
These same blue eyes, abrim with tears,
Through depths of love look into mine.
A parting, tender, soft and low,
With arms that cling and lips that cleave 。 。 ﹡
Ah me! it's all so long ago,
Yet seems so sweet this Christmas Eve.

Just thirty years ago, again . . .
We say a bitter, *last* good-bye;
Our lips are white with wrath and pain;
Our little children cling and cry.
Whose was the fault? it matters not,
For man and woman both deceive;
It's buried now and all forgot,
Forgiven, too, this Christmas Eve.

And she (God pity me) is dead;
Our children men and women grown.
I like to think that they are wed,
With little children of their own,

THE TRAPPER'S CHRISTMAS EVE

That crowd around their Christmas tree . . .
I would not ever have them grieve,
Or shed a single tear for me,
To mar their joy this Christmas Eve.

Stripped to the buff and gaunt and still
Lies all the land in grim distress.
Like lost soul wailing, long and shrill,
A wolf-howl cleaves the emptiness.
Then hushed as Death is everything.
The moon rides haggard and forlorn . . .
" O hark the herald angels sing! "
God bless all men — it's Christmas morn.

THE WORLD'S ALL RIGHT

*B*E *honest, kindly, simple, true;*
*   Seek good in all, scorn but pretence;*
Whatever sorrow come to you,
Believe in Life's Beneficence!

The World's all right; serene I sit,
And cease to puzzle over it.
There's much that's mighty strange, no doubt;
But Nature knows what she's about;
And in a million years or so
We'll know more than to-day we know.
Old Evolution's under way —
        What ho! the World's all right, I say.

Could things be other than they are?
All's in its place, from mote to star.
The thistledown that flits and flies
Could drift no hair-breadth otherwise.
What is, must be; with rhythmic laws
All Nature chimes, Effect and Cause.
The sand-grain and the sun obey —
        What ho! the World's all right, I say.

THE WORLD'S ALL RIGHT

Just try to get the Cosmic touch,
The sense that " you " don't matter much.
A million stars are in the sky;
A million planets plunge and die;
A million million men are sped;
A million million wait ahead.
Each plays his part and has his day —
   What ho! the World's all right, I say.

Just try to get the Chemic view:
A million million lives made " you."
In lives a million you will be
Immortal down Eternity;
Immortal on this earth to range,
With never death, but ever change.
You always were, and will be aye —
   What ho! the World's all right, I say.

Be glad! And do not blindly grope
For Truth that lies beyond our scope:
A sober plot informeth all
Of Life's uproarious carnival.
Your day is such a little one,
A gnat that lives from sun to sun;
Yet gnat and you have parts to play —
   What ho! the World's all right, I say.

THE WORLD'S ALL RIGHT

And though it's written from the start,
Just act your best your little part.
Just be as happy as you can,
And serve your kind, and die — a man.
Just live the good that in you lies,
And seek no guerdon of the skies;
Just make your Heaven here, to-day —
      What ho! the World's all right, I say.

Remember! in Creation's swing
The Race and not the man's the thing.
There's battle, murder, sudden death,
And pestilence, with poisoned breath.
Yet quick forgotten are such woes;
On, on the stream of Being flows.
Truth, Beauty, Love uphold their sway —
      What ho! the World's all right, I say.

The World's all right; serene I sit,
And joy that I am part of it;
And put my trust in Nature's plan,
And try to aid her all I can;
Content to pass, if in my place
I've served the uplift of the Race.
Truth! Beauty! Love! O Radiant Day —
      What ho! the World's all right, I say.

THE BALDNESS OF CHEWED EAR

WHEN Chewed-ear Jenkins got hitched up to
Guinneyveer McGee,
His flowin' locks, ye recollect, wuz frivolous an' free;
But in old Hymen's jack-pot, it's a most amazin' thing,
Them flowin' locks jest disappeared like snow-balls in
the Spring;
Jest seemed to wilt an' fade away like dead leaves in
the Fall,
An' left old Chewed-ear balder than a white-washed can-
non ball.

Now Missis Chewed-ear Jenkins, that wuz Guinneyveer
McGee,
Wuz jest about as fine a draw as ever made a pair;
But when the boys got joshin' an' suggested it was she
That must be inflooenshul for the old man's slump in
hair —
Why! Missis Chewed-ear Jenkins jest went clean up
in the air.

118

THE BALDNESS OF CHEWED EAR

" To demonstrate," sez she that night, " the lovin' wife
   I am,
I've bought a dozen bottles of Bink's Anty-Dandruff
   Balm.
'Twill make yer hair jest sprout an' curl like squash-
   vines in the sun,
An' I'm propose to sling it on till every drop is done."
That hit old Chewed-ear's funny side, so he lays back
   an' hollers:
" The day you raise a hair, old girl, you'll git a thou-
   sand dollars."

Now, whether 'twas the prize or not 'tis mighty hard
   to say,
But Chewed-ear didn't seem to have much comfort from
   that day.
With bottles of that dandruff dope she followed at his
   heels,
An' sprinkled an' massaged him even when he ate his
   meals.
She waked him from his beauty sleep with tender, lovin'
   care.
An' rubbed an' scrubbed assiduous, yet never sign of hair.

Well, naturally all the boys soon tumbled to the joke,

An' at the Wow-wow's Social 'twas Cold-deck Davis spoke:

" The little woman's working mighty hard on Chewed-ear's crown;

Let's give her for a three-fifth's share a hundred dollars down.

We stand to make five hundred clear — boys, drink in whiskey straight:

' The Chewed-ear Jenkins Hirsute Propagation Syndicate.' "

The boys wuz on, an' soon chipped in the necessary dust;

They primed up a committy to negotiate the deal;

Then Missis Jenkins yielded, bein' rather in disgust,

An' all wuz signed an' witnessed, an' invested with a seal.

They rounded up old Chewed-ear, an' they broke it what they'd done;

Allowed they'd bought an interest in his chance of raisin' hair;

They yanked his hat off anxiouslike, opinin' one by one

Their magnifyin' glasses showed fine prospects everywhere.

They bought Hairlene, an' Thatchem, an' Jay's Capillery Juice,

THE BALDNESS OF CHEWED EAR

An' Seven Something Sisters, an' Macassar an' Bay Rum,
An' everyone insisted on his speshul right to sluice
His speshul line of lotion onto Chewed-ear's cranium.
They only got the merrier the more the old man roared,
An' shares in " Jenkins Hirsute " went sky-highin' on
    the board.

The Syndicate wuz hopeful that they'd demonstrate the
    pay,
An' Missis Jenkins laboured in her perseverin' way.
The boys discussed on " surface rights," an' " out-crops "
    an' so on,
An' planned to have it " crown " surveyed, an' blue prints
    of it drawn.
They ran a base line, sluiced an' yelled, an' everyone wuz
    glad,
Except the balance of the property, an' he wuz " mad."
" It gives me pain," he interjects, " to squash yer glowin'
    dream,
But you wuz fools when you got in on this here ' Hir-
    sute ' scheme.
You'll never raise a hair on me," when lo! that very
    night,
Preparin' to retire he got a most onpleasant fright:
For on that shinin' dome of his, so prominently bare,
He felt the baby outcrop of a second growth of hair.

A thousand dollars! Sufferin' Cæsar! Well, it must
be saved!

He grabbed his razor recklesslike, an' shaved an' shaved
an' shaved.

An' when his head was smooth again he gives a mighty
sigh,

An' sneaks away, an' buys some Hair Destroyer on the
sly.

So there wuz Missis Jenkins with " Restorer " wagin'
fight,

An' Chewed-ear with " Destroyer " circumventin' her at
night.

The battle wuz a mighty one; his nerves wuz on the
strain,

An' yet in spite of all he did that hair began to gain.

The situation grew intense, so quietly one day,

He gave his share-holders the slip, an' made his get-
a-way.

Jest like a criminal he skipped, an' aimed to defalcate

The Chewed-ear Jenkins Hirsute Propagation Syndicate.

His guilty secret burned him, an' he sought the city's din:

" I've got to get a wig," sez he, " to cover up my sin.

It's growin', growin' night an' day; it's most amazin'
hair ";

An' when he looked at it that night, he shuddered with
despair.

He shuddered an' suppressed a cry at what his optics
    seen —
For on my word of honour, boys, that hair wuz growin'
    green.

At first he guessed he'd get some dye, an' try to dye
    it black;
An' then he saw 'twas Nemmysis wuz layin' on his track.
He must jest face the music, an' confess the thing he
    done,
An' pay the boys an' Guinneyveer the money they had
    won.
An' then there came a big idee — it thrilled him like
    a shock;
Why not control the Syndicate by buyin' up the Stock?

An' so next day he hurried back with smoothly shaven
    pate,
An' for a hundred dollars he bought up the Syndicate.
'Twas mighty frenzied finance an' the boys set up a roar,
But " Hirsutes " from the market wuz withdrawn for
    evermore.
An' to this day in Nuggetsville they tell the tale how
    slick
The Syndicate sold out too soon, and Chewed-ear turned
    the trick.

THE MOTHER

THERE will be a singing in your heart,
  There will be a rapture in your eyes;
You will be a woman set apart,
You will be so wonderful and wise.
You will sleep, and when from dreams you start,
As of one that wakes in Paradise,
There will be a singing in your heart,
There will be a rapture in your eyes.

There will be a moaning in your heart,
There will be an anguish in your eyes;
You will see your dearest ones depart,
You will hear their quivering good-byes.
Yours will be the heart-ache and the smart,
Tears that scald and lonely sacrifice;
There will be a moaning in your heart,
There will be an anguish in your eyes.

There will come a glory in your eyes,
There will come a peace within your heart;
Sitting 'neath the quiet evening skies,
Time will dry the tear and dull the smart.

THE MOTHER

You will know that you have played your part;
Yours shall be the love that never dies:
You, with Heaven's peace within your heart,
You, with God's own glory in your eyes.

THE DREAMER

THE lone man gazed and gazed upon his gold,
    His sweat, his blood, the wage of weary days;
But now how sweet, how doubly sweet to hold
All gay and gleamy to the campfire blaze.
The evening sky was sinister and cold;
The willows shivered, wanly lay the snow;
The uncommiserating land, so old,
So worn, so grey, so niggard in its woe,
Peered through its ragged shroud. The lone man sighed,
Poured back the gaudy dust into its poke,
Gazed at the seething river listless-eyed,
Loaded his corn-cob pipe as if to smoke;
Then crushed with weariness and hardship crept
Into his ragged robe, and swiftly slept.

   .   .   .   .

Hour after hour went by; a shadow slipped
From vasts of shadow to the camp-fire flame;
Gripping a rifle with a deadly aim,
A gaunt and hairy man with wolfish eyes . . .

   *   *   *   *   *

THE DREAMER

The sleeper dreamed, and lo! this was his dream:
He rode a streaming horse across a moor.
Sudden 'mid pit-black night a lightning gleam
Showed him a way-side inn, forlorn and poor.
A sullen host unbarred the creaking door,
And led him to a dim and dreary room;
Wherein he sat and poked the fire a-roar,
So that weird shadows jigged athwart the gloom.
He ordered wine. 'Od's blood! but he was tired.
What matter! Charles was crushed and George was
    King;
His party high in power; how he aspired!
Red guineas packed his purse, too tight to ring.
The fire-light gleamed upon his silken hose,
His silver buckles and his powdered wig.
What ho! more wine! He drank, he slowly rose.
What made the shadows dance that madcap jig?
He clutched the candle, steered his way to bed,
And in a trice was sleeping like the dead.

Across the room there crept, so shadow soft,
His sullen host, with naked knife a-gleam,
(A gaunt and hairy man with wolfish eyes.) . . .
And as he lay, the sleeper dreamed a dream.

     *   *   *   *   *

THE DREAMER

'Twas in a ruder land, a wilder day.
A rival princeling sat upon his throne,
Within a dungeon, dark and foul he lay,
With chains that bit and festered to the bone.
They haled him harshly to a vaulted room,
Where One gazed on him with malignant eye;
And in that devil-face he read his doom,
Knowing that ere the dawn-light he must die.
Well, he was sorrow-glutted; let them bring
Their prize assassins to the bloody work.
His kingdom lost, yet would he die a King,
Fearless and proud, as when he faced the Turk.
Ah God! the glory of that great Crusade!
The bannered pomp, the gleam, the splendid urge!
The crash of reeking combat, blade to blade!
The reeling ranks, blood-avid and a-surge!
For long he thought; then feeling o'er him creep
Vast weariness, he fell into a sleep.

    .   .   .   .

The cell door opened; soft the headsman came,
Within his hand a mighty axe a-gleam,
(A gaunt and hairy man with wolfish eyes,) . . .
And as he lay, the sleeper dreamed a dream.

    *   *   *   *

THE DREAMER

'Twas in a land unkempt of life's red dawn;
Where in his sanded cave he dwelt alone;
Sleeping by day, or sometimes worked upon
His flint-head arrows and his knives of stone;
By night stole forth and slew the savage boar,
So that he loomed a hunter of loud fame,
And many a skin of wolf and wild-cat wore,
And counted many a flint-head to his name;
Wherefore he walked the envy of the band,
Hated and feared, but matchless in his skill.
Till lo! one night deep in that shaggy land,
He tracked a yearling bear and made his kill;
Then over-worn he rested by a stream,
And sank into a sleep too deep for dream.

   .   .   .   .

Hunting his food a rival caveman crept
Through those dark woods, and marked him where he
    lay;
Cowered and crawled upon him as he slept,
Poising a mighty stone aloft to slay —
(A gaunt and hairy man with wolfish eyes.) . . .

     *   *   *   *   *

THE DREAMER

The great stone crashed. The Dreamer shrieked and
    woke,
And saw, fear-blinded, in his dripping cell,
A gaunt and hairy man, who with one stroke
Swung a great ax of steel that flashed and fell . . .

So that he woke amid his bedroom gloom,
And saw, hair-poised, a naked, thirsting knife,
A gaunt and hairy man with eyes of doom —
And then the blade plunged down to drink his life . . .
So that he woke, wrenched back his robe, and looked,
And saw beside his dying fire upstart
A gaunt and hairy man with finger crooked —
A rifle rang, a bullet searched his heart . . .

    *   *   *   *   *

The morning sky was sinister and cold.
Grotesque the Dreamer sprawled, and did not rise
For long and long there gazed upon some gold
A gaunt and hairy man with wolfish eyes.

AT THIRTY-FIVE

THREE score and ten, the psalmist saith,
    And half my course is well-nigh run;
I've had my flout at dusty death,
I've had my whack of feast and fun.
I've mocked at those who prate and preach;
I've laughed with any man alive;
But now with sobered heart I reach
The Great Divide of Thirty-five.

And looking back I must confess
I've little cause to feel elate.
I've played the mummer more or less;
I fumbled fortune, flouted fate.
I've vastly dreamed and little done;
I've idly watched my brothers strive:
Oh, I have loitered in the sun
By primrose paths to Thirty-five!

And those who matched me in the race,
Well, some are out and trampled down;
The others jog with sober pace;
Yet one wins delicate renown.

AT THIRTY-FIVE

O midnight feast and famished dawn!
O gay, hard life, with hope alive!
O golden youth, forever gone,
How sweet you seem at Thirty-five!

Each of our lives is just a book
As absolute as Holy Writ;
We humbly read, and may not look
Ahead, nor change one word of it.
And here are joys and here are pains;
And here we fail and here we thrive;
O wondrous volume! what remains
When we reach chapter Thirty-five?

The very best, I dare to hope,
Ere Fate writes Finis to the tome;
A wiser head, a wider scope,
And for the gipsy heart, a home;
A songful home, with loved ones near,
With joy, with sunshine all alive:
Watch me grow younger every year —
Old Age! thy name is Thirty-five!

THE SQUAW MAN

THE cow-moose comes to water, and the beaver's
    overbold,
The net is in the eddy of the stream;
The teepee stars the vivid sward with russet, red and
    gold,
And in the velvet gloom the fire's a-gleam.
The night is ripe with quiet, rich with incense of the
    pine;
From sanctuary lake I hear the loon;
The peaks are bright against the blue, and drenched
    with sunset wine,
And like a silver bubble is the moon.

Cloud-high I climbed but yesterday; a hundred miles
    around
I looked to see a rival fire a-gleam.
As in a crystal lens it lay, a land without a bound,
All lure, and virgin vastitude, and dream.
The great sky soared exultantly, the great earth bared
    its breast,
All river-veined and patterned with the pine;

THE SQUAW MAN

The heedless hordes of caribou were streaming to the
    West,
A land of lustrous mystery — and mine.

Yea, mine to frame my Odyssey: Oh, little do they know
My conquest and the kingdom that I keep!
The meadows of the musk-ox, where the laughing
    grasses grow,
The rivers where the careless conies leap.
Beyond the silent Circle, where white men are fierce
    and few,
I lord it, and I mock at man-made law;
Like a flame upon the water is my little light canoe,
And yonder in the fireglow is my squaw.

A squaw man! yes, that's what I am; sneer at me if you
    will.
I've gone the grilling pace that cannot last;
With bawdry, bridge and brandy — Oh, I've drank
    enough to kill
A dozen such as you, but that is past.
I've swung round to my senses, found the place where
    I belong;
The City made a madman out of me;
But here beyond the Circle, where there's neither right
    or wrong,
I leap from life's straight-jacket, and I'm free.

THE SQUAW MAN

Yet ever in the far forlorn, by trails of lone desire;
Yet ever in the dawn's white leer of hate;
Yet ever by the dripping kill, beside the drowsy fire,
There comes the fierce heart-hunger for a mate.
There comes the mad blood-clamour for a woman's
    clinging hand,
Love-humid eyes, the velvet of a breast;
And so I sought the Bonnet-plumes, and chose from out
    the band
The girl I thought the sweetest and the best.

O wistful women I have loved before my dark disgrace!
O women fair and rare in my home land!
Dear ladies, if I saw you now I'd turn away my face,
Then crawl to kiss your foot-prints in the sand!
And yet — that day the rifle jammed — a wounded moose
    at bay —
A roar, a charge . . . I faced it with my knife:
A shot from out the willow-scrub, and there the monster
    lay. . . .
Yes, little Laughing Eyes, you saved my life.

The man must have the woman, and we're all brutes
    more or less,
Since first the male ape shinned the family tree;
And yet I think I love her with a husband's tenderness,
And yet I know that she would die for me.

THE SQUAW MAN

Oh, if I left you, Laughing Eyes, and nevermore came
back,

God help you, girl! I know what you would
do. . . .

I see the lake wan in the moon, and from the shadow
black,

There drifts a little, *empty* birch canoe.

We're here beyond the Circle, where there's never wrong
nor right;

We aren't spliced according to the law;

But by the gods I hail you on this hushed and holy
night

As the mother of my children, and my squaw.

I see your little slender face set in the firelight glow;

I pray that I may never make it sad;

I hear you croon a baby song, all slumber-soft and low —

God bless you, little Laughing Eyes! I'm glad.

HOME AND LOVE

JUST Home and Love! the words are small
  Four little letters unto each;
And yet you will not find in all
The wide and gracious range of speech
Two more so tenderly complete:
When angels talk in Heaven above,
I'm sure they have no words more sweet
   Than Home and Love.

Just Home and Love! it's hard to guess
Which of the two were best to gain;
Home without Love is bitterness;
Love without Home is often pain.
No! each alone will seldom do;
Somehow they travel hand and glove:
If you win one you must have two,
   Both Home and Love.

And if you've both, well then I'm sure
You ought to sing the whole day long;
It doesn't matter if you're poor
With these to make divine your song.

HOME AND LOVE

And so I praisefully repeat,
When angels talk in Heaven above,
There are no words more simply sweet
Than Home and Love.

I'M SCARED OF IT ALL

I'M scared of it all, God's truth! so I am;
   It's too big and brutal for me.
My nerve's on the raw and I don't give a damn
For all the " hoorah " that I see.
I'm pinned between subway and overhead train,
Where automobillies swoop down:
Oh, I want to go back to the timber again —
I'm scared of the terrible town.

I want to go back to my lean, ashen plains;
My rivers that flash into foam;
My ultimate valleys where solitude reigns;
My trail from Fort Churchill to Nome.
My forests packed full of mysterious gloom,
My ice-fields agrind and aglare:
The city is deadfalled with danger and doom —
I know that I'm safer up there.

I watch the wan faces that flash in the street;
All kinds and all classes I see.
Yet never a one in the million I meet,
Has the smile of a comrade for me.

I'M SCARED OF IT ALL

Just jaded and panting like dogs in a pack;
Just tensed and intent on the goal:
O God! but I'm lonesome — I wish I was back,
Up there in the land of the Pole.

I wish I was back on the Hunger Plateaus,
And seeking the lost caribou;
I wish I was up where the Coppermine flows
To the kick of my little canoe.
I'd like to be far on some weariful shore,
In the Land of the Blizzard and Bear;
Oh, I wish I was snug in the Arctic once more,
For I know I am safer up there!

I prowl in the canyons of dismal unrest;
I cringe — I'm so weak and so small.
I can't get my bearings, I'm crushed and oppressed
With the haste and the waste of it all.
The slaves and the madman, the lust and the sweat,
The fear in the faces I see;
The getting, the spending, the fever, the fret —
It's too bleeding cruel for me.

I feel it's all wrong, but I can't tell you why —
The palace, the hovel next door;
The insolent towers that sprawl to the sky,
The crush and the rush and the roar.

I'M SCARED OF IT ALL

I'm trapped like a fox and I fear for my pelt;
I cower in the crash and the glare;
Oh, I want to be back in the avalanche belt,
For I know that it's safer up there!

I'm scared of it all: Oh, afar I can hear
The voice of my solitudes call!
We're nothing but brute with a little veneer,
And nature is best after all.
There's tumult and terror abroad in the street;
There's menace and doom in the air;
I've got to get back to my thousand-mile beat;
The trail where the cougar and silver-tip meet;
The snows and the camp-fire, with wolves at my feet,
        Good-bye, for it's safer up there.

        To be forming good habits up there;
        To be starving on rabbits up there;
        In your hunger and woe,
        Though it's sixty below,
        Oh, I know that it's safer up there!

A SONG OF SUCCESS

H O! we were strong, we were swift, we were brave.
   Youth was a challenge, and Life was a fight.
All that was best in us gladly we gave,
Sprang from the rally, and leapt for the height.
Smiling is Love in a foam of Spring flowers:
Harden our hearts to him — on let us press!
Oh, what a triumph and pride shall be ours!
See where it beacons, the star of success!

Cares seem to crowd on us — so much to do;
New fields to conquer, and time's on the wing.
Grey hairs are showing, a wrinkle or two;
Somehow our footstep is losing its spring.
Pleasure's forsaken us, Love ceased to smile;
Youth has been funeralled; Age travels fast.
Sometimes we wonder: is it worth while?
There! we have gained to the summit at last.

Aye, we have triumphed! Now must we haste,
Revel in victory . . . why! what is wrong?
Life's choicest vintage is flat to the taste —
Are we too late? Have we laboured too long?

A SONG OF SUCCESS

Wealth, power, fame we hold . . . ah! but the
    truth:
Would we not give this vain glory of ours
For one mad, glad year of glorious youth,
Life in the Springtide, and Love in the flowers.

143

THE SONG OF THE CAMP FIRE

I

HEED me, feed me, I am hungry, I am red-tongued
    with desire;
Boughs of balsam, slabs of cedar, gummy fagots of the
    pine,
Heap them on me, let me hug them to my eager heart
    of fire,
Roaring, soaring up to heaven as a symbol and a sign.
Bring me knots of sunny maple, silver birch and
    tamarack;
Leaping, sweeping, I will lap them with my ardent
    wings of flame;
I will kindle them to glory, I will beat the darkness
    back;
Streaming, gleaming, I will goad them to my glory and
    my fame.
Bring me gnarly limbs of live-oak, aid me in my fren-
    zied fight;
Strips of iron-wood, scaly blue-gum, writhing redly in
    my hold;
With my lunge of lurid lances, with my whips that flail
    the night,
They will burgeon into beauty, they will foliate in gold.

THE SONG OF THE CAMP FIRE

Let me star the dim sierras, stab with light the inland
    seas;
Roaming wind and roaring darkness! seek no mercy at
    my hands;
I will mock the marly heavens, lamp the purple prairies,
I will flaunt my deathless banners down the far, un-
    houseled lands.
In the vast and vaulted pine-gloom where the pillared
    forests frown,
By the sullen, bestial rivers running where God only
    knows,
On the starlit coral beaches when the combers thunder
    down,
In the death-spell of the barrens, in the shudder of the
    snows;
In a blazing belt of triumph from the palm-leaf to the
    pine,
As a symbol of defiance lo! the wilderness I span;
And my beacons burn exultant as an everlasting sign
Of unending domination, of the mastery of Man;
I, the Life, the fierce Uplifter, I that weaned him from
    the mire;
I, the angel and the devil, I, the tyrant and the slave;
I, the Spirit of the Struggle; I, the mighty God of Fire;
I, the Maker and Destroyer; I, the Giver and the
    Grave.

THE SONG OF THE CAMP FIRE

II

Gather round me, boy and grey-beard, frontiersman of
 every kind.

Few are you, and far and lonely, yet an army forms
 behind:

By your camp-fires shall they know you, ashes scattered
 to the wind.

Peer into my heart of solace, break your bannock at my
 blaze;

Smoking, stretched in lazy shelter, build your castles
 as you gaze;

Or, it may be, deep in dreaming, think of dim, unhappy
 days.

Let my warmth and glow caress you, for your trails are
 grim and hard;

Let my arms of comfort press you, hunger-hewn and
 battle-scarred:

O my lovers! how I bless you with your lives so madly
 marred!

For you seek the silent spaces, and their secret lore you
 glean:

For you win the savage races, and the brutish Wild you
 wean;

And I gladden desert places, where camp-fire has never
 been.

THE SONG OF THE CAMP FIRE

From the Pole unto the Tropics is there trail ye have
    not dared?
And because you hold death lightly, so by death shall
    you be spared,
(As the sages of the ages in their pages have declared.)

On the roaring Arkilinik in a leaky bark canoe;
Up the cloud of Mount McKinley, where the avalanche
    leaps through;
In the furnace of Death Valley, when the mirage glim-
    mers blue.

Now a smudge of wiry willows on the weary Kusko-
    quim;
Now a flare of gummy pine-knots where Vancouver's
    scaur is grim;
Now a gleam of sunny ceiba, when the Cuban beaches
    dim.

Always, always God's Great Open: lo! I burn with
    keener light
In the corridors of silence, in the vestibules of night;
'Mid the ferns and grasses gleaming, was there ever gem
    so bright?

THE SONG OF THE CAMP FIRE

Not for weaklings, not for women, like my brother of
the hearth;
Ring your songs of wrath around me, I was made for
manful mirth,
In the lusty, gusty greatness, on the bald spots of the
earth.

Men, my masters! men, my lovers! ye have fought and
ye have bled;
Gather round my ruddy embers, softly glowing is my
bed;
By my heart of solace dreaming, rest ye and be comforted!

III

I am dying, O my masters! by my fitful flame ye sleep;
My purple plumes of glory droop forlorn.
Grey ashes choke and cloak me, and above the pines
there creep
The stealthy silver moccasins of morn.
There comes a countless army, it's the Legion of the
Light;
It tramps in gleaming triumph round the world;
And before its jewelled lances all the shadows of the
night
Back in to abysmal darknesses are hurled.

148

THE SONG OF THE CAMP FIRE

Leap to life again, my lovers! ye must toil and never
        tire;
    The day of daring, doing, brightens clear,
When the bed of spicy cedar and the jovial camp-fire
    Must only be a memory of cheer.
There is hope and golden promise in the vast portentous
            dawn;
    There is glamour in the glad, effluent sky:
Go and leave me; I will dream of you and love you
            when you're gone;
    I have served you, O my masters! let me die.

A little heap of ashes, grey and sodden by the rain,
    Wind-scattered, blurred and blotted by the snow:
Let that be all to tell of me, and glorious again,
    Ye things of greening gladness, leap and glow!
A black scar in the sunshine by the palm-leaf or the pine,
    Blind to the night and dead to all desire;
Yet oh, of life and uplift what a symbol and a sign!
Yet oh, of power and conquest what a destiny is mine!
A little heap of ashes — Yea! a miracle divine,
    The foot-print of a god, all-radiant Fire.

HER LETTER

"I'M taking pen in hand this night, and hard it is for me;

My poor old fingers tremble so, my hand is stiff and slow,

And even with my glasses on I'm troubled sore to see. . . .

You'd little know your mother, boy; you'd little, little know.

You mind how brisk and bright I was, how straight and trim and smart;

'Tis weariful I am the now, and bent and frail and grey.

I'm waiting at the road's end, lad; and all that's in my heart,

Is just to see my boy again before I'm called away."

"Oh well I mind the sorry day you crossed the gurly sea;

'Twas like the heart was torn from me, a waeful wife was I.

You said that you'd be home again in two years, maybe three;

But nigh a score of years have gone, and still the years
    go by.
I know it's cruel hard for you, you've bairnies of your
    own;
I know the siller's hard to win, and folks have used
    you ill:
But oh, think of your mother, lad, that's waiting by her
    lone!
And even if you canna come — *just write and say you
    will."*

" Aye, even though there's little hope, just promise that
    you'll try.
It's weary, weary waiting, lad; just say you'll come next
    year.
I'm thinking there will be no ' next '; I'm thinking soon
    I'll lie
With all the ones I've laid away . . . but oh, the
    hope will cheer!
You know you're all that's left to me, and we are seas
    apart;
But if you'll only *say* you'll come, then will I hope and
    pray.
I'm waiting by the grave-side, lad; and all that's in my
    heart
Is just to see my boy again before I'm called away."

THE MAN WHO KNEW

THE Dreamer visioned Life as it might be,
   And from his dream forthright a picture grew,
A painting all the people thronged to see,
And joyed therein — till came the Man Who Knew,
Saying: " 'Tis bad! Why do ye gape, ye fools!
He painteth not according to the schools."

The Dreamer probed Life's mystery of woe,
And in a book he sought to give the clue;
The people read, and saw that it was so,
And read again — then came the Man Who Knew,
Saying: "Ye witless ones! this book is vile:
It hath not got the rudiments of style."

Love smote the Dreamer's lips, and silver clear
He sang a song so sweet, so tender true,
That all the market-place was thrilled to hear,
And listened rapt — till came the Man Who Knew,
Saying: " His technique's wrong; he singeth ill.
Waste not your time." The singer's voice was still.

THE MAN WHO KNEW

And then the people roused as if from sleep,
Crying: "What care we if it be not Art!
Hath he not charmed us, made us laugh and weep?
Come, let us crown him where he sits apart."
Then, with his picture spurned, his book unread,
His song unsung, they found their Dreamer — *dead.*

THE LOGGER

IN the moonless, misty night, with my little pipe alight,
    I am sitting by the camp-fire's fading cheer;
Oh, the dew is falling chill on the dim, deer-haunted
       hill,
    And the breakers in the bay are moaning drear.
The toilful hours are sped, the boys are long abed,
    And I alone a weary vigil keep;
In the sightless, sullen sky I can hear the night-hawk cry,
    And the frogs in frenzied chorus from the creek.

And somehow the embers' glow brings me back the long
      ago,
    The days of merry laughter and light song;
When I sped the hours away with the gayest of the gay
    In the giddy whirl of fashion's festal throng.
Oh, I ran a grilling race and I little recked the pace,
    For the lust of youth ran riot in my blood;
But at last I made a stand in this God-forsaken land
    Of the pine-tree and the mountain and the flood.

THE LOGGER

And now I've got to stay, with an overdraft to pay,
    For pleasure in the past with future pain;
And I'm not the chap to whine, for if the chance were
        mine
    I know I'd choose the old life once again.
With its woman's eyes a-shine, and its flood of golden
        wine;
    Its fever and its frolic and its fun;
The old life with its din, its laughter and its sin —
    And chuck me in the gutter when it's done.

Ah, well! it's past and gone, and the memory is wan,
    That conjures up each old familiar face;
And here by fortune hurled, I am dead to all the world,
    And I've learned to lose my pride and keep my
        place.
My ways are hard and rough, and my arms are strong
        and tough,
    And I hew the dizzy pine till darkness falls;
And sometimes I take a dive, just to keep my heart alive,
    Among the gay saloons and dancing halls.

In the distant, dinful town just a little drink to drown
    The cares that crowd and canker in my brain;
Just a little joy to still set my pulses all a-thrill,
    Then back to brutish labour once again.

And things will go on so until one day I shall know
    That Death has got me cinched beyond a doubt;
Then I'll crawl away from sight, and morosely in the
      night
    My weary, wasted life will peter out.

Then the boys will gather round, and they'll launch me
      in the ground,
    And pile the stones the timber wolf to foil;
And the moaning pine will wave overhead a nameless
      grave,
    Where the black snake in the sunshine loves to coil.
And they'll leave me there alone, and perhaps with
      softened tone
    Speak of me sometimes in the camp-fire's glow,
As a played-out, broken chum, who has gone to King-
      dom Come,
    And who went the pace in England long ago.

THE PASSING OF THE YEAR

MY glass is filled, my pipe is lit,
  My den is all a cosy glow;
And snug before the fire I sit,
  And wait to *feel* the old year go.
I dedicate to solemn thought
  Amid my too-unthinking days,
This sober moment, sadly fraught
  With much of blame, with little praise.

Old Year! upon the Stage of Time
  You stand to bow your last adieu;
A moment, and the prompter's chime
  Will ring the curtain down on you.
Your mien is sad, your step is slow;
  You falter as a Sage in pain;
Yet turn, Old Year, before you go,
  And face your audience again.

That sphinx-like face, remote, austere,
  Let us all read, whate'er the cost:
O Maiden! why that bitter tear?
  Is it for dear one you have lost?

THE PASSING OF THE YEAR

Is it for fond illusion gone?
  For trusted lover proved untrue?
O sweet girl-face, so sad, so wan
  What hath the Old Year meant to you?

And you, O neighbour on my right
  So sleek, so prosperously clad!
What see you in that aged wight
  That makes your smile so gay and glad?
What opportunity unmissed?
  What golden gain, what pride of place?
What splendid hope? O Optimist!
  What read you in that withered face?

And You, deep shrinking in the gloom,
  What find you in that filmy gaze?
What menace of a tragic doom?
  What dark, condemning yesterdays?
What urge to crime, what evil done?
  What cold, confronting shape of fear?
O haggard, haunted, hidden One
  What see you in the dying year?

And so from face to face I flit,
  The countless eyes that stare and stare;
Some are with approbation lit,
  And some are shadowed with despair.

THE PASSING OF THE YEAR

Some show a smile and some a frown;
  Some joy and hope, some pain and woe:
Enough! Oh, ring the curtain down!
  Old weary year! it's time to go.

My pipe is out, my glass is dry;
  My fire is almost ashes too;
But once again, before you go,
  And I prepare to meet the New:
Old Year! a parting word that's true,
  For we've been comrades, you and I —
I thank God for each day of you;
  There! bless you now! Old Year, good-bye!

THE GHOSTS

SMITH, great writer of stories, drank; found it im-
mortalised his pen;
Fused in his brain-pan, else a blank, heavens of glory
now and then;
Gave him the magical genius touch; God-given power
to gouge out, fling
Flat in your face a soul-thought — Bing! Twiddle
your heart-strings in his clutch.
"Bah!" said Smith, "let my body lie stripped to the
buff in swinish shame,
If I can blaze in the radiant sky out of adoring stars
my name.
Sober am I nonentitized; drunk am I more than half a
god.
Well, let the flesh be sacrificed; spirit shall speak and
shame the clod.
Who would not gladly, gladly give Life to do one thing
that will live?"

Smith had a friend, we'll call him Brown; dearer than
brothers were those two.
When in the wassail Smith would drown, Brown would
rescue and pull him through.

THE GHOSTS

When Brown was needful Smith would lend; so it fell
    as the years went by,
Each on the other would depend: then at the last Smith
    came to die.

There Brown sat in the sick man's room, still as a stone
    in his despair;
Smith bent on him his eyes of doom, shook back his lion
    mane of hair;
Said: " Is there one in my chosen line, writer of forth-
    right tales my peer?
Look in that little desk of mine; there is a package, bring
    it here.
Story of stories, gem of all; essence and triumph, key
    and clue;
Tale of a loving woman's fall; soul swept hell-ward, and
    God! it's true.
I was the man — Oh, yes, I've paid, paid with mighty and
    mordant pain.
Look! here's the masterpiece I've made out of my sin,
    my manhood slain.
Art supreme! yet the world would stare, know my mis-
    tress and blaze my shame.
I have a wife and daughter — there! take it and thrust
    it in the flame."

THE GHOSTS

Brown answered: " Master, you have dipped pen in your heart, your phrases sear.

Ruthless, unflinching, you have stripped naked your soul and set it here.

Have I not loved you well and true? See! between us the shadows drift;

This bit of blood and tears means You — oh, let me have it, a parting gift.

Sacred I'll hold it, a trust divine; sacred your honour, her dark despair;

Never shall it see printed line: here, by the living God I swear."

Brown on a Bible laid his hand; Smith, great writer of stories, sighed:

"Comrade, I trust you, and understand. Keep my secret!" And so he died.

Smith was buried — up soared his sales; lured you his books in every store;

Exquisite, whimsy, heart-wrung tales; men devoured them and craved for more.

So when it slyly got about Brown had a posthumous manuscript,

Jones, the publisher, sought him out, into his pocket deep he dipped.

THE GHOSTS

"A thousand dollars?" Brown shook his head. "The story is not for sale," he said.

Jones went away, then others came. Tempted and taunted, Brown was true.
Guarded at friendship's shrine the fame of the unpublished story grew and grew.
It's a long, long lane that has no end, but some lanes end in the Potter's field;
Smith to Brown had been more than friend: patron, protector, spur and shield.
Poor, loving-wistful, dreamy Brown, long and lean, with a smile askew,
Friendless he wandered up and down, gaunt as a wolf, as hungry too.
Brown with his lilt of saucy rhyme, Brown with his tilt of tender mirth
Garretless in the gloom and grime, singing his glad, mad songs of earth:
So at last with a faith divine, down and down to the Hunger-line.

There as he stood in a woeful plight, tears a-freeze on his sharp cheek-bones,
Who should chance to behold his plight, but the publisher, the plethoric Jones;

Peered at him for a little while, held out a bill: "*Now,*
   will you sell?"
Brown scanned it with his twisted smile: "A thousand
   dollars! you go to hell!"

Brown enrolled in the homeless host, sleeping anywhere,
   anywhen;
Suffered, strove, became a ghost, slave of the lamp for
   other men;
For What's-his-name and So-and-so in the abyss his soul
   he stripped,
Yet in his want, his worst of woe, held he fast to the
   manuscript.
Then one day as he chewed his pen, half in hunger and
   half despair,
Creaked the door of his garret den; Dick, his brother,
   was standing there.
Down on the pallet bed he sank, ashen his face, his voice
   a wail:
"Save me, brother! I've robbed the bank; to-morrow
   it's ruin, capture, gaol.
Yet there's a chance: I could to-day pay back the money,
   save our name;
You have a manuscript, they say, worth a thousand —
   think, man! the shame. . . ."
Brown with his heart pain-pierced the while, with his
   stern, starved face, and his lips stone-pale,

Shuddered and smiled his twisted smile: "Brother, I
    guess you go to gaol."

While poor Brown in the leer of dawn wrestled with
    God for the sacred fire,
Came there a woman weak and wan, out of the mob, the
    murk, the mire;
Frail as a reed, a fellow ghost, weary with woe, with
    sorrowing;
Two pale souls in the legion lost; lo! Love bent with a
    tender wing,
Taught them a joy so deep, so true, it seemed that the
    whole-world fabric shook,
Thrilled and dissolved in radiant dew: then Brown made
    him a golden book,
Full of the faith that Life is good, that the earth is a
    dream divinely fair,
Lauding his gem of womanhood in many a lyric rich
    and rare;
Took it to Jones, who shook his head: "I will consider
    it," he said.

While he considered, Brown's wife lay clutched in the
    tentacles of pain;
Then came the doctor, grave and grey; spoke of decline,
    of nervous strain;

Hinted Egypt, the South of France — Brown with ter-
 ror was tiger-gripped.
Where was the money? What the chance? Pitiful
 God! . . . the manuscript!
A thousand dollars! his only hope! he gazed and gazed
 at the garret wall. . . .
Reached at last for the envelope, turned to his wife
 and told her all.
Told of his friend, his promise true; told like his very
 heart would break:
" Oh, my dearest! what shall I do? shall I not sell it
 for your sake? "
Ghostlike she lay, as still as doom; turned to the wall
 her weary head;
Icy-cold in the pallid gloom, silent as death . . . at
 last she said:
" Do! my husband? Keep your vow! Guard his secret and let me die. . . .
Oh, my dear, I must tell you now — *the woman he
 loved and wronged was I;*
Darling! I haven't long to live: I never told you —
 forgive, forgive! "

For a long, long time Brown did not speak; sat bleak-
 browed in the wretched room;
Slowly a tear stole down his cheek, and he kissed her hand
 in the dismal gloom.

THE GHOSTS

To break his oath, to brand her shame; his well-loved
    friend, his worshipped wife;
To keep his vow, to save her name, yet at the cost of
    what? Her life!
A moment's space did he hesitate, a moment of pain and
    dread and doubt,
Then he broke the seals, and, stern as fate, unfolded the
    sheets and spread them out. . . .
On his knees by her side he limply sank, peering amazed
    — *each page was blank.*

(For oh, the supremest of our art are the stories we do
    not dare to tell,
Locked in the silence of the heart, for the awful records
    of Heav'n and Hell.)

Yet those two in the silence there, seemed less weariful
    than before.
Hark! a step on the garret stair, a postman knocks at the
    flimsy door.
·' Registered letter!" Brown thrills with fear; opens,
    and reads, then bends above:
" Glorious tidings! Egypt, dear! The book is accepted
    — life and love."

167

GOOD-BYE, LITTLE CABIN

O DEAR little cabin, I've loved you so long,
  And now I must bid you good-bye!
I've filled you with laughter, I've thrilled you with song,
And sometimes I've wished I could cry.
Your walls they have witnessed a weariful fight,
And rung to a won Waterloo:
But oh, in my triumph I'm dreary to-night —
Good-bye, little cabin, to you!

Your roof is bewhiskered, your floor is a-slant,
Your walls seem to sag and to swing;
I'm trying to find just your faults, but I can't —
You poor, tired, heart-broken old thing!
I've seen when you've been the best friend that I had,
Your light like a gem on the snow;
You're sort of a part of me — Gee! but I'm sad;
I hate, little cabin, to go.

Below your cracked window red raspberries climb;
A hornet's nest hangs from a beam;
Your rafters are scribbled with adage and rhyme,
And dimmed with tobacco and dream.

GOOD-BYE, LITTLE CABIN

"Each day has its laugh," and "Don't worry, just
    work."
Such mottoes reproachfully shine.
Old calendars dangle — what memories lurk
About you, dear cabin of mine!

I hear the world-call and the clang of the fight;
I hear the hoarse cry of my kind;
Yet well do I know, as I quit you to-night,
It's Youth that I'm leaving behind.
And often I'll think of you, empty and black,
Moose antlers nailed over your door:
Oh, if I should perish my ghost will come back
To dwell in you, cabin, once more!

How cold, still and lonely, how weary you seem!
A last wistful look and I'll go.
Oh, will you remember the lad with his dream!
The lad that you comforted so.
The shadows enfold you, it's drawing to-night;
The evening star needles the sky:
And huh! but it's stinging and stabbing my sight —
God bless you, old cabin, good-bye!

HEART O' THE NORTH

AND when I come to the dim trail-end,
    I who have been Life's rover,
This is all I would ask, my friend,
    Over and over and over:

A little space on a stony hill
    With never another near me,
Sky o' the North that's vast and still,
    With a single star to cheer me;

Star that gleams on a moss-grey stone
    Graven by those who love me —
There would I lie alone, alone,
    With a single pine above me;

Pine that the north wind whinneys through —
    Oh, I have been Life's lover!
But there I'd lie and listen to
    Eternity passing over.

THE SCRIBE'S PRAYER

WHEN from my fumbling hand the tired pen
falls,
And in the twilight weary droops my head;
While to my quiet heart a still voice calls,
Calls me to join my kindred of the Dead:
Grant that I may, O Lord, ere rest be mine,
Write to Thy praise one radiant, ringing line.

For all of worth that in this clay abides,
The leaping rapture and the ardent flame,
The hope, the high resolve, the faith that guides:
All, all is Thine, and liveth in Thy name:
Lord, have I dallied with the sacred fire?
Lord, have I trailed Thy glory in the mire!

E'en as a toper from the dram-shop reeling,
Sees in his garret's blackness, dazzling fair,
All that he might have been, and, heart-sick, kneel-
ing,
Sobs in the passion of a vast despair:
So my ideal self haunts me alway —
When the accounting comes, how shall I pay?

THE SCRIBE'S PRAYER

For in the dark I grope, nor understand;
And in my heart fight selfishness and sin:
Yet, Lord, I do not seek Thy helping hand;
Rather let me my own salvation win:
Let me through strife and penitential pain
Onward and upward to the heights attain.

Yea, let me live my life, its meaning seek;
Bear myself fitly in the ringing fight;
Strive to be strong that I may aid the weak;
Dare to be true — O God! the Light, the Light!
Cometh the Dark so soon. I've mocked Thy Word;
Yet do I know Thy Love: have mercy, Lord. . . .

FINIS

Rhymes of a Red Cross Man

To the Memory of
MY BROTHER,
LIEUTENANT ALBERT SERVICE
CANADIAN INFANTRY
KILLED IN ACTION, FRANCE
August, 1916.

CONTENTS

CONTENTS

FOREWORD

I've tinkered at my bits of rhymes
In weary, woeful, waiting times;
In doleful hours of battle-din,
Ere yet they brought the wounded in;
Through vigils of the fateful night,
In lousy barns by candle-light;
In dug-outs, sagging and aflood,
On stretchers stiff and bleared with blood;
By ragged grove, by ruined road,
By hearths accurst where Love abode;
By broken altars, blackened shrines
I've tinkered at my bits of rhymes.

I've solaced me with scraps of song
The desolated ways along:
Through sickly fields all shrapnel-sown,
And meadows reaped by death alone;
By blazing cross and splintered spire,
By headless Virgin in the mire;
By gardens gashed amid their bloom,
By gutted grave, by shattered tomb;
Beside the dying and the dead,

FOREWORD

Where rocket green and rocket red,
In trembling pools of poising light,
With flowers of flame festoon the night.
Ah me! by what dark ways of wrong
I've cheered my heart with scraps of song.

So here's my sheaf of war-won verse,
And some is bad, and some is worse.
And if at times I curse a bit,
You needn't read that part of it;
For through it all like horror runs
The red resentment of the guns.
And you yourself would mutter when
You took the things that once were men,
And sped them through that zone of hate
To where the dripping surgeons wait;
And wonder too if in God's sight
War ever, ever can be right.

Yet may it not be, crime and war
But effort misdirected are?
And if there's good in war and crime,
There may be in my bits of rhyme,
My songs from out the slaughter mill:
So take or leave them as you will.

THE CALL

(France, August first, 1914)

Far and near, high and clear,
　　Hark to the call of War!
Over the gorse and the golden dells,
Ringing and swinging of clamorous bells,
Praying and saying of wild farewells:
　　War! War! War!

High and low, all must go:
　　Hark to the shout of War!
Leave to the women the harvest yield;
Gird ye, men, for the sinister field;
A sabre instead of a scythe to wield:
　　War! Red War!

Rich and poor, lord and boor,
　　Hark to the blast of War!
Tinker and tailor and millionaire,
Actor in triumph and priest in prayer,

9

THE CALL

Comrades now in the hell out there,
Sweep to the fire of War!

Prince and page, sot and sage,
Hark to the roar of War!
Poet, professor and circus clown,
Chimney-sweeper and fop o' the town,
Into the pot and be melted down:
Into the pot of War!

Women all, hear the call,
The pitiless call of War!
Look your last on your dearest ones,
Brothers and husbands, fathers, sons:
Swift they go to the ravenous guns,
The gluttonous guns of War.

Everywhere thrill the air
The maniac bells of War.
There will be little of sleeping to-night;
There will be wailing and weeping to-night;
Death's red sickle is reaping to-night:
War! War! War!

THE FOOL

" But it isn't playing the game," he said,
And he slammed his books away;
" The Latin and Greek I've got in my head
Will do for a duller day."
" Rubbish! " I cried; " The bugle's call
Isn't for lads from school."
D'ye think he'd listen?   Oh, not at all:
So I called him a fool, a fool.

Now there's his dog by his empty bed,
And the flute he used to play,
And his favourite bat . . . but Dick he's dead,
Somewhere in France, they say:
Dick with his rapture of song and sun,
Dick of the yellow hair,
Dicky whose life had but begun,
Carrion-cold out there.

Look at his prizes all in a row:
Surely a hint of fame.
Now he's finished with,— nothing to show:

THE FOOL

Doesn't it seem a shame?
Look from the window!   All you see
Was to be his one day:
Forest and furrow, lawn and lea,
And he goes and chucks it away.

Chucks it away to die in the dark:
Somebody saw him fall,
Part of him mud, part of him blood,
The rest of him — not at all.
And yet I'll bet he was never afraid,
And he went as the best of 'em go,
For his hand was clenched on his broken blade,
And his face was turned to the foe.

And I called him a fool . . . oh how blind
   was I !
And the cup of my grief's abrim.
Will Glory o' England ever die
So long as we've lads like him?
So long as we've fond and fearless fools,
Who, spurning fortune and fame,
Turn out with the rallying cry of their schools,
Just bent on playing the game.

THE FOOL

A fool! Ah no! He was more than wise.
His was the proudest part.
He died with the glory of faith in his eyes,
And the glory of love in his heart.
And though there's never a grave to tell,
Nor a cross to mark his fall,
Thank God! we know that he " batted well "
In the last great Game of all.

THE VOLUNTEER

Sez I: My Country calls? Well, let it call.
I grins perlitely and declines wiv thanks.
Go, let 'em plaster every blighted wall,
'Ere's *one* they don't stampede into the ranks.
Them politicians with their greasy ways;
Them empire-grabbers — fight for 'em? No
        fear!
I've seen this mess a-comin' from the days
Of Algyserious and Aggydear:
      I've felt me passion rise and swell,
      But . . . wot the 'ell, Bill? Wot the 'ell?

Sez I: My Country? Mine? I likes their
      cheek.
Me mud-bespattered by the cars they drive,
Wot makes my measly thirty bob a week,
And sweats red blood to keep meself alive!
Fight for the right to slave that they may spend,
Them in their mansions, me 'ere in my slum?
No, let 'em fight wot's something to defend:

THE VOLUNTEER

But me, I've nothin'—let the Kaiser come.
    And so I cusses 'ard and well,
    But . . . wot the 'ell, Bill? Wot the 'ell?

Sez I: If they would do the decent thing,
And shield the missis and the little 'uns,
Why, even *I* might shout " God save the King,"
And face the chances of them 'ungry guns.
But we've got three, another on the way;
It's that wot makes me snarl and set me jor:
The wife and nippers, wot of 'em, I say,
If I gets knocked out in this blasted war?
    Gets proper busted by a shell,
    But . . . wot the 'ell, Bill? Wot the 'ell?

Ay, wot the 'ell's the use of all this talk?
To-day some boys in blue was passin' me,
And some of 'em they 'ad no legs to walk,
And some of 'em they 'ad no eyes to see.
And — well, I couldn't look 'em in the face,
And so I'm goin', goin' to declare
I'm under forty-one and take me place
To face the music with the bunch out there.
    A fool, you say! Maybe you're right.
    I'll 'ave no peace unless I fight.
    I've ceased to think; I only know
    I've gotta go, Bill, gotta go.

THE CONVALESCENT

, . . So I walked among the willows very
    quietly all night;
There was no moon at all, at all; no timid star
    alight;
There was no light at all, at all; I wint from
    tree to tree,
And I called him as his mother called, but he
    nivver answered me.

Oh I called him all the night-time, as I walked
    the wood alone;
And I listened and I listened, but I nivver heard
    a moan;
Then I found him at the dawnin', when the
    sorry sky was red:
I was lookin' for the livin', but I only found
    the dead.

16

THE CONVALESCENT

Sure I know that it was Shamus by the silver
    cross he wore;
But the bugles they were callin', and I heard
    the cannon roar.
Oh I had no time to tarry, so I said a little
    prayer,
And I clasped his hands together, and I left him
    lyin' there.

Now the birds are singin', singin', and I'm
    home in Donegal,
And it's Springtime, and I'm thinkin' that I
    only dreamed it all;
I dreamed about that evil wood, all crowded
    with its dead,
Where I knelt beside me brother when the
    battle-dawn was red.

Where I prayed beside me brother ere I wint
    to fight anew:
Such dreams as these are evil dreams; I can't
    believe it's true.
Where all is love and laughter, sure it's hard to
    think of loss . . .
But mother's sayin' nothin', and she clasps —
    a silver cross.

THE MAN FROM ATHABASKA

Oh the wife she tried to tell me that 'twas
    nothing but the thrumming
Of a wood-pecker a-rapping on the hollow of a
    tree;
And she thought that I was fooling when I said
    it was the drumming
Of the mustering of legions, and 'twas calling
    unto me;
'Twas calling me to pull my freight and hop
    across the sea.

And a-mending of my fish-nets sure I started
    up in wonder,
For I heard a savage roaring and 'twas coming
    from afar;
Oh the wife she tried to tell me that 'twas
    only summer thunder,

THE MAN FROM ATHABASKA

And she laughed a bit sarcastic when I told her
    it was War;
'Twas the chariots of battle where the mighty
    armies are.

Then down the lake came Half-breed Tom with
    russet sail a-flying,
And the word he said was " War " again, so
    what was I to do?
Oh the dogs they took to howling, and the
    missis took to crying,
As I flung my silver foxes in the little birch
    canoe:
Yes, the old girl stood a-blubbing till an island
    hid the view.

Says the factor: " Mike, you're crazy!   They
    have soldier men a-plenty.
You're as grizzled as a badger, and you're sixty
    year or so."
" But I haven't missed a scrap," says I, " since
    I was one and twenty.
And shall I miss the biggest?   You can bet your
    whiskers — no! "
So I sold my furs and started . . . and that's
    eighteen months ago.

THE MAN FROM ATHABASKA

For I joined the Foreign Legion, and they put
  me for a starter
In the trenches of the Argonne with the Boche
  a step away;
And the partner on my right hand was an
  apache from Montmartre;
On my left there was a millionaire from Pitts-
  burg, U. S. A.
(Poor fellow! They collected him in bits the
  other day.)

But I'm sprier than a chipmunk, save a touch
  of the lumbago,
And they calls me Old Methoosalah, and
  blagues me all the day.
I'm their exhibition sniper, and they work me
  like a Dago,
And laugh to see me plug a Boche a half a mile
  away.
Oh I hold the highest record in the regiment,
  they say.

And at night they gather round me, and I tell
  them of my roaming
In the Country of the Crepuscule beside the
  Frozen Sea,

THE MAN FROM ATHABASKA

Where the musk-ox runs unchallenged, and the
  cariboo goes homing;
And they sit like little children, just as quiet as
  can be:
Men of every crime and colour, how they
  harken unto me!

And I tell them of the Furland, of the tumpline
  and the paddle,
Of secret rivers loitering, that no one will explore;
And I tell them of the ranges, of the pack-strap
  and the saddle,
And they fill their pipes in silence, and their
  eyes beseech for more;
While above the star-shells fizzle and the high
  explosives roar.

And I tell of lakes fish-haunted, where the big
  bull moose are calling,
And forests still as sepulchres with never trail
  or track;
And valleys packed with purple gloom, and
  mountain peaks appalling,

THE MAN FROM ATHABASKA

And I tell them of my cabin on the shore at
    Fond du Lac;
And I find myself a-thinking: Sure I wish that
    I was back.

So I brag of bear and beaver while the batter-
    ies are roaring,
And the fellows on the firing steps are blazing
    at the foe;
And I yarn of fur and feather when the *mar-
    mites* are a-soaring,
And they listen to my stories, seven *poilus* in a
    row,
Seven lean and lousy *poilus* with their cigarettes
    aglow.

And I tell them when it's over how I'll hike
    for Athabaska;
And those seven greasy *poilus* they are crazy
    to go too.
And I'll give the wife the " pickle-tub " I prom-
    ised, and I'll ask her
The price of mink and marten, and the run of
    cariboo,
And I'll get my traps in order, and I'll start to
    work anew.

22

THE MAN FROM ATHABASKA

For I've had my fill of fighting, and I've seen
    a nation scattered,
And an army swung to slaughter, and a river
    red with gore,
And a city all a-smoulder, and . . . as if it
    really mattered,
For the lake is yonder dreaming, and my cabin's
    on the shore;
And the dogs are leaping madly, and the wife is
    singing gladly,
And I'll rest in Athabaska, and I'll leave it
    nevermore.

THE RED RETREAT

Tramp, tramp, the grim road, the road from
Mons to Wipers
(I've 'ammered out this ditty with me bruised
and bleedin' feet);
Tramp, tramp, the dim road — we didn't 'ave
no pipers,
And bellies that was 'oller was the drums we 'ad
to beat.
Tramp, tramp, the bad road, the bits o' kiddies
cryin' there,
The fell birds a-flyin' there, the 'ouses all
aflame;
Tramp, tramp, the sad road, the pals I left
a-lyin' there,
Red there, and dead there. . . . Oh blimy,
it's a shame!

A-singin' " 'Oo's Yer Lady Friend? " we started
out from 'Arver,
A-singin' till our froats was dry — we didn't.
care a 'ang;

THE RED RETREAT

The Frenchies 'ow they lined the way, and slung
  us their palaver,
And all we knowed to arnser was the one word
  " vang ";
They gave us booze and caporal, and cheered
  for us like crazy,
And all the pretty gels was out to kiss us as we
  passed;
And 'ow they all went dotty when we 'owled the
  Marcelaisey!
Oh, Gawd! Them was the 'appy days, the
  days too good to last.

We started out for God Knows Where, we
  started out a-roarin';
We 'ollered: " 'Ere We Are Again," and
  'struth! but we was dry.
The dust was gummin' up our ears, and 'ow the
  sweat was pourin';
The road was long, the sun was like a brazier
  in the sky.
We wondered where the 'Uns was — we wasn't
  long a-wonderin',
For down a scruff of 'ill-side they rushes like a
  flood;

Then oh! 'twas music 'eavenly, our batteries
    a-thunderin',
And arms and legs went soarin' in the fountain
    of their blood.

For on they came like bee-swarms, a-hochin'
    and a-singin';
We pumped the bullets into 'em, we couldn't
    miss a shot.
But though we mowed 'em down like grass,
    like grass was they a-springin',
And all our 'ands was blistered, for our rifles
    was so 'ot.
We roared with battle-fury, and we lammed the
    stuffin' out of 'em,
And then we fixed our bay'nets and we spitted
    'em like meat.
You should 'ave 'eard the beggars squeal; you
    should 'ave seen the rout of 'em,
And 'ow we cussed and wondered when the
    word came: Retreat!

Retreat! That was the 'ell of it. It fair up-
    set our 'abits,
A-runnin' from them blighters over 'alf the
    roads of France;

THE RED RETREAT

A-scurryin' before 'em like a lot of blurry rabbits,
And knowin' we could smash 'em if we just 'ad
  'alf a chance.
Retreat!   That was the bitter bit, a-limpin' and
  a-blunderin';
All day and night a-hoofin' it and sleepin' on
  our feet;
A-fightin' rear guard actions for a bit o' rest,
  and wonderin'
If sugar beets or mangels was the 'olesomest
  to eat.

Ho yus, there isn't many left that started out
  so cheerily;
There was no bands a-playin' and we 'ad no
  autmobeels.
Our tummies they was 'oller, and our 'eads was
  'angin' wearily,
And if we stopped to light a fag the 'Uns was
  on our 'eels.
That rotten road!   I can't forget the kids and
  mothers flyin' there,
The bits of barns a-blazin' and the 'orrid sights
  I sor;

THE RED RETREAT

The stiffs that lined the wayside, me own pals
a-lyin' there,
Their faces covered over wiv a little 'eap of
stror.

Tramp, tramp, the red road, the wicked bullets
'ummin'
(I've panted out this ditty with me 'ot 'ard
breath.)
Tramp, tramp, the dread road, the Boches all
a-comin',
The lootin' and the shootin' and the shrieks
o' death.
Tramp, tramp, the fell road, the mad 'orde pur-
suin' there,
And 'ow we 'urled it back again, them grim,
grey waves;
Tramp, tramp, the 'ell road, the 'orror and the
ruin there,
The graves of me mateys there, the grim, sour
graves.

THE HAGGIS OF PRIVATE MC PHEE

" Hae ye heard whit ma auld mither's postit
  tae me?
It fair maks me hamesick," says Private Mc-
  Phee.
" And whit did she send ye?" says Private
  McPhun,
As he cockit his rifle and bleezed at a Hun.
" A haggis! A *Haggis!*" says Private Mc-
  Phee;
" The brawest big haggis I ever did see.
And think! it's the morn when fond memory
  turns
Tae haggis and whuskey — the Birthday o'
  Burns.
We maun find a dram; then we'll ca' in the rest
O' the lads, and we'll hae a Burns' Nicht wi'
  the best."

" Be ready at sundoon," snapped Sergeant Mc-
        Cole;
" I want you two men for the List'nin' Patrol."
Then Private McPhee looked at Private Mc-
        Phun:
" I'm thinkin', ma lad, we're confoundedly
        done."
Then Private McPhun looked at Private Mc-
        Phee:
" I'm thinkin' auld chap, it's a' aff wi' oor
        spree."
But up spoke their crony, wee Wullie McNair:
" Jist lea' yer braw haggis for me tae prepare;
And as for the dram, if I search the camp
        roun',
We maun hae a drappie tae jist haud it doon.
Sae rin, lads, and think, though the nicht it be
        black,
O' the haggis that's waitin' ye when ye get
        back."

My! but it wis waesome on Naebuddy's Land,
And the deid they were rottin' on every hand.
And the rockets like corpse candles hauntit the
        sky,

And the winds o' destruction went shudderin'
by.
There wis skelpin' o' bullets and skirlin' o'
shells,
And breengin' o' bombs and a thoosand death-
knells;
But cooryin' doon in a Jack Johnson hole
Little fashed the twa men o' the List'nin' Patrol.
For sweeter than honey and bricht as a gem
Wis the thocht o' the haggis that waitit for
them.

Yet alas! in oor moments o' sunniest cheer
Calamity's aften maist cruelly near.
And while the twa talked o' their puddin'
divine
The Boches below them were howkin' a mine.
And while the twa cracked o' the feast they
would hae,
The fuse it wis burnin' and burnin' away.
Then sudden a roar like the thunner o' doom,
A hell-leap o' flame . . . then the wheesht o'
the tomb.

"Haw, Jock! Are ye hurtit?" says Private
    McPhun.

"Ay, Geordie, they've got me; I'm fearin' I'm
    done.

It's ma leg; I'm jist thinkin' it's aff at the knee;

Ye'd best gang and leave me," says Private
    McPhee.

"Oh leave ye I wunna," says Private Mc-
    Phun;

"And leave ye I canna, for though I micht run,

It's no faur I wud gang, it's no muckle I'd see:

I'm blindit, and that's whit's the maitter wi'
    me."

Then Private McPhee sadly shakit his heid:

"If we bide here for lang, we'll be bidin' for
    deid.

And yet, Geordie lad, I could gang weel con-
    tent

If I'd tasted that haggis ma auld mither sent."

"That's droll," says McPhun; "ye've jist
    speakit ma mind.

Oh I ken it's a terrible thing tae be blind;

And yet it's no that that embitters ma lot —

It's missin' that braw muckle haggis ye've got."

For a while they were silent; then up once again

PRIVATE MC PHEE

Spoke Private McPhee, though he whussilt wi'
    pain:
"And why should we miss it? Between you
    and me
We've legs for tae run, and we've eyes for tae
    see.
You lend me your shanks and I'll lend you ma
    sicht,
And we'll baith hae a kyte-fu' o' haggis the
    nicht."

Oh the sky it wis dourlike and dreepin' a wee,
When Private McPhun gruppit Private Mc-
    Phee.
Oh the glaur it wis fylin' and crieshin' the
    grun',
When Private McPhee guidit Private Mc-
    Phun.
"Keep clear o' them corpses — they're maybe
    no deid!
Haud on! There's a big muckle crater aheid.
Look oot! There's a sap; we'll be haein' a
    coup.
A staur-shell! For Godsake! Doun, lad, on
    yer daup.

Bear aff tae yer richt. . . . Aw yer jist daein'
fine:
Before the nicht's feenished on haggis we'll
dine."

There wis death and destruction on every hand;
There wis havoc and horror on Naebuddy's
Land.
And the shells bickered doun wi' a crump and
a glare,
And the hameless wee bullets were dingin' the
air.
Yet on they went staggerin', cooryin' doun
When the stutter and cluck o' a Maxim crept
roun'.
And the legs o' McPhun they were sturdy and
stoot,
And McPhee on his back kept a bonnie look-oot.
"On, on, ma brave lad! We're no faur frae
the goal;
I can hear the braw sweerin' o' Sergeant Mc-
Cole."

PRIVATE MC PHEE

But strength has its leemit, and Private Mc-
    Phun,
Wi' a sab and a curse fell his length on the
    grun'.
Then Private McPhee shoutit doon in his ear:
" Jist think o' the haggis! I smell it from here.
It's gushin' wi' juice, it's embaumin' the air;
It's steamin' for us, and we're — jist — aboot
    — there."
Then Private McPhun answers: " Dommit,
    auld chap!
For the sake o' that haggis I'll gang till I drap."
And he gets on his feet wi' a heave and a
    strain,
And onward he staggers in passion and pain.
And the flare and the glare and the fury in-
    crease,
Till you'd think they'd jist taken a' hell on a
    lease.
And on they go reelin' in peetifu' plight,
And someone is shoutin' away on their right;
And someone is runnin', and noo they can hear
A sound like a prayer and a sound like a cheer;
And swift through the crash and the flash and
    the din,
The lads o' the Hielands are bringin' them in.

" They're baith sairly woundit, but is it no droll
Hoo they rave aboot haggis? " says Sergeant
  McCole.
When hirplin alang comes wee Wullie McNair,
And they a' wonnert why he wis greetin' sae
  sair.
And he says: " I'd jist liftit it oot o' the pot,
And there it lay steamin' and savoury hot,
When sudden I dooked at the fleech o' a shell,
And it — *drapped on the haggis and dinged it
  tae hell.*"

And oh but the lads were fair taken aback;
Then sudden the order wis passed tae attack,
And up from the trenches like lions they leapt,
And on through the nicht like a torrent they
  swept.
On, on, wi' their bayonets thirstin' before!
On, on tae the foe wi' a rush and a roar!
And wild to the welkin their battle-cry rang,
And doon on the Boches like tigers they sprang,
And there wisna a man but had death in his ee,
For he thocht o' the haggis o' Private McPhee.

THE LARK

From wrath-red dawn to wrath-red dawn,
The guns have brayed without abate;
And now the sick sun looks upon
The bleared, blood-boltered fields of hate
As if it loathed to rise again.
How strange the hush! Yet sudden, hark!
From yon down-trodden gold of grain,
The leaping rapture of a lark.

A fusillade of melody,
That sprays us from yon trench of sky;
A new amazing enemy
We cannot silence though we try;
A battery on radiant wings,
That from yon gap of golden fleece
Hurls at us hopes of such strange things
As joy and home and love and peace.

THE LARK

Pure heart of song! do you not know
That we are making earth a hell?
Or is it that you try to show
Life still is joy and all is well?
Brave little wings!   Ah, not in vain
You beat into that bit of blue:
Lo! we who pant in war's red rain
Lift shining eyes, see Heaven too.

THE ODYSSEY OF 'ERBERT
'IGGINS

Me and Ed and a stretcher
Out on the nootral ground.
(If there's one dead corpse, I'll betcher
There's a 'undred smellin' around.)
Me and Eddie O'Brian,
Both of the R. A. M. C.
" It's a 'ell of a night
For a soul to take flight,"
As Eddie remarks to me.
Me and Ed crawlin' 'omeward,
Thinkin' our job is done,
When sudden and clear,
Wot do we 'ear:
'Owl of a wounded 'Un.

" Got to take 'im," snaps Eddy;
" Got to take all we can.
'E may be a Germ
Wiv the 'eart of a worm,
But, blarst 'im! ain't 'e a man?"
So 'e sloshes out fixin' a dressin'

THE ODYSSEY OF 'ERBERT 'IGGINS

('E'd always a medical knack),
When that wounded 'Un
'E rolls to 'is gun,
And 'e plugs me pal in the back.

Now what would you do? I arst you.
There was me slaughtered mate.
There was that 'Un
(I'd collered 'is gun),
A-snarlin' 'is 'ymn of 'ate.
Wot did I do? 'Ere, whisper . . .
'E'd a shiny bald top to 'is 'ead,
But when I got through,
Between me and you,
It was 'orrid and jaggy and red.

" 'Ang on like a limpet, Eddy.
Thank Gord! you ain't dead after all."
It's slow and it's sure and it's steady
(Which is 'ard, for 'e's big and I'm small).
The rockets are shootin' and shinin',
It's rainin' a perishin' flood,
The bullets are buzzin' and whinin',
And I'm up to me stern in the mud.
There's all kinds of 'owlin' and 'ootin';
It's black as a bucket of tar;
Oh, I'm doin' my bit,

40

But I'm 'avin' a fit,
And I wish I was 'ome wiv Mar.

" Stick on like a plaster, Eddy.
Old sport, you're a-slackin' your grip."
Gord! But I'm crocky already;
My feet, 'ow they slither and slip!
There goes the biff of a bullet.
The Boches have got us for fair.
Another one — *Whut!*
The son of a slut!
'E managed to miss by a 'air.
'Ow! Wot was it jabbed at me shoulder?
Gave it a dooce of a wrench.
Is it Eddy or me
Wot's a-bleedin' so free?
Crust! but it's long to the trench.
I ain't just as strong as a Sandow,
And Ed ain't a flapper by far;
I'm blamed if I understand 'ow
We've managed to get where we are.
But 'ere's for a bit of a breather.
" Steady there, Ed, 'arf a mo'.
Old pal, it's all right;
It's a 'ell of a fight,
But are we down-'earted? No-o-o."

41

THE ODYSSEY OF 'ERBERT 'IGGINS

Now war is a funny thing, ain't it?
It's the rummiest sort of a go.
For when it's most real,
It's then that you feel
You're a-watchin' a cinema show.
'Ere's me wot's a barber's assistant.
Hey, presto! It's somewheres in France,
And I'm 'ere in a pit
Where a coal-box 'as 'it,
And it's all like a giddy romance.

The ruddy quick-firers are spittin',
The 'eavies are bellowin' 'ate,
And 'ere I am cashooly sittin',
And 'oldin' the 'ead of me mate.
Them gharstly green star-shells is beamin',
'Ot shrapnel is poppin' like rain,
And I'm sayin': " Bert 'Iggins, you're dreamin',
And you'll wake up in 'Ampstead again.
You'll wake up and 'ear yourself sayin':
' Would you like, sir, to 'ave a shampoo?'
'Stead of sheddin' yer blood
In the rain and the mud,
Which is some'ow the right thing to do;
Which is some'ow yer 'oary-eyed dooty,
Wot you're doin' the best wot you can,
For 'Ampstead and 'ome and beauty,

THE ODYSSEY OF 'ERBERT 'IGGINS

And you've been and you've slaughtered a man.
A feller wot punctured your partner;
Oh, you 'ammered 'im 'ard on the 'ead,
And you still see 'is eyes
Starin' bang at the skies,
And you ain't even sorry 'e's dead.
But you wish you was back in your diggin's
Asleep on your mouldy old stror.
Oh, you're doin' yer bit, 'Erbert 'Iggins,
But you ain't just enjoyin' the war."

" 'Ang on like a hoctopus, Eddy.
It's us for the bomb-belt again.
Except for the shrap
Which 'as 'it me a tap,
I'm feelin' as right as the rain.
It's my silly old feet wot are slippin',
It's as dark as a 'ogs'ead o' sin,
But don't be oneasy, my pippin,
I'm goin' to pilot you in.
It's my silly old 'ead wot is reelin'.
The bullets is buzzin' like bees.
Me shoulder's red-'ot,
And I'm bleedin' a lot,
And me legs is on'inged at the knees.
But we're staggerin' nearer and nearer.

THE ODYSSEY OF 'ERBERT 'IGGINS

Just stick it, old sport, play the game.
I make 'em out clearer and clearer,
Our trenches a-snappin' with flame.
Oh, we're stumblin' closer and closer.
'Ang on there, lad! Just one more try.
Did you say: Put you down? Damn it, no,
    sir!
I'll carry you in if I die.
By cracky! old feller, they've seen us.
They're sendin' out stretchers for two.
Let's give 'em the hoorah between us
('Anged lucky we aren't booked through).
My flipper is mashed to a jelly.
A bullet 'as tickled your spleen.
We've shed lots of gore
And we're leakin' some more,
But — wot a hoccasion it's been!
Ho! 'Ere comes the rescuin' party.
They're crawlin' out cautious and slow.
Come! Buck up and greet 'em, my 'earty,
Shoulder to shoulder — so.
They mustn't think we was down-'earted.
Old pal, we was never down-'earted.
If they arsts us if we was down-'earted
We'll 'owl in their fyces: 'No-o-o!'

44

A SONG OF WINTER WEATHER

It isn't the foe that we fear;
It isn't the bullets that whine;
It isn't the business career
Of a shell, or the bust of a mine;
It isn't the snipers who seek
To nip our young hopes in the bud:
No, it isn't the guns,
And it isn't the Huns —
It's the *mud,*

   mud,

     mud.

It isn't the *mêlée* we mind.
That often is rather good fun.
It isn't the shrapnel we find
Obtrusive when rained by the ton;
It isn't the bounce of the bombs
That gives us a positive pain:
It's the strafing we get
When the weather is wet —

45

A SONG OF WINTER WEATHER

It's the *rain,*
>> *rain,*
>>>> *rain.*

It isn't because we lack grit
We shrink from the horrors of war.
We don't mind the battle a bit;
In fact that is what we are for;
It isn't the rum-jars and things
Make us wish we were back in the fold:
It's the fingers that freeze
In the boreal breeze —
It's the *cold,*
>> *cold,*
>>>> *cold.*

Oh, the rain, the mud, and the cold,
The cold, the mud, and the rain;
With weather at zero it's hard for a hero
From language that's rude to refrain.
With porridgy muck to the knees,
With sky that's a-pouring a flood,
Sure the worst of our foes
Are the pains and the woes
Of the *rain,*
>> the *cold,*
>>>> and the *mud.*

46

TIPPERARY DAYS

Oh, weren't they the fine boys! You never
    saw the beat of them,
Singing all together with their throats bronze-
    bare;
Fighting-fit and mirth-mad, music in the feet of
    them,
Swinging on to glory and the wrath out there.
Laughing by and chaffing by, frolic in the smiles
    of them,
On the road, the white road, all the afternoon;
Strangers in a strange land, miles and miles and
    miles of them,
Battle-bound and heart-high, and singing this
    tune:

> *It's a long way to Tipperary,*
> *It's a long way to go;*
> *It's a long way to Tipperary,*
> *And the sweetest girl I know.*
> *Good-bye, Piccadilly,*
> *Farewell, Lester Square:*

47

TIPPERARY DAYS

It's a long, long way to Tipperary,
But my heart's right there.

" Come, Yvonne and Juliette! Come, Mimi,
and cheer for them!
Throw them flowers and kisses as they pass
you by.
Aren't they the lovely lads! Haven't you a
tear for them
Going out so gallantly to dare and die?
What is it they're singing so? Some high hymn
of Motherland?
Some immortal chanson of their Faith and
King?
Marseillaise or Brabançon, anthem of that
other land,
Dears, let us remember it, that song they
sing:

" C'est un chemin long ' to Tepararee,'
C'est un chemin long, c'est vrai;
C'est un chemin long ' to Tepararee,'
Et la belle fille qu'je connais.
Bonjour, Peekadeely!
Au revoir, Lestaire Squaire!
C'est un chemin long ' to Tepararee,'
Mais mon coeur ' ees zaire.' "

48

TIPPERARY DAYS

The gallant old " Contemptibles! " There
    isn't much remains of them,
So full of fun and fitness, and a-singing in their
    pride;
For some are cold as clabber and the corby picks
    the brains of them,
And some are back in Blighty, and a-wishing
    they had died.
And yet it seems but yesterday, that great, glad
    sight of them,
Swinging on to battle as the sky grew black and
    black;
But oh their glee and glory, and the great, grim
    fight of them! —
Just whistle Tipperary and it all comes back:

> *It's a long way to Tipperary*
> *(Which means " 'ome " anywhere);*
> *It's a long way to Tipperary*
> *(And the things wot make you care).*
> *Good-bye, Piccadilly*
> *('Ow I 'opes my folks is well);*
> *It's a long, long way to Tipperary —*
> *('R! Ain't War just 'ell?)*

FLEURETTE

(The Wounded Canadian Speaks)

My leg? It's off at the knee.
Do I miss it? Well, some. You see
I've had it since I was born;
And lately a devilish corn.
(I rather chuckle with glee
To think how I've fooled that corn.)

But I'll hobble around all right.
It isn't that, it's my face.
Oh I know I'm a hideous sight,
Hardly a thing in place;
Sort of gargoyle, you'd say.
Nurse won't give me a glass,
But I see the folks as they pass
Shudder and turn away;
Turn away in distress . . .
Mirror enough, I guess.

I'm gay! You bet I *am* gay;
But I wasn't a while ago.
If you'd seen me even to-day,
The darndest picture of woe,

FLEURETTE

With this Caliban mug of mine,
So ravaged and raw and red,
Turned to the wall — in fine,
Wishing that I was dead. . . .
What has happened since then,
Since I lay with my face to the wall,
The most despairing of men?
Listen!   I'll tell you all.

That *poilu* across the way,
With the shrapnel wound in his head,
Has a sister: she came to-day
To sit awhile by his bed.
All morning I heard him fret:
" Oh, when will she come, Fleurette? "

Then sudden, a joyous cry;
The tripping of little feet;
The softest, tenderest sigh;
A voice so fresh and sweet;
Clear as a silver bell,
Fresh as the morning dews:
" *C'est toi, c'est toi, Marcel!*
Mon frère, comme je suis heureuse! "

So over the blanket's rim
I raised my terrible face,

FLEURETTE

And I saw — how I envied him!
A girl of such delicate grace;
Sixteen, all laughter and love;
As gay as a linnet, and yet
As tenderly sweet as a dove;
Half woman, half child — Fleurette.

Then I turned to the wall again.
(I was awfully blue, you see,)
And I thought with a bitter pain:
"Such visions are not for me."
So there like a log I lay,
All hidden, I thought from view,
When sudden I heard her say:
"Ah! Who is that *malheureux?*"
Then briefly I heard him tell
(However he came to know)
How I'd smothered a bomb that fell
Into the trench, and so
None of my men were hit,
Though it busted me up a bit.

Well, I didn't quiver an eye,
And he chattered and there she sat;
And I fancied I heard her sigh —
But I wouldn't just swear to that.
And maybe she wasn't so bright,

FLEURETTE

Though she talked in a merry strain,
And I closed my eyes ever so tight,
Yet I saw her ever so plain:
Her dear little tilted nose,
Her delicate, dimpled chin,
Her mouth like a budding rose,
And the glistening pearls within;
Her eyes like the violet:
Such a rare little queen — Fleurette.

And at last when she rose to go,
The light was a little dim,
And I ventured to peep, and so
I saw her, graceful and slim,
And she kissed him and kissed him, and oh
How I envied and envied him!

So when she was gone I said
In rather a dreary voice
To him of the opposite bed:
" Ah, friend, how you must rejoice!
But me, I'm a thing of dread.
For me nevermore the bliss,
The thrill of a woman's kiss."

Then I stopped, for lo! she was there,
And a great light shone in her eyes.

FLEURETTE

And me! I could only stare,
I was taken so by surprise,
When gently she bent her head:
" *May I kiss you, Sergeant?* " she said.

Then she kissed my burning lips
With her mouth like a scented flower,
And I thrilled to the finger-tips,
And I hadn't even the power
To say: " God bless you, dear! "
And I felt such a precious tear
Fall on my withered cheek,
And darn it! I couldn't speak.

And so she went sadly away,
And I knew that my eyes were wet.
Ah, not to my dying day
Will I forget, forget!
Can you wonder now I am gay?
God bless her, that little Fleurette!

FUNK

When your marrer bone seems 'oller,
And you're glad you ain't no taller,
And you're all a-shakin' like you 'ad the chills;
When your skin creeps like a pullet's,
And you're duckin' all the bullets,
And you're green as gorgonzola round the gills;
When your legs seem made of jelly,
And you're squeamish in the belly,
And you want to turn about and do a bunk:
For Gawd's sake, kid, don't show it!
Don't let your mateys know it —
You're just sufferin' from funk, funk, funk.

Of course there's no denyin'
That it ain't so easy tryin'
To grin and grip your rifle by the butt,
When the 'ole world rips asunder,
And you sees yer pal go under,
As a bunch of shrapnel sprays 'im on the nut;

FUNK

I admit it's 'ard contrivin'
When you 'ears the shells arrivin',
To discover you're a bloomin' bit o' spunk;
But, my lad, you've got to do it,
And your God will see you through it,
For wot 'E 'ates is funk, funk, funk.

So stand up, son; look gritty,
And just 'um a lively ditty,
And only be afraid to be afraid;
Just 'old yer rifle steady,
And 'ave yer bay'nit ready,
For that's the way good soldier-men is made.
And if you 'as to die,
As it sometimes 'appens, why,
Far better die a 'ero than a skunk;
A-doin' of yer bit,
And so — to 'ell with it,
There ain't no bloomin' funk, funk, funk.

OUR HERO

" Flowers, only flowers — bring me dainty
      posies,
Blossoms for forgetfulness," that was all he
      said;
So we sacked our gardens, violets and roses,
Lilies white and bluebells laid we on his bed.
Soft his pale hands touched them, tenderly
      caressing;
Soft into his tired eyes came a little light;
Such a wistful love-look, gentle as a blessing;
There amid the flowers waited he the night.

" I would have you raise me; I can see the West
      then:
I would see the sun set once before I go."
So he lay a-gazing, seemed to be at rest then,
Quiet as a spirit in the golden glow.
So he lay a-watching rosy castles crumbling,
Moats of blinding amber, bastions of flame,
Rugged rifts of opal, crimson turrets tumbling;
So he lay a-dreaming till the shadows came.

OUR HERO

"Open wide the window; there's a lark a-
    singing;
There's a glad lark singing in the evening sky.
How it's wild with rapture, radiantly winging:
Oh it's good to hear that when one has to die.
I am horror-haunted from the hell they found
    me;
I am battle-broken, all I want is rest.
Ah! It's good to die so, blossoms all around
    me,
And a kind lark singing in the golden West.

"Flowers, song and sunshine, just one thing is
    wanting,
Just the happy laughter of a little child."
So we brought our dearest, Doris all-en-
    chanting;
Tenderly he kissed her; radiant he smiled.
"In the golden peace-time you will tell the
    story
How for you and yours, sweet, bitter deaths
    were ours. . . .
God bless little children!" So he passed to
    glory,
So we left him sleeping, still amid the flow'rs.

MY MATE

I've been sittin' starin', starin' at 'is muddy pair
    of boots,
And tryin' to convince meself it's 'im.
(Look out there, lad! That sniper —'e's a
    dysey when 'e shoots;
'E'll be layin' of you out the same as Jim.)
Jim as lies there in the dug-out wiv 'is blanket
    round 'is 'ead,
To keep 'is brains from mixin' wiv the mud;
And 'is face as white as putty, and 'is over-
    coat all red,
Like 'e's spilt a bloomin' paint-pot — but it's
    blood.

And I'm tryin' to remember of a time we wasn't
    pals.
'Ow often we've played 'ookey, 'im and me;
And sometimes it was music-'alls, and some-
    times it was gals,

MY MATE

And even there we 'ad no disagree.
For when 'e copped Mariar Jones, the one I
   liked the best,
I shook 'is 'and and loaned 'im 'arf a quid;
I saw 'im through the parson's job, I 'elped 'im
   make 'is nest,
I even stood god-farther to the kid.

So when the war broke out, sez 'e: "Well,
   wot abaht it, Joe?"
"Well, wot abaht it, lad?" sez I to 'im.
'Is missis made a awful fuss, but 'e was mad
   to go,
('E always was 'igh-sperrited was Jim).
Well, none of it's been 'eaven, and the most
   of it's been 'ell,
But we've shared our baccy, and we've 'alved
   our bread.
We'd all the luck at Wipers, and we shaved
   through Noove Chapelle,
And . . . that snipin' barstard gits 'im on the
   'ead.

MY MATE

Now wot I wants to know is, why it wasn't
    me was took?
I've only got meself, 'e stands for three.
I'm plainer than a louse, while 'e was 'andsome
    as a dook;
'E always *was* a better man than me.
'E was goin' 'ome next Toosday; 'e was 'appy
    as a lark,
And 'e'd just received a letter from 'is kid;
And 'e struck a match to show me, as we stood
    there in the dark,
When . . . that bleedin' bullet got 'im on the
    lid.

'E was killed so awful sudden that 'e 'adn't
    time to die.
'E sorto jumped, and came down wiv a thud.
Them corpsy-lookin' star-shells kept a-streamin'
    in the sky,
And there 'e lay like nothin' in the mud.
And there 'e lay so quiet wiv no mansard to 'is
    'ead,
And I'm sick, and blamed if I can understand:
The pots of 'alf and 'alf we've 'ad, and *zip!*
    like that —'e's dead,
Wiv the letter of 'is nipper in 'is 'and.

MY MATE

There's some as fights for freedom and there's
    some as fights for fun,
But me, my lad, I fights for bleedin' 'ate.
You can blame the war and blast it, but I 'opes
    it won't be done
Till I gets the bloomin' blood-price for me
    mate.
It'll take a bit o' bayonet to level up for Jim;
Then if I'm spared I think I'll 'ave a bid,
Wiv 'er that was Mariar Jones to take the
    place of 'im,
To sorter be a farther to 'is kid.

MILKING TIME

There's a drip of honeysuckle in the deep green
    lane;
There's old Martin jogging homeward on his
    worn old wain;
There are cherry petals falling, and a cuckoo
    calling, calling,
And a score of larks (God bless 'em) . . .
    but it's all pain, pain.
For you see I am not really there at all, not
    at all;
For you see I'm in the trenches where the
    crump-crumps fall;
And the bits o' shells are screaming and it's
    only blessed dreaming
That in fancy I am seeming back in old Saint
    Pol.

Oh I've thought of it so often since I've come
    down here;
And I never dreamt that any place could be
    so dear;

MILKING TIME

The silvered whinstone houses, and the rosy
    men in blouses,
And the kindly, white-capped women with their
    eyes spring-clear.
And mother's sitting knitting where her roses
    climb,
And the angelus is calling with a soft, soft
    chime,
And the sea-wind comes caressing, and the
    light's a golden blessing,
And Yvonne, Yvonne is guessing that it's milk-
    ing time.

Oh it's Sunday, for she's wearing of her broid-
    ered gown;
And she draws the pasture pickets and the cows
    come down;
And their feet are powdered yellow, and their
    voices honey-mellow,
And they bring a scent of clover, and their eyes
    are brown.
And Yvonne is dreaming after, but her eyes are
    blue;
And her lips are made for laughter, and her
    white teeth too;

MILKING TIME

And her mouth is like a cherry, and a dimple
    mocking merry
Is lurking in the very cheek she turns to you.

So I walk beside her kindly, and she laughs at
    me;
And I heap her arms with lilac from the lilac
    tree;
And a golden light is welling, and a golden
    peace is dwelling,
And a thousand birds are telling how it's good
    to be.
And what are pouting lips for if they can't be
    kissed?
And I've filled her arms with blossom so she
    can't resist;
And the cows are sadly straying, and her mother
    must be saying
That Yvonne is long delaying . . . *God!
How close that missed!*

A nice polite reminder that the Boche are nigh;
That we're here to fight like devils, and if
    need-be die;

MILKING TIME

That from kissing pretty wenches to the fran-
tic firing-benches
Of the battered, tattered trenches is a far, far
cry.
Yet still I'm sitting dreaming in the glare and
grime;
And once again I'm hearing of them church-
bells chime;
And how I wonder whether in the golden summer weather
We will fetch the cows together when it's milking time. . . .
    (English voice, months later) : —
"*Ow Bill! A rottin' Frenchy. Whew! 'E
ain't 'arf prime.*"

YOUNG FELLOW MY LAD

" Where are you going, Young Fellow My Lad,
On this glittering morn of May? "
" I'm going to join the Colours, Dad;
They're looking for men, they say."
" But you're only a boy, Young Fellow My Lad;
You aren't obliged to go."
" I'm seventeen and a quarter, Dad,
And ever so strong, you know."

 . . . . . .

" So you're off to France, Young Fellow My
  Lad,
And you're looking so fit and bright."
" I'm terribly sorry to leave you, Dad,
But I feel that I'm doing right."
" God bless you and keep you, Young Fellow
  My Lad,
You're all of my life, you know."
" Don't worry. I'll soon be back, dear Dad,
And I'm awfully proud to go."

 . . . . . .

YOUNG FELLOW MY LAD

" Why don't you write, Young Fellow My Lad?
I watch for the post each day;
And I miss you so, and I'm awfully sad,
And it's months since you went away.
And I've had the fire in the parlour lit,
And I'm keeping it burning bright
Till my boy comes home; and here I sit
Into the quiet night."

.   .   .   .   .   .

" What is the matter, Young Fellow My Lad?
No letter again to-day.
Why did the postman look so sad,
And sigh as he turned away?
I hear them tell that we've gained new ground,
But a terrible price we've paid:
God grant, my boy, that you're safe and sound;
But oh I'm afraid, afraid."

.   .   .   .   .

YOUNG FELLOW MY LAD

They've told me the truth, Young Fellow My
  Lad:
You'll never come back again:
(Oh God! the dreams and the dreams I've had,
And the hopes I've nursed in vain!)
For you passed in the night, Young Fellow My
  Lad,
And you proved in the cruel test
Of the screaming shell and the battle hell
That my boy was one of the best.

"So you'll live, you'll live, Young Fellow My
  Lad,
In the gleam of the evening star,
In the wood-note wild and the laugh of the
  child,
In all sweet things that are.
And you'll never die, my wonderful boy,
While life is noble and true;
For all our beauty and hope and joy
We will owe to our lads like you."

A SONG OF THE SANDBAGS

No, Bill, I'm not a-spooning out no patriotic
    tosh
(The cove be'ind the sandbags ain't a death-or-
    glory cuss).
And though I strafes 'em good and 'ard I doesn't
    'ate the Boche,
I guess they're mostly decent, just the same as
    most of us.
I guess they loves their 'omes and kids as much
    as you or me;
And just the same as you or me they'd rather
    shake than fight;
And if we'd 'appened to be born at Berlin-on-
    the-Spree,
We'd be out there with 'Ans and Fritz, dead
    sure that we was right.

    A-standin' up to the sandbags
    It's funny the thoughts wot come;
    Starin' into the darkness,

A SONG OF THE SANDBAGS

'Earin' the bullets 'um;
(*Zing! Zip! Ping! Rip!*
'Ark 'ow the bullets 'um!)
A-leanin' against the sandbags
Wiv me rifle under me ear,
Oh, I've 'ad more thoughts on a sentry-go
Than I used to 'ave in a year.

I wonder, Bill, if 'Ans and Fritz is wonderin'
  like me
Wot's at the bottom of it all?   Wot all the
  slaughter's for?
'E thinks 'e's right (of course 'e ain't) but this
  we both agree,
If them as made it 'ad to fight, there wouldn't be
  no war.
If them as lies in feather beds while we kips in
  the mud;
If them as makes their fortoons while we fights
  for 'em like 'ell;
If them as slings their pot of ink just 'ad to sling
  their blood:
By Crust!   I'm thinkin' there 'ud be another
  tale to tell.

Shiverin' up to the sandbags,
With a hicicle 'stead of a spine,

A SONG OF THE SANDBAGS

Don't it seem funny the things you think
'Ere in the firin' line:
(*Whee! Whut! Ziz! Zut!*
Lord! 'Ow the bullets whine!)
Hunkerin' down when a star-shell
Cracks in a sputter of light,
You can jaw to yer soul by the sandbags
Most any old time o' night.

They talks o' England's glory and a-'oldin' of
our trade,
Of Empire and 'igh destiny until we're fair flim-
flammed;
But if it's for the likes o' that that bloody war
is made,
Then wot I say is: Empire and 'igh destiny be
damned!
There's only one good cause, Bill, for poor
blokes like us to fight:
That's self-defence, for 'earth and 'ome, and
them that bears our name;
And that's wot I'm a-doin' by the sandbags 'ere
to-night. . . .
But Fritz out there will tell you 'e's a-doin' of
the same.

A SONG OF THE SANDBAGS

Starin' over the sandbags,
Sick of the 'ole damn thing;
Firin' to keep meself awake,
'Earin' the bullets sing.
(*Hiss!   Twang!   Tsing!   Pang!*
Saucy the bullets sing.)
Dreamin' 'ere by the sandbags
Of a day when war will cease,
When 'Ans and Fritz and Bill and me
Will clink our mugs in fraternity,
And the Brotherhood of Labour will be
The Brotherhood of Peace.

ON THE WIRE

O God, take the sun from the sky!
It's burning me, scorching me up.
God, can't You hear my cry?
Water!   A poor, little cup!
It's laughing, the cursed sun!
See how it swells and swells
Fierce as a hundred hells!
God, will it never have done?
It's searing the flesh on my bones;
It's beating with hammers red
My eyeballs into my head;
It's parching my very moans.
See!   It's the size of the sky,
And the sky is a torrent of fire,
Foaming on me as I lie
Here on the wire . . . the wire. . . .

Of the thousands that wheeze and hum
Heedlessly over my head,
Why can't a bullet come,
Pierce to my brain instead,

74

ON THE WIRE

Blacken forever my brain,
Finish forever my pain?
Here in the hellish glare
Why must I suffer so?
Is it God doesn't care?
Is it God doesn't know?
Oh, to be killed outright,
Clean in the clash of the fight!
That is a golden death,
That is a boon; but this . . .
Drawing an anguished breath
Under a hot abyss,
Under a stooping sky
Of seething, sulphurous fire,
Scorching me up as I lie
Here on the wire . . . the wire. . . .

Hasten, O God, Thy night!
Hide from my eyes the sight
Of the body I stare and see
Shattered so hideously.
I can't believe that it's mine.
My body was white and sweet,
Flawless and fair and fine,
Shapely from head to feet;
Oh no, I can never be

ON THE WIRE

The thing of horror I see
Under the rifle fire,
Trussed on the wire . . . the wire. . . .

Of night and of death I dream;
Night that will bring me peace,
Coolness and starry gleam,
Stillness and death's release:
Ages and ages have passed,—
Lo! it is night at last.
Night! but the guns roar out.
Night! but the hosts attack.
Red and yellow and black
Geysers of doom upspout.
Silver and green and red
Star-shells hover and spread.
Yonder off to the right
Fiercely kindles the fight;
Roaring near and more near,
Thundering now in my ear;
Close to me, close . . . Oh, hark!
Someone moans in the dark.
I hear, but I cannot see,
I hear as the rest retire,
Someone is caught like me,
Caught on the wire . . . the wire. . . .

ON THE WIRE

Again the shuddering dawn,
Weird and wicked and wan;
Again, and I've not yet gone.
The man whom I heard is dead.
Now I can understand:
A bullet hole in his head,
A pistol gripped in his hand.
Well, he knew what to do,—
Yes, and now I know too. . . .

Hark the resentful guns!
Oh, how thankful am I
To think my beloved ones
Will never know how I die!
I've suffered more than my share;
I'm shattered beyond repair;
I've fought like a man the fight,
And now I demand the right
(God! how his fingers cling!)
To do without shame this thing.
Good! there's a bullet still;
Now I'm ready to fire;
Blame me, God, if You will,
Here on the wire . . . the wire. . . .

BILL'S GRAVE

I'm gatherin' flowers by the wayside to lay on
    the grave of Bill;
I've sneaked away from the billet, 'cause Jim
    wouldn't understand;
'E'd call me a silly fat'ead, and larf till it made
    'im ill,
To see me 'ere in the cornfield, wiv a big bookay
    in me 'and.

For Jim and me we are rough uns, but Bill was
    one o' the best;
We 'listed and learned together to larf at the
    wust wot comes;
Then Bill copped a packet proper, and took 'is
    departure West,
So sudden 'e 'adn't a minit to say good-bye to
    'is chums.

78

BILL'S GRAVE

And they took me to where 'e was planted, a
    sort of a measly mound,
And, thinks I, 'ow Bill would be tickled, bein' so
    soft and queer,
If I gathered a bunch o' them wild-flowers, and
    sort of arranged them round
Like a kind of a bloody headpiece . . . and
    that's the reason I'm 'ere.

But not for the love of glory I wouldn't 'ave Jim
    to know.
'E'd call me a slobberin' Cissy, and larf till 'is
    sides was sore;
I'd 'ave larfed at meself too, it isn't so long
    ago;
But some'ow it changes a feller, 'avin' a taste o'
    war.

It 'elps a man to be 'elpful, to know wot 'is pals
    is worth
(Them golden poppies is blazin' like lamps some
    fairy 'as lit);
I'm fond o' them big white dysies. . . . Now
    Jim's o' the salt o' the earth;
But 'e 'as got a tongue wot's a terror, and 'e
    ain't sentimental a bit.

BILL'S GRAVE

I likes them blue chaps wot's 'idin' so shylike
    among the corn.
Won't Bill be glad!   We was allus thicker 'n
    thieves, us three.
Why! 'Oo's that singin' so 'earty? *Jim!* And
    as sure as I'm born
'E's there in the giddy cornfields, a-gatherin'
    flowers like me.

Quick!   Drop me posy be'ind me.   I watches
    'im for a while,
Then I says: " Wot 'o, there, Chummy! Wot
    price the little bookay? "
And 'e starts like a bloke wot's guilty, and 'e
    says with a sheepish smile:
" She's a bit of orl right, the widder wot keeps
    the estaminay."

So 'e goes away in a 'urry, and I wishes 'im
    best o' luck,
And I picks up me bunch o' wild-flowers, and the
    light's gettin' sorto dim,

BILL'S GRAVE

When I makes me way to the boneyard, and
    . . . I stares like a man wot's stuck,
For wot do I see? *Bill's grave-mound strewn*
    with the flowers of Jim.

Of course I won't never tell 'im, bein' a tactical
    lad;
And Jim parley-voos to the widder: " Trez
    beans, lamoor; compree? "
Oh, 'e'd die of shame if 'e knew I knew; but say!
    won't Bill be glad
When 'e stares through the bleedin' clods and
    sees the blossoms of Jim and me?

JEAN DESPREZ

Oh ye whose hearts are resonant, and ring to
    War's romance,
Hear ye the story of a boy, a peasant boy of
    France;
A lad uncouth and warped with toil, yet who,
    when trial came,
Could feel within his soul upleap and soar the
    sacred flame;
Could stand upright, and scorn and smite, as
    only heroes may:
Oh, harken! Let me try to tell the tale of Jean
    Desprez.

With fire and sword the Teuton horde was
    ravaging the land,
And there was darkness and despair, grim death
    on every hand;
Red fields of slaughter sloping down to ruin's
    black abyss;

82

JEAN DESPREZ

The wolves of war ran evil-fanged, and little did
    they miss.
And on they came with fear and flame, to burn
    and loot and slay,
Until they reached the red-roofed croft, the
    home of Jean Desprez.

" Rout out the village, one and all! " the Uhlan
    Captain said.
" Behold!   Some hand has fired a shot.   My
    trumpeter is dead.
Now shall they Prussian vengeance know; now
    shall they rue the day,
For by this sacred German slain, ten of these
    dogs shall pay."
They drove the cowering peasants forth, women
    and babes and men,
And from the last, with many a jeer, the Cap-
    tain chose he ten;
Ten simple peasants, bowed with toil; they
    stood, they knew not why,
Against the grey wall of the church, hearing
    their children cry;

Hearing their wives and mothers wail, with faces
    dazed they stood.
A moment only. . . . *Ready! Fire!* They
    weltered in their blood.

But there was one who gazed unseen, who heard
    the frenzied cries,
Who saw these men in sabots fall before their
    children's eyes;
A Zouave wounded in a ditch, and knowing
    death was nigh,
He laughed with joy: "Ah! here is where I
    settle ere I die."
He clutched his rifle once again, and long he
    aimed and well. . . .
A shot! Beside his victims ten the Uhlan Cap-
    tain fell.

They dragged the wounded Zouave out; their
    rage was like a flame.
With bayonets they pinned him down, until their
    Major came.
A blonde, full-blooded man he was, and arrogant
    of eye;

JEAN DESPREZ

He stared to see with shattered skull his favourite Captain lie.
" Nay, do not finish him so quick, this foreign
swine," he cried;
" Go nail him to the big church door: he shall
be crucified."

With bayonets through hands and feet they
nailed the Zouave there,
And there was anguish in his eyes, and horror
in his stare;
" Water! A single drop!" he moaned; but
how they jeered at him,
And mocked him with an empty cup, and saw
his sight grow dim;
And as in agony of death with blood his lips
were wet,
The Prussian Major gaily laughed, and lit a
cigarette.

But mid the white-faced villagers who cowered
in horror by,
Was one who saw the woeful sight, who heard
the woeful cry:

"Water!   One little drop, I beg!   For love of
  Christ who died. . . ."
It was the little Jean Desprez who turned and
  stole aside;
It was the little bare-foot boy who came with
  cup abrim
And walked up to the dying man, and gave the
  drink to him.

A roar of rage!   They seize the boy; they tear
  him fast away.
The Prussian Major swings around; no longer
  is he gay.
His teeth are wolfishly agleam; his face all dark
  with spite:
"Go, shoot the brat," he snarls, "that dare
  defy our Prussian might.
Yet stay! I have another thought.   I'll kindly
  be, and spare;
Quick! give the lad a rifle charged, and set him
  squarely there,
And bid him shoot, and shoot to kill.   Haste!
  Make him understand
The dying dog he fain would save shall perish
  by his hand.

And all his kindred they shall see, and all shall
    curse his name,
Who bought his life at such a cost, the price of
    death and shame."

They brought the boy, wild-eyed with fear; they
    made him understand;
They stood him by the dying man, a rifle in his
    hand.
" Make haste! " said they; " the time is short,
    and you must kill or die."
The Major puffed his cigarette, amusement in
    his eye.
And then the dying Zouave heard, and raised his
    weary head:
" Shoot, son, 'twill be the best for both; shoot
    swift and straight," he said.
" Fire first and last, and do not flinch; for lost
    to hope am I;
And I will murmur: *Vive La France!* and
    bless you ere I die."

Half-blind with blows the boy stood there; he
    seemed to swoon and sway;

JEAN DESPREZ

Then in that moment woke the soul of little Jean
    Desprez.
He saw the woods go sheening down; the larks
    were singing clear;
And oh! the scents and sounds of spring, how
    sweet they were! how dear!
He felt the scent of new-mown hay, a soft breeze
    fanned his brow;
O God! the paths of peace and toil! How
    precious were they now!
The summer days and summer ways, how bright
    with hope and bliss!
The autumn such a dream of gold . . . and all
    must end in this:
This shining rifle in his hand, that shambles all
    around;
The Zouave there with dying glare; the blood
    upon the ground;
The brutal faces round him ringed, the evil eyes
    aflame;
That Prussian bully standing by, as if he watched
    a game.
" Make haste and shoot," the Major sneered;
    " a minute more I give;
A minute more to kill your friend, if you your-
    self would live."

JEAN DESPREZ

They only saw a bare-foot boy, with blanched
    and twitching face;
They did not see within his eyes the glory of his
    race;
The glory of a million men who for fair France
    have died,
The splendour of self-sacrifice that will not be
    denied.
Yet . . . he was but a peasant lad, and oh! but
    life was sweet. . . .
" Your minute's nearly gone, my lad," he heard
    a voice repeat.
" Shoot!   Shoot! " the dying Zouave moaned;
    " Shoot!   Shoot! " the soldiers said.
Then Jean Desprez reached out and shot . . .
    the Prussian Major dead!

GOING HOME

I'm goin' 'ome to Blighty — ain't I glad to 'ave
   the chance!
I'm loaded up wiv fightin', and I've 'ad my fill
   o' France;
I'm feelin' so excited-like, I want to sing and
   dance,
   For I'm goin' 'ome to Blighty in the mawnin'.

I'm goin' 'ome to Blighty: can you wonder as
   I'm gay?
I've got a wound I wouldn't sell for 'alf a year
   o' pay;
A harm that's mashed to jelly in the nicest sort
   o' way,
   For it takes me 'ome to Blighty in the mawnin'.

'Ow everlastin' keen I was on gettin' to the
   front!
I'd ginger for a dozen, and I 'elped to bear the
   brunt;
But Cheese and Crust! I'm crazy, now I've
   done me little stunt,
      To sniff the air of Blighty in the mawnin'.

90

GOING HOME

I've looked upon the wine that's white, and on
    the wine that's red;
I've looked on cider flowin', till it fairly turned
    me 'ead;
But oh, the finest scoff will be, when all is done
    and said,
    A pint o' Bass in Blighty in the mawnin'.

I'm goin' back to Blighty, which I left to strafe
    the 'Un;
I've fought in bloody battles, and I've 'ad a 'eap
    of fun;
But now me flipper's busted, and I think me
    dooty's done,
    And I'll kiss me gel in Blighty in the mawnin'.

Oh, there be furrin' lands to see, and some of 'em
    be fine;
And there be furrin' gels to kiss, and scented
    furrin' wine;
But there's no land like England, and no other
    gel like mine:
    Thank Gawd for dear old Blighty in the
    mawnin'.

COCOTTE

When a girl's sixteen, and as poor as she's pretty,
And she hasn't a friend and she hasn't a home,
Heigh-ho!   She's as safe in Paris city
As a lamb night-strayed where the wild wolves
        roam;
And that was I; oh, it's seven years now
(Some water's run down the Seine since then),
And I've almost forgotten the pangs and the
        tears now,
And I've almost taken the measure of men.

Oh, I found me a lover who loved me only,
Artist and poet, and almost a boy.
And my heart was bruised, and my life was
        lonely,
And him I adored with a wonderful joy.
If he'd come to me with his pockets empty,
How we'd have laughed in a garret gay!
But he was rich, and in radiant plenty
We lived in a villa at Viroflay.
Then came the War, and of bliss bereft me;
Then came the call, and he went away;

COCOTTE

All that he had in the world he left me,
With the rose-wreathed villa at Viroflay.
Then came the news and the tragic story:
My hero, my splendid lover was dead,
Sword in hand on the field of glory,
And he died with my name on his lips, they said.

So here am I in my widow's mourning,
The weeds I've really no right to wear;
And women fix me with eyes of scorning,
Call me "cocotte," but I do not care.
And men look at me with eyes that borrow
The brightness of love, but I turn away;
Alone, say I, I will live with Sorrow,
In my little villa at Viroflay.

And lo! I'm living alone with *Pity*,
And they say that pity from love's not far;
Let me tell you all: last week in the city
I took the metro at Saint Lazare;
And the carriage was crowded to overflowing,
And when there entered at Chateaudun
Two wounded *poilus* with medals showing,
I eagerly gave my seat to one.

You should have seen them: they'd slipped
    death's clutches,

93

COCOTTE

But sadder a sight you will rarely find;
One had a leg off and walked on crutches,
The other, a bit of a boy, was blind.
And they both sat down, and the lad was trying
To grope his way as a blind man tries;
And half of the women around were crying,
And some of the men had tears in their eyes.

How he stirred me, this blind boy, clinging
Just like a child to his crippled chum.
But I did not cry.   Oh no; a singing
Came to my heart for a year so dumb,
Then I knew that at three-and-twenty
There is wonderful work to be done,
Comfort and kindness and joy in plenty,
Peace and light and love to be won.

Oh, thought I, could mine eyes be given
To one who will live in the dark alway!
To love and to serve —'twould make life
    Heaven
Here in my villa at Viroflay.
So I left my *poilus:* and now you wonder
Why to-day I am so elate. . . .
Look!   In the glory of sunshine yonder
They're bringing my blind boy in at the gate.

MY BAY'NIT

When first I left Blighty they gave me a bay'nit
And told me it 'ad to be smothered wiv gore;
But blimey!   I 'aven't been able to stain it,
So far as I've gone wiv the vintage of war.
For ain't it a fraud! when a Boche and yours
                 truly
Gits into a mix in the grit and the grime,
'E jerks up 'is 'ands wiv a yell and 'e's duly
                    Part of me outfit every time.

                Left, right, Hans and Fritz!
                Goose step, keep up yer mits!
                Oh my,   Ain't it a shyme!
                Part of me outfit every time.

At toasting a biscuit me bay'nit's a dandy;
I've used it to open a bully beef can;
For pokin' the fire it comes in werry 'andy;
For any old thing but for stickin' a man.
'Ow often I've said: " 'Ere, I'm goin' to
        press you

95

MY BAY'NIT

Into a 'Un till you're seasoned for prime,'
And fiercely I rushes to do it, but bless you!
> Part of me outfit every time.

> Lor, yus; *don't* they look glad?
> Right O! 'Owl Kamerad!
> Oh my, always the syme!
> Part of me outfit every time.

I'm 'untin' for someone to christen me bay'nit,
Some nice juicy Chewton wot's fightin' in France;
I'm fairly down-'earted —'ow *can* yer explain
    it?
I keeps gettin' prisoners every chance.
As soon as they sees me they ups and surrenders,
Extended like monkeys wot's tryin' to climb;
And I uses me bay'nit — to slit their sus-
    penders —
> Part of me outfit every time.

> Four 'Uns; lor, wot a bag!
> 'Ere, Fritz, sample a fag!
> Oh my, ain't it a gyme!
> Part of me outfit every time.

CARRY ON!

It's easy to fight when everything's right,
And you're mad with the thrill and the glory;
It's easy to cheer when victory's near,
And wallow in fields that are gory.
It's a different song when everything's wrong.
When you're feeling infernally mortal;
When it's ten against one, and hope there is
              none,
Buck up, little soldier, and chortle:

        Carry on!   Carry on!
    There isn't much punch in your blow.
You're glaring and staring and hitting out blind;
You're muddy and bloody, but never you mind.
        Carry on!   Carry on!
    You haven't the ghost of a show.
It's looking like death, but while you've a breath,
        Carry on, my son!   Carry on!

97

CARRY ON!

And so in the strife of the battle of life
It's easy to fight when you're winning;
It's easy to slave, and starve and be brave,
When the dawn of success is beginning.
But the man who can meet despair and defeat
With a cheer, there's the man of God's choos-
ing;
The man who can fight to Heaven's own height
Is the man who can fight when he's losing.

   Carry on! Carry on!
  Things never were looming so black.
But show that you haven't a cowardly streak,
And though you're unlucky you never are weak.
   Carry on! Carry on!
  Brace up for another attack.
It's looking like hell, but — you never can tell:
   Carry on, old man! Carry on!

There are some who drift out in the deserts of
   doubt,
And some who in brutishness wallow;
There are others, I know, who in piety go
Because of a Heaven to follow.
But to labour with zest, and to give of your best,

CARRY ON!

For the sweetness and joy of the giving;
To help folks along with a hand and a song;
Why, there's the real sunshine of living.

Carry on!   Carry on!
Fight the good fight and true;
Believe in your mission, greet life with a cheer;
There's big work to do, and that's why you
are here.
Carry on!   Carry on!
Let the world be the better for you;
And at last when you die, let this be your cry:
Carry on, my soul!   Carry on!

OVER THE PARAPET

All day long when the shells sail over
I stand at the sandbags and take my chance;
But at night, at night I'm a reckless rover,
And over the parapet gleams Romance.
Romance! Romance! How I've dreamed it,
    writing
Dreary old records of money and mart,
Me with my head chuckful of fighting
And the blood of vikings to thrill my heart.

But little I thought that my time was coming,
Sudden and splendid, supreme and soon;
And here I am with the bullets humming
As I crawl and I curse the light of the moon.
Out alone, for adventure thirsting,
Out in mysterious No Man's Land;
Prone with the dead when a star-shell, bursting,
Flares on the horrors on every hand.
There are ruby stars and they drip and wiggle;
And the grasses gleam in a light blood-red;
There are emerald stars, and their tails they
    wriggle,

OVER THE PARAPET

And ghastly they glare on the face of the dead.
But the worst of all are the stars of whiteness,
That spill in a pool of pearly flame,
Pretty as gems in their silver brightness,
And etching a man for a bullet's aim.

Yet oh, it's great to be here with danger,
Here in the weird, death-pregnant dark,
In the devil's pasture a stealthy ranger,
When the moon is decently hiding.   Hark!
What was that?   Was it just the shiver
Of an eerie wind or a clammy hand?
The rustle of grass, or the passing quiver
Of one of the ghosts of No Man's Land?

It's only at night when the ghosts awaken,
And gibber and whisper horrible things;
For to every foot of this God-forsaken
Zone of jeopard some horror clings.
Ugh!   What was that?   It felt like a jelly,
That flattish mound in the noisome grass;
You three big rats running free of its belly,
Out of my way and let me pass!

But if there's horror, there's beauty, wonder;
The trench lights gleam and the rockets play.

OVER THE PARAPET

That flood of magnificent orange yonder
Is a battery blazing miles away.
With a rush and a singing a great shell passes;
The rifles resentfully bicker and brawl,
And here I crouch in the dew-drenched grasses,
And look and listen and love it all.

God! What a life! But I must make haste
    now,
Before the shadow of night be spent.
It's little the time there is to waste now,
If I'd do the job for which I was sent.
My bombs are right and my clippers ready,
And I wriggle out to the chosen place,
When I hear a rustle . . . Steady! . . .
    Steady!
Who am I staring slap in the face?

There in the dark I can hear him breathing,
A foot away, and as still as death;
And my heart beats hard, and my brain is seeth-
    ing,
And I know he's a Hun by the smell of his breath.
Then: "Will you surrender?" I whisper
    hoarsely,
For it's death, swift death to utter a cry.

OVER THE PARAPET

" English   schwein-hund! "   he   murmurs
    coarsely.
" Then we'll fight it out in the dark," say I.

So we grip and we slip and we trip and wrestle
There in the gutter of No Man's Land;
And I feel my nails in his wind-pipe nestle,
And he tries to gouge, but I bite his hand.
And he tries to squeal, but I squeeze him tighter:
" Now," I say, " I can kill you fine;
But tell me first, you Teutonic blighter!
Have   you   any   children?"   He   answers:
    " Nein."

Nine!   Well, I cannot kill such a father,
So I tie his hands and I leave him there.
Do I finish my little job?   Well, rather;
And I get home safe with some light to spare.
Heigh-ho! by day it's just prosy duty,
Doing the same old song and dance;
But oh! with the night — joy, glory, beauty:
Over the parapet — Life, Romance!

THE BALLAD OF SOULFUL SAM

You want me to tell you a story, a yarn of the
 firin' line,
Of our thin red kharki 'eroes, out there where
 the bullets whine;
Out there where the bombs are bustin', and the
 cannons like 'ell-doors slam —
Just order another drink, boys, and I'll tell you
 of Soulful Sam.

Oh, Sam, he was never 'ilarious, though I've 'ad
 some mates as was wus;
He 'adn't C. B. on his programme, he never was
 known to cuss.
For a card or a skirt or a beer-mug he 'adn't a
 friendly word;
But when it came down to Scriptures, say!
 Wasn't he just a bird!

He always 'ad tracts in his pocket, the which he
 would haste to present,
And though the fellers would use them in ways
 that they never was meant,

THE BALLAD OF SOULFUL SAM

I used to read 'em religious, and frequent I've
    been impressed
By some of them bundles of 'oly dope he carried
    around in his vest.

For I — and oh, 'ow I shudder at the 'orror the
    word conveys!
'Ave been — let me whisper it 'oarsely — a gam-
    bler 'alf of me days;
A gambler, you 'ear — a gambler. It makes
    me wishful to weep,
And yet 'ow it's true, my brethren! — I'd
    rather gamble than sleep.

I've gambled the 'ole world over, from Monte
    Carlo to Maine;
From Dawson City to Dover, from San Fran-
    cisco to Spain.
Cards! They 'ave been me ruin. They've
    taken me pride and me pelf,
And when I'd no one to play with — why, I'd
    go and I'd play by meself.

And Sam 'e would sit and watch me, as I shuf-
    fled a greasy deck,
And 'e'd say: "You're bound to Perdition,"
    And I'd answer: "Git off me neck!"

And that's 'ow we came to get friendly, though
    built on a different plan,
Me wot's a desprite gambler, 'im sich a good
    young man.

But on to me tale. Just imagine . . . Dark-
    ness! The battle-front!
The furious 'Uns attackin'! Us ones a-bearin'
    the brunt!
Me crouchin' be'ind a sandbag, tryin' 'ard to keep
    calm,
When I 'ears someone singin' a 'ymn toon;
    be'old! it is Soulful Sam.

Yes; right in the crash of the combat, in the
    fury of flash and flame,
'E was shootin' and singin' serenely as if 'e en-
    joyed the same.
And there in the 'eat of the battle, as the 'ordes
    of demons attacked,
He dipped down into 'is tunic, and 'e 'anded me
    out a tract.

Then a star-shell flared, and I read it: Oh,
    Flee From the Wrath to Come!
Nice cheerful subject, I tell yer, when you're
    'earin' the bullets 'um.

THE BALLAD OF SOULFUL SAM

And before I 'ad time to thank 'im, just one of
    them bits of lead
Comes slingin' along in a 'urry, and it 'its my
    partner. . . . Dead?

No, siree! not by a long sight!   For it plugged
    'im 'ard on the chest,
Just where 'e'd tracts for a army corps stowed
    away in 'is vest.
On its mission of death that bullet 'ustled
    along, and it caved
A 'ole in them tracts to 'is 'ide, boys — but the
    life o' me pal was saved.

And there as 'e showed me in triumph, and
    'orror was chokin' me breath,
On came another bullet on its 'orrible mission of
    death;
On through the night it cavorted, seekin' its
    'aven of rest,
And it zipped through a crack in the sandbags,
    and it wolloped me bang on the breast.

Was I killed, do you ask? Oh no, boys. Why
    am I sittin' 'ere

THE BALLAD OF SOULFUL SAM

Gazin' with mournful vision at a mug long
    empty of beer?
With a throat as dry as a — oh, thanky! I
    don't much mind if I do.
Beer with a dash of 'ollands, that's my particular
    brew.

Yes, that was a terrible moment. It 'ammered
    me 'ard o'er the 'eart;
It bowled me down like a nine-pin, and I looked
    for the gore to start;
And I saw in the flash of a moment, in that
    thunder of hate and strife,
Me wretched past like a pitchur — the sins of a
    gambler's life.

For I 'ad no tracts to save me, to thwart that mad
    missile's doom;
I 'ad no pious pamphlets to 'elp me to cheat the
    tomb;
I 'ad no 'oly leaflets to baffle a bullet's aim;
I'd only — a deck of cards, boys, but . . . *it
seemed to do just the same*.

ONLY A BOCHE

We brought him in from between the lines: we'd
    better have let him lie;
For what's the use of risking one's skin for a
    tyke that's going to die?
What's the use of tearing him loose under a
    gruelling fire,
When he's shot in the head, and worse than
    dead, and all messed up on the wire?

However, I say, we brought him in.   *Diable!*
    The mud was bad;
The trench was crooked and greasy and high,
    and oh, what a time we had!
And often we slipped, and often we tripped, but
    never he made a moan;
And how we were wet with blood and with
    sweat! but we carried him in like our own.

ONLY A BOCHE

Now there he lies in the dug-out dim, awaiting
 the ambulance,
And the doctor shrugs his shoulders at him, and
 remarks, " He hasn't a chance."
And we squat and smoke at our game of bridge
 on the glistening, straw-packed floor,
And above our oaths we can hear his breath deep-
 drawn in a kind of snore.

For the dressing station is long and low, and
 the candles gutter dim,
And the mean light falls on the cold clay walls
 and our faces bristly and grim;
And we flap our cards on the lousy straw, and we
 laugh and jibe as we play,
And you'd never know that the cursed foe was
 less than a mile away.
As we con our cards in the rancid gloom, oppressed by that snoring breath,
You'd never dream that our broad roof-beam
 was swept by the broom of death.

Heigh-ho! My turn for the dummy hand; I
 rise and I stretch a bit;
The fetid air is making me yawn, and my cigarette's unlit,

ONLY A BOCHE

So I go to the nearest candle flame, and the man
  we brought is there,
And his face is white in the shabby light, and I
  stand at his feet and stare.
Stand for awhile, and quietly stare: for strange
  though it seems to be,
The dying Boche on the stretcher there has a
  queer resemblance to me.

It gives one a kind of a turn, you know, to come
  on a thing like that.
It's just as if I were lying there, with a turban
  of blood for a hat,
Lying there in a coat grey-green instead of a
  coat grey-blue,
With one of my eyes all shot away, and my brain
  half tumbling through;
Lying there with a chest that heaves like a bellows up and down,
And a cheek as white as snow on a grave, and
  lips that are coffee brown.

And confound him, too! He wears, like me, on
  his finger a wedding ring,
And around his neck, as around my own, by a
  greasy bit of string,

ONLY A BOCHE

A locket hangs with a woman's face, and I turn
    it about to see:
Just as I thought . . . on the other side the
    faces of children three;
Clustered together cherub-like, three little laugh-
    ing girls,
With the usual tiny rosebud mouths and the usual
    silken curls.
"Zut!" I say.   "He has beaten me; for me, I
    have only two,"
And I push the locket beneath his shirt, feel-
    ing a little blue.

Oh, it isn't cheerful to see a man, the marvellous
    work of God,
Crushed in the mutilation mill, crushed to a
    smeary clod;
Oh, it isn't cheerful to hear him moan; but it
    isn't that I mind,
It isn't the anguish that goes with him, it's the
    anguish he leaves behind.
For his going opens a tragic door that gives on a
    world of pain,
And the death he dies, those who live and love,
    will die again and again.

ONLY A BOCHE

So here I am at my cards once more, but it's kind
    of spoiling my play,
Thinking of those three brats of his so many a
    mile away.
War is war, and he's only a Boche, and we all of
    us take our chance;
But all the same I'll be mighty glad when I'm
    hearing the ambulance.
One foe the less, but all the same I'm heartily
    glad I'm not
The man who gave him his broken head, the
    sniper who fired the shot.

No trumps you make it, I think you said?
    You'll pardon me if I err;
For a moment I thought of other things . . .
    Mon Dieu! Quelle vache de guerre.

PILGRIMS

For oh, when the war will be over
We'll go and we'll look for our dead;
We'll go when the bee's on the clover,
And the plume of the poppy is red:
We'll go when the year's at its gayest,
When meadows are laughing with flow'rs;
And there where the crosses are greyest,
We'll seek for the cross that is ours.

For they cry to us: *Friends, we are lonely,*
A-weary the night and the day;
But come in the blossom-time only,
Come when our graves will be gay:
When daffodils all are a-blowing,
And larks are a-thrilling the skies,
Oh, come with the hearts of you glowing,
And the joy of the Spring in your eyes.

PILGRIMS

But never, oh, never come sighing,
For ours was the Splendid Release;
And oh, but 'twas joy in the dying
To know we were winning you Peace!
So come when the valleys are sheening,
And fledged with the promise of grain;
And here where our graves will be greening,
Just smile and be happy again.

And so, when the war will be over,
We'll seek for the Wonderful One;
And maiden will look for her lover,
And mother will look for her son;
And there will be end to our grieving,
And gladness will gleam over loss,
As — glory beyond all believing!
We point . . . to a name on a cross.

MY PRISONER

We was in a crump-'ole, 'im and me;
Fightin' wiv our bayonets was we;
Fightin' 'ard as 'ell we was,
Fightin' fierce as fire because
It was 'im or me as must be downed;
'E was twice as big as me;
I was 'arf the weight of 'e;
We was like a terryer and a 'ound.

'Struth! But 'e was sich a 'andsome bloke.
Me, I'm 'andsome as a chunk o' coke.
Did I give it 'im? Not 'arf!
Why, it fairly made me laugh,
'Cos 'is bloomin' bellows wasn't sound.
Couldn't fight for monkey nuts.
Soon I gets 'im in the guts,
There 'e lies a-floppin' on the ground.

116

MY PRISONER

In I goes to finish up the job.
Quick 'e throws 'is 'ands above 'is nob;
Speakin' English good as me:
" 'Tain't no use to kill," says 'e;
" Can't yer tyke me prisoner instead? "
" Why, I'd like to, sir," says I;
" But — yer knows the reason why:
If we pokes our noses out we're dead.

" Sorry, sir.   Then on the other 'and
(As a gent like you must understand),
If I 'olds you longer 'ere,
Wiv yer pals so werry near,
It's me 'oo'll 'ave a free trip to Berlin;
If I lets yer go away,
Why, you'll fight another day:
See the sitooation I am in.

" Anyway I'll tell you wot I'll do,
Bein' kind and seein' as it's you,
Knowin' 'ow it's cold, the feel
Of a 'alf a yard o' steel,
I'll let yer 'ave a rifle ball instead;
Now, jist think yerself in luck. . . .
'Ere, ol' man!   You keep 'em stuck,
Them saucy dooks o' yours, above yer 'ead."

MY PRISONER

'Ow 'is mits shot up it made me smile!
'Ow 'e seemed to ponder for a while!
Then 'e says : " It seems a shyme,
Me, a man wot's known ter Fyme :
Give me blocks of stone, I'll give yer gods.
Whereas, pardon me, I'm sure
You, my friend, are still obscure. . . ."
" In war," says I, " that makes no blurry odds."

Then says 'e : " I've painted picters too. . . .
Oh, dear God!   The work I planned to do,
And to think this is the end!"
" 'Ere," says I, " my hartist friend,
Don't you give yerself no friskin' airs.
Picters, statoos, is that why
You should be let off to die?
That the best ye done?   Just say yer prayers."

Once again 'e seems ter think awhile.
Then 'e smiles a werry 'aughty smile :
" Why, no, sir, it's not the best;
There's a locket next me breast,
Picter of a gel 'oo's eyes are blue.
That's the best I've done," says 'e.
" That's me darter, aged three. . . ."
" Blimy!" says I, " I've a nipper, too."

MY PRISONER

Straight I chucks my rifle to one side;
Shows 'im wiv a lovin' farther's pride
Me own little Mary Jane.
Proud 'e shows me 'is Elaine,
And we talks as friendly as can be;
Then I 'elps 'im on 'is way,
'Opes 'e's sife at 'ome to-day,
Wonders —*'ow would 'e 'ave treated me?*

TRI-COLOUR

Poppies, you try to tell me, glowing there in the
wheat;
Poppies! Ah no! You mock me: It's blood,
I tell you, it's blood.
It's gleaming wet in the grasses; it's glist'ning
warm in the wheat;
It dabbles the ferns and the clover; it brims in
an angry flood;
It leaps to the startled heavens; it smothers the
sun; it cries
With scarlet voices of triumph from blossom and
bough and blade.
See the bright horror of it! It's roaring out
of the skies,
And the whole red world is a-welter. . . .
O God! I'm afraid! I'm afraid!

Cornflowers, you say, just cornflowers, gemming
the golden grain;
Ah no! You can't deceive me. Can't I believe my eyes?
Look! It's the dead, my comrades, stark on the
dreadful plain,

TRI-COLOUR

All in their dark-blue blouses, staring up at the
   skies.
Comrades of canteen laughter, dumb in the yel-
   low wheat.
See how they sprawl and huddle!   See how their
   brows are white!
Goaded on to the shambles, there in death and
   defeat. . . .
Father of Pity, hide them!   Hasten, O God,
   Thy night!

Lilies (the light is waning), only lilies you say,
Nestling and softly shining there where the
   spear-grass waves.
No, my friend, I know better; brighter I see than
   day:
It's the poor little wooden crosses over their
   quiet graves.
Oh, how they're gleaming, gleaming!   See!
   Each cross has a crown.
Yes, it's true I am dying; little will be the
   loss. . . .
Darkness . . . but look!   In Heaven a light,
   and it's shining down. . . .
God's accolade!   Lift me up, friends.   I'm go-
   ing to win — *my Cross*.

A POT OF TEA

You make it in your mess-tin by the brazier's
    rosy gleam;
You watch it cloud, then settle amber clear;
You lift it with your bay'nit, and you sniff the
    fragrant steam;
The very breath of it is ripe with cheer.
You're awful cold and dirty, and a-cursin' of
    your lot;
You scoff the blushin' 'alf of it, so rich and rip-
    pin' 'ot;
It bucks you up like anythink, just seems to touch
    the spot:
    God bless the man that first discovered
    Tea!

Since I came out to fight in France, which ain't
    the other day,
I think I've drunk enough to float a barge;
All kinds of fancy foreign dope, from caffy and
    doo lay,
To rum they serves you out before a charge.

A POT OF TEA

In back rooms of estaminays I've gurgled pints
        of cham;
I've swilled down mugs of cider till I've felt a
        bloomin' dam;
But 'struth! they all ain't in it with the vintage
        of Assam:
    God bless the man that first invented Tea!

I think them lazy lumps o' gods wot kips on as-
        phodel
Swigs nectar that's a flavour of Oolong;
I only wish them sons o' guns a-grillin' down in
        'ell
Could 'ave their daily ration of Suchong.
Hurrah! I'm off to battle, which is 'ell and
        'eaven too;
And if I don't give some poor bloke a sexton's
        job to do,
To-night, by Fritz's campfire, won't I 'ave a gor-
        geous brew
    (For fightin' mustn't interfere with Tea).
To-night we'll all be tellin' of the Boches that
        we slew,
    As we drink the giddy victory in Tea.

THE REVELATION

The same old sprint in the morning, boys, to the
same old din and smut;
Chained all day to the same old desk, down in
the same old rut;
Posting the same old greasy books, catching the
same old train:
Oh, how will I manage to stick it all, if I ever
get back again?

We've bidden good-bye to life in a cage, we're
finished with pushing a pen;
They're pumping us full of bellicose rage, they're
showing us how to be men.
We're only beginning to find ourselves; we're
wonders of brawn and thew;
But when we go back to our Sissy jobs,— oh,
what are we going to do?

For shoulders curved with the counter stoop will
be carried erect and square;
And faces white from the office light will be
bronzed by the open air;

THE REVELATION

And we'll walk with the stride of a new-born
    pride, with a new-found joy in our eyes,
Scornful men who have diced with death under
    the naked skies.

And when we get back to the dreary grind, and
    the bald-headed boss's call,
Don't you think that the dingy window-blind, and
    the dingier office wall,
Will suddenly melt to a vision of space, of vio-
    lent, flame-scarred night?
Then . . . oh, the joy of the danger-thrill, and
    oh, the roar of the fight!

Don't you think as we peddle a card of pins the
    counter will fade away,
And again we'll be seeing the sand-bag rims, and
    the barb-wire's misty grey?
As a flat voice asks for a pound of tea, don't you
    fancy we'll hear instead
The night-wind moan and the soothing drone of
    the packet that's overhead?

Don't you guess that the things we're seeing now
    will haunt us through all the years;
Heaven and hell rolled into one, glory and blood
    and tears;

THE REVELATION

Life's pattern picked with a scarlet thread, where
    once we wove with a grey
To remind us all how we played our part in the
    shock of an epic day?

Oh, we're booked for the Great Adventure now,
    we're pledged to the Real Romance;
We'll find ourselves or we'll lose ourselves some-
    where in giddy old France;
We'll know the zest of the fighter's life; the best
    that we have we'll give;
We'll hunger and thirst; we'll die . . . but first
    — we'll live; by the gods, we'll live!

We'll breathe free air and we'll bivouac under
    the starry sky;
We'll march with men and we'll fight with men,
    and we'll see men laugh and die;
We'll know such joy as we never dreamed; we'll
    fathom the deeps of pain:
But the hardest bit of it all will be — when we
    come back home again.

THE REVELATION

For some of us smirk in a chiffon shop, and some
  of us teach in a school;
Some of us help with the seat of our pants to
  polish an office stool;
The merits of somebody's soap or jam some of
  us seek to explain,
But all of us wonder what we'll do when we have
  to go back again.

GRAND-PÈRE

And so when he reached my bed
The General made a stand:
" My brave young fellow," he said,
   " I would shake your hand."

So I lifted my arm, the right,
With never a hand at all;
Only a stump, a sight
    Fit to appal.

" Well, well.   Now that's too bad!
That's sorrowful luck," he said;
" But there!   You give me, my lad,
   The left instead."

So from under the blanket's rim
I raised and showed him the other,
A snag as ugly and grim
    As its ugly brother.

GRAND-PÈRE

He looked at each jagged wrist;
He looked, but he did not speak;
And then he bent down and kissed
    Me on either cheek.

You wonder now I don't mind
I hadn't a hand to offer. . . .
They tell me (you know I'm blind)
    '*Twas Grand-père Joffre.*

SON

He hurried away, young heart of joy, under our
    Devon sky!
And I watched him go, my beautiful boy, and a
    weary woman was I.
For my hair is grey, and his was gold; he'd the
    best of his life to live;
And I'd loved him so, and I'm old, I'm old; and
    he's all I had to give.

Ah yes, he was proud and swift and gay, but
    oh how my eyes were dim!
With the sun in his heart he went away, but he
    took the sun with him.
For look!   How the leaves are falling now, and
    the winter won't be long. . . .
Oh boy, my boy with the sunny brow, and the
    lips of love and of song!

SON

How we used to sit at the day's sweet end, we
    two by the firelight's gleam,
And we'd drift to the Valley of Let's Pretend,
    on the beautiful river of Dream.
Oh dear little heart! All wealth untold would
    I gladly, gladly pay
Could I just for a moment closely hold that
    golden head to my grey.

For I gaze in the fire, and I'm seeing there a
    child, and he waves to me;
And I run and I hold him up in the air, and he
    laughs and shouts with glee;
A little bundle of love and mirth, crying:
    " Come, Mumsie dear! "
Ah me! If he called from the ends of the earth
    I know that my heart would hear.

.   .   ;   .   .   .

Yet the thought comes thrilling through all my
    pain: how worthier could he die?
Yea, a loss like that is a glorious gain, and piti-
    ful proud am I.

SON

For Peace must be bought with blood and tears,
　　and the boys of our hearts must pay;
And so in our joy of the after-years, let us bless
　　them every day.

And though I know there's a hasty grave with a
　　poor little cross at its head,
And the gold of his youth he so gladly gave, yet
　　to me he'll never be dead.
And the sun in my Devon lane will be gay, and
　　my boy will be with me still,
So I'm finding the heart to smile and say: "Oh
　　God, if it be Thy Will!"

THE BLACK DUDEEN

Humping it here in the dug-out,
Sucking me black dudeen,
I'd like to say in a general way,
There's nothing like Nickyteen;
There's nothing like Nickyteen, me boys,
Be it pipes or snipes or cigars;
So be sure that a bloke
Has plenty to smoke,
If you wants him to fight your wars.

When I've eat my fill and my belt is snug,
I begin to think of my baccy plug.
I whittle a fill in my horny palm,
And the bowl of me old clay pipe I cram.
I trim the edges, I tamp it down,
I nurse a light with an anxious frown;
I begin to draw, and my cheeks tuck in,
And all my face is a blissful grin;
And up in a cloud the good smoke goes,
And the good pipe glimmers and fades and
    glows;

THE BLACK DUDEEN

In its throat it chuckles a cheery song,
For I likes it hot and I likes it strong.
Oh, it's good is grub when you're feeling hollow,
But the best of a meal's the smoke to follow.

There was Micky and me on a night patrol,
Having to hide in a fizz-bang hole;
And sure I thought I was worse than dead
Wi' them crump-crumps hustlin' over me head.
Sure I thought 'twas the dirty spot,
Hammer and tongs till the air was hot.
And mind you, water up to your knees.
And cold! A monkey of brass would freeze.
And if we ventured our noses out
A " typewriter " clattered its pills about.
The field of glory! Well, I don't think!
I'd sooner be safe and snug in clink.

Then Micky, he goes and he cops one bad,
He always was having ill-luck, poor lad.
Says he: " Old chummy, I'm booked right
    through;
Death and me 'as a wrongday voo.
But . . . 'aven't you got a pinch of shag? —
I'd sell me perishin' soul for a fag."
And there he shivered and cussed his luck,

THE BLACK DUDEEN

So I gave him me old black pipe to suck.
And he heaves a sigh, and he takes to it
Like a babby takes to his mammy's tit;
Like an infant takes to his mother's breast
Poor little Micky! he went to rest.

But the dawn was near, though the night was
      black,
So I left him there and I started back.
And I laughed as the silly old bullets came,
For the bullet ain't made wot's got me name.
Yet some of 'em buzzed onhealthily near,
And one little blighter just chipped me ear.
But there! I got to the trench all right,
When sudden I jumped wi' a start o' fright,
And a word that doesn't look well in type:
I'd clean forgotten me old clay pipe.

So I had to do it all over again,
Crawling out on that filthy plain.
Through shells and bombs and bullets and all —
Only this time — I do not crawl.
I run like a man wot's missing a train,
Or a tom-cat caught in a plump of rain.
I hear the spit of a quick-fire gun
Tickle my heels, but I run, I run.

THE BLACK DUDEEN

Through crash and crackle, and flicker and flame,
(Oh, the packet ain't issued wot's got me name!)
I run like a man that's no ideer
Of hunting around for a sooveneer.
I run bang into a German chap,
And he stares like an owl, so I bash his map.
And just to show him that I'm his boss,
I gives him a kick on the parados.
And I marches him back with me all serene,
With, *tucked in me gub, me old dudeen.*

Sitting here in the trenches
Me heart's a-splittin' with spleen,
For a parcel o' lead comes missing me head,
But it smashes me old dudeen.
God blast that red-headed sniper!
I'll give him somethin' to snipe;
Before the war's through
Just see how I do
That blighter that smashed me pipe.

THE LITTLE PIOU-PIOU *

Oh, some of us lolled in the château,
And some of us slinked in the slum;
But now we are here with a song and a cheer
To serve at the sign of the drum.
They put us in trousers of scarlet,
In big sloppy ulsters of blue;
In boots that are flat, a box of a hat,
And they call us the little piou-piou,
   Piou-piou,
The laughing and quaffing piou-piou,
The swinging and singing piou-piou;
And so with a rattle we march to the battle,
The weary but cheery piou-piou.

> *Encore un petit verre de vin,*
> *Pour nous mettre en route;*
> *Encore un petit verre de vin*
> *Pour nous mettre en train.*

They drive us head-on for the slaughter;
We haven't got much of a chance;
The issue looks bad, but we're awfully glad
To battle and die for La France.
For some must be killed, that is certain;

* The French "Tommy."

137

THE LITTLE PIOU-PIOU

There's only one's duty to do;
So we leap to the fray in the glorious way
They expect of the little piou-piou.
En avant!
The way of the gallant piou-piou,
The dashing and smashing piou-piou;
The way grim and gory that leads us to glory
Is the way of the little piou-piou.

Allons, enfants de la Patrie,
Le jour de gloire est arrivé.

To-day you would scarce recognise us,
Such veterans war-wise are we;
So grimy and hard, so calloused and scarred,
So " crummy," yet gay as can be.
We've finished with trousers of scarlet,
They're giving us breeches of blue,
With a helmet instead of a cap on our head,
Yet still we're the little piou-piou.
Nous les aurons!
The jesting, unresting piou-piou;
The cheering, unfearing piou-piou;
The keep-your-head-level and fight-like-the-devil;
The dying, defying piou-piou.

À la bayonette!   Jusqu'à la mort!
Sonnez la charge, clairons!

BILL THE BOMBER

The poppies gleamed like bloody pools through
    cotton-woolly mist;
The Captain kept a-lookin' at the watch upon his
    wrist;
And there we smoked and squatted, as we
    watched the shrapnel flame;
'Twas wonnerful, I'm tellin' you, how fast them
    bullets came.
'Twas weary work the waiting, though; I tried
    to sleep a wink,
For waitin' means a-thinkin', and it doesn't do to
    think.
So I closed my eyes a little, and I had a niceish
    dream
Of a-standin' by a dresser with a dish of Devon
    cream;
But I hadn't time to sample it, for suddenlike I
    woke:
" Come on, me lads!" the Captain says, 'n I
    climbed out through the smoke.

We spread out in the open: it was like a bath of
    lead;

But the boys they cheered and hollered fit to raise
    the bloody dead,
Till a beastly bullet copped 'em, then they lay
    without a sound,
And it's odd — we didn't seem to heed them
    corpses on the ground.
And I kept on thinkin', thinkin', as the bullets
    faster flew,
How they picks the werry best men, and they lets
    the rotters through;
So indiscriminatin' like, they spares a man of sin,
And a rare lad wots a husband and a father gets
    done in.
And while havin' these reflections and advancin'
    on the run,
A bullet biffs me shoulder, and says I : " That's
    number one."

Well, it downed me for a jiffy, but I didn't lose
    me calm,
For I knew that I was needed : I'm a bomber,
    so I am.
I 'ad lost me cap and rifle, but I " carried on "
    because
I 'ad me bombs and knew that they was needed,
    so they was.

BILL THE BOMBER

We didn't 'ave no singin' now, nor many men to
    cheer;
Maybe the shrapnel drowned 'em, crashin' out
    so werry near;
And the Maxims got us sideways, and the bullets
    faster flew,
And I copped one on me flipper, and says I:
    " That's number two."

I was pleased it was the left one, for I 'ad me
    bombs, ye see.
And 'twas 'ard if they'd be wasted like, and all
    along o' me.
And I'd lost me 'at and rifle — but I told you
    that before,
So I packed me mit inside me coat and " carried
    on " once more.
But the rumpus it was wicked, and the men were
    scarcer yet,
And I felt me ginger goin', but me jaws I kindo
    set,
And we passed the Boche first trenches, which
    was 'eapin' 'igh with dead,
And we started for their second, which was fifty
    feet ahead;
When something like a 'ammer smashed me sav-
    age on the knee,

And down I came all muck and blood: Says I:
   "That's number three."

So there I lay all 'elpless like, and bloody sick at
   that,
And worryin' like anythink, because I'd lost
   me 'at;
And thinkin' of me missis, and the partin' words
   she said:
"If you gets killed, write quick, ol' man, and tell
   me as you're dead."
And lookin' at me bunch o' bombs — that was
   the 'ardest blow,
To think I'd never 'ave the chance to 'url them at
   the foe.
And there was all our boys in front, a-fightin'
   there like mad,
And me as could 'ave 'elped 'em wiv the lovely
   bombs I 'ad.
And so I cussed and cussed, and then I struggled
   back again,
Into that bit of battered trench, packed solid with
   its slain.

Now as I lay a-lyin' there and blastin' of me lot,
And wishin' I could just dispose of all them
   bombs I'd got,

BILL THE BOMBER

I sees within the doorway of a shy, retirin' dug-
out
Six Boches all a-grinnin', and their Captain stuck
'is mug out;
And they 'ad a nice machine gun, and I twigged
what they was at;
And they fixed it on a tripod, and I watched 'em
like a cat;
And they got it in position, and they seemed so
werry glad,
Like they'd got us in a death-trap, which, con-
demn their souls! they 'ad.
For there our boys was fightin' fifty yards in
front, and 'ere
This lousy bunch of Boches they 'ad got us in
the rear.

Oh it set me blood a-boilin' and I quite forgot
me pain,
So I started crawlin', crawlin' over all them
mounds of slain;
And them barstards was so busy-like they 'ad no
eyes for me,
And me bleedin' leg was draggin', but me right
arm it was free. . . .
And now they 'ave it all in shape, and swingin'
sweet and clear;

And now they're all excited like, but — I am
    drawin' near;
And now they 'ave it loaded up, and now they're
    takin' aim. . . .
Rat-tat-tat-tat!   Oh here, says I, is where I join
    the game.
And my right arm it goes swingin', and a bomb it
    goes a-slingin',
And that " typewriter " goes wingin' in a thun-
    derbolt of flame.

Then these Boches, wot was left of 'em, they
    tumbled down their 'ole,
And up I climbed a mound of dead, and down
    on them I stole.
And oh that blessed moment when I heard their
    frightened yell,
And I laughed down in that dug-out, ere I
    bombed their souls to hell.
And now I'm in the hospital, surprised that I'm
    alive;
We started out a thousand men, we came back
    thirty-five.
And I'm minus of a trotter, but I'm most amazin'
    gay,
For me bombs they wasn't wasted, though, you
    might say, " thrown away."

THE WHISTLE OF SANDY
McGRAW

You may talk o' your lutes and your dulcimers
    fine,
Your harps and your tabors and cymbals and a'.
But here in the trenches jist gie me for mine
The wee penny whistle o' Sandy McGraw.
Oh, it's: "Sandy, ma lad, will you lilt us a
    tune?"
And Sandy is willin' and trillin' like mad;
Sae silvery sweet that we a' throng aroun',
And some o' it's gay, but the maist o' it's sad.
Jist the wee simple airs that sink intae your
    hert,
And grup ye wi' love and wi' longin' for hame;
And ye glour like an owl till you're feelin' the
    stert
O' a tear, and you blink wi' a feelin' o' shame.
For his song's o' the heather, and here in the
    dirt
You listen and dream o' a land that's sae braw,

And he mak's you forget a' the harm and the
    hurt,
For he pipes like a laverock, does Sandy Mc-
    Graw.

     .   .   .

At Eepers I mind me when rank upon rank
We rose from the trenches and swept like the
    gale,
Till the rapid-fire guns got us fell on the flank
And the murderin' bullets came swishin' like
    hail:
Till a' that were left o' us faltered and broke;
Till it seemed for a moment a panicky rout,
When shrill through the fume and the flash and
    the smoke
The wee valiant voice o' a whistle piped out.
The Campbells are Comin': Then into the
    fray
We bounded wi' bayonets reekin' and raw,
And oh we fair revelled in glory that day,
Jist thanks to the whistle o' Sandy McGraw.

     .   .   .   .

At Loose, it wis after a sconnersome fecht,
On the field o' the slain I wis crawlin' aboot;
And the rockets were burnin' red holes in the
    nicht;

And the guns they were veciously thunderin'
    oot;
When sudden I heard a bit sound like a sigh,
And there in a crump-hole a kiltie I saw:
" Whit ails ye, ma lad?   Are ye woundit? "
    says I.
" I've lost ma wee whustle," says Sandy Mc-
    Graw.
" 'Twas oot by yon bing where we pressed the
    attack,
It drapped frae ma pooch, and between noo
    and dawn
There isna much time so I'm jist crawlin'
    back. . . ."
" Ye're daft, man! " I telt him, but Sandy wis
    gone.

Weel, I waited a wee, then I crawled oot
    masel,
And the big stuff wis gorin' and roarin' around,
And I seemed tae be under the oxter o' hell,
And Creation wis crackin' tae bits by the sound.
And I says in ma mind: " Gang ye back, ye
    auld fule! "

When I thrilled tae a note that wis saucy and
    sma';
And there in a crater, collected and cool,
Wi' his wee penny whistle wis Sandy McGraw.
Ay, there he wis playin' as gleg as could be,
And listenin' hard wis a spectacled Boche;
Then Sandy turned roon' and he noddit tae
    me,
And he says: "Dinna blab on me, Sergeant
    McTosh.
The auld chap is deein'. He likes me tae play.
It's makin' him happy. Jist see his een shine!"
And thrillin' and sweet in the hert o' the fray
Wee Sandy wis playin' *The Watch on the
    Rhine.*

.   .   .   .   .   .

The last scene o' a'—'twas the day that we
    took
That bit o' black ruin they ca' Labbiesell.
It seemed the hale hillside jist shivered and
    shook,
And the red skies were roarin' and spewin' oot
    shell.
And the Sergeants were cursin' tae keep us
    in hand,

148

And hard on the leash we were strainin' like
    dugs,
When upward we shot at the word o' com-
    mand,
And the bullets were dingin' their songs in oor
    lugs.
And onward we swept wi' a yell and a cheer,
And a' wis destruction, confusion and din,
And we knew that the trench o' the Boches wis
    near,
And it seemed jist the safest bit hole tae be in.
So we a' tumbled doon, and the Boches were
    there,
And they held up their hands, and they yelled:
    " Kamarad ! "
And I merched aff wi' ten, wi' their palms in
    the air,
And my! I wis prood-like, and my! I wis
    glad.
And I thocht: if ma lassie could see me jist
    then. . . .
When sudden I sobered at somethin' I saw,
And I stopped and I stared, and I halted ma
    men,
For there on a stretcher wis Sandy McGraw.

WHISTLE OF SANDY MC GRAW

Weel, he looks in ma face, jist as game as ye
    please:
" Ye ken hoo I hate tae be workin'," says he;
" But noo I can play in the street for bawbees,
Wi' baith o' ma legs taken aff at the knee."
And though I could see he wis rackit wi' pain,
He reached for his whistle and stertit tae
    play;
And quaverin' sweet wis the pensive refrain:
The flowers o' the forest are a' wede awae.
Then sudden he stoppit: " Man, wis it no
    grand
Hoo we took a' them trenches?" . . . He
    shakit his heid:
" I'll — no — play — nae — mair ——" feebly
    doon frae his hand
Slipped the wee penny whistle and — *Sandy wis
    deid.*

  . . . .

And so you may talk o' your Steinways and
    Strads,
Your wonderful organs and brasses sae braw;
But oot in the trenches jist gie me, ma lads,
Yon wee penny whistle o' Sandy McGraw.

THE STRETCHER-BEARER

My stretcher is one scarlet stain,
And as I tries to scrape it clean,
I tell you wot — I'm sick with pain
For all I've 'eard, for all I've seen;
Around me is the 'ellish night,
And as the war's red rim I trace,
I wonder if in 'Eaven's height,
Our God don't turn away 'Is Face.

I don't care 'oose the Crime may be;
I 'olds no brief for kin or clan;
I 'ymns no 'ate: I only see
As man destroys his brother man;
I waves no flag: I only know,
As 'ere beside the dead I wait,
A million 'earts is weighed with woe,
A million 'omes is desolate.

In drippin' darkness, far and near,
All night I've sought them woeful ones.

THE STRETCHER-BEARER

Dawn shudders up and still I 'ear
The crimson chorus of the guns.
Look! like a ball of blood the sun
'Angs o'er the scene of wrath and wrong. . . .
" Quick!   Stretcher-bearers on the run! "
O Prince of Peace!   'Ow long, 'ow long?

WOUNDED

Is it not strange?   A year ago to-day,
With scarce a thought beyond the hum-drum
    round,
I did my decent job and earned my pay;
Was averagely happy, I'll be bound.
Ay, in my little groove I was content,
Seeing my life run smoothly to the end,
With prosy days in stolid labour spent,
And jolly nights, a pipe, a glass, a friend.
In God's good time a hearth fire's cosy gleam,
A wife and kids, and all a fellow needs;
When presto! like a bubble goes my dream:
I leap upon the Stage of Splendid Deeds.
I yell with rage; I wallow deep in gore:
I, that was clerk in a drysalter's store.

Stranger than any book I've ever read.
Here on the reeking battlefield I lie,
Under the stars, propped up with smeary dead,

WOUNDED

Like too, if no one takes me in, to die.
Hit on the arms, legs, liver, lungs and gall;
Damn glad there's nothing more of me to hit;
But calm, and feeling never pain at all,
And full of wonder at the turn of it.
For of the dead around me three are mine,
Three foemen vanquished in the whirl of fight;
So if I die I have no right to whine,
I feel I've done my little bit all right.
I don't know how — but there the beggars are,
As dead as herrings pickled in a jar.

And here am I, worse wounded than I thought;
For in the fight a bullet bee-like stings;
You never heed; the air is metal-hot,
And all alive with little flicking wings.
But on you charge. You see the fellows fall;
Your pal was by your side, fair fighting-mad;
You turn to him, and lo! no pal at all;
You wonder vaguely if he's copped it bad.
But on you charge. The heavens vomit death;
And vicious death is besoming the ground.
You're blind with sweat; you're dazed, and out
     of breath,
And though you yell, you cannot hear a sound.

WOUNDED

But on you charge.   Oh, War's a rousing game!
Around you smoky clouds like ogres tower;
The earth is rowelled deep with spurs of flame,
And on your helmet stones and ashes shower.
But on you charge. It's odd! You have no
    fear.
Machine-gun bullets whip and lash your path;
Red, yellow, black the smoky giants rear;
The shrapnel rips, the heavens roar in wrath.
But on you charge.   Barbed wire all trampled
    down.
The ground all gored and rent as by a blast;
Grim heaps of grey where once were heaps
    of brown;
A ragged ditch — the Hun first line at last.
All smashed to hell.   Their second right ahead,
So on you charge.   There's nothing else to do.
More reeking holes, blood, barbed wire, grue-
    some dead;
(Your puttee strap's undone — that worries
    you).
You glare around.   You think you're all alone.
But no; your chums come surging left and
    right.
The nearest chap flops down without a groan,
His face still snarling with the rage of fight.

WOUNDED

Ha! here's the second trench — just like the
 first,
Only a little more so, more " laid out ";
More pounded, flame-corroded, death-accurst;
A pretty piece of work, beyond a doubt.
Now for the third, and there your job is done,
So on you charge. You never stop to think.
Your cursed puttee's trailing as you run;
You feel you'd sell your soul to have a drink.
The acrid air is full of cracking whips.
You wonder how it is you're going still.
You foam with rage. Oh, God! to be at grips
With someone you can rush and crush and
 kill.
Your sleeve is dripping blood; you're seeing
 red;
You're battle-mad; your turn is coming now.
See! there's the jagged barbed wire straight
 ahead,
And there's the trench — you'll get there any-
 how.
Your puttee catches on a strand of wire,
And down you go; perhaps it saves your life,
For over sandbag rims you see 'em fire,
Crop-headed chaps, their eyes ablaze with
 strife.

WOUNDED

You crawl, you cower; then once again you
plunge
With all your comrades roaring at your heels.
Have at 'em, lads! You stab, you jab, you
lunge;
A blaze of glory, then the red world reels.
A crash of triumph, then . . . you're faint a
bit . . .
That cursed puttee! Now to fasten it. . . .

Well, that's the charge. And now I'm here
alone.
I've built a little wall of Hun on Hun,
To shield me from the leaden bees that drone
(It saves me worry, and it hurts 'em none).
The only thing I'm wondering is when
Some stretcher-men will stroll along my way?
It isn't much that's left of me, but then
Where life is, hope is, so at least they say.
Well, if I'm spared I'll be the happy lad.
I tell you I won't envy any king.
I've stood the racket, and I'm proud and glad;
I've had my crowning hour. Oh, War's the
thing!

WOUNDED

It gives us common, working chaps our chance,
A taste of glory, chivalry, romance.

Ay, War, they say, is hell; it's heaven, too.
It lets a man discover what he's worth.
It takes his measure, shows what he can do,
Gives him a joy like nothing else on earth.
It fans in him a flame that otherwise
Would flicker out, these drab, discordant days;
It teaches him in pain and sacrifice
Faith, fortitude, grim courage past all praise.
Yes, War is good.   So here beside my slain,
A happy wreck I wait amid the din;
For even if I perish mine's the gain. . . .
Hi, there, you fellows! *Won't* you take me
        in?
Give me a fag to smoke upon the way. . . .
We've taken La Boiselle!   The hell, you say!
Well, that would make a corpse sit up and
        grin. . . .
Lead on!   I'll live to fight another day.

FAITH

Since all that is was ever bound to be;
Since grim, eternal laws our Being bind;
And both the riddle and the answer find,
And both the carnage and the calm decree;
Since plain within the Book of Destiny
Is written all the journey of mankind
Inexorably to the end; since blind
And mortal puppets playing parts are we:

Then let's have faith; good cometh out of ill;
The power that shaped the strife shall end the
     strife;
Then let's bow down before the Unknown Will;
Fight on, believing all is well with life;
Seeing within the worst of War's red rage
The gleam, the glory of the Golden Age.

THE COWARD

'Ave you seen Bill's mug in the Noos to-day?
'E's gyned the Victoriar Cross, they say;
Little Bill wot would grizzle and run away,
    If you 'it 'im a swipe on the jawr.
'E's slaughtered the Kaiser's men in tons;
'E's captured one of their quick-fire guns,
And 'e 'adn't no practice in killin' 'Uns
    Afore 'e went off to the war.

    Little Bill wot I nussed in 'is by-by clothes;
    Little Bill wot told me 'is childish woes;
    'Ow often I've tidied 'is pore little nose
        Wiv the 'em of me pinnyfore.
    And now all the papers 'is praises ring,
    And 'e's been and 'e's shaken the 'and of
        the King
    And I sawr 'im to-day in the ward, pore
        thing,
        Where they're patchin' 'im up once
        more.

THE COWARD

And 'e says: "Wot d'ye think of it, Lizer
      Ann?"
And I says: "Well, I can't make it out, old
      man;
You'd 'ook it as soon as a scrap began,
  When you was a bit of a kid."
And 'e whispers: "'Ere, on the quiet, Liz,
They're makin' too much of the 'ole damn biz,
And the papers is printin' me ugly phiz,
   But . . . I'm 'anged if I know wot I did.

"Oh, the Captain comes and 'e says: 'Look
     'ere!
They're far too quiet out there: it's queer.
They're up to somethin'—'oo'll volunteer
  To crawl in the dark and see?'
Then I felt me 'eart like a 'ammer go,
And up jumps a chap and 'e says: 'Right
     O!'
But I chips in straight, and I says 'Oh no!
  'E's a missis and kids — take me.'

  "And the next I knew I was sneakin' out,
  And the oozy corpses was all about,
  And I felt so scared I wanted to shout,
    And me skin fair prickled wiv fear;

THE COWARD

And I sez: 'You coward! You 'ad no
    right
To take on the job of a man this night,'
Yet still I kept creepin' till ('orrid sight!)
    The trench of the 'Uns was near.

" It was all so dark, it was all so still;
Yet somethin' pushed me against me will;
'Ow I wanted to turn! Yet I crawled until
    I was seein' a dim light shine.
Then thinks I: ' I'll just go a little bit,
And see wot the doose I can make of it,'
And it seemed to come from the mouth of a pit:
    ' Christmas! ' sez I, ' a *mine.*'

" Then 'ere's the part wot I can't explain:
I wanted to make for 'ome again,
But somethin' was blazin' inside me brain,
    So I crawled to the trench instead;
Then I saw the bullet 'ead of a 'Un,
And 'e stood by a rapid-firer gun,
And I lifted a rock and I 'it 'im one,
    And 'e dropped like a chunk o' lead.

" Then all the 'Uns that was underground,
Comes up with a rush and on with a bound,

THE COWARD

And I swings that giddy old Maxim round
  And belts 'em solid and square.
You see I was off me chump wiv fear:
' If I'm sellin' me life,' sez I, ' it's dear.'
And the trench was narrow and they was
      near,
  So I peppered the brutes for fair.

" So I 'eld 'em back and I yelled wiv fright,
And the boys attacked and we 'ad a fight,
And we ' captured a section o' trench ' that
      night
  Which we didn't expect to get;
And they found me there with me Maxim gun,
And I'd laid out a score if I'd laid out one,
And I fainted away when the thing was done,
  And I 'aven't got over it yet."

So that's the 'istory Bill told me.
Of course it's all on the strict Q. T.;
It wouldn't do to get out, you see,
  As 'e hacted against 'is will.
But 'e's convalescin' wiv all 'is might,
And 'e 'opes to be fit for another fight —
Say! Ain't 'e a bit of the real all right?
  Wot's the matter with Bill!

MISSIS MORIARTY'S BOY

Missis Moriarty called last week, and says she
    to me, says she:
" Sure the heart of me's broken entirely now —
    it's the fortunate woman you are;
You've still got your Dinnis to cheer up your
    home, but me Patsy boy where is he?
Lyin' alone, cold as a stone, kilt in the weariful
    wahr.
Oh, I'm seein' him now as I looked on him
    last, wid his hair all curly and bright,
And the wonderful, tenderful heart he had, and
    his eyes as he wint away,
Shinin' and lookin' down on me from the pride
    of his proper height:
Sure I'll remember me boy like that if I live
    to me dyin' day."

And just as she spoke them very same words
    me Dinnis came in at the door,
Came in from McGonigle's ould shebeen, came
    in from drinkin' his pay;
And Missis Moriarty looked at him, and she
    didn't say anny more,

But she wrapped her head in her ould black
    shawl, and she quietly wint away.
And what was I thinkin', I ask ye now, as I
    put me Dinnis to bed,
Wid him ravin' and cursin' one half of the
    night, as cold by his side I sat;
Was I thinkin' the poor ould woman she was
    wid her Patsy slaughtered and dead?
Was I weepin' for Missis Moriarty? I'm not
    so sure about that.

Missis Moriarty goes about wid a shinin' look
    on her face;
Wid her grey hair under her ould black shawl,
    and the eyes of her mother-mild;
Some say she's a little bit off her head; but
    annyway it's the case,
Her timper's so swate that you nivver would tell
    she'd be losin' her only child.
And I think, as I wait up ivery night for me
    Dinnis to come home blind,
And I'm hearin' his stumblin' foot on the stair
    along about half-past three:
Sure there's many a way of breakin' a heart, and
    I haven't made up me mind —
Would I be Missis Moriarty, or Missis Mori-
    arty me?

MY FOE

A Belgian Priest-Soldier Speaks: —

Gurr! You *cochon!* Stand and fight!
Show your mettle! Snarl and bite!
Spawn of an accursed race,
Turn and meet me face to face!
Here amid the wreck and rout
Let us grip and have it out!
Here where ruins rock and reel
Let us settle, steel to steel!
Look! Our houses, how they spit
Sparks from brands your friends have lit.
See! Our gutters running red,
Bright with blood your friends have shed.
Hark! Amid your drunken brawl
How our maidens shriek and call.
Why have *you* come here alone,
To this hearth's blood-spattered stone?
Come to ravish, come to loot,
Come to play the ghoulish brute.

MY FOE

Ah, indeed!   We well are met,
Bayonet to bayonet.
God!   I never killed a man:
Now I'll do the best I can.
Rip you to the evil heart,
Laugh to see the life-blood start.
Bah!   You swine!   I hate you so.
Show you mercy?   No! . . . and no! . . .

There!   I've done it.   See!   He lies
Death a-staring from his eyes;
Glazing eyeballs, panting breath,
How it's horrible, is Death!
Plucking at his bloody lips
With his trembling finger-tips;
Choking in a dreadful way
As if he would something say
In that uncouth tongue of his. . . .
Oh, how horrible Death is!

How I wish that he would die!
So unnerved, unmanned am I.
See!   His twitching face is white!
See!   His bubbling blood is bright.
Why do I not shout with glee?

MY FOE

What strange spell is over me?
There he lies; the fight was fair;
Let me toss my cap in air.
Why am I so silent? Why
Do I pray for him to die?
Where is all my vengeful joy?
Ugh! *My foe is but a boy.*

I'd a brother of his age
Perished in the war's red rage;
Perished in the Ypres hell:
Oh, I loved my brother well.
And though I be hard and grim,
How it makes me think of him!
He had just such flaxen hair
As the lad that's lying there.
Just such frank blue eyes were his. . . .
God! How horrible war is!

I have reason to be gay:
There is one less foe to slay.
I have reason to be glad:
Yet — my foe is such a lad.
So I watch in dull amaze,
See his dying eyes a-glaze,

MY FOE

See his face grow glorified,
See his hands outstretched and wide
To that bit of ruined wall
Where the flames have ceased to crawl,
Where amid the crumbling bricks
Hangs *a blackened crucifix*.

Now, oh now I understand.
Quick I press it in his hand,
Close his feeble finger-tips,
Hold it to his faltering lips.
As I watch his welling blood
I would stem it if I could.
God of Pity, let him live!
God of Love, forgive, forgive.

.   .   .   .   .

His face looked strangely, as he died,
Like that of One they crucified.
And in the pocket of his coat
I found a letter; thus he wrote:
The things I've seen! Oh, mother dear,
I'm wondering can God be here?
To-night amid the drunken brawl
I saw a Cross hung on a wall;

MY FOE

I'll seek it now, and there alone
Perhaps I may atone, atone. . . .

Ah no! 'Tis I who must atone.
No other saw but God alone;
Yet how can I forget the sight
Of that face so woeful white!
Dead I kissed him as he lay,
Knelt by him and tried to pray;
Left him lying there at rest,
Crucifix upon his breast.

Not for him the pity be.
Ye who pity, pity me,
Crawling now the ways I trod,
Blood-guilty in sight of God.

MY JOB

I've got a little job on 'and, the time is drawin'
    nigh;
At seven by the Captain's watch I'm due to go
    and do it;
I wants to 'ave it nice and neat, and pleasin' to
    the eye,
And I 'opes the God of soldier men will see me
    safely through it.
Because, you see, it's somethin' I 'ave never done
    before;
And till you 'as experience noo stunts is always
    tryin';
The chances is I'll never 'ave to do it any
    more:
At seven by the Captain's watch my little job
    is . . . *dyin'*.

I've got a little note to write; I'd best begin
    it now.
I ain't much good at writin' notes, but here
    goes: "Dearest Mother,
I've been in many 'ot old 'do's'; I've scraped
    through safe some'ow,

MY JOB

But now I'm on the very point of tacklin' an-
    other.
A little job of hand-grenades; they called for
    volunteers.
They picked me out; I'm proud of it; it seems
    a trifle dicky.
If anythin' should 'appen, well, there ain't no
    call for tears,
And so . . . I 'opes this finds you well.— Your
    werry lovin' Micky."

I've got a little score to settle wiv them swine
    out there.
I've 'ad so many of me pals done in it's quite
    upset me.
I've seen so much of bloody death I don't seem
    for to care,
If I can only even up, how soon the blighters
    get me.
I'm sorry for them perishers that corpses in a
    bed;
I only 'opes mine's short and sweet, no linger-
    longer-lyin';
I've made a mess of life, but now I'll try to
    make instead . . .
It's seven sharp. Good-bye, old pals! . . . *a
decent job in dyin'.*

THE SONG OF THE PACIFIST

What do they matter, our headlong hates, when
    we take the toll of our Dead?
Think ye our glory and gain will pay for the
    torrent of blood we have shed?
By the cheers of our Victory will the heart of
    the mother be comforted?

If by the Victory all we mean is a broken and
    brooding foe;
Is the pomp and power of a glitt'ring hour, and
    a truce for an age or so:
By the clay-cold hand on the broken blade we
    have smitten a bootless blow!

If by the Triumph we only prove that the sword
    we sheathe is bright;
That justice and truth and love endure; that
    freedom's throned on the height;
That the feebler folks shall be unafraid; that
    Might shall never be Right;

THE SONG OF THE PACIFIST

If this be all: by the blood-drenched plains, by
    the havoc of fire and fear,
By the rending roar of the War of Wars, by
    the Dead so doubly dear. . . .
Then our Victory is a vast defeat, and it mocks
    us as we cheer.

Victory! there can be but one, hallowed in every
    land:
When by the graves of our common dead we
    who were foemen stand;
And in the hush of our common grief hand is
    tendered to hand.

Triumph! Yes, when out of the dust in the
    splendour of their release
The spirits of those who fell go forth and they
    hallow our hearts to peace,
And, brothers in pain, with world-wide voice,
    we clamour that War shall cease.

Glory! Ay, when from blackest loss shall be
    born most radiant gain;
When over the gory fields shall rise a star that
    never shall wane:

THE SONG OF THE PACIFIST

Then, and then only, our Dead shall know that
    they have not fall'n in vain.

When our children's children shall talk of
    War as a madness that may not be;
When we thank our God for our grief to-day,
    and blazon from sea to sea
In the name of the Dead the banner of Peace
    . . . that will be Victory.

THE TWINS

There were two brothers, John and James,
And when the town went up in flames,
To save the house of James dashed John,
Then turned, and lo! his own was gone.

And when the great World War began,
To volunteer John promptly ran;
And while he learned live bombs to lob,
James stayed at home and — sneaked his job.

John came home with a missing limb;
That didn't seem to worry him;
But oh, it set his brain awhirl
To find that James had — sneaked his girl!

Time passed. John tried his grief to drown;
To-day James owns one-half the town;
His army contracts riches yield;
And John? Well, *search the Potter's Field.*

THE SONG OF THE
SOLDIER-BORN

Give me the scorn of the stars and a peak de-
fiant;
Wail of the pines and a wind with the shout of
a giant;
Night and a trail unknown and a heart re-
liant.

Give me to live and love in the old, bold fashion;
A soldier's billet at night and a soldier's ration;
A heart that leaps to the fight with a soldier's
passion.

For I hold as a simple faith there's no denying:
The trade of a soldier's the only trade worth
plying;
The death of a soldier's the only death worth
dying.

THE SONG OF THE SOLDIER-BORN

So let me go and leave your safety behind
    me;
Go to the spaces of hazard where nothing shall
    bind me;
Go till the word is War — and then you will
    find me.

Then you will call me and claim me because
    you will need me;
Cheer me and gird me and into the battle-wrath
    speed me. . . .
And when it's over, spurn me and no longer
    heed me.

For guile and a purse gold-greased are the
    arms you carry;
With deeds of paper you fight and with pens
    you parry;
You call on the hounds of the law your foes
    to harry.

You with your " Art for its own sake," posing
    and prinking;
You with your " Live and be merry," eating
    and drinking;

THE SONG OF THE SOLDIER-BORN

You with your " Peace at all hazard," from
   bright blood shrinking.

Fools! I will tell you now: though the red
   rain patters,
And a million of men go down, it's little it
   matters. . . .
There's the Flag upflung to the stars, though
   it streams in tatters.

There's a glory gold never can buy to yearn
   and to cry for;
There's a hope that's as old as the sky to suffer
   and sigh for;
There's a faith that out-dazzles the sun to
   martyr and die for.

Ah no! it's my dream that War will never be
   ended;
That men will perish like men, and valour be
   splendid;
That the Flag by the sword will be served,
   and honour defended.

THE SONG OF THE SOLDIER-BORN

That the tale of my fights will never be ancient
    story;
That though my eye may be dim and my beard
    be hoary,
I'll die as a soldier dies on the Field of
    Glory.

So give me a strong right arm for a wrong's
    swift righting;
Stave of a song on my lips as my sword is
    smiting;
Death in my boots may-be, but fighting,
    fighting.

AFTERNOON TEA

As I was saying . . . (No, thank you; I never
    take cream with my tea;
Cows weren't allowed in the trenches — got out
    of the habit, y'see.)
As I was saying, our Colonel leaped up like a
    youngster of ten:
" Come on, lads! " he shouts, " and we'll show
    'em."　And he sprang to the head of the
    men.
Then some bally thing seemed to trip him, and
    he fell on his face with a slam. . . .
Oh, he died like a true British soldier, and the
    last word he uttered was " Damn! "
And hang it!　I loved the old fellow, and
    something just burst in my brain,
And I cared no more for the bullets than I
    would for a shower of rain.
'Twas an awf'ly funny sensation (I say, this is
    jolly nice tea) ;

I felt as if something had broken; by gad!   I
   was suddenly free.
Free for a glorified moment, beyond regula-
   tions and laws,
Free just to wallow in slaughter, as the chap
   of the Stone Age was.
So on I went joyously nursing a Berserker rage
   of my own,
And though all my chaps were behind me, feel-
   ing most frightf'ly alone;
With the bullets and shells ding-donging, and
   the " krock " and the swish of the shrap;
And I found myself humming " Ben Bolt "
   . . . (Will you pass me the sugar, old
   chap?
Two lumps, please). . . . What was I say-
   ing?   Oh yes, the jolly old dash;
We simply ripped through the barrage, and
   on with a roar and a crash.
My fellows — Old Nick couldn't stop 'em.
   On, on they went with a yell,
Till they tripped on the Boches' sand-bags,—
   nothing much left to tell:
A trench so tattered and battered that even a
   rat couldn't live;

AFTERNOON TEA

Some corpses tangled and mangled, wire you
　　could pass through a sieve.
The jolly old guns had bilked us, cheated us
　　out of our show,
And my fellows were simply yearning for a
　　red mix-up with the foe.
So I shouted to them to follow, and on we went
　　roaring again,
Battle-tuned and exultant, on in the leaden rain.
Then all at once a machine gun barks from a
　　bit of a bank,
And our Major roars in a fury: " We've got
　　to take it on flank."
He was running like fire to lead us, when down
　　like a stone he comes,
As full of " typewriter " bullets as a pudding
　　is full of plums.
So I took his job and we got 'em. . . . By gad !
　　we got 'em like rats ;
Down in a deep shell-crater we fought like
　　Kilkenny cats.
'Twas pleasant just for a moment to be sheltered
　　and out of range,
With someone you *saw* to go for — it made
　　an agreeable change.

And the Boches that missed my bullets, my
    chaps gave a bayonet jolt,
And all the time, I remember, I whistled and
    hummed " Ben Bolt."

Well, that little job was over, so hell for
    leather we ran,
On to the second line trenches,— that's where
    the fun began.
For though we had strafed 'em like fury, there
    still were some Boches about,
And my fellows, teeth set and eyes glaring, like
    terriers routed 'em out.
Then I stumbled on one of their dug-outs, and
    I shouted: " Is anyone there?"
And a voice, " Yes, one; but I'm wounded,"
    came faint up the narrow stair;
And my man was descending before me, when
    sudden a cry! a shot!
(I say, this cake is delicious. You make it
    yourself, do you not?)
My man? Oh, they killed the poor devil; for
    if there was one there was ten;
So after I'd bombed 'em sufficient I went down
    at the head of my men,

And four tried to sneak from a bunk-hole, but
we cornered the rotters all right;
I'd rather not go into details, 'twas messy that
bit of the fight.
But all of it's beastly messy; let's talk of pleas-
anter things:
The skirts that the girls are wearing, ridicu-
lous fluffy things,
So short that they show. . . . Oh, hang it!
Well, if I must, I must.
We cleaned out the second trench line, bomb
and bayonet thrust;
And on we went to the third one, quite cal-
loused to crumping by now;
And some of our fellows who'd passed us were
making a deuce of a row;
And my chaps — well, I just couldn't hold 'em;
(It's strange how it is with gore;
In some ways it's just like whiskey: if you
taste it you must have more.)
Their eyes were like beacons of battle; by gad,
sir! they *couldn't* be calmed,
So I headed 'em bang for the bomb-belt, rac-
ing like billy-be-damned.
Oh, it didn't take long to arrive there, those
who arrived at all;

AFTERNOON TEA

The machine guns were certainly chronic, the
    shindy enough to appal.
Oh yes, I omitted to tell you, I'd wounds on
    the chest and the head.
And my shirt was torn to a gun-rag, and my
    face blood-gummy and red.
I'm thinking I looked like a madman; I fancy
    I felt one too,
Half naked and swinging a rifle. . . . God!
    what a glorious " do."
As I sit here in old Picadilly, sipping my after-
    noon tea,
I see a blind, bullet-chipped devil, and it's hard
    to believe that it's me;
I see a wild, war-damaged demon, smashing
    out left and right,
And humming " Ben Bolt " rather loudly, and
    hugely enjoying the fight.
And as for my men, may God bless 'em! I've
    loved 'em ever since then:
They fought like the shining angels; they're
    the pick o' the land, my men.
And the trench was a reeking shambles, not a
    Boche to be seen alive —
So I thought; but on rounding a traverse I
    came on a covey of five;

AFTERNOON TEA

And four of 'em threw up their flippers, but
    the fifth chap, a sergeant, was game,
And though I'd a bomb and revolver he came
    at me just the same.
A sporty thing that, I tell you; I just couldn't
    blow him to hell,
So I swung to the point of his jaw-bone, and
    down like a ninepin he fell.
And then when I'd brought him to reason, he
    wasn't half bad, that Hun;
He bandaged my head and my short-rib as well
    as the Doc could have done.
So back I went with my Boches, as gay as a two-
    year-old colt,
And it suddenly struck me as rummy, I still
    was a-humming " Ben Bolt."
And now, by Jove! how I've bored you.
    You've just let me babble away;
Let's talk of the things that *matter* — your
    car or the newest play. . . .

THE MOURNERS

I look into the aching womb of night;
I look across the mist that masks the dead;
The moon is tired and gives but little light,
    The stars have gone to bed.

The earth is sick and seems to breathe with pain;
A lost wind whimpers in a mangled tree;
I do not see the foul, corpse-cluttered plain,
    The dead I do not see.

The slain I *would* not see . . . and so I lift
My eyes from out the shambles where they lie;
When lo! a million woman-faces drift
    Like pale leaves through the sky.

The cheeks of some are channelled deep with
       tears;
But some are tearless, with wild eyes that stare
Into the shadow of the coming years
    Of fathomless despair.

THE MOURNERS

And some are young, and some are very old;
And some are rich, some poor beyond belief;
Yet all are strangely like, set in the mould
    Of everlasting grief.

They fill the vast of Heaven, face on face;
And then I see one weeping with the rest,
Whose eyes beseech me for a moment's
    space. . . .
    Oh eyes I love the best!

Nay, I but dream.   The sky is all forlorn,
And there's the plain of battle writhing red:
God pity them, the women-folk who mourn!
    How happy are the dead!

L'ENVOI

My job is done; my rhymes are ranked and
    ready,
My word-battalions marching verse by verse;
Here stanza-companies are none too steady;
There print-platoons are weak, but might be
    worse.
And as in marshalled order I review them,
My type-brigades, unfearful of the fray,
My eyes that seek their faults are seeing
    through them
Immortal visions of an epic day.

It seems I'm in a giant bowling-alley;
The hidden heavies round me crash and thud;
A spire snaps like a pipe-stem in the valley;
The rising sun is like a ball of blood.
Along the road the " fantassins " are pouring,
And some are gay as fire, and some steel-
    stern. . . .

L'ENVOI

Then back again I see the red tide pouring,
Along the reeking road from Hebuterne.

And once again I seek Hill Sixty-Seven,
The Hun lines grey and peaceful in my sight;
When suddenly the rosy air is riven —
A "coal-box" blots the "boyou" on my right.
Or else to evil Carnoy I am stealing,
Past sentinels who hail with bated breath;
Where not a cigarette spark's dim revealing
May hint our mission in that zone of death.

I see across the shrapnel-seeded meadows
The jagged rubble-heap of La Boiselle;
Blood-guilty Fricourt brooding in the shadows,
And Thiepval's château empty as a shell.
Down Albert's riven streets the moon is leer-
        ing;
The Hanging Virgin takes its bitter ray;
And all the road from Hamel I am hearing
The silver rage of bugles over Bray.

L'ENVOI

Once more within the sky's deep sapphire
    hollow
I sight a swimming Taube, a fairy thing;
I watch the angry shell flame flash and follow
In feather puffs that flick a tilted wing;
And then it fades, with shrapnel mirror's
    flashing;
The flashes bloom to blossoms lily gold;
The batteries are rancorously crashing,
And life is just as full as it can hold.

Oh spacious days of glory and of grieving!
Oh sounding hours of lustre and of loss!
Let us be glad we lived you, still believing
The God who gave the cannon gave the Cross.
Let us be sure amid these seething passions,
The lusts of blood and hate our souls abhor:
The Power that Order out of Chaos fashions
Smites fiercest in the wrath-red forge of
    War. . . .
Have faith! Fight on! Amid the battle-hell
Love triumphs, Freedom beacons, all is well.

Ballads of a Bohemian

CONTENTS

7

BOOK TWO
EARLY SUMMER
I

II

III

IV

V

BOOK THREE
LATE SUMMER
I

CONTENTS

9

BOOK FOUR

WINTER

I

PRELUDE

Alas! upon some starry height,
The Gods of Excellence to please,
This hand of mine will never smite
The Harp of High Serenities.
Mere minstrel of the street am I,
To whom a careless coin you fling;
But who, beneath the bitter sky,
Blue-lipped, yet insolent of eye,
Can shrill a song of Spring;
A song of merry mansard days,
The cheery chimney-tops among;
Of rolics and of roundelays
When we were young . . . when we were young;
A song of love and lilac nights,
Of wit, of wisdom and of wine;
Of Folly whirling on the Heights,
Of hunger and of hope divine;
Of Blanche, Suzette and Celestine,
And all that gay and tender band
Who shared with us the fat, the lean,
The hazard of Illusion-land;
When scores of Philistines we slew
As mightily with brush and pen
We sought to make the world anew,
And scorned the gods of other men;
When we were fools divinely wise,

Who held it rapturous to strive;
When Art was sacred in our eyes,
And it was Heav'n to be alive. . . .

O days of glamor, glory, truth,
To you to-night I raise my glass;
O freehold of immortal youth,
Bohemia, the lost, alas!
O laughing lads who led the romp,
Respectable you've grown, I'm told;
Your heads you bow to power and pomp,
You've learned to know the worth of gold.
O merry maids who shared our cheer,
Your eyes are dim, your locks are gray;
And as you scrub I sadly fear
Your daughters speed the dance to-day.
O windmill land and crescent moon!
O Columbine and Pierrette!
To you my old guitar I tune
Ere I forget, ere I forget. . . .

So come, good men who toil and tire,
Who smoke and sip the kindly cup,
Ring round about the tavern fire
Ere yet you drink your liquor up;
And hear my simple songs of earth,
Of youth and truth and living things;
Of poverty and proper mirth,
Of rags and rich imaginings;
Of cock-a-hoop, blue-heavened days,
Of hearts elate and eager breath,

Of wonder, worship, pity, praise,
Of sorrow, sacrifice and death;
Of lusting, laughter, passion, pain,
Of lights that lure and dreams that thrall . . .
And if a golden word I gain,
Oh, kindly folks, God save you all!
And if you shake your heads in blame . . .
Good friends, God love you all the same.

BOOK ONE

SPRING

I

MONTPARNASSE,
April 1914.

All day the sun has shone into my little attic, a bitter sunshine that brightened yet did not warm. And so as I toiled and toiled doggedly enough, many were the looks I cast at the three faggots I had saved to cook my evening meal. Now, however, my supper is over, my pipe alight, and as I stretch my legs before the embers I have at last a glow of comfort, a glimpse of peace.

MY GARRET

Here is my Garret up five flights of stairs;
Here's where I deal in dreams and ply in fancies,
Here is the wonder-shop of all my wares,
My sounding sonnets and my red romances.
Here's where I challenge Fate and ring my rhymes,
And grope at glory — aye, and starve at times.

Here is my Stronghold: stout of heart am I,
Greeting each dawn as songful as a linnet;
And when at night on yon poor bed I lie
(Blessing the world and every soul that's in it),
Here's where I thank the Lord no shadow bars
My skylight's vision of the valiant stars.

17

Here is my Palace tapestried with dreams.
Ah! though to-night ten *sous* are all my treasure,
While in my gaze immortal beauty gleams,
Am I not dowered with wealth beyond all measure?
Though in my ragged coat my songs I sing,
King of my soul, I envy not the king.

Here is my Haven: it's so quiet here;
Only the scratch of pen, the candle's flutter;
Shabby and bare and small, but O how dear!
Mark you — my table with my work a-clutter,
My shelf of tattered books along the wall,
My bed, my broken chair — that's nearly all.

Only four faded walls, yet mine, all mine.
Oh, you fine folks, a pauper scorns your pity.
Look, where above me stars of rapture shine;
See, where below me gleams the siren city . . .
Am I not rich? — a millionaire no less,
If wealth be told in terms of Happiness.

Ten *sous*. . . . . I think one can sing best of poverty when
one is holding it at arm's length. I'm sure that when I
wrote these lines, fortune had for a moment tweaked me by
the nose. To-night, however, I am truly down to ten *sous*.
It is for that I have stayed in my room all day, rolled in
my blankets and clutching my pen with clammy fingers.
I must work, work, work. I must finish my book before
poverty crushes me. I am not only writing for my living
but for my life. Even to-day my Muse was mutinous. For
hours and hours anxiously I stared at a paper that was blank;

nervously I paced up and down my garret; bitterly I flung
myself on my bed.   Then suddenly it all came.   Line after
line I wrote with hardly a halt.   So I made another of my
Ballads of the Boulevards.   Here it is:

JULOT THE *APACHE*

You've heard of Julot the *apache,* and Gigolette, his
    môme. . . .
Montmartre was their hunting-ground, but Belville
    was their home.
A little chap just like a boy, with smudgy black
    mustache,—
Yet there was nothing juvenile in Julot the *apache.*
From head to heel as tough as steel, as nimble as
    a cat,
With every trick of twist and kick, a master of
    savate.
And Gigolette was tall and fair, as stupid as a cow,
With three combs in the greasy hair she banged
    upon her brow.
You'd see her on the Place Pigalle on any afternoon,
A primitive and strapping wench as brazen as the
    moon.
And yet there is a tale that's told of Clichy after
    dark,
And two *gendarmes* who swung their arms with
    Julot for a mark.
And oh, but they'd have got him too; they banged
    and blazed away,

When like a flash a woman leapt between them and
    their prey.
She took the medicine meant for him; she came
    down with a crash . . .
" Quick now, and make your get-away, O Julot the
    apache! " . . .
But no! He turned, ran swiftly back, his arms
    around her met;
They nabbed him sobbing like a kid, and kissing
    Gigolette.

Now I'm a reckless painter chap who loves a jam-
    boree,
And one night in Cyrano's bar I got upon a spree;
And there were trollops all about, and crooks of
    every kind,
But though the place was reeling round I didn't
    seem to mind.
Till down I sank, and all was blank when in the
    bleary dawn
I woke up in my studio to find — my money gone;
Three hundred francs I'd scraped and squeezed to
    pay my quarter's rent.
" Some one has pinched my wad," I wailed; " it
    never has been spent."
And as I racked my brains to seek how I could raise
    some more,
Before my cruel landlord kicked me cowering from
    the door:
A knock . . . " Come in," I gruffly groaned; I did
    not raise my head,

Then lo! I heard a husky voice, a swift and silky
 tread:
" You got so blind, last night, *mon vieux,* I collared
 all your cash —
Three hundred francs. . . . There! *Nom de
Dieu,"* said Julot the *apache.*

And that was how I came to know Julot and Gigo-
 lette,
And we would talk and drink a *bock,* and smoke a
 cigarette.
And I would meditate upon the artistry of crime,
And he would tell of cracking cribs and cops and
 doing time;
Or else when he was flush of funds he'd carelessly
 explain
He'd biffed some bloated *bourgeois* on the border of
 the Seine.
So gentle and polite he was, just like a man of peace,
And not a desperado and the terror of the police.

Now one day in a *bistro* that's behind the Place
 Vendôme
I came on Julot the *apache,* and Gigolette his
 môme.
And as they looked so very grave, says I to them,
 says I,
" Come on and have a little glass, it's good to rinse
 the eye.
You both look mighty serious; you've something on
 the heart."

" Ah, yes," said Julot the *apache,* " we've some-
    thing to impart.
When such things come to folks like us, it isn't very
    gay . . .
It's Gigolette — she tells me that a *gosse* is on the
    way."
Then Gigolette, she looked at me with eyes like
    stones of gall:
" If we were honest folks," said she, " I wouldn't
    mind at all.
But then . . . you know the life we lead; well, any-
    way I mean
(That is, providing it's a girl) to call her Angeline."
" Cheer up," said I; " it's all in life.   There's gold
    within the dross.
Come on, we'll drink another *verre* to Angeline the
    gosse."

And so the weary winter passed, and then one April
    morn
The worthy Julot came at last to say the babe was
    born.
" I'd like to chuck it in the Seine," he sourly snarled,
    " and yet
I guess I'll have to let it live, because of Gigolette."
I only laughed, for sure I saw his spite was all a bluff,
And he was prouder than a prince behind his manner
    gruff.
Yet every day he'd blast the brat with curses deep
    and grim,
And swear to me that Gigolette no longer thought
    of *him.*

And then one night he dropped the mask; his eyes
    were sick with dread,
And when I offered him a smoke he groaned and
    shook his head:
"I'm all upset; it's Angeline . . . she's covered
    with a rash . . .
She'll maybe die, my little *gosse*," cried Julot the
    apache.

But Angeline, I joy to say, came through the test
    all right,
Though Julot, so they tell me, watched beside her
    day and night.
And when I saw him next, says he: "Come up and
    dine with me.
We'll buy a beefsteak on the way, a bottle and some
    brie."
And so I had a merry night within his humble home,
And laughed with Angeline the *gosse* and Gigolette
    the *môme*.
And every time that Julot used a word the least
    obscene,
How Gigolette would frown at him and point to
    Angeline:
Oh, such a little innocent, with hair of silken floss,
I do not wonder they were proud of Angeline the
    gosse.
And when her arms were round his neck, then Julot
    says to me:
"I must work harder now, *mon vieux,* since I've to
    work for three."

He worked so very hard indeed, the police dropped
  in one day,
And for a year behind the bars they put him safe
  away.

So dark and silent now, their home; they'd gone —
  I wondered where,
Till in a laundry near I saw a child with shining hair;
And o'er the tub a strapping wench, her arms in
  soapy foam;
Lo! it was Angeline the *gosse*, and Gigolette the
  môme.
And so I kept an eye on them and saw that all went
  right,
Until at last came Julot home, half crazy with de-
  light.
And when he'd kissed them both, says he: " I've had
  my fill this time.
I'm on the honest now, I am; I'm all fed up with
  crime.
You mark my words, the page I turn is going to be
  clean,
I swear it on the head of her, my little Angeline."

And so, to finish up my tale, this morning as I
  strolled
Along the boulevard I heard a voice I knew of old.
I saw a rosy little man with walrus-like mus-
  tache . . .
I stopped, I stared. . . . By all the gods! 'twas
  Julot the *apache*.

"I'm in the garden way," he said, "and doing
    mighty well;
I've half an acre under glass, and heaps of truck to
    sell.
Come out and see. Oh come, my friend, on Sunday,
    wet or shine . . .
Say! — *it's the First Communion of that little girl
    of mine.*"

II

Chez Moi, Montparnasse,
The same evening.

To-day is an anniversary. A year ago to-day I kicked
over an office stool and came to Paris thinking to make a
living by my pen. I was twenty then, and in my pocket
I had twenty pounds. Of that, my ten *sous* are all that
remain. And so to-night I am going to spend them, not
prudently on bread, but prodigally on beer.

As I stroll down the Boul' Mich' the lingering light
has all the exquisite tenderness of violet; the trees are in
their first translucent green; beneath them the lamps are
lit with purest gold, and from the Little Luxembourg comes
a silver jangle of tiny voices. Taking the gay side of the
street, I enter a café. Although it isn't its true name, I
choose to call my café —

L'ESCARGOT D'OR

O Tavern of the Golden Snail!
Ten *sous* have I, so I'll regale;

Ten *sous* your amber brew to sip
(Eight for the *bock* and two the tip),
And so I'll sit the evening long,
And smoke my pipe and watch the throng,
The giddy crowd that drains and drinks,
I'll watch it quiet as a sphinx;
And who among them all shall buy
For ten poor *sous* such joy as I?
As I who, snugly tucked away,
Look on it all as on a play,
A frolic scene of love and fun,
To please an audience of One.

O Tavern of the Golden Snail!
You've stuff indeed for many a tale.
All eyes, all ears, I nothing miss:
Two lovers lean to clasp and kiss;
The merry students sing and shout,
The nimble *garçons* dart about;
Lo! here come Mimi and Musette
With: "*S'il vous plait, une cigarette?*"
Marcel and Rudolf, Schaunard too,
Behold the old rapscallion crew,
With flowing tie and shaggy head . . .
Who says Bohemia is dead?
Oh shades of Murger! prank and clown,
And I will watch and write it down.

O Tavern of the Golden Snail!
What crackling throats have gulped your ale!
What sons of Fame from far and near

Have glowed and mellowed in your cheer!
Within this corner where I sit
Banville and Coppée clashed their wit;
And hither too, to dream and drain,
And drown despair, came poor Verlaine.
Here Wilde would talk and Synge would muse,
Maybe like me with just ten *sous*.
Ah! one is lucky, is one not?
With ghosts so rare to drain a pot!
So may your custom never fail,
O Tavern of the Golden Snail!

There! my pipe is out. Let me light it again and consider.
I have no illusions about myself. I am not fool enough to
think I am a poet, but I have a knack of rhyme and I love
to make verses. Mine is a tootling, tin-whistle music.
Humbly and afar I follow in the footsteps of Praed and
Lampson, of Field and Riley, hoping that in time my Muse
may bring me bread and butter. So far, however, it has
been all kicks and no coppers. And to-night I am at the
end of my tether. I wish I knew where to-morrow's breakfast was coming from. Well, since rhyming's been my ruin,
let me rhyme to the bitter end.

IT IS LATER THAN YOU THINK

Lone amid the café's cheer,
Sad of heart am I to-night;
Dolefully I drink my beer,
But no single line I write.
There's the wretched rent to pay,

Yet I glower at pen and ink:
Oh, inspire me, Muse, I pray,
It is later than you think!

Hello! there's a pregnant phrase.
Bravo! let me write it down;
Hold it with a hopeful gaze,
Gauge it with a fretful frown;
Tune it to my lyric lyre . . .
Ah! upon starvation's brink,
How the words are dark and dire:
It is later than you think.

Weigh them well. . . . Behold yon band,
Students drinking by the door,
Madly merry, *bock* in hand,
Saucers stacked to mark their score.
Get you gone, you jolly scamps;
Let your parting glasses clink;
Seek your long neglected lamps:
It is later than you think.

Look again: yon dainty blonde,
All allure and golden grace,
Oh so willing to respond
Should you turn a smiling face.
Play your part, poor pretty doll;
Feast and frolic, pose and prink;
There's the Morgue to end it all,
And it's later than you think.

Yon's a playwright — mark his face,
Puffed and purple, tense and tired;
Pasha-like he holds his place,
Hated, envied and admired.
How you gobble life, my friend;
Wine, and woman soft and pink!
Well, each tether has its end:
Sir, it's later than you think.

See yon living scarecrow pass
With a wild and wolfish stare
At each empty absinthe glass,
As if he saw Heaven there.
Poor damned wretch, to end your pain
There is still the Greater Drink.
Yonder waits the sanguine Seine . . .
It is later than you think.

Lastly, you who read; aye, you
Who this very line may scan:
Think of all you planned to do . . .
Have you done the best you can?
See! the tavern lights are low;
Black's the night, and how you shrink!
God! and is it time to go?
Ah! the clock is always slow;
It is later than you think;
Sadly later than you think;
Far, far later than you think.

Scarcely do I scribble that last line on the back of an old envelope when a voice hails me. It is a fellow free-lance, a short-story man called MacBean. He is having a feast of *Marennes* and he asks me to join him.

MacBean is a Scotsman with the soul of an Irishman. He has a keen, lean, spectacled face, and if it were not for his gray hair he might be taken for a student of theology. However, there is nothing of the Puritan in MacBean. He loves wine and women, and money melts in his fingers.

He has lived so long in the Quarter he looks at life from the Parisian angle. His knowledge of literature is such that he might be a Professor, but he would rather be a vagabond of letters. We talk shop. We discuss the American short story, but MacBean vows they do these things better in France. He says that some of the *contes* printed every day in the *Journal* are worthy of Maupassant. After that he buys more beer, and we roam airily over the fields of literature, plucking here and there a blossom of quotation. A fine talk, vivid and eager. It puts me into a kind of glow.

MacBean pays the bill from a handful of big notes, and the thought of my own empty pockets for a moment damps me. However, when we rise to go, it is well after midnight, and I am in a pleasant daze. The rest of the evening may be summed up in the following jingle:

NOCTAMBULE

Zut! it's two o'clock.
See! the lights are jumping.
Finish up your *bock,*
Time we all were humping.
Waiters stack the chairs,

Pile them on the tables;
Let us to our lairs
Underneath the gables.

Up the old Boul' Mich'
Climb with steps erratic.
Steady . . . how I wish
I was in my attic!
Full am I with cheer;
In my heart the joy stirs;
Couldn't be the beer,
Must have been the oysters.

In obscene array
Garbage cans spill over;
How I wish that they
Smelled as sweet as clover!
Charing women wait;
Cafés drop their shutters;
Rats perambulate
Up and down the gutters.

Down the darkened street
Market carts are creeping;
Horse with wary feet,
Red-faced driver sleeping.
Loads of vivid greens,
Carrots, leeks, potatoes,
Cabbages and beans,
Turnips and tomatoes.

Pair of dapper chaps,
Cigarettes and sashes,
Stare at me, perhaps
Desperate *Apachès*.
" Needn't bother me,
Jolly well you know it;
*Parceque je suis
Quartier Latin poète*.

" Give you villanelles,
Madrigals and lyrics;
Ballades and rondels,
Odes and panegyrics.
Poet pinched and poor,
Pricked by cold and hunger;
Trouble's troubadour,
Misery's balladmonger."

Think how queer it is!
Every move I'm making,
Cosmic gravity's
Center I am shaking;
Oh, how droll to feel
(As I now am feeling),
Even as I reel,
All the world is reeling.

Reeling too the stars,
Neptune and Uranus,
Jupiter and Mars,
Mercury and Venus;

Suns and moons with me,
As I'm homeward straying,
All in sympathy
Swaying, swaying, swaying.

Lord! I've got a head.
Well, it's not surprising.
I must gain my bed
Ere the sun be rising;
When the merry lark
In the sky is soaring,
I'll refuse to hark,
I'll be snoring, snoring.

Strike a sulphur match . . .
Ha! at last my garret.
Fumble at the latch,
Close the door and bar it.
Bed, you graciously
Wait, despite my scorning . . .
So, bibaciously
Mad old world, good morning.

III

My Garret, Montparnasse,
April.

INSOMNIA

Heigh ho! to sleep I vainly try;
Since twelve I haven't closed an eye,

And now it's three, and as I lie,
From Notre Dame to St. Denis
The bells of Paris chime to me;
" You're young," they say, " and strong and free."

I do not turn with sighs and groans
To ease my limbs, to rest my bones,
As if my bed were stuffed with stones,
No peevish murmur tips my tongue —
Ah no! for every sound upflung
Says: " Lad, you're free and strong and young."

And so beneath the sheet's caress
My body purrs with happiness;
Joy bubbles in my veins. . . . Ah yes,
My very blood that leaps along
Is chiming in a joyous song,
Because I'm young and free and strong.

   Maybe it is the springtide.   I am so happy I am afraid.
The sense of living fills me with exultation.   I want to
sing, to dance; I am dithyrambic with delight.

I think the moon must be to blame:
It fills the room with fairy flame;
It paints the wall, it seems to pour
A dappled flood upon the floor.
I rise and through the window stare . . .
Ye gods! how marvelously fair!
From Montrouge to the Martyr's Hill,

A silver city rapt and still;
Dim, drowsy deeps of opal haze,
And spire and dome in diamond blaze;
The little lisping leaves of spring
Like sequins softly glimmering;
Each roof a plaque of argent sheen,
A gauzy gulf the space between;
Each chimney-top a thing of grace,
Where merry moonbeams prank and chase;
And all that sordid was and mean,
Just Beauty, deathless and serene.

O magic city of a dream!
From glory unto glory gleam;
And I will gaze and pity those
Who on their pillows drowse and doze . . .
And as I've nothing else to do,
Of tea I'll make a rousing brew,
And coax my pipes until they croon,
And chant a ditty to the moon.

There! my tea is black and strong. Inspiration comes
with every sip. Now for the moon.

The moon peeped out behind the hill
As yellow as an apricot;
Then up and up it climbed until
Into the sky it fairly got;
The sky was vast and violet;
The poor moon seemed to faint in fright,

And pale it grew and paler yet,
Like fine old silver, rinsed and bright.
And yet it climbed so bravely on
Until it mounted heaven-high;
Then earthward it serenely shone,
A silver sovereign of the sky,
A bland sultana of the night,
Surveying realms of lily light.

MOON SONG

A child saw in the morning skies
The dissipated-looking moon,
And opened wide her big blue eyes,
And cried: " Look, look, my lost balloon! "
And clapped her rosy hands with glee:
" Quick, mother!   Bring it back to me."

A poet in a lilied pond
Espied the moon's reflected charms,
And ravished by that beauty blonde,
Leapt out to clasp her in his arms.
And as he'd never learnt to swim,
Poor fool! that was the end of him.

A rustic glimpsed amid the trees
The bluff moon caught as in a snare.
" They say it do be made of cheese,"
Said Giles, " and that a chap bides there. . . .
That Blue Boar ale be strong, I vow —
The lad's a-winkin' at me now."

Two lovers watched the new moon hold
The old moon in her bright embrace.
Said she: "There's mother, pale and old,
And drawing near her resting place."
Said he: "Be mine, and with me wed,"
Moon-high she stared . . . she shook her head.

A soldier saw with dying eyes
The bleared moon like a ball of blood,
And thought of how in other skies,
So pearly bright on leaf and bud
Like peace its soft white beams had lain;
Like Peace! . . . He closed his eyes again.

Child, lover, poet, soldier, clown,
Ah yes, old Moon, what things you've seen!
I marvel now, as you look down,
How can your face be so serene?
And tranquil still you'll make your round,
Old Moon, when we are underground.

"And now, blow out your candle, lad, and get to bed.
See, the dawn is in the sky. Open your window and let
its freshness rouge your cheek. You've earned your rest.
Sleep."

Aye, but before I do so, let me read again the last of
my *Ballads*.

THE SEWING-GIRL

The humble garret where I dwell
Is in that Quarter called the Latin;
It isn't spacious — truth to tell,
There's hardly room to swing a cat in.
But what of that! It's there I fight
For food and fame, my Muse inviting,
And all the day and half the night
You'll find me writing, writing, writing.

Now, it was in the month of May
As, wrestling with a rhyme rheumatic,
I chanced to look across the way,
And lo! within a neighbor attic,
A hand drew back the window shade,
And there, a picture glad and glowing,
I saw a sweet and slender maid,
And she was sewing, sewing, sewing.

So poor the room, so small, so scant,
Yet somehow oh, so bright and airy.
There was a pink geranium plant,
Likewise a very pert canary.
And in the maiden's heart it seemed
Some fount of gladness must be springing,
For as alone I sadly dreamed
I heard her singing, singing, singing.

THE SEWING-GIRL

God love her! how it cheered me then
To see her there so brave and pretty;
So she with needle, I with pen,
We slaved and sang above the city.
And as across my streams of ink
I watched her from a poet's distance,
She stitched and sang . . . I scarcely think
She was aware of my existence.

And then one day she sang no more.
That put me out, there's no denying.
I looked — she labored as before,
But, bless me! she was crying, crying.
Her poor canary chirped in vain;
Her pink geranium drooped in sorrow;
" Of course," said I, " she'll sing again.
Maybe," I sighed, " she will to-morrow."

Poor child; 'twas finished with her song:
Day after day her tears were flowing;
And as I wondered what was wrong
She pined and peaked above her sewing.
And then one day the blind she drew,
Ah! though I sought with vain endeavor
To pierce the darkness, well I knew
My sewing-girl had gone for ever.

And as I sit alone to-night
My eyes unto her room are turning . . .
I'd give the sum of all I write
Once more to see her candle burning,

Once more to glimpse her happy face,
And while my rhymes of cheer I'm ringing,
Across the sunny sweep of space
To hear her singing, singing, singing.

Heigh ho! I realize I am very weary. It's nice to be so
tired, and to know one can sleep as long as one wants. The
morning sunlight floods in at my window, so I draw the
blind, and throw myself on my bed. . . .

IV

My Garret, Montparnasse,
April.

Hurrah! As I opened my eyes this morning to a hard,
unfeeling world, little did I think what a surprise awaited
me. A big blue envelope had been pushed under my door.
Another rejection, I thought, and I took it up distastefully.
The next moment I was staring at my first cheque.

It was an express order for two hundred francs, in payment
of a bit of verse. . . . So to-day I will celebrate. I will
lunch at the D'Harcourt, I will dine on the Grand Boulevard,
I will go to the theater.

Well, here's the thing that has turned the tide for me.
It is somewhat in the vein of "Sourdough" Service, the
Yukon bard. I don't think much of his stuff, but they
say he makes heaps of money. I can well believe it, for
he drives a Hispano-Suiza in the Bois every afternoon. The
other night he was with a crowd at the Dome Café, a chubby
chap who sits in a corner and seldom speaks. I was dis-

appointed. I thought he was a big, hairy man who swore like a trooper and mixed brandy with his beer. He only drank Vichy, poor fellow!

LUCILLE

Of course you've heard of the *Nancy Lee,* and how
    she sailed away
On her famous quest of the Arctic flea, to the wilds
    of Hudson's Bay?
For it was a foreign Prince's whim to collect this
    tiny cuss,
And a golden quid was no more to him than a
    copper to coves like us.
So we sailed away and our hearts were gay as we
    gazed on the gorgeous scene;
And we laughed with glee as we caught the flea of
    the wolf and the wolverine;
Yea, our hearts were light as the parasite of the
    ermine rat we slew,
And the great musk ox, and the silver fox, and the
    moose and the caribou.
And we laughed with zest as the insect pest of the
    marmot crowned our zeal,
And the wary mink and the wily " link," and the
    walrus and the seal.
And with eyes aglow on the scornful snow we danced
    a rigadoon,
Round the lonesome lair of the Arctic hare, by the
    light of the silver moon.

But the time was nigh to homeward hie, when,
    imagine our despair!
For the best of the lot we hadn't got — the flea of
    the polar bear.
Oh, his face was long and his breath was strong, as
    the Skipper he says to me:
" I wants you to linger 'ere, my lad, by the shores
    of the Hartic Sea;
I wants you to 'unt the polar bear the perishin'
    winter through,
And if flea ye find of its breed and kind, there's a
    'undred quid for you."
But I shook my head: " No, Cap," I said; " it's
    yourself I'd like to please,
But I tells ye flat I wouldn't do that if ye went on
    yer bended knees."
Then the Captain spat in the seething brine, and
    he says: " Good luck to you,
If it can't be did for a 'undred quid, supposin' we
    call it two? "
So that was why they said good-by, and they sailed
    and left me there —
Alone, alone in the Arctic Zone to hunt for the
    polar bear.

Oh, the days were slow and packed with woe, till I
    thought they would never end;
And I used to sit when the fire was lit, with my
    pipe for my only friend.
And I tried to sing some rollicky thing, but my song
    broke off in a prayer,

And I'd drowse and dream by the driftwood gleam;
    I'd dream of a polar bear;
I'd dream of a cloudlike polar bear that blotted the
    stars on high,
With ravenous jaws and flenzing claws, and the
    flames of hell in his eye.
And I'd trap around on the frozen ground, as a
    proper hunter ought,
And beasts I'd find of every kind, but never the one
    I sought.
Never a track in the white ice-pack that humped
    and heaved and flawed,
Till I came to think: "Why, strike me pink! if
    the creature ain't a fraud."
And then one night in the waning light, as I hurried
    home to sup,
I hears a roar by the cabin door, and a great white
    hulk heaves up.
So my rifle flashed, and a bullet crashed; dead, dead
    as a stone fell he,
And I gave a cheer, for there in his ear —Gosh ding
    me! — a tiny flea.

At last, at last! Oh, I clutched it fast, and I gazed
    on it with pride;
And I thrust it into a biscuit-tin, and I shut it safe
    inside;
With a lid of glass for the light to pass, and space
    to leap and play;
Oh, it kept alive; yea, seemed to thrive, as I watched
    it night and day.

And I used to sit and sing to it, and I shielded it
 from harm,
And many a hearty feed it had on the heft of my
 hairy arm.
For you'll never know in that land of snow how lonesome a man can feel;
So I made a fuss of the little cuss, and I christened
 it " Lucille."
But the longest winter has its end, and the ice went
 out to sea,
And I saw one day a ship in the bay, and there was
 the *Nancy Lee*.
So a boat was lowered and I went aboard, and they
 opened wide their eyes —
Yes, they gave a cheer when the truth was clear,
 and they saw my precious prize.
And then it was all like a giddy dream; but to cut
 my story short,
We sailed away on the fifth of May to the foreign
 Prince's court;
To a palmy land and a palace grand, and the little
 Prince was there,
And a fat Princess in a satin dress with a crown of
 gold on her hair.
And they showed me into a shiny room, just him
 and her and me,
And the Prince he was pleased and friendly-like,
 and he calls for drinks for three.
And I shows them my battered biscuit-tin, and I
 makes my modest spiel,

And they laughed, they did, when I opened the lid,
    and out there popped Lucille.

Oh, the Prince was glad, I could soon see that, and
    the Princess she was too;
And Lucille waltzed round on the tablecloth as she
    often used to do.
And the Prince pulled out a purse of gold, and he
    put it in my hand;
And he says: " It was worth all that, I'm told, to
    stay in that nasty land."
And then he turned with a sudden cry, and he
    clutched at his royal beard;
And the Princess screamed, and well she might —
    for Lucille had disappeared.

" She must be here," said his Noble Nibbs, so we
    hunted all around;
Oh, we searched that place, but never a trace of the
    little beast we found.
So I shook my head, and I glumly said: " Gol darn
    the saucy cuss!
It's mighty queer, but she isn't here; so . . . she
    must be on one of us.
You'll pardon me if I make so free, but — there's
    just one thing to do:
If you'll kindly go for a half a mo' I'll search me
    garments through."
Then all alone on the shiny throne I stripped from
    head to heel;

In vain, in vain; it was very plain that I hadn't got
   Lucille.
So I garbed again, and I told the Prince, and he
   scratched his august head;
" I suppose if she hasn't selected you, it must be
   me," he said.
So *he* retired; but he soon came back, and his fea-
   tures showed distress:
" Oh, it isn't you and it isn't me." . . . Then we
   looked at the Princess.
So *she* retired; and we heard a scream, and she
   opened wide the door;
And her fingers twain were pinched to pain, but a
   radiant smile she wore:
" It's here," she cries, " our precious prize. Oh, I
   found it right away. . . ."
Then I ran to her with a shout of joy, but I choked
   with a wild dismay.
I clutched the back of the golden throne, and the
   room began to reel . . .
What she held to me was, ah yes! a flea, but . . .
   it wasn't my Lucille.

After all, I did not celebrate. I sat on the terrace of the
Café Napolitain on the Grand Boulevard, half hypnotized
by the passing crowd. And as I sat I fell into conversation
with a god-like stranger who sipped some golden ambrosia.
He told me he was an actor and introduced me to his bever-
age, which he called a " Suze-Anni." He soon left me, but
the effect of the golden liquid remained, and there came

over me a desire to write. *C'était plus fort que moi.* So instead of going to the Folies Bergère I spent all evening in the Omnium Bar near the Bourse, and wrote the following:

ON THE BOULEVARD

Oh, it's pleasant sitting here,
Seeing all the people pass;
You beside your *bock* of beer,
I behind my *demi-tasse.*
Chatting of no matter what.
You the Mummer, I the Bard;
Oh, it's jolly, is it not? —
Sitting on the Boulevard.

More amusing than a book,
If a chap has eyes to see;
For, no matter where I look,
Stories, stories jump at me.
Moving tales my pen might write;
Poems plain on every face;
Monologues you could recite
With inimitable grace.

(Ah! Imagination's power)
See yon *demi-mondaine* there,
Idly toying with a flower,
Smiling with a pensive air . . .
Well, her smile is but a mask,
For I saw within her muff

Such a wicked little flask:
Vitriol — ugh! the beastly stuff.

Now look back beside the bar.
See yon curled and scented *beau*,
Puffing at a fine cigar —
Sale espèce de maquereau.
Well (of course, it's all surmise),
It's for him she holds her place;
When he passes she will rise,
Dash the vitriol in his face.

Quick they'll carry him away,
Pack him in a Red Cross car;
Her they'll hurry, so they say,
To the cells of St. Lazare.
What will happen then, you ask?
What will all the sequel be?
Ah! Imagination's task
Isn't easy . . . let me see . . .

She will go to jail, no doubt,
For a year, or maybe two;
Then as soon as she gets out
Start her bawdy life anew.
He will lie within a ward,
Harmless as a man can be,
With his face grotesquely scarred,
And his eyes that cannot see.

Then amid the city's din
He will stand against a wall,

With around his neck a tin
Into which the pennies fall.
She will pass (I see it plain,
Like a cinematograph),
She will halt and turn again,
Look and look, and maybe laugh.

Well, I'm not so sure of that —
Whether she will laugh or cry.
He will hold a battered hat
To the lady passing by.
He will smile a cringing smile,
And into his grimy hold,
With a laugh (or sob) the while,
She will drop a piece of gold.

" Bless you, lady," he will say,
And get grandly drunk that night.
She will come and come each day,
Fascinated by the sight.
Then somehow he'll get to know
(Maybe by some kindly friend)
Who she is, and so . . . and so
Bring my story to an end.

How his heart will burst with hate!
He will curse and he will cry.
He will wait and wait and wait,
Till again she passes by.
Then like tiger from its lair
He will leap from out his place,

Down her, clutch her by the hair,
Smear the vitriol on her face.

(Ah! Imagination rare)
See . . . he takes his hat to go;
Now he's level with her chair;
Now she rises up to throw. . . .
God! and she has done it too . . .
Oh, those screams; those hideous screams!
I imagined and . . . it's true:
How his face will haunt my dreams!

What a sight!   It makes me sick.
Seems I am to blame somehow.
Garçon, fetch a brandy quick . . .
There!   I'm feeling better now.
Let's collaborate, we two,
You the Mummer, I the Bard;
Oh, what ripping stuff we'll do,
Sitting on the Boulevard!

It is strange how one works easily at times. I wrote
this so quickly that I might almost say I had reached the
end before I had come to the beginning. In such a mood
I wonder why everybody does not write poetry. Get a
Roget's *Thesaurus,* a rhyming dictionary: sit before your
typewriter with a strong glass of coffee at your elbow, and
just click the stuff off.

FACILITY

So easy 'tis to make a rhyme,
That did the world but know it,
Your coachman might Parnassus climb,
Your butler be a poet.

Then, oh, how charming it would be
If, when in haste hysteric
You called the page, you learned that he
Was grappling with a lyric.

Or else what rapture it would yield,
When cook sent up the salad,
To find within its depths concealed
A touching little ballad.

Or if for tea and toast you yearned,
What joy to find upon it
The chambermaid had coyly laid
A palpitating sonnet.

Your baker could the fashion set;
Your butcher might respond well;
With every tart a triolet,
With every chop a rondel.

Your tailor's bill . . . well, I'll be blowed!
Dear chap! I never knowed him . . .
He's gone and written me an ode,
Instead of what I *owed* him.

So easy 'tis to rhyme . . . yet stay!
Oh, terrible misgiving!
Please do not give the game away . . .
I've got to make my living.

V

MY GARRET
May 1914.

GOLDEN DAYS

Another day of toil and strife,
Another page so white,
Within that fateful Log of Life
That I and all must write;
Another page without a stain
To make of as I may,
That done, I shall not see again
Until the Judgment Day.

Ah, could I, could I backward turn
The pages of that Book,
How often would I blench and burn!
How often loathe to look!
What pages would be meanly scrolled;
What smeared as if with mud;
A few, maybe, might gleam like gold,
Some scarlet seem as blood.

O Record grave, God guide my hand
And make me worthy be,

Since what I write to-day shall stand
To all eternity;
Aye, teach me, Lord of Life, I pray,
As I salute the sun,
To bear myself that every day
May be a Golden One.

I awoke this morning to see the bright sunshine flooding
my garret. No chamber in the palace of a king could
have been more fair. How I sang as I dressed! How I
lingered over my coffee, savoring every drop! How care-
fully I packed my pipe, gazing serenely over the roofs of
Paris.

Never is the city so lovely as in this month of May, when
all the trees are in the fullness of their foliage. As I look, I
feel a freshness of vision in my eyes. Wonder wakes in
me. The simplest things move me to delight.

THE JOY OF LITTLE THINGS

It's good the great green earth to roam,
Where sights of awe the soul inspire;
But oh, it's best, the coming home,
The crackle of one's own hearth-fire!
You've hob-nobbed with the solemn Past;
You've seen the pageantry of kings;
Yet oh, how sweet to gain at last
The peace and rest of Little Things!

Perhaps you're counted with the Great;
You strain and strive with mighty men;
Your hand is on the helm of State;
Colossus-like you stride . . . and then
There comes a pause, a shining hour,
A dog that leaps, a hand that clings:
O Titan, turn from pomp and power;
Give all your heart to Little Things.

Go couch you childwise in the grass,
Believing it's some jungle strange,
Where mighty monsters peer and pass,
Where beetles roam and spiders range.
'Mid gloom and gleam of leaf and blade,
What dragons rasp their painted wings!
O magic world of shine and shade!
O beauty land of Little Things!

I sometimes wonder, after all,
Amid this tangled web of fate,
If what is great may not be small,
And what is small may not be great.
So wondering I go my way,
Yet in my heart contentment sings . . .
O may I ever see, I pray,
God's grace and love in Little Things.

So give to me, I only beg,
A little roof to call my own,
A little cider in the keg,
A little meat upon the bone;

A little garden by the sea,
A little boat that dips and swings . . .
Take wealth, take fame, but leave to me,
O Lord of Life, just Little Things.

Yesterday I finished my tenth ballad. When I have done about a score I will seek a publisher. If I cannot find one, I will earn, beg or steal the money to get them printed. Then if they do not sell I will hawk them from door to door. Oh, I'll succeed, I know I'll succeed. And yet I don't want an easy success; give me the joy of the fight, the thrill of the adventure. Here's my last ballad:

THE ABSINTHE DRINKERS

He's yonder, on the terrace of the Café de la Paix,
The little wizened Spanish man, I see him every day.
He's sitting with his Pernod on his customary chair;
He's staring at the passers with his customary stare.
He never takes his piercing eyes from off that mov-
       ing throng,
That current cosmopolitan meandering along:
Dark diplomats from Martinique, pale Rastas from
       Peru,
An Englishman from Bloomsbury, a Yank from
       Kalamazoo;
A poet from Montmartre's heights, a dapper little
       Jap,
Exotic citizens of all the countries on the map;

A tourist horde from every land that's underneath
    the sun —
That little wizened Spanish man, he misses never
    one.
Oh, foul or fair he's always there, and many a drink
    he buys,
And there's a fire of red desire within his hollow
    eyes.
And sipping of my Pernod, and a-knowing what I
    know,
Sometimes I want to shriek aloud and give away
    the show.
I've lost my nerve; he's haunting me; he's like a
    beast of prey,
That Spanish man that's watching at the Café de
    la Paix.

Say! Listen and I'll tell you all . . . the day was
    growing dim,
And I was with my Pernod at the table next to him;
And he was sitting soberly as if he were asleep,
When suddenly he seemed to tense, like tiger for a
    leap.
And then he swung around to me, his hand went to
    his hip,
My heart was beating like a gong — my arm was
    in his grip;
His eyes were glaring into mine; aye, though I
    shrank with fear,
His fetid breath was on my face, his voice was in
    my ear:

" Excuse my *brusquerie*," he hissed; " but, sir, do
    you suppose —
That portly man who passed us had a *wen upon
    his nose?* "

And then at last it dawned on me, the fellow must
    be mad;
And when I soothingly replied: " I do not think
    he had,"
The little wizened Spanish man subsided in his chair,
And shrouded in his raven cloak resumed his owlish
    stare.
But when I tried to slip away he turned and glared
    at me,
And oh, that fishlike face of his was sinister to see:
" Forgive me if I startled you; of course you think
    I'm queer;
No doubt you wonder who I am, so solitary here;
You question why the passers-by I piercingly
    review . . .
Well, listen, my bibacious friend, I'll tell my tale
    to you.

" It happened twenty years ago, and in another land:
A maiden young and beautiful, two suitors for her
    hand.
My rival was the lucky one; I vowed I would repay;
Revenge has mellowed in my heart, it's rotten ripe
    to-day.
My happy rival skipped away, vamoosed, he left
    no trace;

And so I'm waiting, waiting here to meet him face
    to face;
For has it not been ever said that all the world one
    day
Will pass in pilgrimage before the Café de la Paix?"

"But, sir," I made remonstrance, "if it's twenty
    years ago,
You'd scarcely recognize him now, he must have
    altered so."
The little wizened Spanish man he laughed a hideous
    laugh,
And from his cloak he quickly drew a faded photo-
    graph.
"You're right," said he, "but there are traits (oh,
    this you must allow)
That never change; Lopez was fat, he must be fatter
    now.
His paunch is senatorial, he cannot see his toes,
I'm sure of it; and then, behold! that wen upon his
    nose.
I'm looking for a man like that.   I'll wait and wait
    until . . ."
"What will you do?" I sharply cried; he answered
    me: "Why, kill!
He robbed me of my happiness — nay, stranger, do
    not start;
I'll firmly and politely put — a bullet in his heart."

And then that little Spanish man, with big cigar
    alight,

Uprose and shook my trembling hand and vanished
in the night.
And I went home and thought of him and had a
dreadful dream
Of portly men with each a wen, and woke up with
. a scream.
And sure enough, next morning, as I prowled the
Boulevard,
A portly man with wenny nose roamed into my
regard;
Then like a flash I ran to him and clutched him by
the arm:
" Oh, sir," said I, " I do not wish to see you come
to harm;
But if your life you value aught, I beg, entreat and
pray —
Don't pass before the terrace of the Café de la
Paix."
That portly man he looked at me with such a
startled air,
Then bolted like a rabbit down the rue Mich-
audière.
" Ha! ha! I've saved a life," I thought; and laughed
in my relief,
And straightway joined the Spanish man o'er his
apéritif.
And thus each day I dodged about and kept the
strictest guard
For portly men with each a wen upon the Boulevard.
And then I hailed my Spanish pal, and sitting in the
sun,

We ordered many Pernods and we drank them every
 one.
And sternly he would stare and stare until my hand
 would shake,
And grimly he would glare and glare until my heart
 would quake.
And I would say: "Alphonso, lad, I must expos-
 tulate;
Why keep alive for twenty years the furnace of
 your hate?
Perhaps his wedded life was hell; and you, at least,
 are free . . ."
" That's where you've got it wrong," he snarled;
 " the fool she took was *me*.
My rival sneaked, threw up the sponge, betrayed
 himself a churl:
'Twas he who got the happiness, I only got — the
 girl."
With that he looked so devil-like he made me creep
 and shrink,
And there was nothing else to do but buy another
 drink.

Now yonder like a blot of ink he sits across the way,
Upon the smiling terrace of the Café de la Paix;
That little wizened Spanish man, his face is ghastly
 white,
His eyes are staring, staring like a tiger's in the
 night.
I know within his evil heart the fires of hate are
 fanned,

I know his automatic's ready waiting to his hand.
I know a tragedy is near. I dread, I have no
    peace . . .
Oh, don't you think I ought to go and call upon the
    police?
Look there . . . he's rising up . . . my God! He
    leaps from out his place . . .
Yon millionaire from Argentine . . . the two are
    face to face . . .
A shot! A shriek! A heavy fall! A huddled
    heap! Oh, see
The little wizened Spanish man is dancing in his
    glee. . . .
I'm sick . . . I'm faint . . . I'm going mad. . . .
    Oh, please take me away . . .
There's BLOOD upon the terrace of the Café de la
    Paix. . . .

And now I'll leave my work and sally forth. The city
is *en fête*. I'll join the crowd and laugh and sing with the
best.

The sunshine seeks my little room
To tell me Paris streets are gay;
That children cry the lily bloom
All up and down the leafy way;
That half the town is mad with May,
With flame of flag and boom of bell:
For Carnival is King to-day;
So pen and page, awhile farewell.

BOOK TWO

EARLY SUMMER

I

THE RELEASE

To-day within a grog-shop near
I saw a newly captured linnet,
Who beat against his cage in fear,
And fell exhausted every minute;
And when I asked the fellow there
If he to sell the bird were willing,
He told me with a careless air
That I could have it for a shilling.

And so I bought it, cage and all
(Although I went without my dinner),
And where some trees were fairly tall
And houses shrank and smoke was thinner,
The tiny door I open threw,
As down upon the grass I sank me:
Poor little chap! How quick he flew . . .
He didn't even wait to thank me.

Life's like a cage; we beat the bars,
We bruise our breasts, we struggle vainly;
Up to the glory of the stars
We strain with flutterings ungainly.

And then — God opens wide the door;
Our wondrous wings are arched for flying;
We poise, we part, we sing, we soar . . .
Light, freedom, love. . . . Fools call it — Dying.

Yes, that wretched little bird haunted me. I had to
let it go. Since I have seized my own liberty I am a fanatic
for freedom. It is now a year ago I launched on my great
adventure. I have had hard times, been hungry, cold,
weary. I have worked harder than ever I did and dis-
couragement has slapped me on the face. Yet the year
has been the happiest of my life.

And all because I am free. By reason of filthy money
no one can say to me: Do this, or do that. "Master"
doesn't exist in my vocabulary. I can look any man in the
face and tell him to go to the devil. I belong to myself.
I am not for sale. It's glorious to feel like that. It sweet-
ens the dry crust and warms the heart in the icy wind. For
that I will hunger and go threadbare; for that I will live
austerely and deny myself all pleasure. After health, the
best thing in life is freedom.

Here is the last of my ballads. It is by way of being an
experiment. Its theme is commonplace, its language that
of everyday. It is a bit of realism in rhyme.

THE WEE SHOP

She risked her all, they told me, bravely sinking
The pinched economies of thirty years;
And there the little shop was, meek and shrinking,
The sum of all her dreams and hopes and fears.

Ere it was opened I would see them in it,
The gray-haired dame, the daughter with her crutch;
So fond, so happy, hoarding every minute,
Like artists, for the final tender touch.

The opening day! I'm sure that to their seeming
Was never shop so wonderful as theirs;
With pyramids of jam-jars rubbed to gleaming;
Such vivid cans of peaches, prunes and pears;
And chocolate, and biscuits in glass cases,
And bon-bon bottles, many-hued and bright;
Yet nothing half so radiant as their faces,
Their eyes of hope, excitement and delight.

I entered: how they waited all a-flutter!
How awkwardly they weighed my acid-drops!
And then with all the thanks a tongue could utter
They bowed me from the kindliest of shops.
I'm sure that night their customers they num-
    bered;
Discussed them all in happy, breathless speech;
And though quite worn and weary, ere they slum-
    bered,
Sent heavenward a little prayer for each.

And so I watched with interest redoubled
That little shop, spent in it all I had;
And when I saw it empty I was troubled,
And when I saw them busy I was glad.
And when I dared to ask how things were going,
They told me, with a fine and gallant smile:

" Not badly . . . slow at first . . . There's never
   knowing . . .
'Twill surely pick up in a little while."

I'd often see them through the winter weather,
Behind the shutters by a light's faint speck,
Poring o'er books, their faces close together,
The lame girl's arm around her mother's neck.
They dressed their windows not one time but twenty,
Each change more pinched, more desperately neat;
Alas! I wondered if behind that plenty
The two who owned it had enough to eat.

Ah, who would dare to sing of tea and coffee?
The sadness of a stock unsold and dead;
The petty tragedy of melting toffee,
The sordid pathos of stale gingerbread.
Ignoble themes! And yet — those haggard faces!
Within that little shop. . . . Oh, here I say
One does not need to look in lofty places
For tragic themes, they're round us every day.

And so I saw their agony, their fighting,
Their eyes of fear, their heartbreak, their despair;
And there the little shop is, black and blighting,
And all the world goes by and does not care.
They say she sought her old employer's pity,
Content to take the pittance he would give.
The lame girl? yes, she's working in the city;
She coughs a lot — she hasn't long to live.

· Last night MacBean introduced me to Saxon Dane the Poet. Truly, he is more like a blacksmith than a Bard — a big bearded man whose black eyes brood somberly or flash with sudden fire. We talked of Walt Whitman, and then of others.

"The trouble with poetry," he said, "is that it is too exalted. It has a phraseology of its own; it selects themes that are quite outside of ordinary experience. As a medium of expression it fails to reach the great mass of the people."

Then he added: "To hell with the great mass of the people! What have they got to do with it? Write to please yourself, as if not a single reader existed. The moment a man begins to be conscious of an audience he is artistically damned. You're not a Poet, I hope?"

I meekly assured him I was a mere maker of verse.

"Well," said he, "better good verse than middling poetry. And maybe even the humblest of rhymes has its uses. Happiness is happiness, whether it be inspired by a Rossetti sonnet or a ballad by G. R. Sims. Let each one who has something to say, say it in the best way he can, and abide the result. . . . After all," he went on, "what does it matter? We are living in a pygmy day. With Tennyson and Browning the line of great poets passed away, perhaps for ever. The world to-day is full of little minstrels, who echo one another and who pipe away tunefully enough. But with one exception they do not matter."

I dared to ask who was his one exception. He answered, "Myself, of course."

Here's a bit of light verse which it amused me to write to-day, as I sat in the sun on the terrace of the Closerie de Lilas:

THE PHILISTINE AND THE BOHEMIAN

She was a Philistine spick and span,
He was a bold Bohemian.
She had the *mode,* and the last at that;
He had a cape and a brigand hat.
She was so *riante* and *chic* and trim;
He was so shaggy, unkempt and grim.
On the rue de la Paix she was wont to shine;
The rue de la Gaîté was more his line.
She doted on Barclay and Dell and Caine;
He quoted Mallarmé and Paul Verlaine.
She was a triumph at Tango teas;
At Vorticist's suppers he sought to please.
She thought that Franz Lehar was utterly great;
Of Strauss and Stravinski he'd piously prate.
She loved elegance, he loved art;
They were as wide as the poles apart:
Yet — Cupid and Caprice are hand and glove —
They met at a dinner, they fell in love.

Home he went to his garret bare,
Thrilling with rapture, hope, despair.
Swift he gazed in his looking-glass,
Made a grimace and murmured: " Ass ! "
Seized his scissors and fiercely sheared,
Severed his buccaneering beard;
Grabbed his hair, and clip ! clip ! clip !
Off came a bunch with every snip.
Ran to a tailor's in startled state,

Suits a dozen commanded straight;
Coats and overcoats, pants in pairs,
Everything that a dandy wears;
Socks and collars, and shoes and ties,
Everything that a dandy buys.
Chums looked at him with wondering stare,
Fancied they'd seen him before somewhere;
A Brummell, a D'Orsay, a *beau* so fine,
A shining, immaculate Philistine.

Home she went in a raptured daze,
Looked in a mirror with startled gaze,
Didn't seem to be pleased at all;
Savagely muttered: " Insipid Doll! "
Clutched her hair and a pair of shears,
Cropped and bobbed it behind the ears;
Aimed at a wan and willowy-necked
Sort of a Holman Hunt effect;
Robed in subtile and sage-green tones,
Like the dames of Rossetti and E. Burne-Jones;
Girdled her garments billowing wide,
Moved with an undulating glide;
All her frivolous friends forsook,
Cultivated a soulful look;
Gushed in a voice with a creamy throb
Over some weirdly Futurist daub —
Did all, in short, that a woman can
To be a consummate Bohemian.

A year went past with its hopes and fears,
A year that seemed like a dozen years.

They met once more. . . . Oh, at last! At last!
They rushed together, they stopped aghast.
They looked at each other with blank dismay,
They simply hadn't a word to say.
He thought with a shiver: " Can this be she? "
She thought with a shudder: " This can't be he? "
This simpering dandy, so sleek and spruce;
This languorous lily in garments loose;
They sought to brace from the awful shock:
Taking a seat, they tried to talk.
She spoke of Bergson and Pater's prose,
He prattled of dances and ragtime shows;
She purred of pictures, Matisse, Cezanne,
His tastes to the girls of Kirchner ran;
She raved of Tschaikowsky and Cæsar Franck,
He owned that he was a jazz-band crank!
They made no headway.   Alas! alas!
He thought her a bore, she thought him an ass.
And so they arose and hurriedly fled;
Perish Illusion, Romance, you're dead.
He loved elegance, she loved art,
Better at once to part, to part.

And what is the moral of all this rot?
Don't try to be what you know you're not.
And if you're made on a muttonish plan,
Don't seek to seem a Bohemian;
And if to the goats your feet incline,
Don't try to pass for a Philistine.

II

A SMALL CAFÉ IN A SIDE STREET,
June 1914.

THE BOHEMIAN DREAMS

Because my overcoat's in pawn,
I choose to take my glass
Within a little *bistro* on
The rue du Montparnasse;
The dusty bins with bottles shine,
The counter's lined with zinc,
And there I sit and drink my wine,
And think and think and think.

I think of hoary old Stamboul,
Of Moslem and of Greek,
Of Persian in coat of wool,
Of Kurd and Arab sheikh;
Of all the types of weal and woe,
And as I raise my glass,
Across Galata bridge I know
They pass and pass and pass.

I think of citron-trees aglow,
Of fan-palms shading down,
Of sailors dancing heel and toe
With wenches black and brown;
And though it's all an ocean far
From Yucatan to France,

I'll bet beside the old bazaar
They dance and dance and dance.

I think of Monte Carlo, where
The pallid croupiers call,
And in the gorgeous, guilty air
The gamblers watch the ball;
And as I flick away the foam
With which my beer is crowned,
The wheels beneath the gilded dome
Go round and round and round.

I think of vast Niagara,
Those gulfs of foam a-shine,
Whose mighty roar would stagger a
More prosy bean than mine;
And as the hours I idly spend
Against a greasy wall,
I know that green the waters bend
And fall and fall and fall.

I think of Nijni Novgorod
And Jews who never rest;
And womenfolk with spade and hod
Who slave in Buda-Pest;
Of squat and sturdy Japanese
Who pound the paddy soil,
And as I loaf and smoke at ease
They toil and toil and toil.

I think of shrines in Hindustan,
Of cloistral glooms in Spain,

Of minarets in Ispahan,
Of St. Sophia's fane,
Of convent towers in Palestine,
Of temples in Cathay,
And as I stretch and sip my wine
They pray and pray and pray.

And so my dreams I dwell within,
And visions come and go,
And life is passing like a Cin-
Ematographic Show;
Till just as surely as my pipe
Is underneath my nose,
Amid my visions rich and ripe
I doze and doze and doze.

Alas! it is too true. Once more I am counting the coppers, living on the ragged edge. My manuscripts come back
to me like boomerangs, and I have not the postage, far less
the heart, to send them out again.

MacBean seems to take an interest in my struggles. I
often sit in his room in the rue Saint-Julien-le-Pauvre,
smoking and sipping whisky into the small hours. He
is an old hand, who knows the market and frankly manu-
factures for it.

"Give me short pieces," he says; "things of three verses
that will fill a blank half-page of a magazine. Let them be
sprightly, and, if possible, have a snapper at the end. Give
me that sort of article. I think I can place it for you."

Then he looked through a lot of my verse: "This is
the kind of stuff I might be able to sell," he said:

A DOMESTIC TRAGEDY

Clorinda met me on the way
As I came from the train;
Her face was anything but gay,
In fact, suggested pain.
" Oh hubby, hubby dear ! " she cried,
" I've awful news to tell. . . ."
" What is it, darling? " I replied;
" Your mother — is she well? "

" Oh no! oh no! it is not that,
It's something else," she wailed,
My heart was beating pit-a-pat,
My ruddy visage paled.
Like lightning flash in heaven's dome
The fear within me woke:
" Don't say," I cried, " our little home
Has all gone up in smoke! "

She shook her head.   Oh, swift I clasped
And held her to my breast;
" The children!   Tell me quick," I gasped,
" Believe me, it is best."
Then, then she spoke; 'mid sobs I caught
These words of woe divine:
" It's coo-coo-cook has gone and bought
A new hat just like mine."

At present I am living on bread and milk. By doing this I can rub along for another ten days. The thought pleases me. As long as I have a crust I am master of my destiny. Some day, when I am rich and famous, I shall look back on all this with regret. Yet I think I shall always remain a Bohemian. I hate regularity. The clock was never made for me. I want to eat when I am hungry, sleep when I am weary, drink — well, any old time.

I prefer to be alone. Company is a constraint on my spirit. I never make an engagement if I can avoid it. To do so is to put a mortgage on my future. I like to be able to rise in the morning with the thought that the hours before me are all mine, to spend in my own way — to work, to dream, to watch the unfolding drama of life.

Here is another of my ballads. It is longer than most, and gave me more trouble, though none the better for that.

THE PENCIL SELLER

A pencil, sir; a penny — won't you buy?
I'm cold and wet and tired, a sorry plight;
Don't turn your back, sir; take one just to try;
I haven't made a single sale to-night.
Oh, thank you, sir; but take the pencil too;
I'm not a beggar, I'm a business man.
Pencils I deal in, red and black and blue;
It's hard, but still I do the best I can.
Most days I make enough to pay for bread,
A cup o' coffee, stretching room at night.
One needs so little — to be warm and fed,
A hole to kennel in — oh, one's all right . . .

Excuse me, you're a painter, are you not?
I saw you looking at that dealer's show,
The *croûtes* he has for sale, a shabby lot —
What do I know of Art?   What do I know . . .
Well, look!   That David Strong so well displayed,
" White Sorcery " it's called, all gossamer,
And pale moon-magic and a dancing maid
(You like the little elfin face of her?) —
That's good; but still, the picture as a whole,
The values,— Pah!   He never painted worse;
Perhaps because his fire was lacking coal,
His cupboard bare, no money in his purse.
Perhaps . . . they say he labored hard and long,
And see now, in the harvest of his fame,
When round his pictures people gape and throng,
A scurvy dealer sells this on his name.
A wretched rag, wrung out of want and woe;
A soulless daub, not David Strong a bit,
Unworthy of his art. . . . How should I know?
How should I know?   I'm *Strong* — I painted it.

There now, I didn't mean to let that out.
It came in spite of me — aye, stare and stare.
You think I'm lying, crazy, drunk, no doubt —
Think what you like, it's neither here nor there.
It's hard to tell so terrible a truth,
To gain to glory, yet be such as I.
It's true; that picture's mine, done in my youth,
Up in a garret near the Paris sky.
The child's my daughter; aye, she posed for me.
That's why I come and sit here every night.

The painting's bad, but still — oh, still I see
Her little face all laughing in the light.
So now you understand.— I live in fear
Lest one like you should carry it away;
A poor, pot-boiling thing, but oh, how dear!
" Don't let them buy it, pitying God! " I pray!
And hark ye, sir — sometimes my brain's awhirl.
Some night I'll crash into that window pane
And snatch my picture back, my little girl,
And run and run. . . .
                                    I'm talking wild again;
A crab can't run.   I'm crippled, withered, lame,
Palsied, as good as dead all down one side.
No warning had I when the evil came:
It struck me down in all my strength and pride.
Triumph was mine, I thrilled with perfect power;
Honor was mine, Fame's laurel touched my brow;
Glory was mine — within a little hour
I was a god and . . . what you find me now.

My child, that little, laughing girl you see,
She was my nurse for all ten weary years;
Her joy, her hope, her youth she gave for me;
Her very smiles were masks to hide her tears.
And I, my precious art, so rich, so rare,
Lost, lost to me — what could my heart but break!
Oh, as I lay and wrestled with despair,
I would have killed myself but for her sake. . . .

By luck I had some pictures I could sell,
And so we fought the wolf back from the door;

She painted too, aye, wonderfully well.
We often dreamed of brighter days in store.
And then quite suddenly she seemed to fail;
I saw the shadows darken round her eyes.
So tired she was, so sorrowful, so pale,
And oh, there came a day she could not rise.
The doctor looked at her; he shook his head,
And spoke of wine and grapes and Southern air:
" If you can get her out of this," he said,
" She'll have a fighting chance with proper care."

" With proper care ! "   When he had gone away,
I sat there, trembling, twitching, dazed with grief.
Under my old and ragged coat she lay,
Our room was bare and cold beyond belief.
" Maybe," I thought, " I still can paint a bit,
Some lilies, landscape, anything at all."
Alas !   My brush, I could not steady it.
Down from my fumbling hand I let it fall.
" With proper care "— how could I give her that,
Half of me dead? . . . I crawled down to the
     street.
Cowering beside the wall, I held my hat
And begged of every one I chanced to meet.
I got some pennies, bought her milk and bread,
And so I fought to keep the Doom away;
And yet I saw with agony of dread
My dear one sinking, sinking day by day.
And then I was awakened in the night:
" Please take my hands, I'm cold," I heard her sigh;
And soft she whispered, as she held me tight:

" Oh daddy, we've been happy, you and I ! "
I do not think she suffered any pain,
She breathed so quietly . . . but though I tried,
I could not warm her little hands again :
And so there in the icy dark she died. . . .
The dawn came groping in with fingers gray
And touched me, sitting silent as a stone;
I kissed those piteous lips, as cold as clay —
I did not cry, I did not even moan.
At last I rose, groped down the narrow stair ;
An evil fog was oozing from the sky;
Half-crazed I stumbled on, I knew not where,
Like phantoms were the folks that passed me by.
How long I wandered thus I do not know,
But suddenly I halted, stood stock-still —
Beside a door that spilled a golden glow
I saw a name, *my name,* upon a bill.
" A Sale of Famous Pictures," so it read,
" A Notable Collection, each a gem,
Distinguished Works of Art by painters dead."
The folks were going in, I followed them.
I stood upon the outskirts of the crowd,
I only hoped that none might notice me.
Soon, soon I heard them call my name aloud :
" A ' David Strong,' his *Fête in Brittany.*"
(A brave big picture that, the best I've done,
It glowed and kindled half the hall away,
With all its memories of sea and sun,
Of pipe and bowl, of joyous work and play.
I saw the sardine nets blue as the sky,
I saw the nut-brown fisher-boats put out.)

" Five hundred pounds! " rapped out a voice near
    by;
" Six hundred! " " Seven! " " Eight! " And then
    a shout:
" A thousand pounds! " Oh, how I thrilled to
    hear!
Oh, how the bids went up by leaps, by bounds!
And then a silence; then the auctioneer:
" It's going! Going! Gone! *Three thousand
    pounds!*"
Three thousand pounds! A frenzy leapt in me.
" That picture's mine," I cried; " I'm David Strong.
I painted it, this famished wretch you see;
I did it, I, and sold it for a song.
And in a garret three small hours ago
My daughter died for want of Christian care.
Look, look at me! . . . Is it to mock my woe
You pay three thousand for my picture there? " . . .

O God! I stumbled blindly from the hall;
The city crashed on me, the fiendish sounds
Of cruelty and strife, but over all
" Three thousand pounds! " I heard; " Three thou-
    sand pounds! "

There, that's my story, sir; it isn't gay.
Tales of the Poor are never very bright . . .
You'll look for me next time you pass this way . . .
I hope you'll find me, sir; good-night, good-night.

III

THE LUXEMBOURG,
June 1914.

On a late afternoon, when the sunlight is mellow on the leaves, I often sit near the Fontaine de Medicis, and watch the children at their play. Sometimes I make bits of verse about them, such as:

FI-FI IN BED

Up into the sky I stare;
All the little stars I see;
And I know that God is there
O, how lonely He must be!

    Me, I laugh and leap all day,
    Till my head begins to nod;
    He's so great, He cannot play:
    I am glad I am not God.

        Poor kind God upon His throne,
        Up there in the sky so blue,
        Always, always all alone . . .
        " Please, dear God, I pity You."

Or else, sitting on the terrace of a café on the Boul' Mich', I sip slowly a Dubonnet or a Byrrh, and the charm of the Quarter possesses me. I think of men who have lived and loved there, who have groveled and gloried, who have drunk deep and died. And then I scribble things like this:

GODS IN THE GUTTER

I dreamed I saw three demi-gods who in a café sat,
And one was small and crapulous, and one was large
    and fat;
And one was eaten up with vice and verminous at
    that.

The first he spoke of secret sins, and gems and per-
    fumes rare;
And velvet cats and courtesans voluptuously fair:
" Who is the Sybarite? " I asked.   They answered:
    " Baudelaire."

The second talked in tapestries, by fantasy beguiled;
As frail as bubbles, hard as gems, his pageantries he
    piled;
" This Lord of Language, who is he? "   They whis-
    pered " Oscar Wilde."

The third was staring at his glass from out abysmal
    pain;
With tears his eyes were bitten in beneath his bulb-
    ous brain.
" Who is the sodden wretch? " I said.   They told
    me: " Paul Verlaine."

Oh, Wilde, Verlaine and Baudelaire, their lips were
    wet with wine;
Oh poseur, pimp and libertine!   Oh cynic, sot and
    swine!

Oh votaries of velvet vice! . . . Oh gods of light
    divine!

Oh Baudelaire, Verlaine and Wilde, they knew the
    sinks of shame;
Their sun-aspiring wings they scorched at passion's
    altar flame;
Yet lo! enthroned, enskied they stand, Immortal
    Sons of Fame.

I dreamed I saw three demi-gods who walked with
    feet of clay,
With cruel crosses on their backs, along a miry way;
Who climbed and climbed the bitter steep to which
    men turn and pray.

And while I am on the subject of the Quarter, let me
repeat this, which is included in my Ballads of the Boulevards:

THE DEATH OF MARIE TORO

We're taking Marie Toro to her home in Père-La-
    Chaise;
We're taking Marie Toro to her last resting-place.
Behold! her hearse is hung with wreaths till every-
    thing is hid
Except the blossoms heaping high upon her coffin lid.
A week ago she roamed the street, a draggle and a
    slut,
A by-word of the Boulevard and everybody's butt;

A week ago she haunted us, we heard her whining
   cry,
We brushed aside the broken blooms she pestered us
   to buy;
A week ago she had not where to rest her weary
   head . . .
But now, oh, follow, follow on, for Marie Toro's
   dead.

Oh Marie, she was once a queen — ah yes, a queen
   of queens.
High-throned above the Carnival she held her splen-
   did sway.
For four-and-twenty crashing hours she knew what
   glory means,
The cheers of half a million throats, the *délire* of a
   day.
Yet she was only one of us, a little sewing-girl,
Though far the loveliest and best of all our laughing
   band;
Then Fortune beckoned; off she danced, amid the
   dizzy whirl,
And we who once might kiss her cheek were proud to
   kiss her hand.
For swiftly as a star she soared; she had her every
   wish;
We saw her roped with pearls of price, with princes
   at her call;
And yet, and yet I think her dreams were of the old
   Boul' Mich',

And yet I'm sure within her heart she loved us best
    of all.
For one night in the Purple Pig, upon the rue Saint-
    Jacques,
We laughed and quaffed . . . a limousine came
    swishing to the door;
Then Raymond Jolicœur cried out: "It's Queen
    Marie come back,
In satin clad to make us glad, and witch our hearts
    once more."
But no, her face was strangely sad, and at the eve-
    ning's end:
"Dear lads," she said; "I love you all, and when
    I'm far away,
Remember, oh, remember, little Marie is your
    friend,
And though the world may lie between, I'm coming
    back some day."
And so she went, and many a boy who's fought his
    way to Fame,
Can look back on the struggle of his garret days and
    bless
The loyal heart, the tender hand, the Providence
    that came
To him and all in hour of need, in sickness and dis-
    tress.
Time passed away. She won their hearts in Lon-
    don, Moscow, Rome;
They worshiped her in Argentine, adored her in
    Brazil;

We smoked our pipes and wondered when she might
    be coming home,
And then we learned the luck had turned, the things
    were going ill.
Her health had failed, her beauty paled, her lovers
    fled away;
And some one saw her in Peru, a common drab at
    last.
So years went by, and faces changed; our beards
    were sadly gray,
And Marie Toro's name became an echo of the past.

You know that old and withered man, that derelict
    of art,
Who for a paltry franc will make a crayon sketch of
    you?
In slouching hat and shabby cloak he looks and is the
    part,
A sodden old Bohemian, without a single *sou*.
A boon companion of the days of Rimbaud and Ver-
    laine,
He broods and broods, and chews the cud of bitter
    souvenirs;
Beneath his mop of grizzled hair his cheeks are
    gouged with pain,
The saffron sockets of his eyes are hollowed out
    with tears.
Well, one night in the D'Harcourt's din I saw him
    in his place,
When suddenly the door was swung, a woman halted
    there;

A woman cowering like a dog, with white and hag-
    gard face,
A broken creature, bent of spine, a daughter of
    Despair.
She looked and looked, as to her breast she held
    some withered bloom;
"Too late! Too late! . . . they all are dead and
    gone," I heard her say.
And once again her weary eyes went round and
    round the room;
"Not one of all I used to know . . ." she turned
    to go away . . .
But quick I saw the old man start: "Ah no!" he
    cried, "not all.
Oh Marie Toro, queen of queens, don't you remem-
    ber Paul?"

"Oh Marie, Marie Toro, in my garret next the sky,
Where many a day and night I've crouched with not
    a crust to eat,
A picture hangs upon the wall a fortune couldn't buy,
A portrait of a girl whose face is pure and angel-
    sweet."
Sadly the woman looked at him: "Alas! it's true,"
    she said;
"That little maid, I knew her once. It's long ago
    — she's dead."
He went to her; he laid his hand upon her wasted
    arm:
"Oh, Marie Toro, come with me, though poor and
    sick am I.

For old times' sake I cannot bear to see you come
    to harm;
Ah! there are memories, God knows, that never,
    never die. . . ."
"Too late!" she sighed; "I've lived my life of
    splendor and of shame;
I've been adored by men of power, I've touched the
    highest height;
I've squandered gold like heaps of dirt — oh, I have
    played the game;
I've had my place within the sun . . . and now I
    face the night.
Look! look! you see I'm lost to hope; I live no mat-
    ter how . . .
To drink and drink and so forget . . . that's all I
    care for now."

And so she went her heedless way, and all our help
    was vain.
She trailed along with tattered shawl and mud-cor-
    roded skirt;
She gnawed a crust and slept beneath the bridges of
    the Seine,
A garbage thing, a composite of alcohol and dirt.
The students learned her story and the cafés knew
    her well,
The Pascal and the Panthéon, the Sufflot and Va-
    chette;
She shuffled round the tables with the flowers she
    tried to sell,
A living mask of misery that no one will forget.

And then last week I missed her, and they found her
    in the street
One morning early, huddled down, for it was freez-
    ing cold;
But when they raised her ragged shawl her face was
    still and sweet;
Some bits of broken bloom were clutched within her
    icy hold.
That's all. . . . Ah yes, they say that saw: her
    blue, wide-open eyes
Were beautiful with joy again, with radiant sur-
    prise. . . .

A week ago she begged for bread; we've bought for
    her a stone,
And a peaceful place in Père-La-Chaise where she'll
    be well alone.
She cost a king his crown, they say; oh, wouldn't she
    be proud
If she could see the wreaths to-day, the coaches and
    the crowd!
So follow, follow, follow on with slow and sober
    tread,
For Marie Toro, gutter waif and queen of queens,
    is dead.

IV

THE CAFÉ DE DEUX MAGOTS,
June 1914.

THE BOHEMIAN

Up in my garret bleak and bare
I tilted back on my broken chair,
And my three old pals were with me there,
　　　Hunger and Thirst and Cold;
Hunger scowled at his scurvy mate:
Cold cowered down by the hollow grate,
And I hated them with a deadly hate
　　　As old as life is old.

So up in my garret that's near the sky
I smiled a smile that was thin and dry:
" You've roomed with me twenty year," said I,
　　　" Hunger and Thirst and Cold;
But now, begone down the broken stair!
I've suffered enough of your spite . . . so there!"
Bang!　Bang!　I slapped on the table bare
　　　A glittering heap of gold.

" Red flames will jewel my wine to-night;
I'll loose my belt that you've lugged so tight;
Ha!　Ha!　Dame Fortune is smiling bright;
　　　The stuff of my brain I've sold;
Canaille of the gutter, up!　Away!
You've battened on me for a bitter-long day;

But I'm driving you forth, and forever and aye,
    Hunger and Thirst and Cold."

So I kicked them out with a scornful roar;
Yet, oh, they turned at the garret door;
Quietly there they spoke once more:
    " The tale is not all told.
It's *au revoir,* but it's not good-by;
We're yours, old chap, till the day you die;
Laugh on, you fool! Oh, you'll never defy
    Hunger and Thirst and Cold."

Hurrah! The crisis in my financial career is over. Once more I have weathered the storm, and never did money jingle so sweetly in my pocket. It was MacBean who delivered me. He arrived at the door of my garret this morning, with a broad grin of pleasure on his face.

" Here," said he; " I've sold some of your rubbish. They'll take more too, of the same sort."

With that he handed me three crisp notes. For a moment I thought that he was paying the money out of his own pocket, as he knew I was desperately hard up; but he showed me the letter enclosing the cheque he had cashed for me.

So we sought the Grand Boulevard, and I had a Pernod, which rose to my head in delicious waves of joy. I talked ecstatic nonsense, and seemed to walk like a god in clouds of gold. We dined on frogs' legs and Vouvray, and then went to see the Revue at the Marigny. A very merry evening.

Such is the life of Bohemia, up and down, fast and feast; its very uncertainty its charm.

Here is my latest ballad, another attempt to express the sentiment of actuality:

THE AUCTION SALE

Her little head just topped the window-sill;
She even mounted on a stool, maybe;
She pressed against the pane, as children will,
And watched us playing, oh so wistfully!
And then I missed her for a month or more,
And idly thought: " She's gone away, no doubt,"
Until a hearse drew up beside the door . . .
I saw a tiny coffin carried out.

And after that, towards dusk I'd often see
Behind the blind another face that looked:
Eyes of a young wife watching anxiously,
Then rushing back to where her dinner cooked.
She often gulped it down alone, I fear,
Within her heart the sadness of despair,
For near to midnight I would vaguely hear
A lurching step, a stumbling on the stair.

These little dramas of the common day!
A man weak-willed and fore-ordained to fail . . .
The window's empty now, they've gone away,
And yonder, see, their furniture's for sale.
To all the world their door is open wide,
And round and round the bargain-hunters roam,
And peer and gloat, like vultures avid-eyed,
Above the corpse of what was once a home.

So reverent I go from room to room,
And see the patient care, the tender touch,

The love that sought to brighten up the gloom,
The woman-courage tested overmuch.
Amid those things so intimate and dear,
Where now the mob invades with brutal tread,
I think: " What happiness is buried here,
What dreams are withered and what hopes are
    dead!"

Oh, woman dear, and were you sweet and glad
Over the lining of your little nest!
What ponderings and proud ideas you had!
What visions of a shrine of peace and rest!
For there's his easy-chair upon the rug,
His reading-lamp, his pipe-rack on the wall,
All that you could devise to make him snug —
And yet you could not hold him with it all.

Ah, patient heart, what homelike joys you planned
To stay him by the dull domestic flame!
Those silken cushions that you worked by hand
When you had time, before the baby came.
Oh, how you wove around him cozy spells,
And schemed so hard to keep him home of nights!
Aye, every touch and turn some story tells
Of sweet conspiracies and dead delights.

And here upon the scratched piano stool,
Tied in a bundle, are the songs you sung;
That cozy that you worked in colored wool,
The Spanish lace you made when you were young,
And lots of modern novels, cheap reprints,

And little dainty knick-knacks everywhere;
And silken bows and curtains of gay chintz . . .
And oh, her tiny crib, her folding chair!

Sweet woman dear, and did your heart not break,
To leave this precious home you made in vain?
Poor shabby things! so prized for old times' sake,
With all their memories of love and pain.
Alas! while shouts the raucous auctioneer,
And rat-faced dames are prying everywhere,
The echo of old joy is all I hear,
All, all I see just heartbreak and despair.

Imagination is the great gift of the gods. Given it, one does not need to look afar for subjects. There is romance in every face.

Those who have Imagination live in a land of enchantment which the eyes of others cannot see. Yet if it brings marvelous joy it also brings exquisite pain. Who lives a hundred lives must die a hundred deaths.

I do not know any of the people who live around me. Sometimes I pass them on the stairs. However, I am going to give my imagination rein, and string some rhymes about them.

Before doing so, having money in my pocket and seeing the prospect of making more, let me blithely chant about

THE JOY OF BEING POOR

I

Let others sing of gold and gear, the joy of being
    rich;
But oh, the days when I was poor, a vagrant in a
    ditch!
When every dawn was like a gem, so radiant and
    rare,
And I had but a single coat, and not a single care;
When I would feast right royally on bacon, bread
    and beer,
And dig into a stack of hay and doze like any
    peer;
When I would wash beside a brook my solitary shirt,
And though it dried upon my back I never took a
    hurt;
When I went romping down the road contemptuous
    of care,
And slapped Adventure on the back — by Gad! we
    were a pair;
When, though my pockets lacked a coin, and though
    my coat was old,
The largess of the stars was mine, and all the sunset
    gold;
When time was only made for fools, and free as air
    was I,
And hard I hit and hard I lived beneath the open
    sky;

When all the roads were one to me, and each had its
    allure . . .
Ye Gods! these were the happy days, the days when I
    was poor.

II

Or else, again, old pal of mine, do you recall the
    times
You struggled with your storyettes, I wrestled with
    my rhymes;
Oh, we were happy, were we not? — we used to live
    so " high "
(A little bit of broken roof between us and the sky) ;
Upon the forge of art we toiled with hammer and
    with tongs;
You told me all your ripping yarns, I sang to you
    my songs.
Our hats were frayed, our jackets patched, our
    boots were down at heel,
But oh, the happy men were we, although we lacked
    a meal.
And if I sold a bit of rhyme, or if you placed a tale,
What feasts we had of tenderloins and apple-tarts
    and ale!
And yet how often we would dine as cheerful as you
    please,
Beside our little friendly fire on coffee, bread and
    cheese.

We lived upon the ragged edge, and grub was never
   sure,
But oh, these were the happy days, the days when
   we were poor.

III

Alas! old man, we're wealthy now, it's sad beyond
   a doubt;
We cannot dodge prosperity, success has found us
   out.
Your eye is very dull and drear, my brow is creased
   with care,
We realize how hard it is to be a millionaire.
The burden's heavy on our backs — you're thinking
   of your rents,
I'm worrying if I'll invest in five or six per cents.
We've limousines, and marble halls, and flunkeys by
   the score,
We play the part . . . but say, old chap, oh, isn't it
   a bore?
We work like slaves, we eat too much, we put on
   evening dress;
We've everything a man can want, I think . . . but
   happiness.

Come, let us sneak away, old chum; forget that we
   are rich,
And earn an honest appetite, and scratch an honest
   itch.

Let's be two jolly garreteers, up seven flights of
    stairs,
And wear old clothes and just pretend we aren't mil-
    lionaires;
And wonder how we'll pay the rent, and scribble
    ream on ream,
And sup on sausages and tea, and laugh and loaf and
    dream.

And when we're tired of that, my friend, oh, you will
    come with me;
And we will seek the sunlit roads that lie beside the
    sea.
We'll know the joy the gipsy knows, the freedom
    nothing mars,
The golden treasure-gates of dawn, the mintage of
    the stars.
We'll smoke our pipes and watch the pot, and feed
    the crackling fire,
And sing like two old jolly boys, and dance to heart's
    desire;
We'll climb the hill and ford the brook and camp
    upon the moor . . .
Old chap, let's haste, I'm mad to taste the Joy of
    Being Poor.

V

My Garret, Montparnasse,
June 1914.

MY NEIGHBORS

To rest my fagged brain now and then,
When wearied of my proper labors,
I lay aside my lagging pen
And get to thinking on my neighbors;
For, oh, around my garret den
There's woe and poverty a-plenty,
And life's so interesting when
A lad is only two-and-twenty.

Now, there's that artist gaunt and wan,
A little card his door adorning;
It reads: " Je ne suis pour personne,"
A very frank and fitting warning.
I fear he's in a sorry plight;
He starves, I think, too proud to borrow,
I hear him moaning every night:
Maybe they'll find him dead to-morrow.

Room 4

THE PAINTER CHAP

He gives me such a bold and curious look,
That young American across the way,

As if he'd like to put me in a book
(Fancies himself a poet, so they say.)
Ah well!   He'll make no " document " of me.
I lock my door.   Ha! ha!   Now none shall see. . . .

Pictures, just pictures piled from roof to floor,
Each one a bit of me, a dream fulfilled,
A vision of the beauty I adore,
My own poor glimpse of glory, passion-thrilled . . .
But now my money's gone, I paint no more.

For three days past I have not tasted food;
The jeweled colors run . . . I reel, I faint;
They tell me that my pictures are no good,
Just crude and childish daubs, a waste of paint.
I burned to throw on canvas all I saw —
Twilight on water, tenderness of trees,
Wet sands at sunset and the smoking seas,
The peace of valleys and the mountain's awe:
Emotion swayed me at the thought of these.
I sought to paint ere I had learned to draw,
And that's the trouble. . . .
                              Ah well! here am I,
Facing my failure after struggle long;
And there they are, my *croutes* that none will buy
(And doubtless they are right and I am wrong);
Well, when one's lost one's faith it's time to die. . . .

This knife will do . . . and now to slash and slash;
Rip them to ribands, rend them every one,
My dreams and visions — tear and stab and gash,

So that their crudeness may be known to none;
Poor, miserable daubs! Ah! there, it's done. . . .

And now to close my little window tight.
Lo! in the dusking sky, serenely set,
The evening star is like a beacon bright.
And see! to keep her tender tryst with night
How Paris veils herself in violet. . . .

Oh, why does God create such men as I? —
All pride and passion and divine desire,
Raw, quivering nerve-stuff and devouring fire,
Foredoomed to failure though they try and try;
Abortive, blindly to destruction hurled;
Unfound, unfit to grapple with the world. . . .

And now to light my wheezy jet of gas;
Chink up the window-crannies and the door,
So that no single breath of air may pass;
So that I'm sealed air-tight from roof to floor.
There, there, that's done; and now there's nothing
        more. . . .

Look at the city's myriad lamps a-shine;
See, the calm moon is launching into space . . .
There will be darkness in these eyes of mine
Ere it can climb to shine upon my face.
Oh, it will find such peace upon my face! . . .

City of Beauty, I have loved you well,
A laugh or two I've had, but many a sigh;

I've run with you the scale from Heav'n to Hell.
Paris, I love you still . . . good-by, good-by.
Thus it all ends — unhappily, alas!
It's time to sleep, and now . . . *blow out the
gas.* . . .

> *Now there's that little* midinette
> *Who goes to work each morning daily;*
> *I choose to call her Blithe Babette,*
> *Because she's always humming gaily;*
> *And though the Goddess " Comme-il-faut "*
> *May look on her with prim expression,*
> *It's Pagan Paris where, you know,*
> *The queen of virtues is Discretion.*

ROOM 6

THE LITTLE WORKGIRL

Three gentlemen live close beside me —
A painter of pictures bizarre,
A poet whose virtues might guide me,
A singer who plays the guitar;
And there on my lintel is Cupid;
I leave my door open, and yet
These gentlemen, aren't they stupid!
They never make love to Babette.

I go to the shop every morning;
I work with my needle and thread;
Silk, satin and velvet adorning,

Then luncheon on coffee and bread.
Then sewing and sewing till seven;
Or else, if the order I get,
I toil and I toil till eleven —
And such is the day of Babette.

It doesn't seem cheerful, I fancy;
The wage is unthinkably small;
And yet there is one thing I can say:
I keep a bright face through it all.
I chaff though my head may be aching;
I sing a gay song to forget;
I laugh though my heart may be breaking —
It's all in the life of Babette.

That gown, O my lady of leisure,
You begged to be " finished in haste."
It gives you an exquisite pleasure,
Your lovers remark on its taste.
Yet . . . oh, the poor little white faces,
The tense midnight toil and the fret . . .
I fear that the foam of its laces
Is salt with the tears of Babette.

It takes a brave heart to be cheery
With no gleam of hope in the sky;
The future's so utterly dreary,
I'm laughing — in case I should cry.
And if, where the gay lights are glowing,
I dine with a man I have met,
And snatch a bright moment — who's going
To blame a poor little Babette?

And you, Friend beyond all the telling,
Although you're an ocean away,
Your pictures, they tell me, are selling,
You're married and settled, they say.
Such happiness one wouldn't barter;
Yet, oh, do you never regret
The Springtide, the roses, Montmartre,
Youth, poverty, love and — Babette?

That blond-haired chap across the way
With sunny smile and voice so mellow,
He sings in some cheap cabaret,
Yet what a gay and charming fellow!
His breath with garlic may be strong,
What matters it? his laugh is jolly;
His day he gives to sleep and song:
His night's made up of song and folly.

ROOM 5

THE CONCERT SINGER

I'm one of these haphazard chaps
Who sit in cafés drinking;
A most improper taste, perhaps,
Yet pleasant, to my thinking.
For, oh, I hate discord and strife;
I'm sadly, weakly human;
And I do think the best of life
Is wine and song and woman.

Now, there's that youngster on my right
Who thinks himself a poet,
And so he toils from morn to night
And vainly hopes to show it;
And there's that dauber on my left,
Within his chamber shrinking —
He looks like one of hope bereft;
He lives on air, I'm thinking.

But me, I love the things that are,
My heart is always merry;
I laugh and tune my old guitar:
Sing ho! and hey-down-derry.
Oh, let them toil their lives away
To gild a tawdry era,
But I'll be gay while yet I may:
Sing tira-lira-lira.

I'm sure you know that picture well,
A monk, all else unheeding,
Within a bare and gloomy cell
A musty volume reading;
While through the window you can see
In sunny glade entrancing,
With cap and bells beneath a tree
A jester dancing, dancing.

Which is the fool and which the sage?
I cannot quite discover;
But you may look in learning's page
And I'll be laughter's lover.

For this our life is none too long,
And hearts were made for gladness;
Let virtue lie in joy and song,
The only sin be sadness.

So let me troll a jolly air,
Come what come will to-morrow;
I'll be no *cabotin* of care,
No *souteneur* of sorrow.
Let those who will indulge in strife,
To my most merry thinking,
The true philosophy of life
Is laughing, loving, drinking.

And there's that weird and ghastly hag
Who walks head bent, with lips a-mutter;
With twitching hands and feet that drag,
And tattered skirts that sweep the gutter.
An outworn harlot, lost to hope,
With staring eyes and hair that's hoary
I hear her gibber, dazed with dope:
I often wonder what's her story.

ROOM 7

THE COCO-FIEND

I look at no one, me;
I pass them on the stair;
Shadows!   I don't see;
Shadows! everywhere.

Haunting, taunting, staring, glaring,
Shadows!   I don't care.
Once my room I gain
Then my life begins.
Shut the door on pain;
How the Devil grins!
Grin with might and main;
Grin and grin in vain;
Here's where Heav'n begins:
Cocaine!   Cocaine!

A whiff!   Ah, that's the thing.
How it makes me gay!
Now I want to sing,
Leap, laugh, play.
Ha!   I've had my fling!
Mistress of a king
In my day.
Just another snuff . . .
Oh, the blessed stuff!
How the wretched room
Rushes from my sight;
Misery and gloom
Melt into delight;
Fear and death and doom
Vanish in the night.
No more cold and pain,
I am young again,
Beautiful again,
Cocaine!   Cocaine!

Oh, I was made to be good, to be good,
For a true man's love and a life that's sweet;

Fireside blessings and motherhood.
Little ones playing around my feet.
How it all unfolds like a magic screen,
Tender and glowing and clear and glad,
The wonderful mother I might have been,
The beautiful children I might have had;
Romping and laughing and shrill with glee,
Oh, I see them now and I see them plain.
Darlings!   Come nestle up close to me,
You comfort me so, and you're just . . . Cocaine.

It's Life that's all to blame:
We can't do what we will;
She robes us with her shame,
She crowns us with her ill.
I do not care, because
I see with bitter calm,
Life made me what I was,
Life makes me what I am.
Could I throw back the years,
It all would be the same;
Hunger and cold and tears,
Misery, fear and shame,
And then the old refrain,
Cocaine!   Cocaine!

A love-child I, so here my mother came,
Where she might live in peace with none to blame.
And how she toiled!   Harder than any slave,
What courage! patient, hopeful, tender, brave.
We had a little room at Lavilette,

So small, so neat, so clean, I see it yet.
Poor mother! sewing, sewing late at night,
Her wasted face beside the candlelight,
This Paris crushed her.   How she used to sigh!
And as I watched her from my bed I knew
She saw red roofs against a primrose sky
And glistening fields and apples dimmed with dew.
Hard times we had.   We counted every *sou,*
We sewed sacks for a living.   I was quick . . .
Four busy hands to work instead of two.
Oh, we were happy there, till she fell sick. . . .

My mother lay, her face turned to the wall,
And I, a girl of sixteen, fair and tall,
Sat by her side, all stricken with despair,
Knelt by her bed and faltered out a prayer.
A doctor's order on the table lay,
Medicine for which, alas! I could not pay;
Medicine to save her life, to soothe her pain.
I sought for something I could sell, in vain . . .
All, all was gone!   The room was cold and bare;
Gone blankets and the cloak I used to wear;
Bare floor and wall and cupboard, every shelf —
Nothing that I could sell . . . except myself.

I sought the street, I could not bear
To hear my mother moaning there.
I clutched the paper in my hand.
'Twas hard.   You cannot understand . . .
I walked as martyr to the flame,
Almost exalted in my shame.

They turned, who heard my voiceless cry,
" For Sale, a virgin, who will buy? "
And so myself I fiercely sold,
And clutched the price, a piece of gold.
Into a pharmacy I pressed;
I took the paper from my breast.
I gave my money . . . how it gleamed!
How precious to my eyes it seemed!
And then I saw the chemist frown,
Quick on the counter throw it down,
Shake with an angry look his head:
" Your *louis d'or* is bad," he said.

Dazed, crushed, I went into the night,
I clutched my gleaming coin so tight.
No, no, I could not well believe
That any one could so deceive.
I tried again and yet again —
Contempt, suspicion and disdain;
Always the same reply I had:
" Get out of this.   Your money's bad."

Heart broken to the room I crept,
To mother's side.   All still . . . she slept . . .
I bent, I sought to raise her head . . .
" Oh, God, have pity! " she was dead.

That's how it all began.
Said I: Revenge is sweet.
So in my guilty span
I've ruined many a man.

They've groveled at my feet,
I've pity had for none;
I've bled them every one.
Oh, I've had interest for
That worthless *louis d'or*.

But now it's over; see,
I care for no one, me;
Only at night sometimes
In dreams I hear the chimes
Of wedding-bells and see
A woman without stain
With children at her knee.
Ah, how you comfort me,
Cocaine! . . .

BOOK THREE

LATE SUMMER

I

MacBean, before he settled down to the manufacture of mercantile fiction, had ideas of a nobler sort, which bore their fruit in a slender book of poems. In subject they are either erotic, mythologic, or descriptive of nature. So polished are they that the mind seems to slide over them: so faultless in form that the critics hailed them with highest praise, and as many as a hundred copies were sold.

Saxon Dane, too, has published a book of poems, but he, on the other hand, defies tradition to an eccentric degree. Originality is his sin. He strains after it in every line. I must confess I think much of the free verse he writes is really prose, and a good deal of it blank verse chopped up into odd lengths. He talks of assonance and color, of stress and pause and accent, and bewilders me with his theories.

He and MacBean represent two extremes, and at night, as we sit in the Café du Dôme, they have the hottest of arguments. As for me, I listen with awe, content that my medium is verse, and that the fashions of Hood, Thackeray and Bret Harte are the fashions of to-day.

Of late I have been doing light stuff, " fillers " for Mac-Bean. Here are three of my specimens:

THE PHILANDERER

Oh, have you forgotten those afternoons
With riot of roses and amber skies,

117

When we thrilled to the joy of a million Junes,
And I sought for your soul in the deeps of your eyes?
I would love you, I promised, forever and aye,
And I meant it too; yet, oh, isn't it odd?
When we met in the Underground to-day
I addressed you as Mary instead of as Maude.

Oh, don't you remember that moonlit sea,
With us on a silver trail afloat,
When I gracefully sank on my bended knee
At the risk of upsetting our little boat?
Oh, I vowed that my life was blighted then,
As friendship you proffered with mournful mien;
But now as I think of your children ten,
I'm glad you refused me, Evangeline.

Oh, is that moment eternal still
When I breathed my love in your shell-like ear,
And you plucked at your fan as a maiden will,
And you blushed so charmingly, Guinivere?
Like a worshiper at your feet I sat;
For a year and a day you made me mad;
But now, alas! you are forty, fat,
And I think: What a lucky escape I had!

Oh, maidens I've set in a sacred shrine,
Oh, Rosamond, Molly and Mignonette,
I've deemed you in turn the most divine,
In turn you've broken my heart . . . and yet
It's easily mended.   What's past is past.
To-day on Lucy I'm going to call;

For I'm sure that I know true love at last,
And *She* is the fairest girl of all.

THE *PETIT VIEUX*

" Sow your wild oats in your youth," so we're always
    told;
But I say with deeper sooth: " Sow them when
    you're old."
I'll be wise till I'm about seventy or so:
Then, by Gad! I'll blossom out as an ancient *beau*.

I'll assume a dashing air, laugh with loud Ha!
    ha! . . .
How my grandchildren will stare at their grand-
    papa!
Their perfection aurioled I will scandalize:
Won't I be a hoary old sinner in their eyes!

Watch me, how I'll learn to chaff barmaids in a bar;
Scotches daily, gayly quaff, puff a fierce cigar.
I will haunt the Tango teas, at the stage-door stand;
Wait for Dolly Dimpleknees, bouquet in my hand.

Then at seventy I'll take flutters at roulette;
While at eighty hope I'll make good at poker yet;
And in fashionable togs to the races go,
Gayest of the gay old dogs, ninety years or so.

" Sow your wild oats while you're young," that's
    what you are told;

Don't believe the foolish tongue — sow 'em when
    you're old.
Till you're threescore years and ten, take my
    humble tip,
Sow your nice tame oats and then . . . Hi, boys!
    Let 'er rip.

MY MASTERPIECE

It's slim and trim and bound in blue;
Its leaves are crisp and edged with gold;
Its words are simple, stalwart too;
Its thoughts are tender, wise and bold.
Its pages scintillate with wit;
Its pathos clutches at my throat:
Oh, how I love each line of it!
That Little Book I Never Wrote.

In dreams I see it praised and prized
By all, from plowman unto peer;
It's pencil-marked and memorized,
It's loaned (and not returned, I fear);
It's worn and torn and travel-tossed,
And even dusky natives quote
That classic that the world has lost,
The Little Book I Never Wrote.

Poor ghost! For homes you've failed to cheer,
For grieving hearts uncomforted,
Don't haunt me now. . . . Alas! I fear

The fire of Inspiration's dead.
A humdrum way I go to-night,
From all I hoped and dreamed remote:
Too late . . . a better man must write
That Little Book I Never Wrote

Talking about writing books, there is a queer character
who shuffles up and down the little streets that neighbor the
Place Maubert, and who, they say, has been engaged on one
for years. Sometimes I see him cowering in some cheap
bouge, and his wild eyes gleam at me through the tangle
of his hair. But I do not think he ever sees me. He
mumbles to himself, and moves like a man in a dream. His
pockets are full of filthy paper on which he writes from
time to time. The students laugh at him and make him
tipsy; the street boys pelt him with ordure; the better cafés
turn him from their doors. But who knows? At least,
this is how I see him:

MY BOOK

Before I drink myself to death,
God, let me finish up my Book!
At night, I fear, I fight for breath,
And wake up whiter than a spook;
And crawl off to a *bistro* near,
And drink until my brain is clear.

Rare Absinthe! Oh, it gives me strength
To write and write; and so I spend
Day after day, until at length
With joy and pain I'll write The End:

Then let this carcase rot; I give
The world my Book — my Book will live.

For every line is tense with truth,
There's hope and joy on every page;
A cheer, a clarion call to Youth,
A hymn, a comforter to Age:
All's there that I was meant to be,
My part divine, the God in me.

It's of my life the golden sum;
Ah! who that reads this Book of mine,
In stormy centuries to come,
Will dream I rooted with the swine?
Behold! I give mankind my best:
What does it matter, all the rest?

It's this that makes sublime my day;
It's this that makes me struggle on.
Oh, let them mock my mortal clay,
My spirit's deathless as the dawn;
Oh, let them shudder as they look . . .
I'll be immortal in my Book.

And so beside the sullen Seine
I fight with dogs for filthy food,
Yet know that from my sin and pain
Will soar serene a Something Good;
Exultantly from shame and wrong
A Right, a Glory and a Song.

How charming it is, this Paris of the summer skies! Each morning I leap up with joy in my heart, all eager to begin the day of work. As I eat my breakfast and smoke my pipe, I ponder over my task. Then in the golden sunshine that floods my little attic I pace up and down, absorbed and forgetful of the world. As I compose I speak the words aloud. There are difficulties to overcome; thoughts that will not fit their mold; rebellious rhymes. Ah! those moments of despair and defeat.

Then suddenly the mind grows lucid, imagination glows, the snarl unravels. In the end is always triumph and success. O delectable *métier*! Who would not be a rhyme-smith in Paris, in Bohemia, in the heart of youth!

I have now finished my twentieth ballad. Five more and they will be done. In quiet corners of cafés, on benches of the Luxembourg, on the sunny Quays I read them over one by one. Here is my latest:

MY HOUR

Day after day behold me plying
My pen within an office drear;
The dullest dog, till homeward hieing,
Then lo! I reign a king of cheer.
A throne have I of padded leather,
A little court of kiddies three,
A wife who smiles whate'er the weather,
A feast of muffins, jam and tea.

The table cleared, a romping battle,
A fairy tale, a " Children, bed,"
A kiss, a hug, a hush of prattle

(God save each little drowsy head!)
A cozy chat with wife a-sewing,
A silver lining clouds that low'r,
Then she too goes, and with her going,
I come again into my Hour.

I poke the fire, I snugly settle,
My pipe I prime with proper care;
The water's purring in the kettle,
Rum, lemon, sugar, all are there.
And now the honest grog is steaming,
And now the trusty briar's aglow:
Alas! in smoking, drinking, dreaming,
How sadly swift the moments go!

Oh, golden hour! 'twixt love and duty,
All others I to others give;
But you are mine to yield to Beauty,
To glean Romance, to greatly live.
For in my easy-chair reclining . . .
I feel the sting of ocean spray;
And yonder wondrously are shining
The Magic Isles of Far Away.

Beyond the comber's crashing thunder
Strange beaches flash into my ken;
On jetties heaped head-high with plunder
I dance and dice with sailor-men.
Strange stars swarm down to burn above me,
Strange shadows haunt, strange voices greet;
Strange women lure and laugh and love me,
And fling their bastards at my feet.

Oh, I would wish the wide world over,
In ports of passion and unrest,
To drink and drain, a tarry rover
With dragons tattooed on my chest,
With haunted eyes that hold red glories
Of foaming seas and crashing shores,
With lips that tell the strangest stories
Of sunken ships and gold moidores;

Till sick of storm and strife and slaughter,
Some ghostly night when hides the moon,
I slip into the milk-warm water
And softly swim the stale lagoon.
Then through some jungle python-haunted,
Or plumed morass, or woodland wild,
I win my way with heart undaunted,
And all the wonder of a child.

The pathless plains shall swoon around me,
The forests frown, the floods appall;
The mountains tiptoe to confound me,
The rivers roar to speed my fall.
Wild dooms shall daunt, and dawns be gory,
And Death shall sit beside my knee;
Till after terror, torment, glory,
I win again the sea, the sea. . . .

Oh, anguish sweet!   Oh, triumph splendid!
Oh, dreams adieu! my pipe is dead.
My glass is dry, my Hour is ended,

It's time indeed I stole to bed.
How peacefully the house is sleeping!
Ah! why should I strange fortunes plan?
To guard the dear ones in my keeping —
That's task enough for any man.

So through dim seas I'll ne'er go spoiling;
The red Tortugas never roam;
Please God! I'll keep the pot a-boiling,
And make at least a happy home.
My children's path shall gleam with roses,
Their grace abound, their joy increase.
And so my Hour divinely closes
With tender thoughts of praise and peace.

II

The Garden of the Luxembourg,
Late July 1914.

When on some scintillating summer morning I leap
lightly up to the seclusion of my garret, I often think of
those lines: " In the brave days when I was twenty-one."

True, I have no loving, kind Lisette to pin her petticoat
across the pane, yet I do live in hope. Am I not in Bohemia
the Magical, Bohemia of Murger, of de Musset, of Verlaine? Shades of Mimi Pinson, of Trilby, of all that immortal line of laughterful grisettes, do not tell me that the
days of love and fun are forever at an end!

Yes, youth is golden, but what of age? Shall it too
not testify to the rhapsody of existence? Let the years between be those of struggle, of sufferance — of disillusion if
you will; but let youth and age affirm the ecstasy of being.

Let us look forward all to a serene sunset, and in the still skies " a late lark singing."

This thought comes to me as, sitting on a bench near the band-stand, I see an old savant who talks to all the children. His clean-shaven face is alive with kindliness; under his tall silk hat his white hair falls to his shoulders. He wears a long black cape over a black frock-coat, very neat linen, and a flowing tie of black silk. I call him " Silvester Bonnard." As I look at him I truly think the best of life are the years between sixty and seventy.

A SONG OF SIXTY-FIVE

Brave Thackeray has trolled of days when he was
    twenty-one,
And bounded up five flights of stairs, a gallant gar-
    reteer;
And yet again in mellow vein when youth was gaily
    run,
Has dipped his nose in Gascon wine, and told of
    Forty Year.
But if I worthy were to sing a richer, rarer time,
I'd tune my pipes before the fire and merrily I'd
    strive
To praise that age when prose again has given way
    to rhyme,
The Indian Summer days of life when I'll be Sixty-
    five;

For then my work will all be done, my voyaging be
    past,

And I'll have earned the right to rest where folding
    hills are green;
So in some glassy anchorage I'll make my cable
    fast,—
Oh, let the seas show all their teeth, I'll sit and smile
    serene.
The storm may bellow round the roof, I'll bide be-
    side the fire,
And many a scene of sail and trail within the flame
    I'll see;
For I'll have worn away the spur of passion and
    desire. : . .
Oh yes, when I am Sixty-five, what peace will come
    to me.

I'll take my breakfast in my bed, I'll rise at half-
    past ten,
When all the world is nicely groomed and full of
    golden song;
I'll smoke a bit and joke a bit, and read the news,
    and then
I'll potter round my peach-trees till I hear the
    luncheon gong.
And after that I think I'll doze an hour, well,
    maybe two,
And then I'll show some kindred soul how well my
    roses thrive;
I'll do the things I never yet have found the time
    to do. . . .
Oh, won't I be the busy man when I am Sixty-five.

I'll revel in my library; I'll read De Morgan's books;
I'll grow so garrulous I fear you'll write me down
    a bore;
I'll watch the ways of ants and bees in quiet sunny
    nooks,
I'll understand Creation as I never did before.
When gossips round the tea-cups talk I'll listen to
    it all;
On smiling days some kindly friend will take me for
    a drive:
I'll own a shaggy collie dog that dashes to my call:
I'll celebrate my second youth when I am Sixty-five.

Ah, though I've twenty years to go, I see myself
    quite plain,
A wrinkling, twinkling, rosy-cheeked, benevolent old
    chap;
I think I'll wear a tartan shawl and lean upon a cane.
I hope that I'll have silver hair beneath a velvet cap.
I see my little grandchildren a-romping round my
    knee;
So gay the scene, I almost wish 'twould hasten to
    arrive.
Let others sing of Youth and Spring, still will it
    seem to me
The golden time's the olden time, some time round
    Sixty-five.

    From old men to children is but a step, and there too,
in the shadow of the Fontaine de Medicis, I spend much
of my time watching the little ones. Childhood, so inno-

cent, so helpless, so trusting, is somehow pathetic to me.

There was one jolly little chap who used to play with a large white Teddy Bear. He was always with his mother, a sweet-faced woman, who followed his every movement with delight. I used to watch them both, and often spoke a few words.

Then one day I missed them, and it struck me I had not seen them for a week, even a month, maybe. After that I looked for them a time or two and soon forgot.

Then this morning I saw the mother in the rue D'Assas. She was alone and in deep black. I wanted to ask after the boy, but there was a look in her face that stopped me.

I do not think she will ever enter the garden of the Luxembourg again.

TEDDY BEAR

O Teddy Bear! with your head awry
And your comical twisted smile,
You rub your eyes — do you wonder why
You've slept such a long, long while?
As you lay so still in the cupboard dim,
And you heard on the roof the rain,
Were you thinking . . . what has become of *him?*
And when will he play again?

Do you sometimes long for a chubby hand,
And a voice so sweetly shrill?
O Teddy Bear! don't you understand
Why the house is awf'ly still?
You sit with your muzzle propped on your paws,
And your whimsical face askew.

Don't wait, don't wait for your friend . . . because
He's sleeping and dreaming too.

Aye, sleeping long. . . . You remember how
He stabbed our hearts with his cries?
And oh, the dew of pain on his brow,
And the deeps of pain in his eyes!
And, Teddy Bear! you remember, too,
As he sighed and sank to his rest,
How all of a sudden he smiled to you,
And he clutched you close to his breast.

I'll put you away, little Teddy Bear,
In the cupboard far from my sight;
Maybe he'll come and he'll kiss you there,
A wee white ghost in the night.
But me, I'll live with my love and pain
A weariful lifetime through;
And my Hope: will I see him again, again?
Ah, God! If I only knew!

After old men and children I am greatly interested in
dogs. I will go out of my way to caress one who shows
any desire to be friendly. There is a very filthy fellow
who collects cigarette stubs on the Boul' Mich', and who is
always followed by a starved yellow cur. The other day
I came across them in a little side street. The man was
stretched on the pavement brutishly drunk and dead to
the world. The dog, lying by his side, seemed to look at
me with sad, imploring eyes. Though all the world despise
that man, I thought, this poor brute loves him and will be
faithful unto death.

From this incident I wrote the verses that follow:

THE OUTLAW

A wild and woeful race he ran
Of lust and sin by land and sea;
Until, abhorred of God and man,
They swung him from the gallows-tree.
And then he climbed the Starry Stair,
And dumb and naked and alone,
With head unbowed and brazen glare,
He stood before the Judgment Throne.

The Keeper of the Records spoke:
" This man, O Lord, has mocked Thy Name.
The weak have wept beneath his yoke,
The strong have fled before his flame.
The blood of babes is on his sword;
His life is evil to the brim:
Look down, decree his doom, O Lord!
Lo! there is none will speak for him."

The golden trumpets blew a blast
That echoed in the crypts of Hell,
For there was Judgment to be passed,
And lips were hushed and silence fell.
The man was mute; he made no stir,
Erect before the Judgment Seat . . .
When all at once a mongrel cur
Crept out and cowered and licked his feet.

It licked his feet with whining cry.
Come Heav'n, come Hell, what did it care?

It leapt, it tried to catch his eye;
Its master, yea, its God was there.
Then, as a thrill of wonder sped
Through throngs of shining seraphim,
The Judge of All looked down and said:
" Lo! here is ONE who pleads for him.

" And who shall love of these the least,
And who by word or look or deed
Shall pity show to bird or beast,
By Me shall have a friend in need.
Aye, though his sin be black as night,
And though he stand 'mid men alone,
He shall be softened in My sight,
And find a pleader by My Throne.

" So let this man to glory win;
From life to life salvation glean;
By pain and sacrifice and sin,
Until he stand before Me — *clean*.
For he who loves the least of these
(And here I say and here repeat)
Shall win himself an angel's pleas
For Mercy at My Judgment Seat."

I take my exercise in the form of walking. It keeps
me fit and leaves me free to think. In this way I have come
to know Paris like my pocket. I have explored its large
and little streets, its stateliness and its slums.

But most of all I love the Quays, between the leafage
and the sunlit Seine. Like shuttles the little steamers dart
up and down, weaving the water into patterns of foam.

Cigar-shaped barges stream under the lacework of the many bridges and make me think of tranquil days and willow-fringed horizons.

But what I love most is the stealing in of night, when the sky takes on that strange elusive purple; when eyes turn to the evening star and marvel at its brightness; when the Eiffel Tower becomes a strange, shadowy stairway yearning in impotent effort to the careless moon.

Here is my latest ballad, short if not very sweet:

THE WALKERS

(He speaks.)

Walking, walking, oh, the joy of walking!
Swinging down the tawny lanes with head held high;
Striding up the green hills, through the heather
    stalking,
Swishing through the woodlands where the brown
    leaves lie;
Marveling at all things — windmills gaily turning,
Apples for the cider-press, ruby-hued and gold;
Tails of rabbits twinkling, scarlet berries burning,
Wedge of geese high-flying in the sky's clear cold,
Light in little windows, field and furrow darkling;
Home again returning, hungry as a hawk;
Whistling up the garden, ruddy-cheeked and
    sparkling,
Oh, but I am happy as I walk, walk, walk!

(She speaks.)

Walking, walking, oh, the curse of walking!

Slouching round the grim square, shuffling up the
    street,
Slinking down the by-way, all my graces hawking,
Offering my body to each man I meet.
Peering in the gin-shop where the lads are drinking,
Trying to look gay-like, crazy with the blues;
Halting in a doorway, shuddering and shrinking
(Oh, my draggled feather and my thin, wet shoes).
Here's a drunken drover: "Hullo, there, old
    dearie!"
No, he only curses, can't be got to talk. . . .
On and on till daylight, famished, wet and weary,
God in Heaven help me as I walk, walk, walk!

III

THE CAFÉ DE LA SOURCE,
Late in July 1914.

The other evening MacBean was in a pessimistic mood.
"Why do you write?" he asked me gloomily.

"Obviously," I said, "to avoid starving. To produce
something that will buy me food, shelter, raiment."

"If you were a millionaire, would you still write?"

"Yes," I said, after a moment's thought. "You get
an idea. It haunts you. It seems to clamor for expression. It begins to obsess you. At last in desperation
you embody it in a poem, an essay, a story. There! it is
disposed of. You are at rest. It troubles you no more.
Yes; if I were a millionaire I should write, if it were only
to escape from my ideas."

"You have given two reasons why men write," said Mac-
Bean: "for gain, for self-expression. Then, again, some

men write to amuse themselves, some because they conceive they have a mission in the world; some because they have real genius, and are conscious they can enrich the literature of all time. I must say I don't know of any belonging to the latter class. We are living in an age of mediocrity. There is no writer of to-day who will be read twenty years after he is dead. That's a truth that must come home to the best of them."

"I guess they're not losing much sleep over it," I said.

"Take novelists," continued MacBean. "The line of first-class novelists ended with Dickens and Thackeray. Then followed some of the second class, Stevenson, Meredith, Hardy. And to-day we have three novelists of the third class, good, capable craftsmen. We can trust ourselves comfortably in their hands. We read and enjoy them, but do you think our children will?"

"Yours won't, anyway," I said.

"Don't be too sure. I may surprise you yet. I may get married and turn *bourgeois.*"

The best thing that could happen to MacBean would be that. It might change his point of view. He is so painfully discouraging. I have never mentioned my ballads to him. He would be sure to throw cold water on them. And as it draws near to its end the thought of my book grows more and more dear to me. How I will get it published I know not; but I will. Then even if it doesn't sell, even if nobody reads it, I will be content. Out of this brief, perishable Me I will have made something concrete, something that will preserve my thought within its dusty covers long after I am dead and dust.

Here is one of my latest:

POOR PETER

Blind Peter Piper used to play
All up and down the city;
I'd often meet him on my way,
And throw a coin for pity.
But all amid his sparkling tones
His ear was quick as any
To catch upon the cobble-stones
The jingle of my penny.

And as upon a day that shone
He piped a merry measure:
" How well you play! " I chanced to say;
Poor Peter glowed with pleasure.
You'd think the words of praise I spoke
Were all the pay he needed;
The artist in the player woke,
The penny lay unheeded.

Now Winter's here; the wind is shrill,
His coat is thin and tattered;
Yet hark! he's playing trill on trill
As if his music mattered.
And somehow though the city looks
Soaked through and through with shadows,
He makes you think of singing brooks
And larks and sunny meadows.

Poor chap! he often starves, they say;
Well, well, I can believe it;

For when you chuck a coin his way
He'll let some street-boy thieve it.
I fear he freezes in the night;
My praise I've long repented,
Yet look! his face is all alight . . .
Blind Peter seems contented.

A day later.

On the terrace of the Closerie de Lilas I came on Saxon
Dane.   He was smoking his big briar and drinking a huge
glass of brown beer.   The tree gave a pleasant shade, and
he had thrown his sombrero on a chair.   I noted how his
high brow was bronzed by the sun and there were golden
lights in his broad beard.   There was something massive
and imposing in the man as he sat there in brooding thought.

MacBean, he told me, was sick and unable to leave his
room.   Rheumatism.   So I bought a cooked chicken and
a bottle of Barsac, and mounting to the apartment of the
invalid, I made him eat and drink.   MacBean was very
despondent, but cheered up greatly.

I think he rather dreads the future.   He cannot save
money, and all he makes he spends.   He has always been
a rover, often tried to settle down but could not.   Now I
think he wishes for security.   I fear, however, it is too late.

THE WISTFUL ONE

I sought the trails of South and North,
I wandered East and West;
But pride and passion drove me forth
And would not let me rest.

And still I seek, as still I roam,
A snug roof overhead;
Four walls, my own; a quiet home. . . .
" You'll have it — *when you're dead.*"

MacBean is one of Bohemia's victims. It is a country
of the young. The old have no place in it. He will gradually lose his grip, go down and down. I am sorry. He is
my nearest approach to a friend. I do not make them
easily. I have deep reserves. I like solitude. I am never
so surrounded by boon companions as when I am all alone.

But though I am a solitary I realize the beauty of friendship, and on looking through my note-book I find the following:

IF YOU HAD A FRIEND

If you had a friend strong, simple, true,
Who knew your faults and who understood;
Who believed in the very best of you,
And who cared for you as a father would;
Who would stick by you to the very end,
Who would smile however the world might frown:
I'm sure you would try to please your friend,
You never would think to throw him down.

And supposing your friend was high and great,
And he lived in a palace rich and tall,
And sat like a King in shining state,
And his praise was loud on the lips of all;
Well then, when he turned to you alone,
And he singled you out from all the crowd,

And he called you up to his golden throne,
Oh, wouldn't you just be jolly proud?

If you had a friend like this, I say,
So sweet and tender, so strong and true,
You'd try to please him in every way,
You'd live at your bravest — now, wouldn't you?
His worth would shine in the words you penned;
You'd shout his praises . . . yet now it's odd!
You tell me you haven't got such a friend;
You haven't?   I wonder . . . *What of God?*

To how few is granted the privilege of doing the work which lies closest to the heart, the work for which one is best fitted.   The happy man is he who knows his limitations, yet bows to no false gods.

MacBean is not happy.   He is overridden by his appetites, and to satisfy them he writes stuff that in his heart he despises.

Saxon Dane is not happy.   His dream exceeds his grasp. His twisted, tortured phrases mock the vague grandiosity of his visions.

I am happy.   My talent is proportioned to my ambition. The things I like to write are the things I like to read.   I prefer the lesser poets to the greater, the cackle of the barnyard fowl to the scream of the eagle.   I lack the divinity of discontent.

True Contentment comes from within.   It dominates circumstance.   It is resignation wedded to philosophy, a Christian quality seldom attained except by the old.

There is such an one I sometimes see being wheeled about in the Luxembourg.   His face is beautiful in its thankfulness.

THE CONTENTED MAN

" How good God is to me," he said;
" For have I not a mansion tall,
With trees and lawns of velvet tread,
And happy helpers at my call?
With beauty is my life abrim,
With tranquil hours and dreams apart;
You wonder that I yield to Him
That best of prayers, a grateful heart?"

" How good God is to me," he said;
" For look! though gone is all my wealth,
How sweet it is to earn one's bread
With brawny arms and brimming health.
Oh, now I know the joy of strife!
To sleep so sound, to wake so fit.
Ah yes, how glorious is life!
I thank Him for each day of it."

" How good God is to me," he said;
" Though health and wealth are gone, it's true;
Things might be worse, I might be dead,
And here I'm living, laughing too.
Serene beneath the evening sky
I wait, and every man's my friend;
God's most contented man am I . . .
He keeps me smiling to the End."

To-day the basin of the Luxembourg is bright with little
boats. Hundreds of happy children romp around it. Little

ones everywhere; yet there is no other city with so many childless homes.

THE SPIRIT OF THE UNBORN BABE

The Spirit of the Unborn Babe peered through the
    window-pane,
Peered through the window-pane that glowed like
    beacon in the night;
For, oh, the sky was desolate and wild with wind
    and rain;
And how the little room was crammed with coziness
    and light!
Except the flirting of the fire there was no sound
    at all;
The Woman sat beside the hearth, her knitting on
    her knee;
The shadow of her husband's head was dancing on
    the wall;
She looked with staring eyes at it, she looked yet
    did not see.
She only saw a childish face that topped the table
    rim,
A little wistful ghost that smiled and vanished quick
    away;
And then because her tender eyes were flooding to
    the brim,
She lowered her head. . . . " Don't sorrow, dear,"
    she heard him softly say;
" It's over now.   We'll try to be as happy as before

(Ah! they who little children have, grant hostages
    to pain).
We gave Life chance to wound us once, but never,
    never more. . . ."
The Spirit of the Unborn Babe fled through the
    night again.

The Spirit of the Unborn Babe went wildered in the
    dark;
Like termagants the winds tore down and whirled
    it with the snow.
And then amid the writhing storm it saw a tiny
    spark,
A window broad, a spacious room all goldenly
    aglow,
A woman slim and Paris-gowned and exquisitely
    fair,
Who smiled with rapture as she watched her jewels
    catch the blaze;
A man in faultless evening dress, young, handsome,
    debonnaire,
Who smoked his cigarette and looked with frank
    admiring gaze.
"Oh, we are happy, sweet," said he; "youth,
    health, and wealth are ours.
What if a thousand toil and sweat that we may live
    at ease!
What if the hands are worn and torn that strew
    our path with flowers!
Ah, well! we did not make the world; let us not
    think of these.

Let's seek the beauty-spots of earth, Dear Heart,
    just you and I;
Let other women bring forth life with sorrow and
    with pain.
Above our door we'll hang the sign: '*No children
    need apply. . . .*' "
The Spirit of the Unborn Babe sped through the
    night again.

The Spirit of the Unborn Babe went whirling on
    and on;
It soared above a city vast, it swept down to a slum;
It saw within a grimy house a light that dimly
    shone;
It peered in through a window-pane and lo! a voice
    said: " Come! "
And so a little girl was born amid the dirt and din,
And lived in spite of everything, for life is or-
    dered so;
A child whose eyes first opened wide to swinishness
    and sin,
A child whose love and innocence met only curse and
    blow.
And so in due and proper course she took the path
    of shame,
And gladly died in hospital, quite old at twenty
    years;
And when God comes to weigh it all, ah! whose shall
    be the blame
For all her maimed and poisoned life, her torture
    and her tears?

For oh, it is not what we do, but what we have not
    done!
And on that day of reckoning, when all is plain and
    clear,
What if we stand before the Throne, blood-guilty
    every one? . . .
Maybe the blackest sins of all are Selfishness and
    Fear.

IV

THE CAFÉ DE LA PAIX,
August 1, 1914.

Paris and I are out of tune. As I sit at this famous corner the faint breeze is stale and weary; stale and weary too
the faces that swirl around me; while overhead the electric
sign of Somebody's Chocolate appears and vanishes with
irritating insistency. The very trees seem artificial, gleaming under the arc-lights with a raw virility that rasps my
nerves.

"Poor little trees," I mutter, "growing in all this grime
and glare, your only dryads the loitering ladies with the
complexions of such brilliant certainty, your only Pipes of
Pan orchestral echoes from the clamorous cafés. Exiles
of the forest! what know you of full-blossomed winds, of
red-embered sunsets, of the gentle admonition of spring
rain! Life, that would fain be a melody, seems here almost
a malady. I crave for the balm of Nature, the anodyne of
solitude, the breath of Mother Earth. Tell me, O wistful
trees, what shall I do?"

Then that stale and weary wind rustles the leaves of the
nearest sycamore, and I am sure it whispers: "Brittany."

So to-morrow I am off, off to the Land of Little Fields.

FINISTÈRE

Hurrah! I'm off to Finistère, to Finistère, to Finistère;
My satchel's swinging on my back, my staff is in my hand;
I've twenty *louis* in my purse, I know the sun and sea are there,
And so I'm starting out to-day to tramp the golden land.
I'll go alone and glorying, with on my lips a song of joy;
I'll leave behind the city with its canker and its care;
I'll swing along so sturdily — oh, won't I be the happy boy!
A-singing on the rocky roads, the roads of Finistère.

Oh, have you been to Finistère, and do you know a whin-gray town
That echoes to the clatter of a thousand wooden shoes?
And have you seen the fisher-girls go galivantin' up and down,
And watched the tawny boats go out, and heard the roaring crews?
Oh, would you sit with pipe and bowl, and dream upon some sunny quay,
Or would you walk the windy heath and drink the cooler air;

Oh, would you seek a cradled cove and tussle with
    the topaz sea! —
Pack up your kit to-morrow, lad, and haste to
    Finistère.

Oh, I will go to Finistère, there's nothing that can
    hold me back.
I'll laugh with Yves and Léon, and I'll chaff with
    Rose and Jeanne;
I'll seek the little, quaint *buvette* that's kept by
    Mother Merdrinac,
Who wears a cap of many frills, and swears just
    like a man.
I'll yarn with hearty, hairy chaps who dance and
    leap and crack their heels;
Who swallow cupfuls of cognac and never turn a
    hair;
I'll watch the nut-brown boats come in with mullet,
    plaice and conger eels,
The jeweled harvest of the sea they reap in
    Finistère.

Yes, I'll come back from Finistère with memories
    of shining days,
Of scaly nets and salty men in overalls of brown;
Of ancient women knitting as they watch the teth-
    ered cattle graze
By little nestling beaches where the gorse goes
    blazing down;
Of headlands silvering the sea, of Calvarys against
    the sky,

Of scorn of angry sunsets, and of Carnac grim and
    bare;
Oh, won't I have the leaping veins, and tawny cheek
    and sparkling eye,
When I come back to Montparnasse and dream of
    Finistère.

Two days later.

Behold me with staff and scrip, footing it merrily in the
Land of Pardons. I have no goal. When I am weary I
stop at some *auberge;* when I am rested I go on again.
Neither do I put any constraint on my spirit. No subduing
of the mind to the task of the moment. I dream to heart's
content.

My dreams stretch into the future. I see myself a singer
of simple songs, a laureate of the under-dog. I will write
books, a score of them. I will voyage far and wide. I
will . . .

But there! Dreams are dangerous. They waste the time
one should spend in making them come true. Yet when we
do make them come true, we find the vision sweeter than
the reality. How much of our happiness do we owe to
dreams? I have in mind one old chap who used to herd
the sheep on my uncle's farm.

OLD DAVID SMAIL

He dreamed away his hours in school;
He sat with such an absent air,
The master reckoned him a fool,
And gave him up in dull despair.

When other lads were making hay
You'd find him loafing by the stream;
He'd take a book and slip away,
And just pretend to fish . . . and dream.

His brothers passed him in the race;
They climbed the hill and clutched the prize.
He did not seem to heed, his face
Was tranquil as the evening skies.

He lived apart, he spoke with few;
Abstractedly through life he went;
Oh, what he dreamed of no one knew,
And yet he seemed to be content.

I see him now, so old and gray,
His eyes with inward vision dim;
And though he faltered on the way,
Somehow I almost envied him.

At last beside his bed I stood:
"And is Life done so soon?" he sighed;
"It's been so rich, so full, so good,
I've loved it all . . ."— and so he died.

Another day.

Framed in hedgerows of emerald, the wheat glows with
a caloric fervor, as if gorged with summer heat. In the
vivid green of pastures old women are herding cows. Calm
and patient are their faces as with gentle industry they
bend over their knitting. One feels that they are necessary
to the landscape.

To gaze at me the field-workers suspend the magnificent lethargy of their labors. The men with the reaping hooks improve the occasion by another pull at the cider bottle under the stook; the women raise apathetic brown faces from the sheaf they are tying; every one is a study in deliberation, though the crop is russet ripe and crying to be cut.

Then on I go again amid high banks overgrown with fern and honeysuckle. Sometimes I come on an old mill that seems to have been constructed by Constable, so charmingly does Nature imitate Art. By the deserted house, half drowned in greenery, the velvety wheel, dipping in the crystal water, seems to protest against this prolongation of its toil.

Then again I come on its brother, the Mill of the Wind, whirling its arms so cheerily, as it turns its great white stones for its master, the floury miller by the door.

These things delight me. I am in a land where Time has lagged, where simple people timorously hug the Past. How far away now seems the welter and swelter of the city, the hectic sophistication of the streets. The sense of wonder is strong in me again, the joy of looking at familiar things as if one were seeing them for the first time.

THE WONDERER

I wish that I could understand
The moving marvel of my Hand;
I watch my fingers turn and twist,
The supple bending of my wrist,
The dainty touch of finger-tip,
The steel intensity of grip;
A tool of exquisite design,
With pride I think: "It's mine! It's mine!"

Then there's the wonder of my Eyes,
Where hills and houses, seas and skies,
In waves of light converge and pass,
And print themselves as on a glass.
Line, form and color live in me;
I am the Beauty that I see;
Ah! I could write a book of size
About the wonder of my Eyes.

What of the wonder of my Heart,
That plays so faithfully its part?
I hear it running sound and sweet;
It does not seem to miss a beat;
Between the cradle and the grave
It never falters, stanch and brave.
Alas! I wish I had the art
To tell the wonder of my Heart.

Then oh! but how can I explain
The wondrous wonder of my Brain?
That marvelous machine that brings
All consciousness of wonderings;
That lets me from myself leap out
And watch my body walk about;
It's hopeless — all my words are vain
To tell the wonder of my Brain.

But do not think, O patient friend,
Who reads these stanzas to the end,
That I myself would glorify. . . .

You're just as wonderful as I,
And all Creation in our view
Is quite as marvelous as you.
Come, let us on the sea-shore stand
And wonder at a grain of sand;
And then into the meadow pass
And marvel at a blade of grass;
Or cast our vision high and far
And thrill with wonder at a star;
A host of stars — night's holy tent
Huge-glittering with wonderment.

If wonder is in great and small,
Then what of Him who made it all?
In eyes and brain and heart and limb
Let's see the wondrous work of Him.
In house and hill and sward and sea,
In bird and beast and flower and tree,
In everything from sun to sod,
The wonder and the awe of God.

August 9, 1914.

For some time the way has been growing wilder. Thick-set hedges have yielded to dykes of stone, and there is every sign that I am approaching the rugged region of the coast. At each point of vantage I can see a Cross, often a relic of the early Christians, stumpy and corroded. Then I come on a slab of gray stone upstanding about fifteen feet. Like a sentinel on that solitary plain it overwhelms me with a sense of mystery.

But as I go on through this desolate land these stones become more and more familiar. Like soldiers they stand in rank, extending over the moor. The sky is cowled with cloud, save where a sullen sunset shoots blood-red rays across the plain. Bathed in that sinister light stands my army of stone, and a wind swooping down seems to wail amid its ranks. As in a glass darkly I can see the skin-clad men, the women with the tangled hair, the beast-like feast, the cowering terror of the night. Then the sunset is cut off suddenly, and a clammy mist shrouds that silent army. So it is almost with a shudder I take my last look at the Stones of Carnac.

But now my pilgrimage is drawing to an end. A painter friend who lives by the sea has asked me to stay with him awhile. Well, I have walked a hundred miles, singing on the way. I have dreamed and dawdled, planned, exulted. I have drunk buckets of cider, and eaten many an omelette that seemed like a golden glorification of its egg. It has all been very sweet, but it will also be sweet to loaf awhile.

OH, IT IS GOOD

Oh, it is good to drink and sup,
And then beside the kindly fire
To smoke and heap the faggots up,
And rest and dream to heart's desire.

Oh, it is good to ride and run,
To roam the greenwood wild and free;
To hunt, to idle in the sun,
To leap into the laughing sea.

Oh, it is good with hand and brain
To gladly till the chosen soil,

And after honest sweat and strain
To see the harvest of one's toil.

Oh, it is good afar to roam,
And seek adventure in strange lands;
Yet oh, so good the coming home,
The velvet love of little hands.

So much is good. . . . We thank Thee, God,
For all the tokens Thou hast given,
That here on earth our feet have trod
Thy little shining trails of Heaven.

V

August 10, 1914.

I am living in a little house so near the sea that at high
tide I can see on my bedroom wall the reflected ripple of
the water. At night I waken to the melodious welter of
waves; or maybe there is a great stillness, and then I know
that the sand and sea-grass are lying naked to the moon.
But soon the tide returns, and once more I hear the roister-
ing of the waves.

Calvert, my friend, is a lover as well as a painter of nature.
He rises with the dawn to see the morning mist kindle to
coral and the sun's edge clear the hill-crest. As he munches
his coarse bread and sips his white wine, what dreams are
his beneath the magic changes of the sky! He will paint
the same scene under a dozen conditions of light. He has
looked so long for Beauty that he has come to see it everywhere.

I love this friendly home of his. A peace steals over my
spirit, and I feel as if I could stay here always. Some day

I hope that I too may have such an one, and that I may write like this:

I HAVE SOME FRIENDS

I have some friends, some worthy friends,
And worthy friends are rare:
These carpet slippers on my feet,
That padded leather chair;
This old and shabby dressing-gown,
So well the worse of wear.

I have some friends, some honest friends,
And honest friends are few;
My pipe of briar, my open fire,
A book that's not too new;
My bed so warm, the nights of storm
I love to listen to.

I have some friends, some good, good friends,
Who faithful are to me:
My wrestling partner when I rise,
The big and burly sea;
My little boat that's riding there
So saucy and so free.

I have some friends, some golden friends,
Whose worth will not decline:
A tawny Irish terrier, a purple shading pine,
A little red-roofed cottage that
So proudly I call mine.

All other friends may come and go,
All other friendships fail;
But these, the friends I've worked to win,
Oh, they will never stale;
And comfort me till Time shall write
The finish to my tale.

Calvert tries to paint more than the thing he sees; he tries to paint behind it, to express its spirit. He believes that Beauty is God made manifest, and that when we discover Him in Nature we discover Him in ourselves.

But Calvert did not always see thus. At one time he was a Pagan, content to paint the outward aspect of things. It was after his little child died he gained in vision. Maybe the thought that the dead are lost to us was too unbearable. He had to believe in a coming together again.

THE QUEST

I sought Him on the purple seas,
I sought Him on the peaks aflame;
Amid the gloom of giant trees
And canyons lone I called His name;
The wasted ways of earth I trod:
In vain! In vain! I found not God.

I sought Him in the hives of men,
The cities grand, the hamlets gray,
The temples old beyond my ken,
The tabernacles of to-day;
All life that is, from cloud to clod
I sought. . . . Alas! I found not God.

Then after roamings far and wide,
In streets and seas and deserts wild,
I came to stand at last beside
The death-bed of my little child.
Lo! as I bent beneath the rod
I raised my eyes . . . and there was God.

A golden mile of sand swings hammock-like between two
tusks of rock. The sea is sleeping sapphire that wakes to
cream and crash upon the beach. There is a majesty in
the detachment of its lazy waves, and it is good in the night
to hear its friendly roar. Good, too, to leap forth with the
first sunshine and fall into its arms, to let it pummel the
body to living ecstasy and send one to breakfast glad-eyed
and glowing.

Behind the house the greensward slopes to a wheat-field
that is like a wall of gold. Here I lie and laze away the
time, or dip into a favorite book, Stevenson's *Letters* or
Belloc's *Path to Rome*. Bees drone in the wild thyme; a
cuckoo keeps calling, a lark spills jeweled melody. Then
there is a seeming silence, but it is the silence of a deeper
sound.

After all, Silence is only man's confession of his deafness.
Like Death, like Eternity, it is a word that means nothing. So lying there I hear the breathing of the trees, the
crepitation of the growing grass, the seething of the sap
and the movements of innumerable insects. Strange how
I think with distaste of the spurious glitter of Paris, of my
garret, even of my poor little book.

I watch the wife of my friend gathering poppies in the
wheat. There is a sadness in her face, for it is only a year
ago they lost their little one. Often I see her steal away to
the village graveyard, sitting silent for long and long.

THE COMFORTER

As I sat by my baby's bed
That's open to the sky,
There fluttered round and round my head
A radiant butterfly.

And as I wept — of hearts that ache
The saddest in the land —
It left a lily for my sake,
And lighted on my hand.

I watched it, oh, so quietly,
And though it rose and flew,
As if it fain would comfort me
It came and came anew.

Now, where my darling lies at rest,
I do not dare to sigh,
For look! there gleams upon my breast
A snow-white butterfly.

My friends will have other children, and if some day they should read this piece of verse, perhaps they will think of the city lad who used to sit under the old fig-tree in the garden and watch the lizards sun themselves on the time-worn wall.

THE OTHER ONE

" Gather around me, children dear;
The wind is high and the night is cold;

Closer, little ones, snuggle near;
Let's seek a story of ages old;
A magic tale of a bygone day,
Of lovely ladies and dragons dread;
Come, for you're all so tired of play,
We'll read till it's time to go to bed."

So they all are glad, and they nestle in,
And squat on the rough old nursery rug,
And they nudge and hush as I begin,
And the fire leaps up and all's so snug;
And there I sit in the big arm-chair,
And how they are eager and sweet and wise,
And they cup their chins in their hands and stare
At the heart of the flame with thoughtful eyes.

And then, as I read by the ruddy glow
And the little ones sit entranced and still . . .
He's drawing near, ah! I know, I know
He's listening too, as he always will.
He's there — he's standing beside my knee;
I see him so well, my wee, wee son. . . .
Oh, children dear, don't look at me —
I'm reading now for — the Other One.

For the firelight glints in his golden hair,
And his wondering eyes are fixed on my face,
And he rests on the arm of my easy-chair,
And the book's a blur and I lose my place:
And I touch my lips to his shining head,
And my voice breaks down and — the story's
     done. . . .

Oh, children, kiss me and go to bed:
Leave me to think of the Other One.

Of the One who will never grow up at all,
Who will always be just a child at play,
Tender and trusting and sweet and small,
Who will never leave me and go away;
Who will never hurt me and give me pain;
Who will comfort me when I'm all alone;
A heart of love that's without a stain,
Always and always my own, my own.

Yet a thought shines out from the dark of pain,
And it gives me hope to be reconciled:
That each of us must be born again,
And live and die as a little child;
So that with souls all shining white,
White as snow and without one sin,
We may come to the Gates of Eternal Light,
Where only children may enter in.

So, gentle mothers, don't ever grieve
Because you have lost, but kiss the rod;
From the depths of your woe be glad, believe
You've given an angel unto God.
Rejoice! You've a child whose youth endures,
Who comes to you when the day is done,
Wistful for love, oh, yours, just yours,
Dearest of all, the Other One.

CATASTROPHE

BRITTANY,
August 14, 1914.

And now I fear I must write in another strain. Up to this time I have been too happy. I have existed in a magic Bohemia, largely of my own making. Hope, faith, enthusiasm have been mine. Each day has had its struggle, its failure, its triumph. However, that is all ended. During the past week we have lived breathlessly. For in spite of the exultant sunshine our spirits have been under a cloud, a deepening shadow of horror and calamity. . . . WAR.

Even as I write, in our little village steeple the bells are ringing madly, and in every little village steeple all over the land. As he hears it the harvester checks his scythe on the swing; the clerk throws down his pen; the shopkeeper puts up his shutters. Only in the cafés there is a clamor of voices and a drowning of care.

For here every man must fight, every home give tribute. There is no question, no appeal. By heredity and discipline all minds are shaped to this great hour. So to-morrow each man will seek his barracks and become a soldier as completely as if he had never been anything else. With the same docility as he dons his baggy red trousers will he let some muddle-headed General hurl him to destruction for some dubious gain. To-day a father, a home-maker; to-morrow fodder for cannon. So they all go without hesitation, without bitterness; and the great military machine that knows not humanity swings them to their fate. I marvel at the sense of duty, the resignation, the sacrifice. It is magnificent, it is FRANCE.

And the Women. Those who wait and weep. Ah! to-day I have not seen one who did not weep. Yes, one.

She was very old, and she stood by her garden gate with her hand on the uplifted latch. As I passed she looked at me with eyes that did not see. She had no doubt sons and grandsons who must fight, and she had good reason, perhaps, to remember the war of *soixante-dix*. When I passed an hour later she was still there, her hand on the uplifted latch.

August 30th.

The men have gone. Only remain graybeards, women and children. Calvert and I have been helping our neighbors to get in the harvest. No doubt we aid; but there with the old men and children a sense of uneasiness and even shame comes over me. I would like to return to Paris, but the railway is mobilized. Each day I grow more discontented. Up there in the red North great things are doing and I am out of it. I am thoroughly unhappy.

Then Calvert comes to me with a plan. He has a Ford car. We will all three go to Paris. He intends to offer himself and his car to the Red Cross. His wife will nurse. So we are very happy at the solution, and to-morrow we are off.

PARIS.

Back again. Closed shutters, deserted streets. How glum everything is! Those who are not mobilized seem uncertain how to turn. Every one buys the papers and reads grimly of disaster. No news is bad news.

I go to my garret as to a beloved friend. Everything is just as I left it, so that it seems I have never been away. I sigh with relief and joy. I will take up my work again. Serene above the storm I will watch and wait. Although I have been brought up in England I am American born. My country is not concerned.

So, going to the Dôme Café, I seek some of my comrades. Strange! They have gone. MacBean, I am told, is in England. By dyeing his hair and lying about his age he has managed to enlist in the Seaforth Highlanders. Saxon Dane too. He has joined the Foreign Legion, and even now may be fighting.

Well, let them go. I will keep out of the mess. But why did they go? I wish I knew. War is murder. Criminal folly. Against Humanity. Imperialism is at the root of it. We are fools and dupes. Yes, I will think and write of other things. . . .

MacBean has enlisted.

I hate violence. I would not willingly cause pain to anything breathing. I would rather be killed than kill I will stand above the Battle and watch it from afar.

Dane is in the Foreign Legion.

How disturbing it all is! One cannot settle down to anything. Every day I meet men who tell the most wonderful stories in the most casual way. I envy them. I too want to have experiences, to live where life's beat is most intense. But that's a poor reason for going to war.

And yet, though I shrink from the idea of fighting, I might in some way help those who are. MacBean and Dane, for example. Sitting lonely in the Dôme, I seem to see their ghosts in the corner. MacBean listening with his keen, sarcastic smile, Saxon Dane banging his great hairy fist on the table till the glasses jump. Where are they now? Living a life that I will never know. When they come back, if they ever do, shall I not feel shamed in their presence? Oh, this filthy war! Things were going on so beautifully. We were all so happy, so full of ambition, of hope; laughing and talking over pipe and bowl, and in our garrets seeking to realize our dreams. Ah, these days will never come again!

Then, as I sit there, Calvert seeks me out.   He has joined
an ambulance corps that is going to the Front.   Will I
come in?

"Yes," I say; " I'll do anything."

So it is all settled.   To-morrow I give up my freedom.

BOOK FOUR

WINTER

I

There is an avenue of noble beeches leading to the Château, and in the shadow of each glimmers the pale oblong of an ambulance. We have to keep them thus concealed, for only yesterday morning a Taube flew over. The beggars are rather partial to Red Cross cars. One of our chaps, taking in a load of wounded, was chased and pelted the other day.

The Château seems all spires and towers, the glorified dream of a Parisian pastrycook. On its terrace figures in khaki are lounging. They are the volunteers, the owner-drivers of the Corps, many of them men of wealth and title. Curious to see one who owns all the coal in two counties proudly signing for his *sou* a day; or another, who lives in a Fifth Avenue palace, contentedly sleeping on the straw-strewn floor of a hovel.

Here is a rhyme I have made of such an one:

PRISCILLA

Jerry MacMullen, the millionaire,
Driving a red-meat bus out there —
How did he win his *Croix de Guerre?*
Bless you, that's all old stuff:
Beast of a night on the Verdun road,
Jerry stuck with a woeful load,

167

Stalled in the mud where the red lights glowed,
Prospect devilish tough.

"Little Priscilla" he called his car,
Best of our battered bunch by far,
Branded with many a bullet scar,
Yet running so sweet and true.
Jerry he loved her, knew her tricks;
Swore: "She's the beat of the best big six,
And if ever I get in a deuce of a fix
Priscilla will pull me through."

"Looks pretty rotten right now," says he;
"Hanged if the devil himself could see.
Priscilla, it's up to you and me
To show 'em what we can do."
Seemed that Priscilla just took the word;
Up with a leap like a horse that's spurred,
On with the joy of a homing bird,
Swift as the wind she flew.

Shell-holes shoot at them out of the night;
A lurch to the left, a wrench to the right,
Hands grim-gripping and teeth clenched tight,
Eyes that glare through the dark.
"Priscilla, you're doing me proud this day;
Hospital's only a league away,
And, honey, I'm longing to hit the hay,
So hurry, old girl. . . . But hark!"

Howl of a shell, harsh, sudden, dread;
Another . . . another. . . . "Strike me dead

If the Huns ain't strafing the road ahead
So the convoy can't get through!
A barrage of shrap, and us alone;
Four rush-cases — you hear 'em moan?
Fierce old messes of blood and bone. . . .
Priscilla, what shall we do?"

Again it seems that Priscilla hears.
With a rush and a roar her way she clears,
Straight at the hell of flame she steers,
Full at its heart of wrath.
Fury of death and dust and din!
Havoc and horror! .She's in, she's in;
She's almost over, she'll win, she'll win!
Woof! Crump! right in the path.

Little Priscilla skids and stops,
Jerry MacMullen sways and flops;
Bang in his map the crash he cops;
Shriek from the car: " Mon Dieu!"
One of the *blessés* hears him say,
Just at the moment he faints away:
" Reckon this isn't my lucky day,
Priscilla, it's up to you."

Sergeant raps on the doctor's door;
" Car in the court with *couchés* four;
Driver dead on the dashboard floor;
Strange how the bunch got here."
" No," says the Doc, " this chap's alive;
But tell me, how could a man contrive

With both arms broken, a car to drive?
Thunder of God! it's queer."

Same little *blessé* makes a spiel;
Says he: "When I saw our driver reel,
A Strange Shape leapt to the driving wheel
And sped us safe through the night."
But Jerry, he says in his drawling tone:
"Rats! Why, Priscilla came in on her own.
Bless her, she did it alone, alone. . . ."
Hanged if I know who's right.

As I am sitting down to my midday meal an orderly gives
me a telegram:

> *Hill 71.   Two couchés.   Send car at once.*

The uptilted country-side is a checker-board of green and
gray, and, except where groves of trees rise like islands,
cultivated to the last acre.   But as we near the firing-line
all efforts to till the land cease, and the ungathered beets of
last year have grown to seed.   Amid rank unkempt fields I
race over a road that is pitted with obus-holes; I pass a
line of guns painted like snakes, and drawn by horses dyed
khaki-color; then soldiers coming from the trenches, mud-
caked and ineffably weary; then a race over a bit of road
that is exposed; then, buried in the hill-side, the dressing
station.

The two wounded are put into my car.   From hip to heel
one is swathed in bandages; the other has a great white
turban on his head, with a red patch on it that spreads and
spreads.   They stare dully, but make no sound.   As I crank
the car there is a shrill screaming noise. . . . About thirty

yards away I hear an explosion like a mine-blast, followed by a sudden belch of coal-black smoke. I stare at it in a dazed way. Then the doctor says: "Don't trouble to analyze your sensations. Better get off. You're only drawing their fire."

Here is one of my experiences:

A CASUALTY

That boy I took in the car last night,
With the body that awfully sagged away,
And the lips blood-crisped, and the eyes flame-
bright,
And the poor hands folded and cold as clay —
Oh, I've thought and I've thought of him all the
day.

For the weary old doctor says to me:
"He'll only last for an hour or so.
Both of his legs below the knee
Blown off by a bomb. . . . So, lad, go slow,
And please remember, he doesn't know."

So I tried to drive with never a jar;
And there was I cursing the road like mad,
When I hears a ghost of a voice from the car:
"Tell me, old chap, have I ' copped it ' bad?"
So I answers "No," and he says, "I'm glad."

"Glad," says he, "for at twenty-two
Life's so splendid, I hate to go.
There's so much good that a chap might do,

And I've fought from the start and I've suffered so.
'Twould be hard to get knocked out now, you know."

" Forget it," says I; then I drove awhile,
And I passed him a cheery word or two;
But he didn't answer for many a mile,
So just as the hospital hove in view,
Says I: " Is there nothing that I can do?"

Then he opens his eyes and he smiles at me;
And he takes my hand in his trembling hold;
" Thank you — you're far too kind," says he:
" I'm awfully comfy — stay . . . let's see:
I fancy my blanket's come unrolled —
My *feet,* please wrap 'em — they're cold . . .
    they're cold."

There is a city that glitters on the plain. Afar off we
can see its tall cathedral spire, and there we often take our
wounded from the little village hospitals to the rail-head.
Tragic little buildings, these emergency hospitals — town-
halls, churches, schools; their cots are never empty, their
surgeons never still.

So every day we get our list of cases and off we go, a long
line of cars swishing through the mud. Then one by one
we branch off to our village hospital, puzzling out the road
on our maps. Arrived there, we load up quickly.

The wounded make no moan. They lie, limp, heavily
bandaged, with bare legs and arms protruding from their
blankets. They do not know where they are going; they
do not care. Like live stock, they are labeled and num-
bered. An orderly brings along their battle-scarred equip-

ment, throwing open their rifles to see that no charge remains. Sometimes they shake our hands and thank us for the drive.

In the streets of the city I see French soldiers wearing the *fourragère*. It is a cord of green, yellow or red, and corresponds to the *Croix de Guerre,* the *Médaille militaire* and the Legion of Honor. The red is the highest of all, and has been granted only to one or two regiments. This incident was told to me by a man who saw it:

THE BLOOD-RED *FOURRAGÈRE*

What was the blackest sight to me
Of all that campaign?
A naked woman tied to a tree
With jagged holes where her breasts should be,
Rotting there in the rain.

On we pressed to the battle fray,
Dogged and dour and spent.
Sudden I heard my Captain say:
"*Voilà!* Kultur has passed this way,
And left us a monument."

So I looked and I saw our Colonel there,
And his grand head, snowed with the years,
Unto the beat of the rain was bare;
And, oh, there was grief in his frozen stare,
And his cheeks were stung with tears!

Then at last he turned from the woeful tree,
And his face like stone was set;

" Go, march the Regiment past," said he,
" That every father and son may see,
And none may ever forget."

Oh, the crimson strands of her hair downpoured
Over her breasts of woe;
And our grim old Colonel leaned on his sword,
And the men filed past with their rifles lowered,
Solemn and sad and slow.

But I'll never forget till the day I die,
As I stood in the driving rain,
And the jaded columns of men slouched by,
How amazement leapt into every eye,
Then fury and grief and pain.

And some would like madmen stand aghast,
With their hands upclenched to the sky;
And some would cross themselves as they passed,
And some would curse in a scalding blast,
And some like children cry.

Yea, some would be sobbing, and some would pray,
And some hurl hateful names;
But the best had never a word to say;
They turned their twitching faces away,
And their eyes were like hot flames.

They passed; then down on his bended knee
The Colonel dropped to the Dead:
" Poor martyred daughter of France!" said he,

" O dearly, dearly avenged you'll be
Or ever a day be sped! "

Now they hold that we are the best of the best,
And each of our men may wear,
Like a gash of crimson across his chest,
As one fierce-proved in the battle-test,
The blood-red *Fourragère*.

For each as he leaps to the top can see,
Like an etching of blood on his brain,
A wife or a mother lashed to a tree,
With two black holes where her breasts should be,
Left to rot in the rain.

So we fight like fiends, and of us they say
That we neither yield nor spare.
Oh, we have the bitterest debt to pay. . . .
Have we paid it? — Look — how we wear to-day
Like a trophy, gallant and proud and gay,
Our blood-red *Fourragère*.

It is often weary waiting at the little *poste de secours*.
Some of us play solitaire, some read a "sixpenny," some
doze or try to talk in bad French to the *poilus*. Around
us is discomfort, dirt and drama.

For my part, I pass the time only too quickly, trying to
put into verse the incidents and ideas that come my way.
In this way I hope to collect quite a lot of stuff which may
some day see itself in print.

Here is one of my efforts:

JIM

Never knew Jim, did you?   Our boy Jim?
Bless you, there was the likely lad;
Supple and straight and long of limb,
Clean as a whistle, and just as glad.
Always laughing, wasn't he, dad?
Joy, pure joy to the heart of him,
And, oh, but the soothering ways he had,
                                        Jim, our Jim!

But I see him best as a tiny tot,
A bonny babe, though it's me that speaks;
Laughing there in his little cot,
With his sunny hair and his apple cheeks.
And my! but the blue, blue eyes he'd got,
And just where his wee mouth dimpled dim
Such a fairy mark like a beauty spot —
                                        That was Jim.

Oh, the war, the war!   How my eyes were wet!
But he says: "Don't be sorrowing, mother dear;
You never knew me to fail you yet,
And I'll be back in a year, a year."
'Twas at Mons he fell, in the first attack;
For so they said, and their eyes were dim;
But I laughed in their faces: "He'll come back,
                                        Will my Jim."

Now, we'd been wedded for twenty year,
And Jim was the only one we'd had;

So when I whispered in father's ear,
He wouldn't believe me — would you, dad?
There! I must hurry . . . hear him cry?
My new little baby. . . . See! that's him.
What are we going to call him?   Why,
                              Jim, just Jim.

Jim! For look at him laughing there
In the same old way in his tiny cot,
With his rosy cheeks and his sunny hair,
And look, just look . . . his beauty spot
In the selfsame place. . . . Oh, I can't explain,
And of course you think it's a mother's whim,
But I know, I know it's my boy again,
                              Same wee Jim.

Just come back as he said he would;
Come with his love and his heart of glee.
Oh, I cried and I cried, but the Lord was good;
From the shadow of Death he set Jim free.
So I'll have him all over again, you see.
Can you wonder my mother-heart's a-brim?
Oh, how happy we're going to be!
                              Aren't we, Jim?

II

IN PICARDY,
January 1915.

The road lies amid a malevolent heath. It seems to lead
us right into the clutch of the enemy; for the star-shells,

that at first were bursting overhead, gradually encircle us. The fields are strangely sinister; the splintered trees are like giant toothpicks. There is a lisping and a twanging overhead.

As we wait at the door of the dugout that serves as a first-aid dressing station, I gaze up into that mysterious dark, so alive with musical vibrations. Then a small shadow detaches itself from the greater shadow, and a gray-bearded sentry says to me: "You'd better come in out of the bullets."

So I keep under cover, and presently they bring my load. Two men drip with sweat as they carry their comrade. I can see that they all three belong to the Foreign Legion. I think for a moment of Saxon Dane. How strange if some day I should carry him! Half fearfully I look at my passenger, but he is a black man. Such things only happen in fiction.

This is what I have written of the finest troops in the Army of France:

KELLY OF THE LEGION

Now Kelly was no fighter;
He loved his pipe and glass;
An easygoing blighter,
Who lived in Montparnasse.
But 'mid the tavern tattle
He heard some guinney say:
" When France goes forth to battle,
The Legion leads the way.

> " *The scourings of creation,*
> *Of every sin and station,*

The men who've known damnation,
Are picked to lead the way."

Well, Kelly joined the Legion;
They marched him day and night;
They rushed him to the region
Where largest loomed the fight.
" Behold your mighty mission,
Your destiny," said they;
" By glorious tradition
The Legion leads the way.

>   *" With tattered banners flying*
>   *With trail of dead and dying,*
>   *On!   On!   All hell defying,*
>   *The Legion sweeps the way."*

With grim, hard-bitten faces,
With jests of savage mirth,
They swept into their places,
The men of iron worth;
Their blooded steel was flashing;
They swung to face the fray;
Then rushing, roaring, crashing,
The Legion cleared the way.

>   *The trail they blazed was gory;*
>   *Few lived to tell the story;*
>   *Through death they plunged to glory;*
>   *But, oh, they cleared the way!*

Now Kelly lay a-dying,
And dimly saw advance,
With split new banners flying,
The *fantassins* of France.
Then up amid the *mêlée*
He rose from where he lay;
" Come on, me boys," says Kelly,
" The Layjun lades the way ! "

> *Aye, while they faltered, doubting*
> *(Such flames of doom were spouting),*
> *He caught them, thrilled them, shouting:*
> *" The Layjun lades the way ! "*

They saw him slip and stumble,
Then stagger on once more;
They marked him trip and tumble,
A mass of grime and gore;
They watched him blindly crawling
Amid hell's own affray,
And calling, calling, calling:
" The Layjun lades the way ! "

> *And even while they wondered,*
> *The battle-wrack was sundered;*
> *To Victory they thundered,*
> *But . . . Kelly led the way.*

Still Kelly kept agoing;
Berserker-like he ran;
His eyes with fury glowing,

A lion of a man;
His rifle madly swinging,
His soul athirst to slay,
His slogan ringing, ringing,
" The Layjun lades the way! "

> *Till in a pit death-baited,*
> *Where Huns with Maxims waited,*
> *He plunged . . . and there, blood-sated,*
> *To death he stabbed his way.*

Now Kelly was a fellow
Who simply loathed a fight:
He loved a tavern mellow,
Grog hot and pipe alight;
I'm sure the Show appalled him,
And yet without dismay,
When Death and Duty called him,
He up and led the way.

> *So in Valhalla drinking*
> *(If heroes meek and shrinking*
> *Are suffered there), I'm thinking*
> *'Tis Kelly leads the way.*

We have just had one of our men killed, a young sculptor
of immense promise.

When one thinks of all the fine work he might have
accomplished, it seems a shame. But, after all, to-morrow
it may be the turn of any of us. If it should be mine, my
chief regret will be for work undone.

Ah! I often think of how I will go back to the Quarter

and take up the old life again.   How sweet it will all seem.
But first I must earn the right.   And if ever I do go back,
how I will find Bohemia changed!   Missing how many a
face!

It was in thinking of our lost comrade I wrote the following:

THE THREE TOMMIES

That Barret, the painter of pictures, what feeling for
color he had!
And Fanning, the maker of music, such melodies
mirthful and mad!
And Harley, the writer of stories, so whimsical, tender and glad!

To hark to their talk in the trenches, high heart unfolding to heart,
Of the day when the war would be over, and each
would be true to his part,
Upbuilding a Palace of Beauty to the wonder and
glory of Art . . .

Yon's Barret, the painter of pictures, yon carcass
that rots on the wire;
His hand with its sensitive cunning is crisped to a
cinder with fire;
His eyes with their magical vision are bubbles of
glutinous mire.

Poor Fanning!   He sought to discover the sym-
phonic note of a shell;

There are bits of him broken and bloody, to show
    you the place where he fell;
I've reason to fear on his exquisite ear the rats have
    been banqueting well.

And speaking of Harley, the writer, I fancy I looked
    on him last,
Sprawling and staring and writhing in the roar of the
    battle blast;
Then a mad gun-team crashed over, and scattered
    his brains as it passed.

Oh, Harley and Fanning and Barret, they were
    bloody good mates o' mine;
Their bodies are empty bottles; Death has guzzled
    the wine;
What's left of them's filth and corruption. . . .
    Where is the Fire Divine?

I'll tell you. . . . At night in the trenches, as I
    watch and I do my part,
Three radiant spirits I'm seeing, high heart reveal-
    ing to heart,
And they're building a peerless palace to the splen-
    dor and triumph of Art.

Yet, alas! for the fame of Barret, the glory he might
    have trailed!
And alas! for the name of Fanning, a star that bea-
    coned and paled,
Poor Harley, obscure and forgotten. . . . Well,
    who shall say that they failed!

No, each did a Something Grander than ever he
    dreamed to do;
And as for the work unfinished, all will be paid their
    due;
The broken ends will be fitted, the balance struck
    will be true.

So painters, and players, and penmen, I tell you:
    Do as you please;
Let your fame outleap on the trumpets, you'll never
    rise up to these —
To three grim and gory Tommies, down, down on
    your bended knees!

Daventry, the sculptor, is buried in a little graveyard
near one of our posts. Just now our section of the line
is quiet, so I often go and sit there. Stretching myself on
a flat stone, I dream for hours.

Silence and solitude! How good the peace of it all seems!
Around me the grasses weave a pattern, and half hide the
hundreds of little wooden crosses. Here is one with a single
name:

AUBREY.

Who was Aubrey I wonder? Then another:

To Our Beloved Comrade.

Then one which has attached to it, in the cheapest of
little frames, the crude water-color daub of a child, three
purple flowers standing in a yellow vase. Below it, painfully printed, I read:

To My Darling Papa — Thy Little Odette.

And beyond the crosses many fresh graves have been dug. With hungry open mouths they wait. Even now I can hear the guns that are going to feed them. Soon there will be more crosses, and more and more. Then they will cease, and wives and mothers will come here to weep.

Ah! Peace so precious must be bought with blood and tears. Let us honor and bless the men who pay, and envy them the manner of their dying; for not all the jeweled orders on the breasts of the living can vie in glory with the little wooden cross the humblest of these has won. . . .

THE TWA JOCKS

Says Bauldy MacGreegor frae Gleska tae Hecky
    MacCrimmon frae Skye:
" That's whit I hate maist aboot fechtin'— it makes
    ye sae deevilish dry;
Noo jist hae a keek at yon ferm-hoose them Gair-
    mans are poundin' sae fine,
Weel, think o' it, doon in the dunnie there's bottles
    and bottles o' wine.
A' hell's fairly belchin' oot yonner, but oh, lad, I'm
    ettlin' tae try. . . ."
*" If it's poose she'll be with ye whateffer," says
    Hecky MacCrimmon frae Skye.*

Says Bauldy MacGreegor frae Gleska: " Whit price
    fur a funeral wreath?
We're dodgin' a' kinds o' destruction, an' jist by the
    skin o' oor teeth.

Here, spread yersel oot on yer belly, and slither
along in the glaur;
Confoond ye, ye big Hielan' deevil! Ye don't real-
ize there's a war.
Ye think that ye're back in Dunvegan, and herdin'
the wee bits o' kye."
" She'll neffer trink wine in Dunfegan," says Hecky
MacCrimmon frae Skye.

Says Bauldy MacGreegor frae Gleska: "Thank
goodness! the ferm-hoose at last;
There's no muckle left but the cellar, an' even that's
vanishin' fast.
Look oot, there's the corpse o' a wumman, sair
mangelt and deid by her lane.
Quick! Strike a match. . . . Whit did I tell ye!
A hale bonny box o' shampane;
Jist knock the heid aff o' a bottle. . . . Haud on,
mon, I'm hearing a cry. . . ."
" She'll think it's a wean that wass greetin'," says
Hecky MacCrimmon frae Skye.

Says Bauldy MacGreegor frae Gleska: "Ma con-
science! I'm hanged but yer richt.
It's yin o' thae waifs of the war-field, a' sobbin' and
shakin' wi' fricht.
Wheesht noo, dear, we're no gaun tae hurt ye.
We're takin' ye hame, my wee doo!
We've got tae get back wi' her, Hecky. Whit
mercy we didna get fou!

We'll no touch a drap o' that likker — that's hard,
    man, ye canna deny. . . ."
"It's the last thing she'll think o' denyin'," says
Hecky MacCrimmon frae Skye.

Says Bauldy MacGreegor frae Gleska: "If I
    should get struck frae the rear,
Ye'll tak' and ye'll shield the wee lassie, and rin for
    the lines like a deer.
God! Wis that the breenge o' a bullet? I'm think-
    in' it's cracket ma spine.
I'm doon on ma knees in the glabber; I'm fearin',
    auld man, I've got mine.
Here, quick! Pit yer erms roon the lassie. Noo,
    rin, lad! good luck and good-by. . . .
"Hoots, mon! it's ye baith she'll be takin'," says
Hecky MacCrimmon frae Skye.

Says Corporal Muckle frae Rannoch: "Is that no'
    a picture tae frame?
Twa sair woundit Jocks wi' a lassie jist like ma wee
    Jeannie at hame.
We're prood o' ye baith, ma brave heroes. We'll
    gie ye a medal, I think."
Says Bauldy MacGreegor frae Gleska: "I'd raither
    ye gied me a drink.
I'll no speak for Private MacCrimmon, but oh, mon,
    I'm perishin' dry. . . ."
"She'll wush that Loch Lefen wass whuskey," says
Hecky MacCrimmon frae Skye.

III

Over the spine of the ridge a horned moon of reddish
hue peers through the splintered, hag-like trees. Where
the trenches are, rockets are rising, green and red. I hear
the coughing of the Maxims, the peevish nagging of the
rifles, the boom of a " heavy " and the hollow sound of its
exploding shell.

Running the car into the shadow of a ruined house, I
try to sleep. But a battery starts to blaze away close by,
and the flame lights up my shelter. Near me some soldiers
are in deep slumber; one stirs in his sleep as a big rat runs
over him, and I know by experience that when one is sleeping a rat feels as heavy as a sheep.

But how *can* one possibly sleep? Out there in the dark
there is the wild tattoo of a thousand rifles; and hark!
that dull roar is the explosion of a mine. There! the purring of the rapid firers. Desperate things are doing. There
will be lots of work for me before this night is over. What
a cursed place!

As I cannot sleep, I think of a story I heard to-day. It
is of a Canadian Colonel, and in my mind I shape it like
this:

HIS BOYS

" I'm going, Billy, old fellow. Hist, lad! Don't
      make any noise.
There's Boches to beat all creation, the pitch of a
      bomb away.

I've fixed the note to your collar, you've got to get
   back to my Boys,
You've got to get back to warn 'em before it's the
   break of day."

The order came to go forward to a trench-line
   traced on the map;
I knew the brass-hats had blundered, I knew and I
   told 'em so;
I knew if I did as they ordered I would tumble into a
   trap,
And I tried to explain, but the answer came like a
   pistol: "Go."

Then I thought of the Boys I commanded — I always called them " my Boys "—
The men of my own recruiting, the lads of my coun-
   tryside;
Tested in many a battle, I knew their sorrows and
   joys,
And I loved them all like a father, with more than a
   father's pride.

To march my Boys to a shambles as soon as the
   dawn of day;
To see them helplessly slaughtered, if all that I
   guessed was true;
My Boys that trusted me blindly, I thought and I
   tried to pray,
And then I arose and I muttered: " It's either them
   or it's you."

I rose and I donned my rain-coat; I buckled my hel-
    met tight.
I remember you watched me, Billy, as I took my
    cane in my hand;
I vaulted over the sandbags into the pitchy night,
Into the pitted valley that served us as No Man's
    Land.

I strode out over the hollow of hate and havoc and
    death,
From the heights the guns were angry, with a
    vengeful snarling of steel;
And once in a moment of stillness I heard hard pant-
    ing breath,
And I turned . . . it was you, old rascal, following
    hard on my heel.

I fancy I cursed you, Billy; but not so much as I
    ought!
And so we went forward together, till we came to
    the valley rim,
And then a star-shell sputtered . . . it was even
    worse than I thought,
For the trench they told me to move in was packed
    with Boche to the brim.

They saw me too, and they got me; they peppered
    me till I fell;
And there I scribbled my message with my life-blood
    ebbing away;
" Now, Billy, you fat old duffer, you've got to get
    back like hell;

And get them to cancel that order before it's the
    dawn of day.

" Billy, old boy, I love you, I kiss your shiny black
    nose;
Now, home there. . . . Hurry, you devil, or I'll cut
    you to ribands. . . . See . . ."
Poor brute! he's off! and I'm dying. . . . I go as a
    soldier goes.
I'm happy. My Boys, God bless 'em! . . . It had
    to be them or me.

Ah! I never was intended for a job like this. I realize
it more and more every day, but I will stick it out till I
break down. To be nervous, over-imaginative, terribly
sensitive to suffering, is a poor equipment for the man who
starts out to drive wounded on the battlefield. I am
haunted by the thought that my car may break down when
I have a load of wounded. Once indeed it did, and a man
died while I waited for help. Now I never look at what
is given me. It might unnerve me.

I have been at it for over six months without a rest.
When an attack has been going on I have worked day and
night, until as I drove I wanted to fall asleep at the wheel.

The winter has been trying; there is rain one day, frost
the next. Mud up to the axles. One sleeps in lousy barns
or dripping dugouts. Cold, hunger, dirt, I know them all
singly and together. My only consolation is that the war
must soon be over, and that I will have helped. When
I have time and am not too tired, I comfort myself with
scribbling.

THE BOOBY-TRAP

I'm crawlin' out in the mangolds to bury wot's left
o' Joe —
Joe, my pal, and a good un (God! 'ow it rains and
rains).
I'm sick o' seein' him lyin' like a 'eap o' offal, and
so
I'm crawlin' out in the beet-field to bury 'is last remains.

'E might' a bin makin' munitions —'e 'adn't no need
to go;
An' I tells 'im strite, but 'e arnsers, " 'Tain't no use
chewin' the fat;
I've got to be doin' me dooty wiv the rest o' the
boys " . . . an' so
Yon's 'im, yon blob on the beet-field wot I'm tryin'
so 'ard to git at.

There was five of us lads from the brickyard; 'Enry
was gassed at Bapome,
Sydney was drowned in a crater, 'Erbert was 'alved
by a shell;
Joe was the pick o' the posy, might 'a bin sifely at
'ome,
Only son of 'is mother, 'er a widder as well.

She used to sell bobbins and buttons —'ad a plice
near the Waterloo Road;

A little, old, bent-over lydy, wiv glasses an' silvery
    'air;
Must tell 'er I planted 'im nicely, cheer 'er up like.
    . . . (Well, I'm blowed,
That bullet near catched me a biffer) — I'll see the
    old gel if I'm spared.

She'll tike it to 'eart, pore ol' lydy, fer 'e was 'er
    'ope and 'er joy;
'Is dad used to drink like a knot-'ole, she kept the
    'ome goin', she did:
She pinched and she scriped fer 'is scoolin', 'e was
    sich a fine 'andsome boy
('Alf Flanders seems packed on me panties) —'e's
    'andsome no longer, pore kid!

This bit o' a board that I'm packin' and draggin'
    around in the mire,
I was tickled to death when I found it. Says I,
    " 'Ere's a nice little glow."
I was chilled and wet through to the marrer, so I
    started to make me a fire;
And then I says: " No; 'ere, Goblimy, it'll do for a
    cross for Joe."

Well, 'ere 'e is. Gawd! 'Ow one chinges a-lyin'
    six weeks in the rain.
Joe, me old pal, 'ow I'm sorry; so 'elp me, I wish I
    could pray.
An' now I 'ad best get a-diggin' 'is grave (it seems
    more like a drain) —

And I 'opes that the Boches won't git me till I gits
    'im safe planted away.

> (*As he touches the body there is a tremen-*
> *dous explosion. He falls back shattered.*)

A booby-trap! Ought to 'a known it! If that's
    not a bastardly trick!
Well, one thing, I won't be long goin'. Gawd!
    I'm a 'ell of a sight.
Wish I'd died fightin' and killin'; that's wot it is
    makes me sick. . . .
Ah, Joe! we'll be pushin' up dysies . . . together,
    old Chummie . . . good-night!

To-day I heard that MacBean had been killed in Belgium.
I believe he turned out a wonderful soldier. Saxon Dane,
too, has been missing for two months. We know what that
means.

It is odd how one gets callous to death, a mediæval
callousness. When we hear that the best of our friends
have gone West, we have a moment of the keenest regret;
but how soon again we find the heart to laugh! The saddest part of loss, I think, is that one so soon gets over it.

Is it that we fail to realize it all? Is it that it seems a
strange and hideous dream, from which we will awake
and rub our eyes?

Oh, how bitter I feel as the days go by! It is creeping
more and more into my verse. Read this:

BONEHEAD BILL

I wonder 'oo and wot 'e was,
    That 'Un I got so slick.

BONEHEAD BILL

ı couldn't see 'is face because
The night was 'ideous thick.
I just made out among the black
A blinkin' wedge o' white;
Then *biff!*   I guess I got 'im *crack* —
The man I killed last night.

I wonder if account o' me
Some wench will go unwed,
And 'eaps o' lives will never be,
Because 'e's stark and dead?
Or if 'is missis damns the war,
And by some candle light,
Tow-headed kids are prayin' for
The Fritz I copped last night.

I wonder, 'struth, I wonder why
I 'ad that 'orful dream?
I saw up in the giddy sky
The gates o' God agleam;
I saw the gates o' 'eaven shine
Wiv everlastin' light:
And then . . . I knew that I'd got mine,
As 'e got 'is last night.

Aye, bang beyond the broodin' mists
Where spawn the mother stars,
I 'ammered wiv me bloody fists
Upon them golden bars;
I 'ammered till a devil's doubt
Fair froze me wiv affright:

To fink wot God would say about
The bloke I corpsed last night.

I 'ushed; I wilted wiv despair,
When, like a rosy flame,
I sees a angel standin' there
'Oo calls me by me name.
'E 'ad such soft, such shiny eyes;
'E 'eld 'is 'and and smiled;
And through the gates o' Paradise
'E led me like a child.

'E led me by them golden palms
Wot 'ems that jeweled street;
And seraphs was a-singin' psalms,
You've no ideer 'ow sweet;
Wiv cheroobs crowdin' closer round
Than peas is in a pod,
'E led me to a shiny mound
Where beams the throne o' God.

And then I 'ears God's werry voice:
" Bill 'agan, 'ave no fear.
Stand up and glory and rejoice
For 'im 'oo led you 'ere."
And in a nip I seemed to see:
Aye, like a flash o' light,
My angel pal I knew to be
The chap I plugged last night.

Now, I don't claim to understand —
They calls me Bonehead Bill;

They shoves a rifle in me 'and,
And show me 'ow to kill.
Me job's to risk me life and limb,
But . . . be it wrong or right,
This cross I'm makin', it's for 'im,
The cove I croaked last night.

IV

A LAPSE OF TIME AND A WORD OF EXPLANATION

THE AMERICAN HOSPITAL, NEUILLY,
January 1919.

Four years have passed and it is winter again. Much
has happened. When I last wrote, on the Somme in 1915,
I was sickening with typhoid fever. All that spring I was
in hospital.

Nevertheless, I was sufficiently recovered to take part
in the Champagne battle in the fall of that year, and to
" carry on " during the following winter. It was at Verdun
I got my first wound.

In the spring of 1917 I again served with my Corps; but
on the entry of the United States into the War I joined
the army of my country. In the Argonne I had my left
arm shot away.

As far as time and health permitted, I kept a record of
these years, and also wrote much verse. All this, however,
has disappeared under circumstances into which there is no
need to enter here. The loss was a cruel one, almost more
so than that of my arm; for I have neither the heart nor the
power to rewrite this material.

And now, in default of something better, I have bundled together this manuscript, and have added to it a few more verses, written in hospitals. Let it represent me. If I can find a publisher for it, *tant mieux*. If not, I will print it at my own cost, and any one who cares for a copy can write to me —

> Stephen Poore,
> 12 *bis,* Rue des Petits Moineaux,
> Paris.

MICHAEL

" There's something in your face, Michael, I've seen
    it all the day;
There's something quare that wasn't there when first
    ye wint away. . . ."

" It's just the Army life, mother, the drill, the left
    and right,
That puts the stiffinin' in yer spine and locks yer jaw
    up tight. . . ."

" There's something in your eyes, Michael, an' how
    they stare and stare —
You're lookin' at me now, me boy, as if I wasn't
    there. . . ."

" It's just the things I've seen, mother, the sights
    that come and come,
A bit o' broken, bloody pulp that used to be a
    chum. . . ."

" There's something on your heart, Michael, that
    makes ye wake at night,
And often when I hear ye moan, I trimble in me
    fright. . . ."

" It's just a man I killed, mother, a mother's son like
    me ;
It seems he's always hauntin' me, he'll never let me
    be. . . ."

" But maybe he was bad, Michael, maybe it was
    right
To kill the inimy you hate in fair and honest
    fight. . . ."

" I did not hate at all, mother; he never did me
    harm ;
I think he was a lad like me, who worked upon a
    farm. . . ."

"And what's it all about, Michael; why did you have
    to go,
A quiet, peaceful lad like you, and we were happy
    so? . . ."

" It's thim that's up above, mother, it's thim that sits
    an' rules ;
We've got to fight the wars they make, it's us as are
    the fools. . . ."

" And what will be the end, Michael, and what's the
    use, I say,

Of fightin' if whoever wins it's us that's got to
    pay? . . ."

" Oh, it will be the end, mother, when lads like him
    and me,
That sweat to feed the ones above, decide that we'll
    be free. . . ."

" And when will that day come, Michael, and when
    will fightin' cease,
And simple folks may till their soil and live and love
    in peace? . . ."

" It's coming soon and soon, mother, it's nearer
    every day,
When only men who work and sweat will have a
    word to say;
When all who earn their honest bread in every land
    and soil
Will claim the Brotherhood of Man, the Comrade-
    ship of Toil;
When we, the Workers, all demand: ' What are we
    fighting for? ' . . .
Then, then we'll end that stupid crime, that devil's
    madness — War."

THE WIFE

" Tell Annie I'll be home in time
To help her with her Christmas-tree."

That's what he wrote, and hark! the chime
Of Christmas bells, and where is he?
And how the house is dark and sad,
And Annie's sobbing on my knee!

The page beside the candle-flame
With cruel type was overfilled;
I read and read until a name
Leapt at me and my heart was stilled:
My eye crept up the column — up
Unto its hateful heading: *Killed*.

And there was Annie on the stair:
" And will he not be long? " she said.
Her eyes were bright and in her hair
She'd twined a bit of riband red;
And every step was daddy's sure,
Till tired out she went to bed.

And there alone I sat so still,
With staring eyes that did not see;
The room was desolate and chill,
And desolate the heart of me;
Outside I heard the news-boys shrill:
" Another Glorious Victory! "

A victory. . . . Ah! what care I?
A thousand victories are vain.
Here in my ruined home I cry
From out my black despair and pain,
I'd rather, rather damned defeat,
And have my man with me again.

They talk to us of pride and power,
Of Empire vast beyond the sea;
As here beside my hearth I cower,
What mean such words as these to me?
Oh, will they lift the clouds that low'r,
Or light my load in years to be?

What matters it to us poor folk?
Who win or lose, it's we who pay.
Oh, I would laugh beneath the yoke
If I had *him* at home to-day;
One's home before one's country comes:
Aye, so a million women say.

" Hush, Annie dear, don't sorrow so."
(How can I tell her?)　" See, we'll light
With tiny star of purest glow
Each little candle pink and white."
(They make mistakes.　I'll tell myself
I did not read that name aright.)
Come, dearest one; come, let us pray
Beside our gleaming Christmas-tree;
Just fold your little hands and say
These words so softly after me:
" God pity mothers in distress,
And little children fatherless."

" *God pity mothers in distress,*
And little children fatherless."

What's that? — a step upon the stair;
A shout! — the door thrown open wide!
My hero and my man is there,
And Annie's leaping by his side. . . .
The room reels round, I faint, I fall. . . .
" O God!   Thy world is glorified."

VICTORY STUFF

What d'ye think, lad; what d'ye think,
As the roaring crowds go by?
As the banners flare and the brasses blare
And the great guns rend the sky?
As the women laugh like they'd all gone mad,
And the champagne glasses clink:
Oh, you're grippin' me hand so tightly, lad,
I'm a-wonderin': what d'ye think?

D'ye think o' the boys we used to know,
And how they'd have topped the fun?
Tom and Charlie, and Jack and Joe —
Gone now, every one.
How they'd have cheered as the joy-bells chime,
And they grabbed each girl for a kiss!
And now — they're rottin' in Flanders slime,
And they gave their lives — for *this*.

Or else d'ye think of the many a time
We wished we too was dead,
Up to our knees in the freezin' grime,
With the fires of hell overhead;

When the youth and the strength of us sapped away,
And we cursed in our rage and pain?
And yet — we haven't a word to say. . . .
We're glad.   We'd do it again.

I'm scared that they pity us.   Come, old boy,
Let's leave them their flags and their fuss.
We'd surely be hatin' to spoil their joy
With the sight of such wrecks as us.
Let's slip away quietly, you and me,
And we'll talk of our chums out there:
You with your eyes that'll never see,
Me that's wheeled in a chair.

WAS IT YOU?

" Hullo, young Jones! with your tie so gay
And your pen behind your ear;
Will you mark my cheque in the usual way?
For I'm overdrawn, I fear."
Then you look at me in a manner bland,
As you turn your ledger's leaves,
And you hand it back with a soft white hand,
And the air of a man who grieves. . . .

" *Was it you, young Jones, was it you I saw*
(And I think I see you yet)
With a live bomb gripped in your grimy paw
And your face to the parapet?
With your lips asnarl and your eyes gone mad
With a fury that thrilled you through. . . .

Oh, I look at you now and I think, my lad,
Was it you, young Jones, was it you?

" Hullo, young Smith, with your well-fed look
And your coat of dapper fit,
Will you recommend me a decent book
With nothing of War in it? "
Then you smile as you polish a finger-nail,
And your eyes serenely roam,
And you suavely hand me a thrilling tale
By a man who stayed at home.

" Was it you, young Smith, was it you I saw
In the battle's storm and stench,
With a roar of rage and a wound red-raw
Leap into the reeking trench?
As you stood like a fiend on the firing-shelf
And you stabbed and hacked and slew. . . .
Oh, I look at you and I ask myself,
Was it you, young Smith, was it you?

" Hullo, old Brown, with your ruddy cheek
And your tummy's rounded swell,
Your garden's looking jolly *chic*
And your kiddies awf'ly well.
Then you beam at me in your cheery way
As you swing your water-can;
And you mop your brow and you blithely say:
' What about golf, old man? '

" Was it you, old Brown, was it you I saw
Like a bull-dog stick to your gun,

A cursing devil of fang and claw
When the rest were on the run?
Your eyes aflame with the battle-hate. . . .
As you sit in the family pew,
And I see you rising to pass the plate,
I ask: Old Brown, was it you?

" Was it me and you?   Was it you and me?
(Is that grammar, or is it not?)
Who groveled in filth and misery,
Who gloried and groused and fought?
Which is the wrong and which is the right?
Which is the false and the true?
The man of peace or the man of fight?
Which is the ME and the YOU? "

V

LES GRANDS MUTILES

I saw three wounded of the war:
And the first had lost his eyes;
And the second went on wheels and had
No legs below the thighs;
And the face of the third was featureless,
And his mouth ran cornerwise.
So I made a rhyme about each one,
And this is how my fancies run.

THE SIGHTLESS MAN

Out of the night a crash,
A roar, a rampart of light;
A flame that leaped like a lash,
Searing forever my sight;
Out of the night a flash,
Then, oh, forever the Night!

Here in the dark I sit,
I who so loved the sun;
Supple and strong and fit,
In the dark till my days be done;
Aye, that's the hell of it,
Stalwart and twenty-one.

Marie is stanch and true,
Willing to be my wife;
Swears she has eyes for two . . .
Aye, but it's long, is Life.
What is a lad to do
With his heart and his brain at strife?

There now, my pipe is out;
No one to give me a light;
I grope and I grope about.
Well, it is nearly night;
Sleep may resolve my doubt,
Help me to reason right. . . .

(He sleeps and dreams.)

I heard them whispering there by the bed . . .
Oh, but the ears of the blind are quick!
Every treacherous word they said
Was a stab of pain and my heart turned sick.
Then lip met lip and they looked at me,
Sitting bent by the fallen fire,
And they laughed to think that I couldn't see;
But I felt the flame of their hot desire.
He's helping Marie to work the farm,
A dashing, upstanding chap, they say;
And look at me with my flabby arm,
And the fat of sloth, and my face of clay —
Look at me as I sit and sit,
By the side of a fire that's seldom lit,
Sagging and weary the livelong day,
When every one else is out on the field,
Sowing the seed for a golden yield,
Or tossing around the new-mown hay. . . .

Oh, the shimmering wheat that frets the sky,
Gold of plenty and blue of hope,
I'm seeing it all with an inner eye
As out of the door I grope and grope.
And I hear my wife and her lover there,
Whispering, whispering, round the rick,
Mocking me and my sightless stare,
As I fumble and stumble everywhere,
Slapping and tapping with my stick;
Old and weary at thirty-one,

Heartsick, wishing it all was done.
Oh, I'll tap my way around to the byre,
And I'll hear the cows as they chew their hay;
There at least there is none to tire,
There at least I am not in the way.
And they'll look at me with their velvet eyes
And I'll stroke their flanks with my woman's hand,
And they'll answer to me with soft replies,
And somehow I fancy they'll understand.
And the horses too, they know me well;
I'm sure that they pity my wretched lot,
And the big fat ram with the jingling bell . . .
Oh, the beasts are the only friends I've got.
And my old dog, too, he loves me more,
I think, than ever he did before.
Thank God for the beasts that are all so kind,
That know and pity the helpless blind!

Ha! they're coming, the loving pair.
My hand's a-shake as my pipe I fill.
What if I steal on them unaware
With a reaping-hook, to kill, to kill? . . .
I'll do it . . . they're there in the mow of hay,
I hear them saying: " He's out of the way! "
Hark! how they're kissing and whispering. . . .
Closer I creep . . . I crouch . . . I spring. . . .

(*He wakes.*)

Ugh! What a horrible dream I've had!
And it isn't real . . . I'm glad, I'm glad!
Marie is good and Marie is true . . .

But now I know what it's best to do.
I'll sell the farm and I'll seek my kind,
I'll live apart with my fellow-blind,
And we'll eat and drink, and we'll laugh and joke,
And we'll talk of our battles, and smoke and smoke;
And brushes of bristle we'll make for sale,
While one of us reads a book of Braille.
And there will be music and dancing too,
And we'll seek to fashion our life anew;
And we'll walk the highways hand in hand,
The Brotherhood of the Sightless Band;
Till the years at last shall bring respite
And our night is lost in the Greater Night.

THE LEGLESS MAN

(The Dark Side)

*My mind goes back to Fumin Wood, and how we
    stuck it out,*
*Eight days of hunger, thirst and cold, mowed down
    by steel and flame;*
*Waist-deep in mud and mad with woe, with dead
    men all about,*
*We fought like fiends and waited for relief that
    never came.*
*Eight days and nights they rolled on us in battle-
    frenzied mass!*
*" Debout les morts!" We hurled them back. By
    God! they did not pass.*

They pinned two medals on my chest, a yellow and
    a brown,
And lovely ladies made me blush, such pretty words
    they said.
I felt a cheerful man, almost, until my eyes went
    down,
And there I saw the blankets — how they sagged
    upon my bed.
And then again I drank the cup of sorrow to the
    dregs:
Oh, they can keep their medals if they give me back
    my legs.

I think of how I used to run and leap and kick the
    ball,
And ride and dance and climb the hills and frolic
    in the sea;
And all the thousand things that now I'll never do
    at all. . . .
Mon Dieu! there's nothing left in life, it often
    seems to me.
And as the nurses lift me up and strap me in my
    chair,
If they would chloroform me off I feel I wouldn't
    care.

Ah yes! we're " heroes all " to-day — they point to
    us with pride;
To-day their hearts go out to us, the tears are in
    their eyes!
But wait a bit; to-morrow they will blindly look
    aside;

No more they'll talk of what they owe, the dues of
    sacrifice
(One hates to be reminded of an everlasting debt).
It's all in human nature.   Ah! the world will soon
    forget.

*My mind goes back to where I lay wound-rotted on
    the plain,*
*And ate the muddy mangold roots, and drank the
    drops of dew,*
*And dragged myself for miles and miles when every
    move was pain,*
*And over me the carrion-crows were retching as they
    flew.*
*Oh, ere I closed my eyes and stuck my rifle in the
    air*
*I wish that those who picked me up had passed and
    left me there.*

(The Bright Side)

Oh, one gets used to everything!
I hum a merry song,
And up the street and round the square
I wheel my chair along;
For look you, how my chest is sound
And how my arms are strong!

Oh, one gets used to anything!
It's awkward at the first,
And jolting o'er the cobbles gives

A man a grievous thirst;
But of all ills that one must bear
That's surely not the worst.

For there's the café open wide,
And there they set me up;
And there I smoke my *caporal*
Above my cider cup;
And play *manille* a while before
I hurry home to sup.

At home the wife is waiting me
With smiles and pigeon-pie;
And little Zi-Zi claps her hands
With laughter loud and high;
And if there's cause to growl, I fail
To see the reason why.

And all the evening by the lamp
I read some tale of crime,
Or play my old accordion
With Marie keeping time,
Until we hear the hour of ten
From out the steeple chime.

Then in the morning bright and soon,
No moment do I lose;
Within my little cobbler's shop
To gain the silver *sous*
(Good luck one has no need of legs
To make a pair of shoes).

And every Sunday — oh, it's then
I am the happy man;
They wheel me to the river-side,
And there with rod and can
I sit and fish and catch a dish
Of *goujons* for the pan.

Aye, one gets used to everything,
And doesn't seem to mind;
Maybe I'm happier than most
Of my two-legged kind;
For look you at the darkest cloud,
Lo! how it's silver-lined.

THE FACELESS MAN

I'm dead.
Officially I'm dead.   Their hope is past.
How long I stood as missing!   Now, at last
                              I'm dead.
Look in my face — no likeness can you see,
No tiny trace of him they knew as " me."
How terrible the change!
Even my eyes are strange.
So keyed are they to pain,
That if I chanced to meet
My mother in the street
She'd look at me in vain.

When she got home I think she'd say:
" I saw the saddest sight to-day —

A *poilu* with no face at all.
Far better in the fight to fall
Than go through life like that, I think.
Poor fellow! how he made me shrink.
No face. Just eyes that seemed to stare
At me with anguish and despair.
This ghastly war! I'm almost cheered
To think my son who disappeared,
My boy so handsome and so gay,
Might have come home like him to-day."

I'm dead. I think it's better to be dead
When little children look at you with dread;
And when you know your coming home again
Will only give the ones who love you pain.
Ah! who can help but shrink? One cannot blame.
They see the hideous husk, not, not the flame
Of sacrifice and love that burns within;
While souls of satyrs, riddled through with sin,
Have bodies fair and excellent to see.
Mon Dieu! how different we all would be
If this our flesh was ordained to express
Our spirit's beauty or its ugliness.

(Oh, you who look at me with fear to-day,
And shrink despite yourselves, and turn away —
It was for you I suffered woe accurst;
For you I braved red battle at its worst;
For you I fought and bled and maimed and slew;
                              For you, for you!
For you I faced hell-fury and despair;

The reeking horror of it all I knew:
I flung myself into the furnace there;
I faced the flame that scorched me with its glare;
I drank unto the dregs the devil's brew —
Look at me now — for *you* and *you* and *you*. . . .)
.   .   .   .   .   .

I'm thinking of the time we said good-by:
We took our dinner in Duval's that night,
Just little Jacqueline, Lucette and I;
We tried our very utmost to be bright.
We laughed.   And yet our eyes, they weren't gay.
I sought all kinds of cheering things to say.
" Don't grieve," I told them.   " Soon the time will
        pass;
My next permission will come quickly round;
We'll all meet at the Gare du Montparnasse;
Three times I've come already, safe and sound."
(But oh, I thought, it's harder every time,
After a home that seems like Paradise,
To go back to the vermin and the slime,
The weariness, the want, the sacrifice.
" Pray God," I said, " the war may soon be done,
But no, oh never, never till we've won! ")

Then to the station quietly we walked;
I had my rifle and my haversack,
My heavy boots, my blankets on my back;
And though it hurt us, cheerfully we talked.
We chatted bravely at the platform gate.
I watched the clock.   My train must go at eight.
One minute to the hour . . . we kissed good-by,

Then, oh, they both broke down, with piteous cry.
I went. . . . Their way was barred; they could not
    pass.
I looked back as the train began to start;
Once more I ran with anguish at my heart
And through the bars I kissed my little lass. . . .

Three years have gone; they've waited day by day.
I never came. I did not even write.
For when I saw my face was such a sight
I thought that I had better . . . stay away.
And so I took the name of one who died,
A friendless friend who perished by my side.
In Prussian prison camps three years of hell
I kept my secret; oh, I kept it well!
And now I'm free, but none shall ever know;
They think I died out there . . . it's better so.

To-day I passed my wife in widow's weeds.
I brushed her arm. She did not even look.
So white, so pinched her face, my heart still bleeds,
And at the touch of her, oh, how I shook!
And then last night I passed the window where
They sat together; I could see them clear,
The lamplight softly gleaming on their hair,
And all the room so full of cozy cheer.
My wife was sewing, while my daughter read;
I even saw my portrait on the wall.
I wanted to rush in, to tell them all;
And then I cursed myself: " You're dead, you're
    dead! "

God! how I watched them from the darkness there,
Clutching the dripping branches of a tree,
Peering as close as ever I might dare,
And sobbing, sobbing, oh, so bitterly!

But no, it's folly; and I mustn't stay.
To-morrow I am going far away.
I'll find a ship and sail before the mast;
In some wild land I'll bury all the past.
I'll live on lonely shores and there forget,
Or tell myself that there has never been
The gay and tender courage of Lucette,
The little loving arms of Jacqueline.

A man lonely upon a lonely isle,
Sometimes I'll look towards the North and smile
To think they're happy, and they both believe
I died for France, and that I lie at rest;
And for my glory's sake they've ceased to grieve,
And hold my memory sacred.   Ah! that's best.
And in that thought I'll find my joy and peace
As there alone I wait the Last Release.

L'ENVOI

We've finished up the filthy war;
We've won what we were fighting for . . .
(Or have we?   I don't know).
But anyway I have my wish:
I'm back upon the old Boul' Mich',
And how my heart's aglow!
Though in my coat's an empty sleeve,
Ah! do not think I ever grieve
(The pension for it, I believe,
Will keep me on the go).

So I'll be free to write and write,
And give my soul to sheer delight,
Till joy is almost pain;
To stand aloof and watch the throng,
And worship youth and sing my song
Of faith and hope again;
To seek for beauty everywhere,
To make each day a living prayer
That life may not be vain.

To sing of things that comfort me,
The joy in mother-eyes, the glee
Of little ones at play;
The blessed gentleness of trees,
Of old men dreaming at their ease
Soft afternoons away;
Of violets and swallows' wings,

Of wondrous, ordinary things
In words of every day.

To rhyme of rich and rainy nights,
When like a legion leap the lights
And take the town with gold;
Of taverns quaint where poets dream,
Of cafés gaudily agleam,
And vice that's overbold;
Of crystal shimmer, silver sheen,
Of soft and soothing nicotine,
Of wine that's rich and old,

Of gutters, chimney-tops and stars,
Of apple-carts and motor-cars,
The sordid and sublime;
Of wealth and misery that meet
In every great and little street,
Of glory and of grime;
Of all the living tide that flows —
From princes down to puppet shows —
I'll make my humble rhyme.

So if you like the sort of thing
Of which I also like to sing,
Just give my stuff a look;
And if you don't, no harm is done —

In writing it I've had my fun;
Good luck to you and every one —
And so

Here ends my book.

INDEX TO FIRST LINES

Neuveau Art

Stinks

Nouveau